The Christic Center

The Christic Center

Life-Giving and Liberating

HAROLD WELLS

ORBIS BOOKS

Maryknoll, New York 10545

Founded in 1970, Orbis Books endeavors to publish works that enlighten the mind, nourish the spirit, and challenge the conscience. The publishing arm of the Maryknoll Fathers and Brothers, Orbis seeks to explore the global dimensions of the Christian faith and mission, to invite dialogue with diverse cultures and religious traditions, and to serve the cause of reconciliation and peace. The books published reflect the opinions of their authors and are not meant to represent the official position of the Maryknoll Society. To obtain more information about Maryknoll and Orbis Books, please visit our website at www.maryknoll.org.

Cover art by Eileen McGuckin, *Christ Pantocrator.* For more of Ms. McGuckin's renditions of classic icons, visit www.saintmarymagdalen.com or write to The Icon Studio, 3041 Broadway, New York, NY 10027.

Library of Congress Cataloging in Publication Data

Wells, Harold.
    The Christic center : life-giving and liberating / Harold Wells.
        p.   cm.
    Includes index.
    ISBN 1-57075-569-8 (pbk.)
    1. Jesus Christ—Person and offices. 2. Theology. I. Title.
BT203.W45 2004
230—dc22

                                        2004006512

For Patricia

SINE QUA NON

CONTENTS

Part III
OTHER INDISPENSABLE CRITERIA
OF THEOLOGICAL ADEQUACY

ACKNOWLEDGMENTS

My thanks, first, to Patricia, my *sine qua non,* the first reader and critic of these pages, companion and conversationalist in all things. A Christian educator and author, no obscurantism or unclarity escapes Pat's eye.

Many thanks are due to my great friend John McTavish, senior pastor at Huntsville, Ontario, dramatist, actor, producer/director of musical productions, and no mean theologian, who read the whole manuscript carefully and offered many suggestions for improvement, especially to the dialogues. I thank him not least for reminding me of Kierkegaard!

Two academic colleagues have read my work critically and offered, with great kindness, important correction and encouragement: Professor Douglas John Hall of McGill University in Montreal, and Professor Don Schweitzer of St. Andrew's College, Saskatoon. My warmest thanks to them for sharing with me their expertise and wisdom.

I am particularly grateful to students of my first-year introduction to systematic theology and my third-year course in doctrine at Emmanuel College, who read (assigned) selected chapters of the manuscript and gave me helpful feedback. Since they, after all, represent the intended audience of the book, both affirmations and critical suggestions were very important.

I am indebted also to numerous men and women who have been my faculty colleagues for over twenty years in the rich environment of Emmanuel College and Toronto School of Theology. Their conversation and colleagueship over many coffees, beers, lunches, and in countless meetings of supervisory, comprehensive, and thesis-proposal meetings have been challenging, stimulating, and supportive. I also owe much to teaching and research assistants whose work over the last several years has freed me up and sometimes been complementary to my own: Karl Koop, Tracy Trothen, Derek Parry, David Zub, Mark Rutledge, Nestor Medina, Rob Fennell, Emmanuel Ofori. I am grateful to the numerous Korean graduate students I have worked with, who have sharpened my sense of "contextuality" in theology. I am indebted to every master's and doctoral student I have directed, who, in the process of being educated, also educated their supervisor. Not least I happily acknowledge that the questions, challenges, and insights of all my students are a constant stimulation to the never-ending, exciting task of theology.

The work would never have been completed without a sabbatical, generously granted by Emmanuel College/Victoria University and its fine leaders:

Principal Peter Wyatt and President Paul Gooch. Their encouragement and support for scholarly research are greatly appreciated.

My thanks also to Robert Ellsberg and Bill Burrows, editor-in-chief and academic editor of Orbis Books, and their highly professional staff, for the many fine books they bring to press (so many of which are found in the notes of this book) and for their hard work and kind encouragement in their assessment and publication of this book.

INTRODUCTION

We need a faith that is life-giving and liberating. In our world of the early twenty-first century, which suffers so profoundly from fear, injustice, and violence, we long for a solid rock on which to stand, wisdom that challenges, guides, and inspires. We need a constructive, humanizing Christianity that lives for justice and peace, that fosters sustainable ways of living. And we need a Christianity that is rationally persuasive to people of our time. The task of Christian theology, as ever, is to inform the church's preaching, teaching, and mission for particular times, places, and circumstances. This book attempts a modest contribution to the ongoing process of thinking and rethinking Christian faith, focusing on the connection of theological method and christology. The connection is obvious, but not often expounded thoroughly and explicitly. Theological method, of course, has to do with the question of the knowledge of God, and since Christians believe they know God through Jesus Christ, method and christology must be intimately related.

In this book I argue that Jesus the Christ is central and foundational for all of Christian faith and Christian action, and therefore also for Christian theology. The rather unusual term *Christic center* emphasizes the point that it is the very person of Christ and not christology as such that is central. Although the centrality of Christ for Christian faith may seem obvious and beyond debate to a great many people, it is necessary to argue this today, over against a number of significant contemporary theologies that would de-center Christ in the life and faith of the church. In some circles, both in liberal Protestantism and Roman Catholicism, "christocentrism" has become a pejorative word. Historic Christianity, presumably centered in Christ, has often been arrogant and imperialistic toward other religions or alien cultures, overwhelmingly sexist, and has helped shape attitudes that contributed to the destruction of the natural environment. Thus we have the "theocentric," or "Reality-centered," or "soteriocentric" theologies that emphasize interreligious dialogue; also the "creation-centered" or "cosmocentric" theologies that stress the ecological concerns and the sacredness of Earth, as well as feminist theologies, some of which would describe themselves as experientially based, and therefore "life-" or "survival-centered." All of these concerns—interreligious understanding and reconciliation, feminism, and the well-being of the natural environment—are strongly affirmed here. We need theology of interreligious dialogue, feminist theology, and ecological theology,

1

and we urgently need them to be broadly appropriated by Christian people. I will contend that, for Christians, these are most successfully defended from within a Christ-centered perspective. The inadequate and destructive "traditional" theologies referred to have not been excessively centered in Christ; on the contrary, they have failed to allow Jesus Christ to be normative and have permitted cultural, philosophical, or ideological forces to reign in theology. I contend here that it is in and through Jesus that we find our true life and liberation. If this were not so, there would be no good reason to continue to call him "the Christ" or to continue to call ourselves "Christ-ians." Our Christian knowledge of God and life in God flows preeminently from Jesus Christ, crucified and risen, who is God's own self-gift and self-disclosure. All of our Christian thought, therefore, coheres in him and finds its inner rationality in him. Because he discloses to us the divine reality and purpose, Jesus frees us from obeisance to all oppressive idols and tyrannical overlords and inspires emancipatory activity at both systemic and personal levels. In our time, when the global market, served by violence, is worshiped as god, Jesus Christ gives us a better direction for a more deeply lived and more sustainable life in this world. In the face of terrorism, whether the massive violence of great nations or of desperate, angry men, Jesus Christ gives us a way of reconciliation, forgiveness, and hope in the face of death. A theology of grace centered in Jesus is able to save us from the self-righteousness that spawns so much arrogance and hatred in our fragile world.

The choice of the words "life-giving" and "liberating" in the title indicates that the method I propose here stands within the young tradition of liberationist theologies. By "liberation-*ist*" (or sometimes "liberative") I mean, broadly speaking, the wide range of critical liberation, feminist, ecological, gay/lesbian, and postcolonial theologies, that is, the contextual and political theologies that have multiplied and flourished as a substantial minority movement throughout the worldwide ecumenical church since the late 1960s. Liberation theology (including that of Latin America) is just one of the many *liberationist* theologies. These theologies by no means constitute a monolithic school, since their very raison d'être is to address the gospel message contextually to many different places and circumstances. While they differ among themselves substantially in their methods, they all share a methodological commitment to relate theologically to the experiences of oppressed and marginalized people, and they are guided in their scriptural interpretations, doctrinal formulations, and social analyses by some version of the "option for the poor." They wish to engage the resources of the Christian faith for a peaceful, equalitarian, just, and ecologically sustainable world, striving in all their theological work to keep these concerns at the forefront. Another way to characterize these theologies in their commonality is to speak of "critical" theology.[1] Critical theologies are alert to the social implications of doctrines and the practical, cultural, and political consequences of theology and ecclesial life. In this book I prefer to emphasize the more positive terms, both of them central to biblical faith: *life* and *liberation*.

The authority and power of Jesus to liberate, known so well to black slaves and other oppressed and marginalized people, derive (I will argue) essentially and primarily from the fact that he was raised up from death, so that, as the black slaves sang, "Jesus won't die no mo'."[2] In the earliest times, too, slaves and other victims of the Roman Empire found hope in this crucified and risen one. The purity and holiness of his love, his courage and compassion, evoke our adoration, but they do so retrospectively in the light of his resurrection. It is precisely the power of the resurrection, gentle and hidden though it is, to save and give hope that has always moved Christians, from the earliest times to the present, to see Christ as the disclosure and incarnation of the divine Wisdom and Word. That is why, in chapter 5, I begin christological reflection with the resurrection. Yet it is also Jesus' death as the holy one of God, detained, tortured, and executed, that qualifies him to speak to all the poor and violated. It was his clear partisanship for them, together with his grace-filled message about God, that evokes the love and worship of Christians on the underside. If African American slaves, both female and male, subject to the most extreme forms of misery and humiliation, sought to "steal away to Jesus," if, as Dwight Hopkins tells us, "the slaves were radically centered on Jesus,"[3] middle-class white Christians should take notice.

Like most works of theology, this is a polemical book. I have a number of undisguised axes to grind. I will contend that some ways of doing theology are better and more "rational" than others, and that theologians should never give up on the claim to be reasonable. Theology must be reasoned, disciplined thought. This implies a broad definition of the rational (discussed in chapter 3) that allows theology to be in dialogue with other disciplines of thought. This concern is not unconnected to our concern for life and liberation, since the rational has every-thing to do with the practical, as well as with the intellectual and theoretical. The oppressed and poor, being up against the extremities of existence, may be more rational than most others in their pursuit of God's truth. Since faith for them is a matter of survival, they cannot afford to get it wrong.

The center and foundation of practical Christian life and freedom—Jesus Christ—must also, then, be the center and foundation of Christian thought. At the same time, our theology must be intentionally contemporary and contextual. No contradiction exists between Christ-centeredness and contextuality, or experi-ence, or liberation. Our belonging to Christ and being centered in him are not some kind of tight straightjacket. "All things are yours," says Paul, since "you belong to Christ and Christ belongs to God" (1 Cor 3:21, 23). Thus, a theology truly based and centered in Christ will be acutely contextual and genuinely lib-erative. Moreover, to argue for a Christ-centered theological method one does not need to be *christomonistic,* that is, so totally focused on Christ as to neglect the Trinity or the Holy Spirit; nor need it imply the neglect of a theology of cre-ation. Rather, to be centered on the Christ is to insist that Jesus, in the power of the Spirit, is the concrete visibility of the triune Creator God among us. Jesus embodies God's reign of justice and peace. He is God's own tangible self-disclosure or revelation, the in-carnation, within created flesh, of God's *agapē* and grace.

It is impossible, therefore, to argue for a Christ-centered method without at the same time exploring the identity and mission of Jesus Christ himself. That is, methodology, or "prolegomenon" to theology, must itself be theological. We cannot begin with some "meta-methodology," outside of actual faith and theology, to talk about how to do theology faithfully. As Karl Barth has taught us, no higher platform or deeper foundation exists that could prescribe for theology how theology should be done. Hence we cannot speak in a purely formal, epistemological manner about revelation and faith without addressing related soteriological and christological issues. Chapter 2 is a substantive discussion of revelation, and chapter 5 of the identity and mission of Jesus Christ with particular focus on his significance for knowledge of God and theological method. The centering of Christians and of Christian worship and mission in Jesus Christ implies the uniqueness of Jesus—the utter uniqueness of this human being, whom alone we call *Emmanuel*. This is the one in whom we trust, the one whom we follow and in whom we hope. That is, we relate to him as to God. In Jesus alone we find God's own being enacted in the acts of a human being. In Jesus' life, ministry, death, and resurrection, we find God's own human existence.

But one must be careful about polemics. A basic conviction underlying this book is that contemporary theology is plagued by a number of false dichotomies and by "party spirit." Readers may be surprised to find this author drawing positively upon authors or theologies that seem to be quite different. How can I quote with enthusiasm from Karl Barth, T. F. Torrance, Hans Frei, and William Placher, yet also from Douglas John Hall, Jon Sobrino, Elizabeth Johnson, and Kim Yong-Bok? How can we appreciate, at the same time, the work of George Grant, Letty Russell, James Cone, Jürgen Moltmann, and Gregory Baum? I regard all of these, together with a number of historical figures (such as the Cappadocian fathers, Luther, Kierkegaard) as my teachers through their written works, and their insights will frequently be cited here. While there are deep similarities among these authors, it would be fatuous to suggest that these people all agreed (or that they would all concur with what I write here) either about theological method or about christology, or that their work can be comfortably harmonized. One can learn much and partly agree with authors with whom one is not particularly aligned. Elisabeth Schüssler Fiorenza, Rosemary Radford Ruether, and Wilfred Cantwell Smith have much to teach us. The reader will also find here sharply critical comments on such figures as George Lindbeck, Chung Hyun Kyung, Sallie McFague, Thomas Berry, and Paul Knitter, but I hope it will be evident that, while disagreeing with them, I greatly appreciate their work. The challenge they bring to the churches is truly a gift. One does not wish to propose some facile eclecticism that dilutes the cogency of these diverse contemporary thinkers. But too much theology goes on in academic ghettoes, where theologians of one stripe listen only to one another while despising members of other schools of thought. I believe that all of these diverse thinkers, and many others, have important contributions to make to the holistic theology we need in our time.

But just how important is theological method? Obviously I think it extremely important, most especially for those who are called to lead, preach, and teach in the decades to come. If theological students are to learn to think theologically for themselves (rather than merely imbibe the theologies of their teachers) for the sake of ministries in a rapidly changing world, methodological reflection is absolutely essential. The articulation of content needs to be disciplined and guided by explicit, intentional method, so that method contributes to and clarifies content. I do not entirely sympathize, therefore, with the comment of Jeffrey Stout: "Preoccupation with method is like clearing your throat: it can go on for only so long before you lose your audience."[4] Of course, we must not get stalled in questions of method and never get on with it. But even as we do so, we have to keep one eye on what we are doing and how we are doing it. I have little sympathy as well with the decision of Jürgen Moltmann (though I greatly admire his work) to articulate his method substantially only at the end of a series of theological volumes.[5] If one hopes to persuade one's reader about theological stances, that reader must be kept informed of how one proceeds and reaches conclusions. Preachers and pastors also, if they hope to convince and lead the intelligent people in their pews, must know how to be accountable for the theological stances they take, and this requires intentional theological method.

Readers will quickly notice something not often found in academic theological works: a number of more-or-less fictional dialogues reflecting (and imperfectly remembering) theological conversations in which I have participated or which I have overheard. I am in good company here. Old Anselm, after all, put theological arguments into conversations with Boso! Abelard too (recounting a dream he had had) created an interfaith dialogue between a philosopher, a Jew, and a Christian![6] And they in turn were taking a leaf from that master of rational discourse Socrates. My use of dialogues here indicates my conviction that theology is not primarily for academics, but is a lively, real life activity in which all Christians engage. *Theology happens* in community, where people struggle together to understand their faith: in Bible study and prayer groups; in committees of churches at local, national, and international levels; in confirmation classes; in pastoral care; and in conversations among friends. Sometimes it happens in moments of tragedy or in the heat of urgent activity, when life-and-death decisions have to be made. Academic theology exists to serve Christian people in their need to live the life of discipleship and to understand and articulate their faith. The dialogues here attempt to illustrate the practical and existential significance of theological questions and aim to stimulate similar discussion among theology students and church members. The dialogues in fact reflect my own memories of doing theology, or of hearing it done, in various situations. They are also meant to heighten our awareness of the personal limitations and perspectives that are part of all reflection. Autobiographical, experiential, and contextual elements (such as one finds in actual conversations) are inevitably woven into theological reflection, and being conscious of that is crucial for "mitigating theology's slide into objectively atrophied forms of teaching."[7]

Of course, I speak out of particular personal experiences and perspectives. And so, to locate myself for the reader, in order that she or he may identify the source of my prejudices and predispositions, I shall indulge briefly in autobiographical comment.

࿇

Raised in a Canadian working-class family in the industrial city of Hamilton, Ontario, I was taken by my mother for a short time to a Salvation Army Sunday School because she and my maternal grandparents were Salvationists. I can still remember singing children's hymns there ("Jesus Loves Me," "Jesus Bids Us Shine," "Tell Me the Stories of Jesus"). But for most of my childhood and adolescence I was nurtured in faith in the United Church of Canada, a more middle-class and quite liberal Protestant denomination, formed in 1925 by a union of Methodists, Presbyterians, and Congregationalists. My other grandparents were devout Methodists before church union, and I have a sense of indebtedness to that tradition of warmhearted piety. I am aware now how important our local church was to a rather precocious, sensitive child: its kind and intelligent, relatively conservative minister, who stayed through all my growing-up years and shaped my theology fundamentally; the dedicated Sunday School teachers, whom I still remember well; Boy Scouts; and youth Bible study. A Sunday School song, sung in a dark room as we gazed at a large screen showing a (rather caucasian) head of Jesus, still plays in my head from time to time:

Turn your eyes upon Jesus
Look full in his wonderful face
And the things of this world will grow strangely dim
In the light of his glory and grace

By the time I reached sixteen, I was running the projector and my girlfriend was playing the piano. My christocentrism may be rooted there. I suppose it could be seen as highly effective "indoctrination." Nevertheless, as I grew up I was surrounded by enough skepticism (that of my father and various friends, arising out of the miseries of the depression, tuberculosis, and the war) that I was capable of questioning Christianity and of passing through some years of rather cynical agnosticism in my later youth. But I had loved Christianity and found it painful to set it aside. When I was still an undergraduate I read Paul Tillich and appreciated his thought about despair and the demonic. He gave me a glimpse of an intellectualy respectable Christianity and opened me up to the possibility of the "dynamics of faith." But it was finally a Christ-centered theology of the cross and of the suffering of God, offered by an intelligent, powerful preacher, that met (but never resolved) my persistent questions about evil and suffering.

The United Church carries forward in various ways the heritages of its founding traditions, including both the liberal social gospel and neo-orthodox thrusts of the early and mid-twentieth century. I appreciate now that the liberality of the United Church assured that I was never tempted to biblical fundamentalism and always assumed the validity of critical biblical studies and of open-minded questioning. But as an undergraduate at McMaster University, I was inspired by the teaching of George Grant, a colourful and larger-than-life (Anglican) Christian intellectual. He was a socialist when I first knew him, yet also a deeply conservative, nationalist political philosopher and critic of modernity. He aroused in me a suspicion of the casual optimism of all things easily "liberal." Afterwards my theological education at Emmanuel College in Toronto, and later graduate studies at Edinburgh, could be characterized as essentially Barthian or, more broadly, neo-orthodox, confirming, in different ways, my suspicion of the superficiality of what is merely modern. The deepening darkness of recent world events in my later life has confirmed an orientation to theology of the cross learned in very different ways from both Grant and Barth.

Yet, through other influences, including that of my working-class family and early experiences in the sphere of menial labour, I was always keenly aware of social injustice and therefore felt an immediate interest in the social gospel as well. I am still convinced that the neo-orthodox theologies offered an important corrective to the rather "thin" liberal theologies that preceded them, and from my early years in ministry I sought to hold together the best of Barth and Reinhold Niebuhr with social gospel heroes, especially Canadian Christian socialist leaders J. S. Woodsworth and Tommy Douglas.

Carrying this combined Barthian and social gospel approach into pastoral ministry, I soon found that the hope theology and the post-Auschwitz *theologia crucis* of Jürgen Moltmannn carried both a depth and a relevance that I felt enriched my own faith and my preaching and practical work in the early 1970s. As a pastor, I was always involved in minor ways in partisan political activity. Going back for doctoral studies at McGill and intensive study of Paul Ricoeur, I was prepared for a university and seminary ministry in southern Africa. Five years at the University of Lesotho, both as lecturer in theology and as chaplain/pastor, brought with it an uncomfortable proximity to severe poverty and political oppression. These were critical years in the struggle against apartheid in neighbouring South Africa. There I was constantly challenged to preach and teach a meaningful message to devout young African Christians who, while they loved Jesus, were seriously skeptical about the role and place of Christianity and the church in their struggle for equality and a decent life. There I found that the South African, American black, and Latin American liberation theologies were exciting, challenging, and profoundly relevant, for both teaching and preaching. At that time (late '70s, early '80s) the theologies of Desmond Tutu, Allan Boesak and James Cone, and of the Latin Americans—Gustavo Gutierrez, Juan Luis Segundo, Jan Sobrino, and José Míguez Bonino—as well as the active proximity of the African National Congress and a congregation made up of poor villagers, students, and university faculty challenged both teacher and students. What made these theologies challenging and acceptable to devout African Christians was that they were not simply modern and Western, but exhibited an undiluted christocentrism, rooted in the beloved scriptures and joined to acute and prophetic social analysis and political commitment. Christian students were severely challenged by Marxist students and faculty, and many of them became "Christian Marxists." In this atmosphere it was great fun to teach a course for undergraduates on Christianity and Marxism and Christian–Marxist dialogue. Members of my congregation, being on the wrong side of the government, were apt to be picked up and jailed, sometimes beaten and tortured. Pastoral responsibility included attempting to visit them, advocating for them, and encouraging and consoling them. I myself (as an expatriate, together with my wife and children) suffered only the honour of being banned from entering the Republic of South Africa.

Since that time, as a pastoral minister and then a professor of theology in Canada, I have attempted to join theological ministry with commitment to various political causes, as a (minor) participant in the New Democratic Party, the peace movement, and the outreach work of the national and local church. After many years of teaching students for ministry (including many Korean, African, as well as Canadian graduate students, who have taught me so much), I am convinced that it is a critical, liberationist theology, unapologetically centered in Christ, that best guides our discipleship and gives integrity, identity, and a place to stand.

PART I

Reflections on Revelation, Faith, and Rationality

CHAPTER 1

Criteria of Theological Adequacy

"I thought I came here to study theology," a student says to me. "But which of all these theologies am I supposed to take seriously? How do you tell the difference between a good theology and a bad theology, or is one as good as another?" The young woman raising the question was beginning her second year of a three-year degree program and was bewildered by the array of approaches, positions, and "answers" that surrounded her in a large ecumenical theological school. Should she believe the Barthians and the postliberals, or the liberationists and the feminists, or the process theologians, or the cosmocentrists, or the liberal Protestants, or the Catholic Rahnerians or Lonerganians? Or is it some combination of these? Apart from whole theologies, which christology, which ecclesiology, which method, and so on? I decide to put the question to my first-year class in systematic theology: How do we recognize a good theology when we see one?—a good discussion opener for a first-year tutorial.

After only a little silence, one young man throws his hat in the ring: "It has to be biblical. We shouldn't be preaching or teaching anything that's not in the Bible."

The rejoinder comes quickly: "Well, what about all the things in the Bible that you wouldn't dare preach? The Bible has all kinds of bad stuff in it, all kinds of violence and bigotry! It isn't the bottom line for me!" So says a middle-aged woman.

After a thoughtful moment, a young woman chimes in: "I'd say a good theology is one that helps me to live well. One that helps me to be loving, and makes me hopeful. It would challenge me to make the world a better place."

"That's too subjective," says the first young man. "Like, whatever makes me feel good! It's also too individualistic. How could you ever have a church based on something so personal? You have to base yourself in the Bible if you expect anybody in the church to take you seriously. And you have to respect tradition too. Otherwise you'll just be making up a whole new religion!"

"I didn't say 'feel good.' I said: 'makes me more loving, more hopeful.' That's different."

The same middle-aged woman, frowning and straining to think and speak at the same time: "Doesn't a good theology fundamentally have something to do with Christ? I mean, if it's a Christian theology, isn't Jesus the bottom line? Kind of like: "What would Jesus do?" or, "What would Jesus say?" Of course, then it would have to be based in the Bible, because that's the only way we know about Jesus."

"Yeah," the young fellow chimes in. Lately it's "What would Jesus drive?"

Now our Korean student enters the conversation, a little hesitantly, since English is not his first language: "I like that idea quite well. Of course, Jesus Christ is very important in the church I come from. But why are there different theologies in different parts of the world? You're right [looking in turn at the other speakers]—if they're good theologies, they help us to live well, and they come from the Bible, and Christ is in the center. But why should there be different theologies in Korea and in Canada, and Latin America, and so on?"

Now a more mature man speaks up. He has a background in philosophy and has had a career as a lawyer. "That's a good point. But there's one other thing to keep in mind: "Does it make sense?" I mean, could I defend it to an intelligent person, especially in a pluralistic society like ours, with so many religions around us? And can I square it with science? Or is it just a lot of nonsense, unsupported by any reasonable arguments? For me, a good theology would have to rationally defensible."

The conversation was actually a little more complicated than that, taking a number of circuitous routes. But it only took a few minutes for the students to identify the issues and the possible answers to the question: How do we recognize a good theology when we see one? Or, we might have asked it a little differently: What guides and disciplines us in the doing of theology, and how do we assess or evaluate theologies? Even more basically: How do we choose the criteria themselves? Is it all a matter of subjective taste and preference? Or can one argue, on some rational basis, for one theology as preferable to another and even for one method as better than another?

This book is about theological method. It is interested in theology as *disciplined thought* and therefore must identify its criteria of theological adequacy. I do not, of course, hope to offer coercive arguments that will force everyone to agree. The students around the seminar table may never agree entirely, but they may clarify their own stances, modify each other's views, and as a result reach a more satisfactory approach. In this book I will propose some answers and will attempt to bring the reader along with me by a process of theological reasoning.

The Praxis Criterion
and the Christic Center

The reader already knows, from the title and the introduction, that I will defend a particular stance regarding theological method. It will be my purpose here to marry the "praxis" or liberative/contextual theologies with christologically centered theologies. Christ-centered theologies, I shall argue, should be praxis- or discipleship-oriented; and praxis theologies should be Christ-centered. In fact they very often are, and here we shall consider why this is necessary and appropriate.

Let me begin to defend this thesis. First, if Christian theology is truly to be "Christ-ian" its center and foundation is Jesus Christ. Jesus, in his life, death, and resurrection is primary norm for all that we do and say in worship and prayer, in Christian discipleship, and therefore also in theology. This is what is meant by the Christic center. Though it seems obvious to many Christians that Christian theology must be Christ-centered, there are many today who think otherwise, and I shall have to discuss this more thoroughly in other chapters. At any rate, the Christic criterion for good theology may be expressed in the question: Is it founded in Jesus Christ? Or: Is it congruent with our best understanding of Jesus Christ? Theology, then, is *disciplined thought*, disciplined from its center and foundation, so that every aspect of faith is illuminated by, and coherent with, Jesus Christ.

But where does praxis come in? I have said that theology is disciplined thought. More specifically, as the *logos* of *theos,* it is disciplined thought about God. Even more, though, it is the disciplined thought of Christ's disciples—the thinking dimension of Christian discipleship within the faith community. Of course, thinking is not the whole of Christian life; it is just one part of it, and probably not the most important part. Being a Christian is not primarily an intellectual matter or a matter of holding certain opinions or beliefs. Being a Christian most essentially entails following Jesus and therefore living in relation to God, and to others, through Jesus. By this I do not mean that it is entirely a moral thing either. Rather, it is about following Christ in his faith and trust in God, in his life of prayer and worship, in his hope, and in his love. Christian faith has this practical character, and theology exists to clarify and enrich the living out of Christian life and discipleship.

The many liberationist theologies that characterize their thought as praxis-oriented may often also be characterized as Christ-centered, but not necessarily. Often the primary norm for these theologies is simply the practical service of justice, peace, and liberty. They insist that a good theology is one that promotes life, love, and hope, and a better world. They are rightly praxis-oriented in that their thinking is always intentionally connected to their action or practice. In the 1970s and '80s, the term "praxis" tended to become a jargon word for practice, or even for activism, but since the term has fallen out of vogue to some degree it may be possible to use it again in its proper sense. Specifically, "praxis" is practice in its dialectical relation with thought. The point about praxis is that what seem to be polar opposites—thought or theory, on the one hand, and action or practice, on the other—are inseparable and mutually informative. According to this line of thought, one does not first work out one's theory at an abstract intellectual level and then apply it to the practical world (since there is no point in having a theory that is irrelevant to practice). Rather, theory is informed by practice, just as practice is informed by theory. Praxis is practical action, but one might define it as *practical action that is informed by theory, in such a way that theory is in turn informed by action.* Action and thought are placed in a circular or dialectical relation. The concept derives in part from Karl Marx's thought, as when he declared in his *Theses on Feuerbach* that "philosophers have only interpreted the world in various ways; the point is to change it."[1] Liberationist theologies take precisely this attitude, as expressed, for example by Elisabeth Schüssler Fiorenza: "feminism is a theory and practice of justice that seeks not just to understand but to change the relationships of marginalization and domination."[2] For Marxist thought, especially the Frankfurt school in the mid-twentieth century,[3] "truth" is a matter not merely of facts and propositions but of praxis; it is about doing. "In practice, man must prove the truth," said Marx, "that is, the reality and power, the this-sidedness of his thinking."[4] One does not need to be a Marxist to reach this insight, since for biblical faith the true God is the One who acts to bring justice and peace, reconciliation and wholeness to the people. To know God, and therefore to know truth, is to do justice (Jer 9:3; 22:16) and believing in Jesus is more than saying, "Lord, Lord!" (Mt 7:21). Praxis-oriented theologies, then, are well rooted in biblical faith. Theology, as thought, must be done with a steady eye on practical matters; and, in circular fashion, action and practice must also be informed by theology. If a theology is destructive and hateful rather than life-giving in its practical consequences, we may very seriously doubt whether it can be "the truth." The praxis criterion for a good theology is expressed in the question: Is it life-giving and liberating?

Have we then two different and equal norms for constructing and evaluating theologies—Jesus Christ, and life-giving, liberating praxis? Are these two conflicting primary norms? The answer, of course, is no. A praxis that is truly life-giving and liberating is congruent with Jesus Christ, and Jesus Christ is, according to Christian faith, the source and ground of true life and liberty. The norms constitute, we may say, a dual bottom line or primary norm. The two must be understood in dialectical relation each to the other. As I have already said, it will be my contention that the authentic basis for a liberative Christian theology is precisely Jesus the Christ, and he himself is, and should be, central—that is, the primary norm of a Christian theology. Jesus Christ reveals God, and in the last analysis it is the true God, as opposed to false deities, that liberates us for life. Christ, then, cannot be separated from life and liberation, and christology itself must be assessed in these terms.

Life, Liberation, and the Christ

Consider the unity of Jesus Christ with life and liberation. It is arguable that in the scriptures, if there is a single central idea or concept associated with Jesus Christ, it is *life*.[5] God raises Jesus from the dead to new life, and promises life at the end. Jesus reveals and incarnates the Creator of life. [6] Jesus, according to the Gospel of John, says: "I have come that you might have life and have it abundantly" (Jn 10:10). Again, we hear on the lips of the Johannine Jesus: "I am . . . the life" (Jn 14:6) and "I am the resurrection and the life" (Jn 11:25). Luke calls Jesus the "author of life" (Acts 3:15). In these texts our earliest Christian forebears testified that in Jesus the Christ they had found true life. *Life* is the opposite of death and means hope in the face of death. *Life* in the vicinity of Jesus means healing and wholeness. *Life* flows from reconciliation with God, the forgiveness of sins and release from overpowering guilt. *Life* means power to grow away from self-centeredness and to grow in love toward our neighbours. *Life* therefore means the end of meaninglessness and despair. *Life* means joy rather than sadness. This is not to deny that following Jesus may lead to suffering, even terrible suffering and death. In some extreme circumstances Christians will find more life in suffering and death than in the service of powers of evil and injustice. The stories of Christian martyrs in every period of church history testify to this. Nor should *life* be confused with our pleasure and convenience in a superficial sense. Still, the Christian faith is not masochistic. Basically, *life* is happiness, hope, and love, at both personal and social levels of existence. For Christian people, then, life and the Christ are inseparable. We may conclude that whatever is not life-giving is not of Christ, and not of God, and that Christ defines for us what true life means.

Liberation too is inseparable from God and from Jesus Christ. The God of Israel, the God of Jesus, is the holy One who liberated the Hebrews slaves in Egypt, and the prophets are overwhelmingly concerned with faithfulness to God through justice and peace. According to Luke, Jesus proclaims: "The Spirit of the Lord is upon me because he has anointed me to bring good news to the poor . . . , to let the oppressed go free" (Lk 4:18). The "option for the poor" or, more broadly, the option for the oppressed or marginalized is not an arbitrary political or ideological preference; it is rightly founded in Jesus. That he brings "good news to the poor," that indeed he is one of them and cares passionately for their well-being and liberation, indicates the unity of Jesus and liberation as normative for theology.[7] The Holy Spirit too, the Spirit of the risen Christ, is also God's power for liberation. Paul proclaims that "the Lord [*kyrios*] is the Spirit, and where the Spirit of the Lord is, there is freedom" (2 Cor 3:17). For John also,

Jesus is not only the "life," but also the "way" and the "truth," and "the truth will make you free" (Jn 8:32). *Liberation,* then, also means personal liberation from sin and guilt through the grace of God's unconditional love and the release from self-centered concern about our own righteousness for a free and vigorous concern for neighbours.

The point is this: our earliest and most fundamental testimonies proclaim, concerning Jesus, that he is the source of true life and liberation. Down through the centuries, and still today, Christian people have continued to believe in him and love him precisely for this reason: he gives us life and liberty. Life and liberation, then, are not alien ideological standards or merely human criteria by which we subordinate Jesus to our own values. The human is not the measure of the divine.[8] Life and freedom, as humanly understood, do not become the measure and criterion of good theology. By lifting up liberation, then, we are not merely vaunting our human autonomy over against God, asserting our right to create or invent ourselves in the typical modern sense.[9] True liberty is not simply the "unlimited freedom to make the world as we want."[10] We worship the One "in whose service is perfect freedom." Life and liberation (at least for Christian people) are derived from and defined precisely in terms of Jesus. The Christ of God discloses to us, in his life and teaching, his death and resurrection, where life and freedom lie. Love, justice, and power come together in him, giving us hope in ultimate victory over oppression and injustice. Specifically, Jesus' own practical option for the poor and oppressed defines for us what life and liberation mean. True life and liberation for the happy, the healthy, and the prosperous cannot be had except in solidarity with those who are poor, sick, or oppressed, because following Jesus means an end, or at least the beginning of the end, of personal selfishness and greed and of the triviality of a life oriented mainly to consumption. In this way he liberates us for life and gives us hope in the deepest sense.

Thus we observe a dialectical tension and unity: Jesus Christ, on the one hand, and human life and liberty, on the other, are not opposed criteria of Christian truth but a dynamic unity. To reiterate a key point: The praxis of what is life-giving and liberating and the Christic center are a dual primary norm for faith and theology; that is, our primary norm of theological adequacy is the life-giving, liberating Christ.

To complicate matters: We note that Christ is not a simple criterion of truth that can be applied in such a way as to solve all our theological problems in one stroke. After all, christology too is controversial and must be done in critical relation to the question of praxis. Similarly, praxis is also not a simple criterion, for the definition of what is life-giving and liberating is also controversial. That is why these two must be kept together and must be seen together also with what might be called the secondary criteria of theological adequacy: scripture, context, and ecclesia.

Primary and Secondary Criteria
of Theological Adequacy

In separate chapters of this book I shall propose at length four questions concerning methodological criteria by which a theology or a particular theological idea or course of action might be evaluated. I have already mentioned the first and primary question concerning the Christic foundation and pointed out that it must be understood in terms of the praxis criterion as well. The other criteria are secondary, as I shall argue, in that they are derived from and must be understood in relation to the primary one about Christ. Though in one sense they seem obvious, they are nevertheless controversial and require considerable clarification:

1. Is it founded in Jesus Christ? (Is it congruent with our best understanding of Jesus Christ, as attested in scripture?)
2. Is it biblical? (Is it supportable in the scripture as a whole, when it is read from its center in Christ, with critical, hermeneutical responsibility?)
3. Is it contextual? (Is it pertinent to the questions, concerns, and crises of our time and place?)
4. Is it ecclesial? (Is it in critical continuity with the church's theological traditions and in dialogue with the whole ecumenical church?)

We note that the first two are circular, in the sense that we cannot have Christ except through scripture, and yet scripture has to be interpreted in light of Christ. Context and ecclesia also have to be understood out of the christological center, using scripture, indicating a certain normative character to the first two. Yet we have another kind of circularity in that Christ and scripture are also inevitably understood within a social context and within the church. These connections will all have to be spelled out in subsequent chapters.

The praxis question, however—Is it life-giving and liberating?—is not simply a fifth question of the same kind. It is formally different from these, in that it resides on the practical side of the theory/practice dialectic and must be placed in dynamic relation to each of the others.

The questions concerning scripture, context, and ecclesia are all complex. By identifying these criteria as secondary, and in this order, I already show my hand as to my own theological preferences and theological location as a certain kind of turn-of-the-century Protestant. I claim no absolute correctness for this construal of theological criteria; however, these are not merely personal or individualistic preferences. I offer them out of the heart of the ecumenical and historic church, arguing that they are congruent with Christian worship and prayer, and the following of Jesus. These criteria, I will argue, are rationally coherent within the wider Christian community. A theologian of another tradition or perspective may order them and articulate them differently, but most would agree that these are key factors of Christian theological discourse. I suggest that, if a theological stance is a good one, and defensible in the Christian community, one will be able to say yes to these four questions concerning criteria. Moreover, each needs to be understood critically in relation to the praxis question: Is it life-giving and liberating?

Is It Reasonable?

I have mentioned most of the classic norms and sources of theology: Christ and scripture, tradition and community, as well as context/experience. What about reason, part of the so-called Wesleyan quadrilateral (scripture, tradition, experience, reason)?[11] Enormous debates have gone on over the centuries about the role of reason in theology, and the question of rationality will be dealt with substantially in chapters 2 and 3. However, "reason" is of a different order than the criteria of theological adequacy mentioned above. One may say that reason is the indispensable ingredient in all theological thought, as in all human thought whatsoever, but it is not a specifically *theological* criterion. Insofar as theology is disciplined thought, like all other disciplines it seeks to be rational and to persuade its listeners by reasonable, intelligible arguments. But more of this later.

A Bewildering Plurality of Theologies

Just why is theological method important? The importance of method for disciplined thought becomes highly visible when we consider the profuse plurality of theologies in the world today, not least within our own North American context, and within any given faith community. Theological method is essential if we are to sort out how and why we differ. The student who asked, "Which of all these theologies am I supposed to take seriously?" put her finger on the problem. It is a fact disturbing to many beginning students in theology, to professors of theology, and to many thinking folk in Christian congregations. I pointed out to the student that neither is there one history, one sociology, one physics, one medicine, or, I understand, one mathematics! To pretend that there is but one theology worth considering—one's own—is to reduce theology to a set of rigid dogmas, and this belies the vitality and intellectual ferment that actually characterize this most exciting of disciplines.

Yet, as I mentioned above, theology claims to be a rational discipline of thought. That is implied by the word itself, for *logos*, an ancient Greek philosophical concept, has essentially to do with "reason." Theology seeks to be a disciplined activity of the human intellect; it is a discipline taught in universities and sometimes called, nostalgically (or derisively), the "queen of the sciences." The Christian church played a decisive role in the foundation of universities in western Christendom, and the reality of the university, which has now spread all over the planet, owes much to the discipline of theology, which sought to see all truth as one and to interpret its world as a universe, a single, integral unity. Thus, Christian theology has traditionally seen itself as *scientia* (Latin, "true knowledge") and in modern times as *Wissenschaft* (German, "science or knowledge") and at one with the truth of philosophy and the natural sciences. Specifically, it is the *scientia Dei,* "knowledge of God." Of course, we no longer inhabit such a simple world; it has become impossible to imagine that Christendom constitutes civilization or that Christian thought, let alone one particular theology, constitutes the whole of worthwhile thought about God. University departments of religion or religious studies (*sciences religieuses*) now inquire into the religious history, practices, and concepts of all humankind, and in these departments Christian theology is usually but one of the subdisciplines of religious studies, which is really a constellation of a large number of specializations, each one vast in itself. This has been a humbling yet salutary experience for Christian theology. If theology wishes to be in touch with reality and truth, it must begin with the realization of its own limitations; and Christian theology now knows that it is the thought of one of many significant religious or faith communities in the world. This is not to say anything for or against its truth content; it is simply to recognize an indisputable fact.

However, while Christian theology may be studied more or less objectively (historically or conceptually) in religious studies, theology is "done" by all Christian people—with greater or lesser degrees of seriousness and commitment. It is done in congregations, in committees of congregations, in Bible study and prayer groups, in presbyteries and synods, by boards and divisions of denominations, and of course by individuals, as an indispensable part of living the Christian faith and carrying out Christian mission. Any definition of theology that restricts it to academic institutions misunderstands theology's true nature, since it has to do essentially with the articulation of faith by a particular faith community. In a scholarly or academic sense it is "done," with greater or lesser degrees of rigour and sophistication, in theological schools or seminaries, but theologians now recognize more and more that their work is the clarification of faith within a confessional community. Anselm of Canterbury knew this very well in the eleventh century. For him theology was *fides quaerens intellectum* ("faith seeking understanding").[12] Doing theology is not, by any means, the whole of the Christian life. It is the thought dimension of Christian life. To augment Anselm's particularly intellectual perspective with the concept of praxis, we need also to speak of love or hope seeking understanding, or action seeking understanding. Nevertheless, theology as such is thought. Faith seeks to understand its own content, to see clearly the internal rationality of its own vision of the real and its own grounds for both prayer and practical action. It is unnerving to do so, however, in a shrinking world within the awareness that many Christians in different parts of the world do this in many different ways, and that Hindus, Buddhists, Jews, Muslims, and others have been inquiring into their own rather different visions of the real with equal sophistication for many centuries, or in same cases for millennia. The faith and thought of reasonable people, then, must be more than an internal, communal discussion; faith and thought must be in conversation with those of other faiths and those outside of faith, just as theology, as a discipline of human thought, must be in conversation with other disciplines. *Intellectus* in our time, therefore, even the *intellectus fidei,* as Anselm well knew, must be *ratio.* It must account for itself to itself and to its faith community, but must also seek to communicate with others outside the community in an intelligible way.

What "faith" or "a faith" is will have to be discussed later and at length. What interests me at this point is that even within any particular faith community there are many theologies. We have long been used to various Catholic, Protestant, and Orthodox theologies (each with its own subspecies) and of Jewish rabbinical thought as well, all of these until recently remarkably sealed off from one another or relating to one another only critically or polemically. But for some decades now these boundaries, especially the Catholic/Protestant division, no longer seem to be the most significant, at least in the West. Conflict zones tend to be within and across these boundaries, between various kinds of conservative evangelical and liberal or postliberal theologies, or between liberation, feminist, and womanist theologies, or between christocentric/trinitarian and pluralist theocentric or soteriocentric theologies, or between traditional substance theologies and process theologies. Then we have the many intentional contextual theologies: Latin American, black American, South African, Korean, Canadian, and so on (all of these are actually plural). These wide varieties and cleavages within Christian theology are just as humbling as the recognition of religious pluralism. When students begin the study of theology in a seminary, they soon learn that they are not simply consuming a body of knowledge and information (though students of physics, chemistry, history, or sociology may still live with such illusions). Rather, they are being invited to "do theology," and to "think theologically." The seminary student is, of course, exposed to various bodies of knowledge and information: historical studies, the findings and debates of a long tradition of biblical scholarship, which is also full of controversy; a rich body of historical/theological thought, which, incidentally, discloses to us that Christianity has always lived with many conflicting theologies; and a great array of contemporary theological understandings that coexist within the community of faith. The pastoral disciplines too include their relatively objective histories and bodies of knowledge and information, but there too controversy reigns. All of the theological subdisciplines have a history of arguments, about which one can learn much. There is some objectivity about all this that can be consumed, and this is indispensable. But "doing theology" in a theological seminary is a matter not of consuming the doctrines explicated by the professors of systematic theology but of learning to think theologically for oneself. If one is going to do Christian ministry of one kind or another over a period of decades into the future, one will be doing it in a swiftly changing world, facing many different circumstances and crises. Within these changing contexts one will have to do one's own theological thinking for the sake of mission and discipleship. While individual students must do this for themselves, one hopes that they will not do it in a merely individualistic manner. One must develop one's own theology within a faith community and in conversation with those outside the community as well. All of this makes it obvious why reflection on method is so absolutely important.

One must say, first, that this plurality of theologies is to be celebrated. It is not the case that one of them is correct and all the others wrong. This is not to suggest a purely relativistic pluralism that takes all theologies and all religions to be equally true. The plurality, however, arises out of a genuine richness. Christian faith and the other religions also arise out of profound experiences and events and are grounded in great classical texts.[13] These texts have a depth and a relevance that transcend particular times and places and (to use a concept of Paul Ricoeur) bear a "surplus of meaning" that surpasses the original intention of the author and reaches beyond the author's time and place. The great traditions, then, have self-renewing power to speak fresh messages to new times and places. But even one era or epoch of history, and a single region of the world, has an infinite number of contexts that are addressed by the texts, so that people of quite different life experience rightly hear the texts and interpret them differently. Faith, which responds to the messages of these great texts, needs to be open to the wisdom that others have found in them. Consider, within Christianity, great contrasting traditions such as the Mennonite tradition and Eastern Orthodoxy. Liturgically, aesthetically, devotionally, intellectually, ethically, and missiologically, these very different traditions (though they lived side by side for centuries) arose and developed out of quite different geographical, historical, economic, political, and cultural circumstances. It would be absurd to say that one of them holds all the truth or that only one of them is faithful to Christ. Since presumably all particular Christian traditions are flawed, one dares to say that each could learn much from the other, that they could be mutually complementary or corrective. One might add that members of particular traditions have special responsibility for the particular insights and strengths they have inherited, to uphold these and to share them. Or consider that, within one large North American Protestant denomination, persons or groups of liberal persuasion and those of conservative evangelical persuasion may also have a good deal to learn from each other, recognizing that each has grown up out of particular experiences and circumstances. No doubt they will genuinely disagee, but they each need to listen to the other with humility and respect and to consider how the richness of a living Word has addressed them differently.

Am I proposing, then, that people of faith no longer claim knowledge of

God? Is theology now simply a private matter of taste and preference? Is it that *I like* liberation theology, and *you like* Whitehead or Barth (rather the way you like heavenly hash, while I prefer pure chocolate ice cream)? Emphatically, I am not calling for a "shopping-mall" approach to theology, where people merely assert their own values and unfounded personal opinions in a kind of "individualism-cum-relativism" that is very common in North American culture.[14] This would be to encourage spiritual and intellectual laziness; in fact, reflection on method is designed precisely to avoid this. We have to ask seriously: How should Mennonites and Eastern Orthodox talk to each other? How do African American liberationists and Canadian Barthians begin to communicate? How can christocentric evangelicals and soteriocentric pluralists possibly exist within the same Christian community of faith? All of these call themselves Christians and often belong to the same churches, yet they have drastically different theological understandings. While it is true that theological variety is to be celebrated and is to be expected, as I have said above, theological plurality also constitutes a major problem in the churches. It is common for church leaders, seeking ecclesial reconciliation, to rejoice publicly in the theological variety or pluralism of their churches, and it is especially easy for people of liberal persuasion to do this. Liberal bishops and moderators regard variety as a spiritual richness and can easily say such things as: "We rejoice in the abundant theological variety that exists among us! Everyone is welcome in our church!" That is, all must be made to feel welcome, and we hope no one leaves. (Our cash-strapped institutions cannot afford to lose anyone.) It is easy to see how this line of thought could degenerate into a kind of casual relativism: "I will believe anything I like, thank you very much, and do not need to defend it to anyone." Or, "You have your faith and I have mine. Why argue about it?"

We need, then, a kind of balanced interaction of firm conviction with openness to others. We need to celebrate plurality but not become complacent in debilitating difference and division. A church with harsh, narrow doctrinal boundaries would hardly be ecclesiastical utopia. Who wants a return to burning or drowning heretics? Yet who could deny that internal theological pluralism is a source of pain and confusion in the Christian *koinōnia*? How can we live with integrity in an atmosphere of creedal chaos?[15] Can we act effectively in mission if we are fundamentally divided about what our faith is? Can we even agree to worship, pray, or participate in sacramental action together, if we are divided about who God is and how God should be addressed, what God has done in Christ, or is doing now in the power of the Holy Spirit? Every faith community (like every political party or civil community) must have some core of commonly held commitment if it is to stand, live, and act as community. A church, therefore, must live and act out of some common center, yet such a center certainly cannot be imposed by an authoritarian ecclesiastical power. The dilemma is a plurality not only of religions but also of theologies.

What Is a "Theology"?

But just what is a theology? When we say there are many theologies, what are we referring to? I am not asking what theology is—relatively an easier question to answer. I am asking, what is a theology? An initial definition might be, simply: a particular configuration of concepts by which people articulate their faith in God. I suggest that in Christianity a theology is a particular understanding of what, or who, "God" is. If a theology is identifiably Christian at all, the reality of God is specifically bound up with Jesus Christ and the Holy Spirit.

Theologies, however, are not systems; they are rarely that neat, and we should be suspicious if they are. They have a habit of coming apart in light of new knowledge or experience and needing to be put back together again. We emphatically do not seek here to build a system of closed and completed concepts. While theologies usually try to be "systematic" in the sense that they seek internal coherence, method in theology should not be seen as a quest for security and completeness, because it offers no guarantee of truth, no simple formula for "getting it right." A theology is appropriately methodical when it is intentional, self-aware, and disciplined by its object of inquiry.

Since a theology is not a system of truth, there is no one correct or finished theology, and we should expect that different individuals and communities will espouse different theologies. Our distinct theologies express that which has grasped us, that which has blessed, liberated, judged, inspired, directed us. To speak descriptively, our theologies differ because they grow, at least in part, out of our differing experiences.[16] They develop in different directions because we have experienced "the divine," or heard the gospel, in different ways. "God," or the "Holy Spirit," has met us in many different circumstances, and it is some specific aspect of the message that has appealed to our imagination, or inspired us to action, or met some personal need. The gospel of God's unconditional love may have met *you* in your great need for forgiveness and self-worth. The gospel of God's solidarity with the oppressed may have met *her* in her struggle for equality and worth as a woman, and *him* as a member of a racial minority, striving for justice for himself and his family in a situation of oppression. The sense of God's will guiding and directing them has met some folk as light and grace, governing and giving direction to what might otherwise be the chaos of their lives. The message of God's suffering unto death, with us and for us, out of inexhaustible love, gives *me* hope and a sense of the goodness of life, in spite of pervasive misery and death in the world. My theology, and his and hers and yours, reflects and articulates the differing ways in which God's truth has reached us in the differing circumstances and experiences of our lives. Realizing this, we may indeed rejoice in the plurality of theologies, may become open and tolerant to one another's particular ways of understanding the message. We may, however, strive for an enriched and balanced theology, one that finds the experience and insights of others complementary to our own. Especially if we are preachers or pastors, we need to do our work out of a theology of sufficient breadth and depth that we have something to say to people in many conditions of life.

At the same time, as I began to suggest above, the plurality of theologies is a problem, and a serious one, since our theologies do not always complement one another. Sometimes they disagree and seriously contradict each other. By our many theologies we can also undermine one another's faith and confidence and relativize one another's sense of the truth. This is where awareness of theological method becomes crucially important. When we seek to communicate across theological barriers, we discover that we are using different standards for distinguishing good from bad theology. We give varying weight or authority to experience, to Christ or scripture, to context, or to tradition. We function with different notions of reason. We use the Bible to authorize our theologies in various ways—as a source of doctrines or concepts, of narrative testimonies, or of symbols and images. We not only have different experiences, but we evaluate the significance of experience differently. That is, we function, sometimes unconsciously and to some degree explicitly, according to different theological methods. Other fundamental differences exist concerning christology and the nature of Christian discipleship. I suggest that we can get inside a theology and understand what makes it tick by asking about three things: the style of discipleship it reflects or generates, its christology, and its method.

1. A theology is distinguishable by the style of discipleship it reflects or generates.

When we label someone as belonging to a school of thought in theology (often a very unkind thing to do) we frequently have in mind the style of Christian life he or she lives. People may actually adopt a theological stance to a large extent because it nurtures a certain lifestyle or a certain social or political commitment. This may be called a "praxis approach" to truth, in which thought and practical action mutually inform each other. In our time critical and liberationist theologies operate with a particular concern for the practical outcome of doctrines and concepts. A certain dialectical circle operates here. Someone may choose, or even create, a theology of a certain kind because of prior personal or social or political commitments, so that the theology *reflects* the prior commitment. Alternatively, a theology may *generate* a practical commitment.

Consider a strongly committed feminist, for whom the feminist movement and concepts have been personally very liberating. Perhaps she had been a victim of male domination or even violence. The adoption of feminist ideas about women's equality was for her a kind of conversion in itself, turning her life around, giving her a whole new self-esteem and opening up unsuspected horizons for her life. She wishes to share this liberation with others and to see feminist values embodied in the society around her. If she then becomes seriously interested in Christianity, the theology she takes up will reflect her prior feminist experience and commitment. One would hope that faith would not become merely instrumental to that prior commitment, but would inform and deepen it.

For another woman, it may work the other way around. Committed all her life to Christ and church, she is a person of deep faith. Serious study of the Bible and exposure to a new context in which women have freedoms and opportunities they never had before may generate in her an openness to feminist theology. This theology in turn will generate in her a new style of Christian discipleship.

This praxis relationship of theology and practical discipleship is not a new thing. To take a famous example, in 1914 the young Karl Barth drastically changed the direction of his theology for what were originally "practical" reasons. He had been a modern liberal pastor, seeking to accommodate Christian faith positively to the dominant modern thought and culture around him. But when the war was declared, his favourite modern theologians all supported the Kaiser's war policy. Barth was shocked. He realized that any theology that could allow for such a dreadful practical, political result must be bad theology (and such theologies did not exist only in Germany!). He became thoroughly disillusioned with those who had taught him theology and began to rethink his faith from the ground up, searching for a theology that did not accommodate easily to the society and its ruling powers and ideologies. This came to mean, for him, a theology rigorously based in the Bible and centered in Jesus Christ, that is, a theology that transcended the dominant views of the culture. Later Barth was a theological leader of the Confessing Church against Nazi ideology, and, contrary to his general reputation as a "conservative" theologian, he remained a political partisan of the left and of the anti-nuclear movement, with clear, practical, political commitments.[17] There is debate as to whether these commitments always found their way consistently into his written academic theology,[18] but then the coherence of thought and action is rarely all that it should be. Barth is just one example; one could find examples of people who moved in quite other directions for critical, practical reasons.

At any rate, I am suggesting that a theology is identifiable by the kind of practical action or style of discipleship it reflects, inspires, or legitimizes. This accounts for the names or labels that are widely used to identify some contemporary theologies, for example, liberationist, feminist, conservative, liberal, radical, ecological, neocolonial, and so on. People's actual lifestyles, ethical attitudes, and political commitments are intimately connected to the ways in which they understand their faith.

2. A theology is distinguishable especially by its christology.

This point is not less important than the preceding one; in fact the two need to be seen together. One could say that theologies are distinguishable by their doctrines of God, and of the Holy Spirit, by their ecclesiology, and so on, and this would be true. Christology, however, has a central, determinative role within any coherent Christian theology, because, for the Christian community, Jesus Christ is universally regarded as revelatory, that is, the preeminent, tangible, visible locus of God's self-revelation. Yet the question remains: Who is Jesus Christ? Is he the incarnation of God, divine and human, or is he one of the many great seers and prophets who have arisen in human history? Is he my personal Lord and Saviour, through whom my sins are forgiven, and because of whom I reach eternal life? Is he our revolutionary political leader, inspiring radical action? Is he my personal healer, consoler, friend? Is he the Christ of the American way of life? Or of black theology? Or the Christ of the feminists, and then again, which feminists? Is it the liberal, harmless Christ of our middle-class neighbourhoods? Or is it several, or none of these? When we have identified a theology's christology, we have gone a good way toward understanding what makes it tick. That is because Jesus Christ is inevitably at the heart of Christian identity. If it is "Christian," our whole theology is tied up with our understanding of the identity of Jesus Christ and the meaning of his work, so that even a theology that seeks to diminish or decenter the place of Christ defines itself within the Christian community in terms of its stance concerning him.

3. A theology is distinguishable by its method.

A theology, at least in its more articulated form, is also identifiable and distinguishable by its method. When speaking of their methods, theologians often speak of "beginning" or "starting point," to indicate what is most formative for them. Classical Protestant theology has given the greatest weight to scripture and enunciates the principle of *sola scriptura,* while Roman Catholic theology has usually valued philosophy and has stressed the weight of tradition, alongside of scripture. Barthians and postliberal Protestants also typically say that they begin with the Bible and are centered in Christ. Feminist theologians, whether Catholic or Protestant, often say that they begin with, and are governed by, "women's experience," and they give varying degrees of importance to Christ and scripture. Liberation and postcolonial theologians in their many varieties often say that they begin with the experience of oppression or marginalization, operate with an explicit social analysis, and usually give great weight to certain liberative aspects of scripture and to the historical Jesus. Process theologians begin with a contemporary scientific perception of the universe as dynamically in process, while ecological theologians may be said to begin with the facts of the ecological crisis and to focus above all on the relevance of faith for their environmental concerns. Particular theologians, perhaps the best of them, may combine a number of these emphases in their thought.

If we want to understand how a theology works, we may ask, Where is its center and starting point? What is normative for this theology? To put it differently: Where is the bottom line? To discern this, we may ask: How is scripture used and interpreted? What is the place of Christ? What are the practical commitments associated with it? What weight is given to tradition and to ecclesial teaching authorites? What place is given to experience and to human reason? To what extent are the circumstances of specific times and places and the multiple crises of our contemporary world brought into relation with faith? These are some of the typical questions of theological method.

Discipleship, christology, and method, then (not necessarily in that order), are key terms for seeing into the heart of a theological position. However, if theology is to continue to claim to be a rational discipline—that is, to be *disciplined thought about God*—it must be more than the mere statement of likes and dislikes, preferences and prejudices. If it is to avoid the shopping mall of lazy religious relativism, it must become explicit about its criteria for truth and its path to knowledge. It must give reasons for thinking this rather than that. I do not suggest that such reasons will ever be strictly demonstrable or coercive, either within the faith community or to the secular world. We would be naive indeed if we thought that Paul Tillich and Pierre Teilhard de Chardin, Rudolf Bultmann and Karl Barth, Hans Frei and Marcus Borg, Lesslie Newbigin and Paul Knitter, Wolfhart Pannenberg and Elisabeth Schüssler Fiorenza, Dwight Hopkins and Robert Jenson (all highly rational people) would ever agree to the validity of one another's reasons. David Kelsey clarified the matter nicely when he wrote:

> But surely theological positions taken as wholes ("Bultmann's theology," "Barth's Dogmatics," or "Tillich's System," etc.) are not arguments, no matter how many arguments they may include . . . rather theological positions taken as wholes might be looked at in a quasi-aesthetic way as a solicitation of mind and imagination to look at Christianity in a certain way.[19]

Nevertheless, if theologians ever give up attempting to give reasons for their theologies and theological methods and admit that it is all a matter of subjective preference or taste, then theology will indeed have fallen into arbitrary irrationality and will certainly have no right to be taken seriously by thoughtful people. Hopefully, even when theologians fail to convince one another, they at least chasten, modify, and discipline one another to more adequate theologies and more appropriate methods.

Nonrational Factors in the Choice of a Theological Method

I have suggested that a theology is identifiable in large measure by its method. But how do we choose a theology or a theological method? We would like to think that our choice is rational, that is, that it is not merely arbitrary but in some sense appropriate or reasonable; and I think we should not give up on this. We want to choose a better, rather than a worse, method and to offer reasons for our choice. Certainly no one will agree to say that his or her method is irrational. Yet it is evident that many factors beyond the purely rational incline us as individuals toward various approaches. It is only rational to acknowledge the functioning of the nonrational in our thinking. We should also keep in mind that it is not only theology that needs to recognize this. The human and social sciences, and even the natural sciences, need to recognize something beyond pure reason operating in their disciplines.[20] As I began to suggest above, all of us have our predilections, arising out of the circumstances of our lives—our fundamental cultural rootedness, our life experience in its broadest sense, and our spiritual or faith experience, our traditional loyalties. It is not simply that some people are wise and intelligent while others are stupid and foolish, or that some have integrity while others are intellectually dishonest. We too readily leap to such accusations when passions are aroused, but this is not helpful to mutual understanding.

To look squarely at the facts of predisposition, point of view, and perspective is wholesome for theology as a discipline and for individuals within it. To acknowledge the role of such subjectivity and to acknowledge the limits of the rational are not optional in our time. Since at least the late eighteenth century, in the period of the later Enlightenment, the human intellect and its capacity to be in touch with objective reality have suffered serious humiliation. Although the epistemological question How do you know? has been asked since philosophy began in the ancient world, it was perhaps Immanuel Kant's *Critique of Pure Reason* (1781) and his suggestion that the human mind is a major contributor to its own perceptions of the external world that moved modern philosophy and theology as well to question their own claims to objective knowledge.

In the century after Kant, and early in the twentieth century, the thought of the post-Kantian, post-Enlightenment "masters of suspicion" (as Paul Ricoeur calls them) has heightened our awareness of the nonrational factors that shape human thought.[21] They may be said to have extended the earlier Cartesian and Kantian doubt about our consciousness of "things" to doubt about consciousness itself. Marx, Nietzsche, Freud, and the thought of other philosophers and sociologists,[22] have made the human and social sciences very skeptical indeed about the objectivity of all claims to knowledge about human and social realities. Karl Marx (1818–1883) has made us aware of "ideology" (used in a pejorative sense) as a false consciousness imposed on society by the ruling class to serve its own interests. He showed us that much of what we think we know rationally is really ideological, and that the dominant modes of social/political perception are subtly imposed on us, sometimes against our own interests: "The ideas of the ruling class are the dominant ideas of every epoch."[23] The fact that Marx himself, however, was able to see through and to criticize these illusions gives us hope that our thought need not be totally mired in ideology. Friedrich Nietzsche (1844–1900) also threw doubt upon the value of human reason to put us in touch with reality, making us suspicious of the moral self-deception of the human psyche that is rampant in our human will for power. Then again, a little later, the great psychiatrist and founder of psychoanalysis Sigmund Freud (1856–1939) taught us about the unconscious mind, the power of illusion, and the psychological self-deception of wish fulfillment to distort our rational perceptions of reality. Each of these masters of suspicion demystified certain nonrational elements of human thought, but they are not entirely discouraging about the powers of human reason, since they themselves began to see through these disguises and to meet guile with "double guile."[24]

Well into the twentieth century, other thinkers heightened our awareness of the limitations of all human thought. In philosophy, Martin Heidegger prepared the ground for what has come to be called "hermeneutical suspicion" with regard to the interpretation of texts. Heidegger was newly aware of the radical historicality of human existence, of the *dasein,* or "being there," in specific historical and cultural contexts. With regard to the interpretation of written texts, he distinguished between sense and meaning and pointed out the semantic autonomy of texts, having in mind the embeddedness of both authors and interpreters in particular contexts.[25]

This heightened realization that the psychological and sociopolitical location and historical and cultural point of view of knowers condition all of our knowing (commonly called "historical consciousness"), together with the discovery in physics of spatiotemporal relativity, has had its bearing even in the natural sciences. Long regarded as the great paragon of rational objectivity, physical science has become aware of shifting paradigms in the scientific vision of the physical universe, and of the selectivity and value judgments that are always part of the process of scientific investigation. Thomas Kuhn argued that even in the physical sciences hermeneutical predispositions are operative as scientists become involved in questions of interpretation.[26]

Today the "hermeneutical suspicion" of liberation theology (building on basic ideas of Marx and others) is a further sharpening of what may be called the postmodern awareness of ideology and self-delusion in theological work. José Míguez Bonino, speaking from a third-world perspective, pointed out in one of the earlier volumes of liberation theology the bias and ideological distortion that occur in the interpretation of the Bible by scholars of the first world: "Very concretely, we cannot receive the interpretation coming from the rich world without suspecting it and, therefore, asking what kind of praxis it supports, reflects, or legitimizes."[27] Again, feminist theology has taught us to be aware of how the Bible has been used as a weapon against women and to look for male bias and domination not only in traditional male interpretations of the scriptures but also in the male authorship of the scriptures themselves:

> The Bible is not only written in the words of men but also serves to legitimate patriarchal power and oppression insofar as it "renders God" male and determines ultimate reality in male terms, which make women invisible or marginal.[28]

The postliberal theology of "language games" and "cultural-linguistic framework" (Lindbeck),[29] borrowing from the philosophy of Wittgenstein, may also be seen as a response to the loss of purely rational foundations for assured knowledge of reality, and as a kind of protective strategy for Christian ecclesial language. Again, very differently, the theocentric or soteriocentric theologies of interfaith dialogue (John Hick, Wilfred Cantwell Smith, Paul Knitter, etc., which will be discussed in another chapter) can also all be seen, in part, as different efforts to come to terms theologically with the awareness of many religions and the humiliation of the intellect that has accompanied the historical consciousness of late modern and postmodern humanity.

The result of such considerations in the sphere of theology and ethics has often been a despairing or cynical relativism, agnosticism, and even nihilism. Much postmodern thought (as we shall discuss later) is a response to the loss of assured rational foundations for human knowing. All claims to truth relativize one another, and to the minds of many no particular version of the truth can be taken seriously. Nihilism (nothing-ism) is an attitude that says that nothing is true; nothing can really be known about reality, especially ultimate reality (agnosticism). Since nothing is true, nothing is really right or wrong in the practical sense. Since nothing is really right or wrong, there can be no victory of righteousness, and therefore there is really nothing to be hoped for. Much of the despair and meaninglessness[30] that afflict great numbers of people in our time derive, I believe, precisely from such an implicit nihilism.

The breakdown of the authority of reason and the accompanying nihilism have been not only acknowledged but celebrated as liberative by postmodernist philosophers since the mid-twentieth century—Michel Foucault, Jacques Derrida, Jean-François Lyotard, and others (figures whom we shall consider in a later chapter)—since they saw discourses of reason as forms of the will to dominate. But for most people, I dare say, the loss of underpinnings for thought and action, or having the carpet pulled out from under their feet, is an unsettling experience. The relativism, agnosticism, and nihilism of some intellectuals is perhaps not as tragic as the appearance of these attitudes among large numbers of people in North American society, including many in our churches. For many people, to believe or think anything in particular in the realm of the religious or ethical is thought to be at best naive and at worst arrogant. Members of Bible study groups in local churches often suggest, in a spirit of broad-minded tolerance, that one interpretation of a biblical passage is as good as any other. In areas of doctrine and belief, "we're all entitled to our own opinions." The cliché that "You have your beliefs and I have mine" is almost as common inside the more liberal faith communities as in interfaith dialogue; and in both circumstances it spells the end both of real dialogue and of the love of truth.

In view of all this it may seem less than helpful to add fuel to the fires of relativism and nihilism by pressing upon students of theology an awareness of the subjectivity, limitations, and locatedness of their theological preferences. Yet this must be faced. It is impossible to go back behind the Age of Enlightenment to some earlier, more innocent era, nor indeed, since the age of suspicion, to the optimism of the Enlightenment itself! Nor can we escape the hermeneutical suspicion that must be applied first to ourselves and then to all other authors and interpreters of texts or doctrines. Failure to face these realities will mean that we will talk past each other in the faith community and fail to offer persuasive theological viewpoints to others. The nonrational factors that come together to shape our theological methods need to be brought out into the open, then, and our actual methods need to be made explicit if we are to commmunicate either inside or outside of faith communities.

Dialogue within a Faith Community

The recognition that partners in theological conversation are often operating from different methods is basic to theological discourse. Such differences create great practical problems in the life of a church that seeks to worship, live, and carry out its mission in a coherent and unified way. I may illustrate my point by depicting an imaginary debate within the church. I have been a party to a number of conversations or debates something like this.

A national Board of World Mission of a large North American Protestant denomination is debating the direction in which the church should move in its mission and outreach policy for Africa. The Reverend Dr. Dennis B. is a man in his early fifties, a senior pastor with a doctorate in historical theology, a former missionary in West Africa. He thinks that the church should put less emphasis, support, and money into political solidarity; economic development; medical, educational, and agricultural work; and interfaith dialogue (which have been the emphases for the past three decades or so) and more into evangelical outreach. He argues that the church should develop partnerships with African churches that are seriously engaged in "spreading the gospel," supporting them financially and with missionary personnel. He believes that the gospel of Jesus Christ should be proclaimed to traditional Africans who have not yet heard it and to African Muslims as well. This is being done forcefully by evangelical and pentecostal churches, he points out, and the Muslims are aggressively spreading their message too. Of course, according to Dennis, we should not entirely discontinue our compassionate medical, agricultural, and educational work. But social and economic development will follow, he thinks, if the gospel is preached and the church planted.

But Ms. Sheila M. vehemently disagrees. She is a slightly younger woman, an influential lay representative of her region of the church, well educated and articulate, a professional in another field. She has taken some courses in religious studies and theology and has done a good deal of reading in contemporary liberation and feminist as well as pluralist theologies. She has been a devoted volunteer for the church for many years. Sheila rejects this kind of evangelistic outreach, which she considers arrogant and imperialistic, and favours instead a greater emphasis on mission as co-operative solidarity with local African people, enabling them through our partnership and advocacy to struggle for systemic social/economic change and to overcome poverty and oppression. Most especially, she would pour church mission money into the anti-AIDS campaign to help meet that enormous and pressing human need. She is certainly not interested in converting people from other religions, an activity she regards as a kind of colonialism, but she would support churches and organizations that promote interreligious dialogue with Muslims and others. As for salvation, she has very little concern about salvation after death. Evangelism for her is "good news for the poor," which means solidarity for human development and social action.

It will be very easy for these two to talk past each other, each using the Bible and each appealing to the authority of Jesus. They come out of very different life experiences and operate with different theological methods. We may observe, to begin with, that Dennis's theology may be described as Christ-centered, and Sheila's can be described as praxis-oriented. They have quite different starting points and different bottom lines for discerning the truth. The basic difference between them about bottom-line norms has a spin off regarding other methodological questions. For example, their disagreement about mission policy reflects different ways of reading and interpreting scripture and different doctrines of what scripture is. When they debate about mission, each of them argues selectively from different favourite missiological texts (Mt 28:19-20 and Lk 4:18-19 respectively). Obviously they have quite different christologies, and they utilize their christologies differently. They have also, therefore, different understandings of salvation, of church, and of mission. They have different visions of the demands of Christian discipleship. Probably they also operate not only with differing social analyses of what is happening in Africa and elsewhere in the world but also with differing ideas about what the role of social analysis should be (if any at all) in theological reflection or in the setting of mission policy.

If Dennis and Sheila and the factions of the church they represent are ever to communicate and work together, they will have to communicate with one another at a fairly deep level. Such dialogue, if sincerely entered into, if it involves genuine listening, will be at least as painful and disturbing to each of them as any between people of different faiths. Probably they will have to begin by breaking down their caricatures of each other, and this is possible if they talk together at length and allow themselves to appreciate each other as persons. Dennis will have to become less self-righteous and indignant toward liberals, whom he regards as faithless and disloyal, willing to abandon anything, superficial in their faith, and therefore co-opted rather easily by alien ideologies and secular humanism. He thinks Sheila is carelessly willing to dissolve away the heart of the historic Christian faith. On the other hand, Sheila will have to be less condescending and superior toward conservatives, who appear to her to be naive, both closed-minded and heavenly minded, out of touch with the reality of today's world, and arrogantly bigoted toward people of other faiths. It is apparent that Sheila and Dennis will have to converse at the level of theological method. It will not suffice for them to discuss their divergent theologies of mission, or even their theologies of salvation or of Christ. When they do so they will soon discover that they operate with different criteria for truth, that they are moving out of different life backgrounds and spiritual experiences, have responded to different aspects of the gospel, and are therefore using different theological methods. No wonder they do not hear each other, shake their heads in amazement at each other, and feel they are speaking different languages.

An *Intra*-Faith Conversation

We may move toward insight into methodological questions by listening in on a conversation between Sheila and Dennis as they struggle to influence the policies of their church. Sheila and Dennis were both rather hot under the collar and lost their tempers a little, red-faced and wagging their fingers at each another on the floor of a large meeting. If they were to meet for coffee after the debate (preferably without an audience) and so engage in a serious conversation about what constitutes authentic Christian mission in our time, we might overhear them making these kinds of points:

1. *"Your understanding of Christian mission is not biblical."*

DENNIS: *I'm sorry, Sheila, but I feel that you're ignoring major elements of the biblical witness simply because they don't fit with your political agenda. We have to submit our minds (and our politics for that matter) to the authority of a truth that transcends our preferences and prejudices. If we purport to be Christian, we simply have to accept the authority of the scriptures. What about Matthew 28:19? "Go and make disciples of all nations." What about Acts 1:8: "You shall be my witnesses, in Judea, in Samaria, and unto the end of the world"? I don't see Africa being excluded from the list here.*

SHEILA: *Oh, and I suppose you have a purely objective interpretation of the Bible and have no political agenda at all, right? Anyway, I can't just accept all verses in the Bible as equally authoritative. You know as well as I do that the Bible is human and fallible, and we all know that New Testament scholarship does not regard all statements attributed to Jesus as authentic. I don't know whether Jesus really said those things. He probably didn't. Anyway, I have to give greater weight to the passages that speak to me, that suggest peace and justice for the whole world. Besides, I think that what I'm saying reflects the general thrust of the Bible as a whole, which is concerned about justice and peace in the world. Call it my politial agenda if you like, but what about the exodus? What about Luke 4 and the liberation of the oppressed? What about Matthew 25 and the care of the poor? You don't think I'm biblical enough? Two can play that game!*

The conversation moves on in that vein for some time, both quoting their favourite texts, each interpreting these texts differently and giving greater weight to their own texts than to the texts of the other. They realize they need to go deeper.

2. "Neither your understanding of Christian mission nor your interpretation of scripture is christologically based."

DENNIS: *Well, I'm not a fundamentalist you know. Of course I don't give equal weight to every little verse in the Bible. But I believe the whole Bible should be interpreted in the light of Jesus Christ. Luther said, "Christ is Lord and King of Scripture." Jesus is Lord, and he clearly commands evangelical mission. "Words of Jesus" or not, it's perfectly plain in Paul and Acts too, as well as the Gospels, that the salvation Jesus offers must be communicated to the whole world. This is the first responsibility of Christian mission. I assume a biblical christology of Jesus as God Incarnate and Saviour of the world. Jesus died for the sins of the whole world and is risen from the dead in order that we might have everlasting life. You seem to have the usual liberal idea that Jesus is just another teacher and example or prophet. As far as I'm concerned, that just throws out the whole gospel of grace. If Jesus is just another lawgiver or example of how good we should be, he's not good news at all, he's bad news! He just adds to the burden of our guilt!*

SHEILA: *OK, calm down. I agree that the whole Bible should be interpreted in the light of Jesus' teaching about love and justice. The Jesus who moves and inspires me is the teacher and example of gracious love. I find God in Jesus, yes. But Jesus is not God. Jesus teaches us about a loving, all forgiving God, one who leads us to justice and peace in this world. I'm sorry, but to say that "Jesus died for our sins" as our "Saviour" makes no sense to me, and I'm not at all sure what I think about the resurrection, whether it really happened or not. I think Jesus "saves" us by showing us the way to struggle for systemic change in the structures of society!*

   Probably Dennis and Sheila will wrestle a while longer about Christ and salvation. They may even alter each other's mind slightly. But continuing to disagree at the christological level, they will probably shift to another kind of
argument that commonly arises in theological discussion:

3. *"Your understanding of Christian mission is out-of-date and out of touch with today's world."*

SHEILA: [Wincing and shaking her head] *Come on, Dennis, be reasonable!
Theology has to change with the times! What you're saying is really out-of-date!
Today we have to take acount of the pluralism of religions in the world. Today
we're working side by side with Muslims, Hindus, and Jews. Some of our kids are
even falling in love with these people and marrying them. And now you want us
to go out and tell them that they're ignorant and their religion is worthless? I
can't believe you feel that way. We can't just go on with this arrogant Christian
imperialism of converting everybody to our religion! We've already done too
much harm that way!*

DENNIS: *Sheila, you're a beautiful person. I like you. But don't tell me to get with
it. I've worked with an African church made up of new converts. And guess what.
They loved Jesus and loved their faith. They had a few complaints, but by and
large they were grateful for what the missionaries brought them. Anyway, as a
Christian it's not my job to be in tune with the spirit of the times. God's truth transcends all times and places. It's not that we don't respect people of other religions. But the religions of the world can't all be true, and if the gospel is true,
then all religion is unbelief! That includes all the crazy religion that keeps cropping up in our churches. The liberal theology that's fashionable today—interfaith
dialogue and liberation theology and feminism and all that—it'll all be out-of-
date ten years from now and we'll have some other theological fad!*

   No doubt Sheila will press her point about how theology actually does
change from one era to another, and even from one place to another, and Dennis
will have to agree, at least in part. He will insist on the great differences between
the world religions and on the necessity of sharing the Christian faith—doing so
respectfully of course. Sheila will agree that Christian faith should be shared, but
in the form of open and vulnerable dialogue, not evangelistic missions and crusades. Despite some growing understanding of each other, they are still in fundamental disagreement about mission.

   There is a fourth kind of argument that often arises in theological discussion
among Christians. It will carry more weight among Roman Catholics than among
Protestants. Among the latter it will tend to be brought out as an argument only
as a last resort, but it may in fact have been substantially operative all along.

4. *"What you are saying is contrary to the understanding of the whole ecumenical church, and the church's long-standing tradition."*

DENNIS: *But you know, Sheila, the church has always known it had to be evangelical. What about Paul, and the great missionaries who evangelized our ancestors, like Patrick and Columba, and the great missionaries of the sixteenth century and the nineteenth century? Do you just say all these people were wrong? Without these missions, Christ would still be unknown to Europeans and North Americans, let alone Africans and Asians. I guess we'd still be Druids worshiping the sun and sacrificing at Stonehenge! Christianity would have remained a tiny sect of Judaism and would eventually disappear. These partner churches of ours in Africa are pretty enthusiastic about evangelical outreach themselves. You ask the African or Korean Christians whether they believe in evangelical mission. They're into it in a big way! They know they wouldn't even exist if previous generations hadn't faithfully carried out the great commission. You yourself, Sheila, [wagging his finger at her] would not be here today talking to me about this if somebody hadn't evangelized you. You tell me to be reasonable, but I don't find your position reasonable at all. I'm sorry, but I think your idea of mission is a recent invention, without the weight of tradition behind it.*

SHEILA: *Well frankly, Dennis, I couldn't care less about tradition. The winners of the theological struggles of the past have often been wrong. They were all men and usually privileged men with power. Some of those missions you talk about were backed up by the Roman army, or British colonial armies, or whatever, and what a lot of misery and oppression they brought to some places! Anyway, I'm not really concerned about being orthodox. It's "orthopraxis" I care about.* [Dennis raises his eyes to heaven] *The bottom line of truth for me is not tradition; it's following Jesus, and that means solidarity with the poor and oppressed!*

DENNIS: [Rolling his eyes again] *O Sheila, spare me the jargon!*

SHEILA: *No Dennis, spare me the dreary orthodoxy! And by the way, I don't grant you that the whole tradition is against me on this. I've got a pretty respectable minority tradition on my side—like the social gospel; the medical, agricultural, and educational missions; Thomas Muenzer, Francis of Assisi, and Jesus; and the Hebrew prophets!*

DENNIS: *There you go again, talking about Jesus as though he's just one more man and not our divine Lord and Saviour!*

We note that the criteria of theological adequacy proposed earlier—Christ, scripture, context, ecclesia—all become operative in this conversation. In different ways both Dennis and Sheila feel that what we have called the "criteria of a good theology" are on their side. In differing ways, they both claim correctness for their view of Christ, their approach to scripture, their perception of context, and their slant on tradition, though they give differing weight to each of these. These are the terms in which Christian theological debate normally proceeds. We note also that neither is merely arbitrary or unreasonable; both argue rationally, offering reasons for thinking as they do. We may find ourselves more in agreement with one than with the other, but I suggest that, in terms of the criteria proposed at the beginning—life-giving and liberating praxis and christological center—neither Sheila nor Dennis holds these together in a satisfactory dynamic unity. As we proceed I will try to show why an appropriate method for Christian theology would do so.

CHAPTER 2

Revelation and Faith
The Knowledge of God as Gift

How can we possibly know anything about God, let alone know God? Only because of the gift of God's self-revelation, and only by faith.

Revelation and faith are the two most basic epistemological concepts for Christian theology and have to be understood together. The terms themselves imply that Christian theology is not founded on observation of the world around us, or philosophical reasoning, nor is it rooted in the depths of our own souls. We know God and God's will and destiny for us through God's speaking a Word of self-disclosure, most decisively in Jesus the Christ. This disclosure is life-giving and liberating. It is not merely metaphysical information, the data for a philosophical worldview. It is a disclosure of God's will and intention for humanity and creation, which is justice, peace, and wholeness. Revelation is always a call to God's *shalom*, and faith is the active response to that call. The knowledge that we claim is faith knowledge, a gift of the Holy Spirit. But revelation and faith are opaque concepts for many people and require elucidation. I begin by suggesting that revelation of God and faith in God are not entirely discontinuous with other kinds of revelation and faith.

"It Was a Revelation!" She Said

"When I heard Chomsky speaking on television about the Iraq war, it was a revelation!" she said. "I already had glimmers of suspicion about what was really going on, but somehow as he spoke, everything came together. As I sat there listening to Chomsky the lights started going on, and by the time he was finished I had a whole new view of the world and knew I had to act on it."

"When my baby was born," the new mother said, "it was a revelation! A whole new range of emotions and feelings! Somehow the whole world seemed different. I'd never felt such wonder and tenderness before, such sheer joy! I felt

I would do anything for my baby. I would even kill for him if I had to!"

Mordecai Richler tells the story of a sixteen-year-old boy, Noah, who has what might be called a breakthrough "revelatory" experience of music:

> The first time Noah had been to a concert the orchestra had played *The Four Seasons* by Vivaldi and he had been so struck by it that he had felt something like pain. He had not suspected that men were capable of such beauty. He had been startled. So he had walked out wondering into the night, not knowing what to make of his discovery. All those stale lies . . . , facts that he had collected like his father did stamps, knowledge, all that passed away, rejected, dwarfed by the entry of beauty into his consciousness. The city, the gaudy night, had whirled around him phantasmagorically but without importance. I didn't know about beauty, he had thought. Nobody ever told me. When he had next been aware of his surroundings he was sitting on a bench on the mountain. It was dawn.[1]

A "revelation" in this secular sense is a breakthrough experience, flashing new insight, lights going on, an Aha!, a mind-changing, life-changing experience. From the perspective of faith, we may indeed discern God's presence in such secular moments of light and truth, since God is not tied down to religion as such or limited to believers.

We may speak of revelation in both subjective and objective senses. On the subjective side, an experience of new truth breaks through to an individual, and his or her whole view of the world is transformed. But the person who received the revelation was confronted by an objectivity—*something . . . someone there,* a set of facts seen in a whole different way which constitutes a kind of intuitive flash of realization; an actual living, breathing, wondrous baby, vulnerable and beautiful; the actually existing, magnificent, joyous music of Vivaldi. When we speak colloquially in this way of a revelation, we mean a breathtaking encounter with something or someone *very real*, so real that other things, in light of it, seem unreal or insignificant. The geopolitical realities interpreted in a new way, the baby himself, the music itself, are revelatory.

These analogies help us to grasp what revelation means theologically and to see that "faith," or response to God's revelation, is not entirely discontinuous with or unlike other breakthrough experiences. Literally, "revelation" means "unveiling" or "disclosure" of something previously hidden.[2] In the scriptures of both testaments it is closely associated with the Word of God, God's speech or communication. When we speak theologically about revelation in a subjective sense, we use words like "conversion" and "faith." In the objective sense we speak of a story, a message that has reached us, a mind-changing, life-changing truth, or better, *a person, someone who confronts us.*

We need to say immediately that for many, perhaps most, Christians, no such memorable, dramatic revelation of God may have occurred in their lives. Many of us have simply been baptized as infants and have grown up within the revelatory tradition of the church, and live within the mystery and beauty of that tradition without remembering a first moment of conversion and faith. This does not necessarily negate the fact that we have really received the revelation; our faith and commitment may be very real, constantly nurtured by worship and prayer, by hearing the preaching of the Word, by receiving the sacrament of holy communion, and by living in Christian community. With some others, who were raised within the life of the church and then left it, or who were never exposed to it at all, a breakthrough revelatory experience can occur later in life. It may be sudden and dramatic or a slowly dawning realization. However it happens, we call it "the work of the Holy Spirit," the divine Reality breathing into us.

However, where revelation in this specifically biblical and Christian sense is concerned, Christians claim a solid, unshakable "objectivity" far beyond their own personal subjective experience. Certain decisive events have occurred in history by which God has spoken and acted in human history. The love and truth disclosed there are constant and unchangeable, more real than we are, and do not depend on anyone's ackowledgment or recognition. "The grass withers, the flower fades, but the Word of our God shall stand forever" (Is 40:8). For Christians this means, objectively and preeminently, the life, death, and resurrection of Jesus, the Word made flesh. When we speak of revelation in a subjective sense, we mean that it is actually received and believed by human beings.[3] Revelation reaches its goal when people actually receive God's Word of grace and promise, of command and of judgment, when people, both individuals and communities, are consoled, encouraged, inspired, led.

Revelation means "God speaks"—not literally that vocalized words come floating down from the sky. The "Word of God" implies radical givenness, something we could never have told ourselves. Though hearing the Word has analogies with the examples given above, it is qualitatively different, for it is something that human beings could never happen upon for themselves, not something we could ever reach by pure rational thought, or find empirically in the world around us or in the depth of our souls. It is neither stargazing, nor soulgazing. It is not the result of religious experience in some general sense, for which human beings have a natural capacity. It comes radically from beyond us as gift. The content of revelation is not the end point of philosophical reflection, nor is Christian faith a philosophical hypothesis. From within faith we know (*a posteriori*, after the fact) that God can be known only as God gives Godself to be known. The holy mystery that confronts us in Jesus Christ discloses One who cannot be summoned to our objective inquiry, who can never become the "object" of our investigative techniques. In faith and theology we speak of the Subject who is beyond and above us, who never comes under our mastery or control. This Reality can only be known as self-gift, as revelation.

We may say, though, that knowledge of God bears some resemblance to the knowledge of persons. A human person too can never be known objectively as an object that comes under our masterful gaze. A person can be known only as she gives herself to be known. Of course, one may observe or investigate or spy upon a person and come to possess a good deal of information *about* her, but really to *know* her, one must enter into relationship. She must disclose herself in conversation, in gestures and activity toward oneself if one is truly to know her. It is commonly said that if we are really to know a person, appreciate the depth and mystery of a person, we must do so in a relationship of love. She must reveal and give of herself; otherwise she simply cannot be known. Not only that, but the person who would know her must enter into a relationship of receptivity and trust—a kind of faith—if mutual knowledge is to be real. This is true also of the God whom we know in Jesus Christ. God has given God's very self to us in Jesus and does so again and again through the Spirit, in Word and sacrament, and can be known only in a relationship of prayer and worship, trust and hope. It is significant that in Hebrew scriptures, the same verb is used about knowing God as knowing one's spouse: "Now the man knew his wife Eve, and she conceived and bore Cain" (Gen 4:1). "Elkanah knew his wife Hannah, and . . . Hannah conceived and bore a son" (1 Sam 1:19-20). So also, to "know God" is not a merely abstract intellectual thing, but a matter of relationality, love, and trust.

Knowledge of God biblically also has an ethical dimension, and this is essential to the praxis dimension of faith. Specifically, to know God is to do justice. Those who think they know God but perpetrate oppression and injustice are self-deceived. The prophet Jeremiah speaks for God in praise of a faithful man, Josiah:

> Did not your father eat and drink and do justice and righteousness?
> Then it was well with him. He judged the cause of the poor and needy;
> then it was well. Is not this to know me? says the Lord. (Jer 22:15-16)

Isaiah too thinks of knowledge of God as practical righteousness. At the end of his great visionary prophecy of universal peace, he declares, on God's behalf: "They will not hurt or destroy in all my holy mountain; for the earth will be full of the knowledge of the Lord, as the waters cover the sea" (Is 11:9). According to Isaiah and Jeremiah, then, living and acting righteously, or at least sincerely attempting to do so (however imperfectly), is essential to knowing God, since loving God means loving justice. In the New Testament, John says something similar about love: "One who loves is of God and knows God . . . for God is Love" (1 Jn 4:7-8). Knowledge of God, then, is relational and practical; it is not merely the possession of academic, metaphysical information. What is given in revelation is not some theory or information about the transcendent. What is given is practical wisdom and relationship.

It is typical for Christians to speak of Jesus Christ as "the revelation of God," since, for Christians, the life, death, and resurrection of Jesus is decisively and incomparably revelatory of God and therefore also discloses the truth about humanity, creation, history, and the future. A good deal will be said elsewhere in this book about Jesus as revelation, but it would be false christomonism (an overly exclusive emphasis on Christ only) to suggest that revelation occured first and only in Jesus of Nazareth. Quite apart from the question of general revelation in the realm of nature, or divine self-disclosure in the other great religious traditions of the world, we know in the Christian tradition that the God revealed in Jesus the Christ was already known before the time of Jesus, and is still known, by the Jews. Revelation as God's redemptive self-disclosure in Jesus has its indispensable, *sine qua non* presupposition in the history of revelation with the people of Israel. There we find established the pattern of God's self-disclosure through prophetic calling, promise, and historical event. The life, death, and resurrection of Jesus as revelatory event have to be understood as continuous with the pattern that we already find in the Hebrew scriptures.

Vocation, Promise, Word Event

While the term "revelation" and its accompanying verbs do not occur very frequently in the Hebrew scriptures (see Gen 35:7; 2 Sam 7:27; Hab 2:19; Job 38:17; Is 22:14; 40:5; etc.), the basic premise is that God communicates, God "speaks." Much more common is the term *dabar* of *Yahweh,* the Word of the Lord, which comes over and over again to patriarchs, judges, or charismatic leaders and prophets: "The Word of the Lord came to Abram" (Gen 15:1); "The Word of the Lord came to Nathan" (2 Sam 7:4); the Word of the Lord you rulers . . ." (Is 1:10); and so on. For our purposes here, it seems useful to focus on two of the earliest and most formative instances of revelation: the call of Abraham and the story of Moses, his calling, and the exodus from Egypt, which may be referred to as "Word events," or events that speak.

It is impossible, of course, to reconstruct a historically factual account of what happened between God and Abraham or between God and Moses. The encounters that we hear about in Genesis and Exodus were surely ineffable and beyond apt description. Besides that, they come to us from a far distant time, were recounted orally, and were later written by ancient people whose mentality was quite different from our own. But these ancient stories of Israel's experiences with God are so important—not only for our faith tradition but for our whole religious and cultural history—that we dare not ignore them. We are told of a holy One who calls and inspires human servants, who establishes covenant with a people, who promises the blessing of a better future, who commands and leads the people toward that future. We hear of God's Word coming to Abraham, who is still regarded by Jews, Christians, and Muslims as their common "father" in faith:

Now the Lord said to Abram, "Go from your country and your kindred and your father's house to the land that I will show you. I will make of you a great nation, and I will bless you, and make your name great, so that you will be a blessing. I will bless those who bless you, and the one who curses you I will curse; and in you all the families of the earth shall be blessed." (Gen 12:1-3)

This leaving behind of country and kindred, setting out to a new land and a whole new life, is remembered by the spiritual descendants of Abraham (Jews, Christians, and Muslims) as the founding event of their peoples and their faith traditions. We should not overlook that people of our own time may often respond to such a story with skepticism. We may imagine the conversation of a confirmation class of bright questioning teenagers reacting to Genesis 12:

Conversation

DEBBIE: *But are we really supposed to believe that God talks to people like this? I've never heard God talk and I don't know anybody else who has. If somebody told me that they heard God talking to them I'd think they were crazy.*

REV. BRIAN: [Stroking his beard] *Yes, one might think that such people were in the grip of auditory hallucations.*

JASON: *And besides, it says God will curse people who curse them. Do we really think God curses people? It sounds like these people made this stuff up to make their own nation sound like the greatest and most important one in the world.*

REV. BRIAN: *It does sound rather like a territorial, tribal god, doesn't it?*

KIM: *Wait a minute! You can't just criticize the Bible like that! I thought this was the Word of God! You make it sound like it's all a pile of . . . rubbish!*

REV. BRIAN: *Oh definitely not rubbish, Kim! And you're right, we should listen to these stories in a spirit of reverence, listening for God's Word. But we can't help criticizing the Bible if it doesn't make sense to us. We'll either reject it as nonsense or find some credible way to understand it and learn from it. But I agree with you, Kim, somebody didn't just make all this up to fool us. There must be something very significant behind it. In fact these old stories, for all their human glitches, are telling us something of earthshaking importance that has had an enormous impact on the whole world.*

DEBBIE: *Really? What's so earthshaking about old fairy tales?*

REV. BRIAN: *Well, three great world faiths had their beginning in some such ancient events as these. Whole civilizations, their moralities and cultures and spirituality, their art and literature, took their beginnings here. A concept of one God, and concepts of time and history and the future, as well. And, most important from our point of view, Jesus came out of this tradition! In fact, the whole world has been blessed through this history, which started with Abraham!*

The young people seem impressed but not entirely convinced. But most of us, in all honesty, need to ask: Does God really speak such quotable words to a human being? Critical study of the Old Testament suggests that the words attributed to God here reflect the later experience and faith of the Jewish community and its own actual history of covenant and blessing. Here the faith community, long centuries after the events of God with Abraham, imaginatively interprets the beginnings of its remarkable national and spiritual history by means of this story of vocation and promise.[4] The story of Abraham reflects Israel's subsequent political and spiritual history. We need not deny, though, that some such revelatory event occurred and that a dim memory of it is recorded here, as it was passed down through many generations by word of mouth. The later history of God with the Hebrew people also tells us of God speaking with people, especially the prophets, and so it should not surprise us that such an experience of God communicating stands at the very beginning of their faith tradition. We will not necessarily accept it in detail as historically factual. What we have to take seriously is the Jews' confession of faith that a divine presence and blessing have accompanied its history and have been with them from the beginning, that God speaks through particular prophetic individuals, and that they are indeed a "called" nation, through whom in truth the whole world has been blessed. The "earth-shaking impact on the whole world" includes the origination of three great world faiths that have shaped civilizations for centuries. The call of Abraham may be said to have initiated a whole new concept of time and of hope for long term history in which God is purposefully at work.

We find the same pattern of calling, command, promise, and event in the story of Moses:

> Moses was keeping the flock of his father-in-law Jethro, the priest of Midian; he led his flock beyond the wilderness, and came to Horeb, the mountain of God. There the angel of the Lord appeared to him in a flame of fire out of a bush; he looked, and the bush was blazing, yet it was not consumed. Then Moses said, "I must turn aside and look at this great sight, and see why the bush is not burned up." When the Lord saw that he had turned aside to see, God called to him out of the bush, "Moses, Moses!" And he said, "Here I am." Then he said, "Come no closer! Remove the sandals from your feet, for the place on which you are standing is holy ground." He said further, "I am the God of your father, the God of Abraham, the God of Isaac, and the God of Jacob." And Moses hid his face, for he was afraid to look at God. (Exod 3:1-6)

Thus we are told of an unspeakable, awesome encounter with a holy One who commands and promises. Was there really a tree burning that was not consumed? Did God speak just these words to Moses? We need not think so. The story is written down much later than the event and in light of other great events that occurred subsequently. We may believe, though, that Moses had an indescribable experience of being addressed by One who spoke directly to him in his particular circumstance of oppression and anger, of longing and hope. We know that fire, in many religious traditions, signifies an epiphany or purifying, purging presence of the divine,[5] and so we may consider the burning bush to be symbolic of a "burning" divine presence impinging on the mind of Moses. Yet even in revelation, God remains mystery. Moses is told to "come no closer." We are told that, on another occasion, Moses beholds only the "back" of God, for "you cannot see my face; for no one shall see me and live" (Exod 33:20). A human being cannot bear to see God.

We should note also that God's revealing is not only *self*-revelation. God also reveals *something*—a purpose and a promise. In the story of Moses and the exodus, God reveals the divine intention for liberty and justice for the enslaved people. We must keep in mind that the story is told from hindsight, from the perspective of the coming liberative event having already occurred. J. Severino Croatto, a Latin American Old Testament theologian, notes:

> the Promise, or the vocation, as narrated, takes for granted the experience of the liberation and the existence of Israel as a people on its land. The Promise expresses in the form of a plan the event which, in reality, engenders the Promise as word. Such is the richness of the Promise or the "vocation." It speaks with a depth not grasped at the time of Abraham and of Moses.[6]

Again, we may accept that something awesome did happen with Moses on the mountain. Whatever precisely happened between God and Moses, what we have in Exodus 3 is the faithful testimony of the Hebrew people to the ineffable presence of the holy One of Israel,[7] who called them to liberty and life. Because they lived within an ongoing tradition of a self-revealing God, they knew that that tradition had a decisive foundation in a revelatory experience of God "speaking." No doubt, oral traditions had been passed down through the generations telling of such encounters. It is reasonable to ask, Where, after all, did the faith of Israel originate, if not in some such awesome experience of being addressed, commanded, and led? And what, or rather who, was revealed, but the gracious, commanding and liberating God, whose self-disclosure totally de-absolutized and desacralized the deified pharaoh of Egypt and all earthly powers and authorities? For Moses, and for all the generations of Jews to come, deity has been henceforth this holy, liberating One, who led, inspired, and empowered the escape into freedom. The events of vocation and promise have been earthshaking indeed.

They have had incomparable impact not only on religious and political consciousness but on the whole history of humankind. Without the burning bush and
the subsequent exodus from Egypt, neither the Hebrew faith tradition nor Christianity would exist. Nor would so-called Christian culture or Western civlization
as we know it. The Islamic faith would never have arisen without this Hebrew,
exodus background, nor the long brilliant history of Islamic civilization, since
Islam too recognizes Moses as a prophet and arose out of a Jewish/Christian
milieu. The antecedent of Christian faith and its originating source is this Hebrew
experience of the self-revealing, holy, and liberating God and the trusting, obedient response to this revelation, which we call faith.

But it was not only the divinely initiated vocation and promise that were revelatory in the early Hebrew experience. It was, above all, the historical event
itself which became the vehicle of revelation for the Hebrew people, and most
specifically the event of the exodus from slavery in Egypt. According to Croatto,
"the Exodus is the key event that models the faith of Israel. Unless we begin from
this central event, neither Israel's faith nor the formation of its religious traditions
and sacred books are understandable."[8]

It is not my purpose here to offer a complete exegesis of the exodus texts—
a massive task—but to explore its significance for the meaning of revelation and
for faith as response to revelation. It was the Jews, says Mircea Eliade, who,
because of their decisive and remarkable liberation from Egypt and the prophetic
tradition that followed, "were the first to discover the meaning of history as the
epiphany of God." Christianity, out of its Hebrew roots, spread throughout the
world its discovery of "personal freedom and continuous time (in place of cyclical time)."[9] The whole world has begun to think of time as moving forward in a
linear manner toward an end or goal. People interpreted the event of liberation as
a divine event, a Word event. The event moved them to believe in and to trust the
God of Abraham, Isaac, and Jacob and to order their lives and society in obedience to God's law; that is, it was the ground of their faith.

But for most of us today, immersed as we are in a critical and modern scientific worldview, the story is fraught with difficulty. We might listen in once
again on our confirmation class, who have read Exodus 1-15 as their week's
homework. They have read of the saving of the infant Moses in the bullrushes by
five courageous women; of the midwives Shiphrah and Puah, who refused to kill
the newborn baby boys; and of the child's mother and sister, and the princess.
They have read of young Moses' rebellion against the beating of a Hebrew slave
and the killing of the Egyptian slave master; his experience of the divine call at
the burning bush; his miraculous deeds and his demands to the pharaoh to release
his people; the horrendous plagues, the Passover, and the death of the Egyptian
firstborn; and finally the dramatic escape across the sea:

> Then Moses stretched out his hand over the sea. The Lord drove the sea
> back by a strong east wind all night, and turned the sea into dry land;

and the waters were divided. The Israelites went into the sea on dry ground, the waters forming a wall for them on their right and on their left. (Exod 14:21-22)

Conversation

REV. BRIAN: *Well, my friends, I hope you all read Exodus 1-15 this week and found it interesting. What did you think of it?*

JASON: *Wow! Awesome! Couldn't possibly believe it, of course, but it makes a really good story!* [Nervous laughter from the others] *I really got off on all that stuff about God sending plagues and drying up the sea!*

KIM: *I don't see why you need to mock it. Why can't God do whatever he likes? If God can create the whole universe, I guess he can arrange for a few plagues, or dry up a little bit of water!*

JASON: *Well, I haven't noticed any miracles lately. How come God didn't send a plague or two to Iraq so the army wouldn't have to go in with their guys firing? A parting of the sea or something like that might have helped out in South America too, or Bosnia, or Rwanda, or Kosovo. If God can do this kind of thing why doesn't he do it more often? Maybe he should have helped out the people in the planes before they crashed in New York and Washington, or the people in the World Trade Center, or the innocent people that got bombed in Afghanistan or Baghdad!*

REV. BRIAN: *Hey, Jason, I had no idea you were so well informed about politics!*

JASON: [A little embarrassed] *Yeah, my parents take me on all these peace marches and political rallies.*

DEBBIE: *I've also got a problem with this type of God. He seems so egotistical, showing off his power and hardening people's hearts. Are we really supposed to bow down to a God like this?*

REV. BRIAN: *You're right, Debbie. It's a very flawed concept of God, isn't it? The God that we meet in Jesus is quite different. On that basis I would criticize the idea of God that is going on in this story. On the other hand, the God who shows up in this story was a huge breakthrough for that time. Here you've got a God who takes sides with little people. This is a holy God of compassion who hates slavery. This was a far cry from the deified pharaoh, and in the name of this holy God, those little people dared to defy the pharaoh. That was earthshaking for the time!*

MATTHEW: *OK, so it was a great breakthrough for the time. But can we take it seriously now? I think the exodus is a great story, but it doesn't seem like it hap-*

pened in this world. Have you ever seen The Ten Commandments *on TV? Moses waves his wand and the water stands up like walls on both sides! Neat stuff, but get real.* [Laughs and smiles]

KIM: [Not amused, flushed with anger] *By the time you guys are finished, there won't be any Bible or Christianity left!*

JASON: [After a brief silence] *Maybe we should believe it, but not take it literally . . . ?*

DEBBIE: *You mean it's all symbols and myths like the Adam and Eve story, to teach us a lesson? Like it never really happened at all?*

JASON: [Shrugging] *Yeah, maybe.*

REV. BRIAN: *Well, I agree we don't have to take it all literally as factual history, and we're right to be critical of its concept of God. But I don't really think it's a myth either. Remember, the Jews are real people with a real religious history. Their story and faith did actually get going somehow. Of course they're not modern, scientific people, so they don't tell it the way we would today. But it's basic to their national memory that somehow things got started in an event of liberation, and their faith is that God had something to do with it.*

KIM: *A little more than "something to do with it," wouldn't you say? I find the story really inspiring. It kind of gets me excited to think what God could do if we believed in him enough.*

REV. BRIAN: *Well, yes. . . . They think of God essentially as their Liberator, you see? They believe that God is at work within human actions and historical events bringing about justice and freedom. We may still believe that, without crediting the spectacular miracles. God can work through natural processes and through people's courage. Like the midwives, defying the pharaoh and refusing to kill the infant boys. And Moses, daring to confront the pharaoh. The miracles tell us that something astounding happened and the people were amazed. We can still be amazed today when great events of liberation happen, either personally or socially. We might even say that wherever people are set free, God is in it. . . .*

The exodus event was central and foundational for the faith of Israel. Following this event, the Decalogue of God's commandments given by Moses opened with the words: "I am the Lord your God who brought you out of Egypt, out of the house of slavery. You shall have no gods beside me" (Exod 20:1-3). Whatever event occurred at the beginning of Israel's national existence, it has to have been such as to account for the exodus-centered covenant faith in a life-giving, people-freeing God. We cannot reconstruct the event and do not need to. But how are we to think of events as revelatory? It is clear enough, as in the conversation above, that most contemporary people do not find miraculous vertical/supernatural interventions very credible. They are far removed from our normal experience of life. Remarkable things may occur, even answers to prayers for healing, for example, but they appear to happen in and through deeply complex, but natural processes. Plagues of locusts, the sudden death of firstborn children, a river flowing with blood, and the timely subsiding of a body of water, no longer appear to us (except in insurance policies) to be "acts of God." We have to think of God's relation to the world and humanity in some other way. Revelation, too, while we must think of it as a presence or inbreaking of a holy transcendence, need not be seen as a supernatural setting aside of the laws of nature. Had twenty-first-century journalists been present to observe and report on the exodus events, probably they would have found a political struggle, perhaps with elements of guerilla violence and bloodshed, elements of luck, and a religiously inspired group of freedom fighters led by a charismatic religious leader. As writers for the secular press they could have interpreted the whole remarkable event quite without reference to God or to miracles. However, such an account would have been entirely inadequate from the point of view of the insiders, the participants in the event, especially as they reflected and pondered upon it some time later. From the vantage point of liberation having been achieved, and the ongoing sense of the presence of their liberating God with them, they looked back and saw the event as an act of God, a mysterious, redemptive event in which something or Someone more than themselves was at work. An event of such profound consequence might, quite reasonably, be interpreted as an event of God. The story as we have it is not, of course, a bare chronicle of events but a "faith-ful" account of events as interpreted. As people of the twenty-first century, we are likely to read the exodus story with quite different eyes than those of ancient readers, and yet the story continues to fascinate and inspire us. We may wish that such supernatural events would occur to liberate Africans or Iraqis or Palestinians today—or disabled folk or people in our own country struggling to live on social assistance. Yet it is often precisely these, whose circumstances most resemble those of the oppressed Hebrews in Egypt, who find hope in this story.

The hermeneutical concepts of Paul Ricoeur and J. Severino Croatto are helpful for an understanding of the exodus event as revelation. Certain historical events, Ricoeur says, are sufficiently rich with meaning and fertile that they generate other events and become foundational for a history of ideas, institutions, and practices. This happens when the event is interpreted and this interpretation becomes the "Word" of the event. The interpretation (e.g., the exodus story as we have it in the Bible) as written text, because of its very richness and depth, takes on a life of its own.[10] "Distantiation" (distancing) occurs between the ancient author and the contemporary reader. Or, as he also expresses it, the text is "polysemic" (it has potential for multiple meanings); it exhibits a surplus or reservoir of meaning.[11] As Ricoeur insists, a responsible exegesis of the text will still explore the "world behind the text" (authorship, date, historical circumstances in which it was written) in order to understand what the author meant to say in that time and place. It is not permissible to make the text say just anything we want it to say. Yet a contemporary reading will also attend to the "world in front of the text," that is, the interpreter's own world of here-and-now. What does it mean for us today? What is the living Word of the ancient event for us? Or, to put it differently, what or who oppresses us today, and how is God seeking to lead us to greater fullness of life?

If we regard the biblical account as "holy scripture," presumably this is because we believe it continues to speak God's Word to us today, so that the exodus was not an event solely for the ancient Hebrews, but continues to be revelatory of God's will for all people. Exodus, then, is still incomplete. While it is a once-upon-a-time actual event, it is also the name of God's ongoing liberating work in the world.

The "hermeneutical circle" (circle of interpretation) to which Croatto refers, or "dialectic of Scripture and context,"[12] so typical of third-world liberationist method and hermeneutics, is another way of stating the point. God's self-revelation, God's leading and inspiration and saving work among us, is a continuing, ongoing reality, as we read the scriptures again and again in ever-changing circumstances. In the Spirit and in expectant faith, we read and reread the story, finding fresh meaning as we put to it the questions that arise out of our own needs and dilemmas. The circularity between the ancient text and our present context becomes in fact a hermeneutical spiral in which the living Word never ceases to be revelatory in new ways. Faith as response to revelation is not, then, a case of believing in authoritative doctrines or concepts (though these may be a helpful part of our thinking) nor even a response to a once-and-for-all revealed-ness in the past. Rather, it is a continuing response to a living and revealing Word which speaks fresh messages to ever-changing contexts. In faith, the text inspires us to look for new exodus events. Thus, faith as response to present revelation, in the Holy Spirit, finds new hope and new guidance and challenges us to play our responsible roles in the remaking of individual lives, and in the making of history.

Revelation, then, is not simply something that happened in past events. It has been especially the liberation theologians of the third world who have found inspiration in the exodus story in our time and guidance for the struggles of their particular contexts. The hermeneutical circle, Croatto points out, runs in two directions. The contemporary context is interpreted in light of the exodus story. The story illuminates and assists in the analysis of what is happening (in his case in Latin America). The context is analyzed and interpreted in light of the biblical Word. But in turn, the present meaning of the biblical Word is illuminated by the circumstances, needs, and questions of the present time. Croatto finds many messages in the story concerning God's compassionate presence in history and God's will for justice and freedom, concerning the mentalities of oppressor and oppressed, and concerning love, violence, vocation, and leadership. As a person of our time, he does not expect that fabulous supernatural interventions will put an end to oppression in Latin America. "It would be ingenuous to hope that the same will happen today in literal form."

> We want to comment on the manifestation of the power of Yahweh, superior to that of the oppressor pharaoh, who can be overcome only by another "power." Now today there is a very clear consciousness that there is no power superior to that of a united and committed "people." When an entire people rejects a tyrant it creates an irremissible "power vacuum." The Hebrews' decision to rebel collectively and to flee . . . insured their success. The pharaoh could do nothing against a united group. But this group was organized and did not hesitate to march because it had been "conscientized" and knew what it had to do, despite the initial resistance and doubt.[13]

Croatto does not claim to be able to describe the strategy of the liberation event in any detail. Obviously it was a political and social event that was interpreted and "indeed should be interpreted for a Christian conscience—as the will of God."[14] It was precisely the revelatory self-disclosure of God to Moses, and through Moses to the people, that decisively conscientized them and thereby undermined the authority of the deified ruler. God's presence and leading as holy, just, and compassionate, liberated the people to play their own responsible roles in the making of a liberated history. "Exodus" is therefore endlessly fertile as inspiration for today's struggles, both social and personal, for groups or individuals, against all kinds of tyrannies.

This is so also in the case of the prophets who followed centuries later. They too—Amos, Hosea, Isaiah, Micah, Jeremiah, Ezekiel—believed that God spoke to them God's own "Word," but, as we said earlier, not simply to provide information about God's mysterious Self. God is always the God of the promise, who commands, judges, and acts, and above all promises a future for which the people both hope and strive. At the same time, the self-revealing God also remains concealed. One of the prophets declares: "Truly, you are a God who hides himself, O God of Israel, the Saviour" (Is 45:15). Again, one could dismiss the prophetic announcements as the delusions of ancient, precritical minds, or as signs of auditory hallucination and mental illness. Yet when one reads their messages one cannot so easily dismiss them, for one finds wisdom and eloquence, courage, hope, and vision for the future. The prophets brought a demanding ethic of justice from the God of exodus. People of faith still discern in their words the Word of God, uttered fallibly, yet powerfully, through flawed human beings.

Of particular interest to Christians is the hope of the prophets for what the God of exodus had in store for the people through the work of a great anointed king, or suffering servant, who would come in the power of God's Spirit to bring justice and peace to the world (e.g., Isaiah chaps. 11, 42, 61). The first Christians identified Jesus as this expected one, the Messiah, the Suffering Servant of God.

Jesus as Revelation

It is within this tradition of God's revelation to Israel and the prophetic hope that Jesus appears, standing in the line of the prophets. His beautiful life of preaching, teaching, and healing is carried out with extraordinary authority. He inspires the faith and love of his disciples and the hatred of the powerful. He is crucified on a Roman cross and dies with forgiveness on his lips. He is raised from the dead. Afterwards, from the perspective of the resurrection, his whole life and death, seen in light of his resurrection, are understood as God's unique and decisive revelation and salvation. We will have to say much more about all of this in a later chapter, but we need to note here something qualitatively different in the story of ongoing revelation.

The New Testament authors proclaim a *decisive* revelatory event, a Word event of a different kind, in the life, death, and resurrection of Jesus. The Letter to the Hebrews puts it this way: "Long ago God spoke to our ancestors in many and various ways by the prophets, but in these last days he has spoken to us by a Son" (Heb 1:1-2). In what appears to be a nascent trinitarianism, the Matthean Jesus says not simply that he reveals "God," but that he, the Son, reveals "the Father," and also that the Father reveals him as the Christ (Mt 16:16). Closely related concepts are light, wisdom, and Word. Paul, after the resurrection, speaks of Jesus as God's light: "For it is the God who said, 'Let light shine out of darkness,' who has shone in our hearts to give the light of the knowledge of the glory of God in the face of Jesus Christ" (2 Cor 4:6). Jesus not only *teaches* wisdom but *is* the Wisdom (*sophia*) of God (1 Cor 1:30). According to John, Jesus not only *brings* light but *is* "the light of the world" (Jn 8:12). Jesus does not, like the prophets, simply *speak* a Word from God but *is,* in his whole life, death, and resurrection, God's own *logos* made flesh (Jn 1:14). Jesus, then, not merely in his teaching and preaching, but in his very person, *incarnates* God's own presence.

We note that the Greek word *apokalypsis* (translated "revelation") very often carries an eschatological connotation; that is, it pertains to the end-time, the time of the fulfilled reign of God. This future orientation of revelation coheres with the revelatory promise in the Hebrew scriptures. Paul writes of waiting for "the revealing of our Lord Jesus Christ" (1 Cor 1:7) and of "the glory that is to be revealed" (Rom 8:18). He writes of Jesus Christ "the revelation of the mystery that was kept secret for long ages but is now disclosed" (Rom 16:25). First Peter speaks of "a salvation ready to be revealed in the last time" (1:5), which is the time when "Jesus Christ will be revealed" (1:7). The apocalyptic book entitled the Revelation of John begins by proclaiming "the revelation of Jesus Christ" as the end-time victory of God's reign over all evil, oppression, and death. It is true, I think, that the first Christians' whole perception of Jesus as revelation, *apokalypsis,* flowed preeminently from the event of the resurrection. His preaching and teaching, his love, compassion, and courage would not in themselves account for their naming him Messiah (Christ), and Word of God made flesh. The resurrection (as I shall argue later) is the *apokalypsis* par excellence. As the sign of God's final victory over evil, injustice, and death, it may be seen as the proleptic (ahead of time) appearance of God's eternal reign, the anticipation of future consummation.[15] As such, the resurrection is *sine qua non* for the proclamation of Jesus as God's decisive self-revelation.

Has revelation ceased since the time of Jesus? Is nothing more to be expected until the consummation of God's eternal reign? Paul certainly did not think so. He believed that he received personal revelations from God, by which he meant guidance and direction for his mission (see 1 Cor 14:6; Gal 1:12; 2:2; Phil 3:15). This can be seen as another way to speak of the guidance of the Holy Spirit. But if Jesus Christ is *the* revelation of God, it follows that ongoing or continuing revelation witnesses to him, or is at least congruent with what we find in him. Alleged revelations are measured according to the "canon" of Jesus himself.

We may draw a distinction here between "original revelation" and "dependent revelation."[16] For biblical faith, the event of the exodus, for example, is original revelation, a decisive liberative, revelatory event, including the call of Moses and the struggle and eventual escape to freedom, which became normative for the Hebrew people for all later discernment of God's Word, presence, and activity. But Jews of later generations, who were not present for the liberation from Egypt, nevertheless receive its revelation, live within its truth, and regularly celebrate it liturgically. Dependent revelation is one of remembrance and imaginative reliving of the event (*anamnēsis*). So also, specifically among Christians, Jesus Christ above all is original revelation and becomes normative for all subsequent alleged revelation. The original revelatory events establish God's identity and purpose. Yet later generations of Christians also receive the revelation in a dependent way, hearing the Word of God through scripture and preaching and celebrating it liturgically and sacramentally.

Revelation, then, is the basic supposition for the Christian knowledge of God. Together with the concept of the Word of God, it is perhaps the most fundamental epistemological concept for Christian theology. We do not speak of it *a priori,* from outside faith. This is not an axiomatic philosophic concept. To receive the knowledge of God is not a natural human possibility, nor is it divinely given information. It is not, then, primarily "propositional." Rather, it is the offer of relationship, of direction, meaning, and hope and can be spoken of only *a posteriori.* Karl Barth wrote with admirable clarity about this:

> We start out from the fact that through His Word God is actually known and will be known again. . . . The question then cannot be posed *in abstracto* but only *in concreto;* not *a priori* but only *a posteriori.* The *in abstracto* and *a priori* question of the possibility of the knowledge of God obviously presupposes the existence of a place outside the knowledge of God itself from which this knowledge can be judged.[17]

In the last analysis, then, no higher or deeper authority exists that can identify or authorize it. It is *believed and acted upon.* It calls forth the response of faith.

Faith, Not Sight

Faith, of course, is correlative to revelation. The concept is unintelligible except as response to a revelation—a Word, a wisdom, a light, by which a person is confronted.

Paul tells us that "we walk by faith, not by sight," yet full of confidence (2 Cor 5:7). Here he reflects the ancient faith of Abraham, who left his home and kindred behind to go to a land he did not know: "It was by faith that Abraham obeyed the call to set out for a country that was the inheritance given to him and his descendants, and that he set out without knowing where he was going" (Heb 11:8). Faith is epistemologically vulnerable. Abraham must have had confidence, but he must have had difficulty explaining his actions to his family and may have had doubts himself. Why must this be so? Why does God ask us to believe what cannot be demonstrated? Is this not an invitation to intellectual dishonesty? Are we not then tempted to believe as a kind of wish fulfillment? Surely preachers and theologians should not encourage people to be gullible, to be less intellectually rigorous than they are able to be. Surely we should not ask for unintelligent faith, for unquestioning credulity! Yet perhaps there is an inner necessity to the vulnerability of faith. The object of inquiry with which we are concerned is God! Not an object among other objects; indeed, not an object at all, but *the Subject*, the ineffable Mystery who lies beyond all epistemological mastery or control. This is the holy One whom we cannot see and still live (Exod 33:20). At the same time the God whom we encounter in the biblical stories, and especially in Jesus, is the gentle, noncoercive God who does not dominate us, does not dominate even our processes of knowing—so much so that Paul can say "God's foolishness is wiser than human wisdom, and God's weakness is stronger than human strength" (1 Cor 1:25).

Many authors have described faith under various headings, and there is no one correct set of categories that adequately characterizes it. I shall speak of Christian faith under four headings: as grounded in experience, as trust and hope, as "following Jesus," and as knowledge.

1. Faith Grounded in Experience

The word "faith" is often used in an unhelpful way by people who give the impression that having faith is (in the words of Mark Twain's Huckleberry Finn) "believing things that you know aren't really true." Faith is sometimes seen as a matter of holding certain opinions simply because we want to, or because we think we ought to, and therefore a kind of excuse for not thinking hard enough, a form of intellectual self-indulgence, or letting some authority do our thinking for us. I recall a confirmation class discussion between some bright, rather skeptical teenagers and their minister, in which the minister was challenged to be clear about what he meant by faith. It went something like this:

Conversation

JASON: *So why do we believe that Jesus rose from the dead? My friends say it's just a fairytale that somebody made up.*

REV. BRIAN: *Well, there are a lot of arguments that scholars have come up with to make it probable or credible, but in the last analysis, I guess it's a matter of faith.*

JASON: *Oh.* [A little disappointed]

DEBBIE: *Heck, by that kind of reasoning I could believe anything that feels good and say it's faith. Our science teacher says it's dishonest to say anything is true if we can't prove it.*

REV. BRIAN: *But we believe lots of things we can't prove scientifically. How about your mother's love? Can you prove that? Or that your favourite music is really beautiful, or that it's wrong to hurt people? If we apply the methods of natural science to all spheres of life, we cut out half of what's important. There are other kinds of reasoning besides scientific or mathematical. There are deeper levels of knowing, and faith is one of them.*

DEBBIE: *Yes, but I can experience those things you mention. I mean, I know my mother loves me because she acts like she does. I can see and hear her. I can't see Jesus rising from the dead.*

REV. BRIAN: *Hmmm. I see your point. True, I can't see Jesus rising from the dead, and I certainly can't prove to anybody else that he did. But I still think my faith in his resurrection is reasonable. I guess what I'm saying is, believing in Jesus is a special kind of experience. The story grabs me, convinces me. Maybe it doesn't knock me right over, but at the end of the day it persuades me. Not the story of the resurrection all by itself, but along with everything else we hear about Jesus—his life, his teaching, his death. My faith isn't based on dry arguments. I feel I meet the risen Christ as he is presented by the witnesses, and I decide to trust the witnesses. It's risky, but it's a little like trusting another person. As a result, a lot of other things in life fall into place. Life makes sense for me. I believe I experience Jesus as alive and present in my life and he changes my whole outlook on life as a result.*

The conversation has a long way to go, and the young people are not necessarily convinced. The whole matter of believing in the resurrection will have to be discussed again later.

But first, a working definition of "faith," so that we know what we are talking about: Christian faith as we hear of it in the New Testament is a believing, trusting, obedient relationship to God in Jesus Christ through the Holy Spirit. It is not faith in God in an abstract sense, but concretely, faith in *this triune God* that we know through Christ and the Spirit. And indeed it is *an experience* that these early witnesses speak of. It is not a case of "believing" or merely assenting to concepts or doctrines that they "take on faith" because some sacred authority has taught them to do so. The disciples, of course, had the unique advantage of knowing and living with a thoroughly fleshly, visible Jesus of Nazareth. His presence with them was, as they tell it, so gracious and powerful that their lives could never be the same again. They believed that his presence was the very grace of God drawing near to them.[18] After his death they claimed to have met him alive again. They said that the power of sin and death had been overcome in him (i.e., he had brought salvation). But later New Testament witnesses who did not know Jesus of Nazareth in the flesh spoke of knowing him through the Holy Spirit (e.g., Paul in 1 Cor 12:3). Even today, Christians often say that they *meet* Jesus Christ, that they encounter him as a personal presence, and that in him they believe they are in touch with the ultimate mystery and meaning of things. Their experience is interpreted experience, of course. It is mediated through scripture and the community of faith. Probably for most people this is not a particularly spooky experience or emotionally very spectacular. It is more likely a deep and quiet experience, one of recognition, of acknowledgment, including typically religious dimensions of awe, of mystery, and of reverence. It may consist in a sense of being powerfully addressed (perhaps through the message of a preacher) or of being unconditionally loved, of having one's life renewed or reoriented, of being deeply challenged or consoled, or of finding that life and the world make sense in a new way. It may happen in the course of a conversation with a believer, or in the context of worship or holy communion. It is not ideas or concepts (though these are involved) nor some kind of *It*, but a *Thou*, which evokes this experience that we call faith.[19] We hear the story of Jesus, of his life, deeds, and teaching, of his death and resurrection, and the story "speaks" to us powerfully and convincingly as a "God story" or a Word event. Indeed, we may say that through the story, God speaks, confronts, and grasps us.

One Christian that I know sometimes likens a meeting with Jesus Christ to being "hit by a Mack truck!" In other words, there is a certain irresistibility about encountering (in the scripture and the church's proclamation) one whose beauty, love, and authority are so overwhelming that one finds oneself acknowledging him as Lord. Someone else told me that at first he dismissed the Jesus story as myth or legend, refusing to take it seriously, but somehow he could not get it out of his mind. Jesus would not go away. His own reasoning processes told him that somehow he had to account for the fact of Jesus, and in the end, explaining away Jesus just wasn't convincing. Others might choose a gentler image than the Mack truck. We could also speak of the experience of wonderful music, say Vivaldi's *Four Seasons,* or the Hungarian Rhapsody, or Tschaikowsky's Violin Concerto in D Minor (perhaps I should mention something of the performances of the Celine Dion, Sarah Brightman, or Enya)—music that sweeps upon the listener, grasping attention, moving emotions, commanding admiration and praise. We don't believe the music is beautiful because someone argued us into it logically on the basis of some premise. Nor could we demonstrate its beauty to someone who did not hear it. So also, the gospel story of Jesus, his life, death, and resurrection, blows us away with the Spirit's gentle persuasive power, claiming our acknowledgment, evoking our love, reorienting our lives. "Let anyone with ears to hear listen!" Jesus frequently says (Mk 4:9; Mt 13:9; Lk 14:35). The One who can so save us, remake us, inspire us to love, liberate us, and give us meaning and hope is precisely what we mean by "the divine."

We must acknowledge, though, that our faith response to Jesus is not always so dramatic. As we mentioned earlier, in every congregation one finds many individuals whose commitment is deep and serious, who perhaps grew up in faith and in the church from infancy, remembering no dramatic moment of conversion. Yet they are continually moved by the Jesus story. Such people often do not speak explicitly of the Holy Spirit, nor even of meeting Jesus. We may name our faith experience in many ways, or even remain relatively inarticulate about it, but it may be real all the same. Then, too, we are aware of some people in the churches whose faith is so very vague or uninformed, or so unexpressed, or so "way out" that we doubt if they can be said to have faith at all. But we could be completely wrong about that. We have to be careful about passing negative judgments about other people's relationship to God. It is not for us to decide who has faith and who has not (especially when people say they have). One important service that theologically educated pastors or teachers may perform is precisely to help Christians understand and name their faith experience.

Christian faith, then, I want to insist, is not a merely groundless subjectivism nor a mere acceptance of external religious authority. It has to do with experiencing, encountering, and responding to One who stands over against us as an objective Other. For Christians this Other is not a vague mystical something, but the person Jesus, the Christ, whose character and deeds are recounted in the Gospels, who is risen and present to us by the Spirit, and, through him, his *Abba* in whom he trusted.

Of course one could still say that one has this kind of experience because one was brought up to have it or because, in our culture, this is the kind of religious experience we are conditioned to have. And there would be truth in that. Had we been brought up in India, for example, we might well have had a kind of Hindu faith, the kind of faith for which a very different culture had equipped us. This is one good reason for taking other people's religious or faith experiences seriously and being open to the wisdom they have to offer. In the meantime, we can speak only of what we know; we can speak only "after the fact"—that it is Jesus and his story that have grasped our minds and our lives.

2. Faith as Trust and Hope

If we peruse the New Testament literature, we find other specific content for the word "faith." The most predominant meaning is trust, and this is inseparable from faith as hope.

In the Synoptic Gospels we find Jesus calling his hearers to "believe the good news" of the coming kingdom. This believing is *believing in* the *basileia* (reign) of God. Jesus frequently tells people, "Your faith has made you whole" (Mk 5:34; Mt 9:22; Lk 8:48). Jesus inspired people to faith and hope in God, which became powerful in their lives. Evidently, Jesus himself had faith, which was essentially trust in his *Abba.* The author of the Letter to the Hebrews calls him the "pioneer and perfecter of our faith" (Heb 12:2). That is, Jesus, as fully human like us, also knew the riskiness and vulnerability of faith. He had faith first. We follow him in his faith in God. Yet, already in the Synoptics, Jesus himself is proclaimed as the object of faith. In the light of his resurrection and of Pentecost, Jesus is seen to be "the Saviour who is Christ the Lord" (Lk 2:10). We are enjoined to follow him, to call him Lord, Christ, Son of God, and to believe *in him* (Mk 9:42; 6:35). Again, in John, we hear "believe in God, believe also in me" (Jn 14:1). For John, Jesus is "the only-begotten Son," given so that "whoever believes in him shall not perish" (3:16).

For Paul, our earliest New Testament author, faith is trusting in God's gracious unconditional love (grace) as this is disclosed especially in Jesus' self-offering by his death on the cross. It is "justification by faith" (Rom 5:1; etc.) or "accepting our acceptance" (Tillich). We are justified (set right, aquitted of our sins, and forgiven) and reconciled to God (2 Cor 5:17, 19) by trustfully accepting God's free offer of justifying, reconciling grace. Faith, again, is not merely assenting intellectually to these ideas or doctrines, but entering into the reconciled relationship. Jesus tells us that such faith is childlike: only those who humble themselves and become like little children will enter God's kingdom (Mt 18:1-4), because the truth here is hidden from the wise and clever but "revealed to babes" (Lk 10:21). This should be taken not as an invitation to sheer gullibility but as a call to trustful humility in the face of the mystery of God. Having faith in and believing in are the same. Faith is not only believing, but *believing in,* in the sense of *trusting in.* "Believing in Jesus" is, logically, much the same as believing in the word, the presence, the integrity of one's mother.

But "trusting in God" *can* seem a rather naive, even childish thing, devoid of life's hard experiences. Obviously it cannot mean some credulous optimism that everything will go well for us and our loved ones, that we will be protected from trouble, pain, sorrow, or death. Rather, faith as trust is something that sustains us through, and in spite of, such things. I well recall a conversation that occurred in a Bible study meeting in my southern African congregation, where a middle-aged white North American woman, an expatriate teacher in that country who was struggling to hold onto her faith, encountered the faith of a middle-aged African Christian man on the subject of trusting God. Tsediso, who had spent time in prison as a political prisoner, had quoted a favourite text: Psalm 56:2: "O Most High, when I am afraid, I put my trust in you. In God, whose word I praise, in God I trust; I am not afraid, what can flesh do to me?"

Conversation

JOAN: *You know, Tsediso, I find it hard to identify with those words about trusting God. I used to be very devout. I prayed every day. Especially I prayed for my son, who was a truck driver, out on those dangerous roads all the time; in fact every single day I prayed to God to protect him from an accident. But then early one morning the minister came to my door with a police report. They'd asked him to come and tell me that my son had been killed during the night when his truck went off a bridge. Well, I'm sorry, that knocked the faith right out of me. I still believe in God in some sense I guess, but I can't say I trust God. I seldom pray any more. I just can't get over feeling that God let me down.*

TSEDISO: *I think I understand how you feel about that. I felt that way the first time I was arrested. I believed I had been doing the right thing. I was fighting for what was right. Then God let me be arrested and thrown into prison. I was sleeping on a cold cement floor with no blankets. They wouldn't allow any visitors. I was so hungry. They wouldn't even let me have my Bible. I couldn't sleep because people were shouting and screaming from other cells. Then they beat me up something awful and did some other terrible things to me. I was so scared I was sure God had abandoned me. But in the dark of the night when I was praying, I knew that I still trusted God. I remembered that something like this, something even worse, happened to his Son. I knew Jesus was with me, and that he was suffering too. I mean it, seriously. I knew Jesus was right there with me in that very cell, and he was getting beat up too. And I knew that they couldn't kill me unless God let them. And I knew it was all right. If they killed me, I'd still be with Jesus.*

The sheer misery and tragedy of so much of our existence, the ghastly, evil things that happen in our world, are more than enough to shake our faith that God is in charge of the world. The kind of doubt expressed above is something that happens to nearly all of us. In fact, faith and doubt may be said to be two sides of the same coin. Precisely because faith is not sight, because faith is vulnerable and risky, we have to face and accept the fact of our doubts. At times we may feel that our doubts are outweighing our faith, and we hold onto faith by our finger-nails, praying "I believe, help my unbelief" (Mk 9:24). A common saying has it: "We are not called to have faith, but to be faithful." Although intellectual hon-esty may sometimes push someone to abandon faith, there is also good reason to remain steadfast, in spite of doubt, holding onto the original experience and insight that brought us to faith in the first place. After a time of struggle, even a "dark night of the soul," faith may return with a new quality, a different under-standing and new vitality. Merely to repress doubt, however, is unhealthy. Paul Tillich pointed out: "In those who rest on their unshakable faith, pharisaism and fanaticism are the unmistakable symptoms of doubt which has been repressed. Doubt is not overcome by repression but by courage."[20]

The reality is, however, that the world as we know and experience it does not correspond to the goodness of God that we see in Christ. Loss of faith can lead to cynicism and despair. Douglas John Hall speaks poignantly of the cyni-cism pervasive in North American culture:

> The cynic can carry on nicely within the officially optimistic society, mouthing the necessary platitudes and going through the motions of business, professional and social life. . . . The open articulation of cyn-icism is contrary to the social code. But the *living* of cynicism is a well-documented phenomenon in North America today. Its most familiar garb is shallow hedonism: the jogger who concentrates on physical well-being and whose devotion to the cult of the body has the conve-nient bonus of squelching persistent questions of the mind; the tourist who is able to find Calcutta and Mexico City "interesting"; the specta-tor who can observe life's pathos with eyes as dry as the glass covering of his television screen.[21]

The alternative, Hall contends, is not a mindless optimism or a false hope but a deeper hope that gives us the courage to look squarely at the darkness of the world. He quotes Reinhold Niebuhr: "There are ultimate problems of life that cannot be fully stated until the answer to them is known. Without the answer to them, men will not allow themselves to contemplate fully the depth of the prob-lem, lest they be driven to despair."[22]

This is why hope is such an essential dimension of faith. The Letter to the Hebrews is the only New Testament text to offer an explicit definition of faith, and here the essential meaning is trust, understood as hope: "Faith is the assur-ance of things hoped for, the evidence of things not seen" (Heb. 11:1). Note that "things not seen" are not so much "things above" as "things ahead" or "things hoped for." Faith as trust and confidence in God's future is linked, then (as in the preaching of the Synoptic Jesus), to the coming reign of God; that is, it is "escha-tological," having to do with the end-time or goal of history. War and famine, imprisonment and torture, disease and early death, environmental disaster—

these things do not correspond to the loving God that we meet in the crucified and risen Jesus. Jürgen Moltmann is the theologian who has made this point most radically:

> Hope's statements of promise, however, must stand in contradiction to the reality which can at present be experienced. They do not result from experiences, but are the condition for the possibility of new experiences. They do not seek to illuminate the reality which exists, but the reality which is coming. . . .
>
> It is in this contradiction that hope must prove its power. Hence eschatology . . . must formulate its statements of hope in contradiction to our present experience of suffering, evil and death.[23]

As in the Synoptic Gospels, faith as hope is anticipatory participation in the wholeness of God's reign now and, as in John, the beginning of eternal life now.

3. Faith as Following Jesus

Faith as following is one of the major emphases of the political and liberation theologies, which emphasize commitment to social justice as faithfulness to Jesus in the service of God's reign. Any genuine faith in the resurrection of Jesus implies serious commitment to follow him. We cannot in fact "believe in" Jesus without believing in his way. Believing in Jesus, then, is not just an opinion about his identity or about something that happened to him; it is faith-fulness or fidelity to Jesus and to what Jesus cared about, namely, God's reign of justice, peace, and wholeness. More than that, faith in Jesus opens up faith in new possibilities for the world. Jon Sobrino writes:

> Jesus makes faith possible. It is told that a power went out from him . . . , a power that was contagious, that could change people . . . this faith is in a God who, coming close, makes us believe in new possibilities actively denied to the poor in history. It is a faith that overcomes fatalism. It is faith in the God of the Kingdom opposed to the idols of the anti-Kingdom.[24]

To acknowledge Jesus as *kyrios* (Lord) is to experience liberation from any false *kyrios*. When the New Testament documents were written, the false *kyrios* was none other than Caesar. To say that Jesus is Lord was to say that Caesar was not. Richard Horsley points out that the first Christians, most especially Paul, deliberately redeployed the key terms of Roman imperial ideology in a way that subtly undermined the oppressive power of Rome. The term *evangel* ("gospel" or "good news"), a Roman announcement of a military victory, was now used to refer to the good news of Jesus' victory over death and all evil powers. The emperor of Rome, who was called not only *kyrios* but also *sōtēr* (Saviour), because he brought "peace on earth" (the *pax Romana* through the terror of military force) was now replaced by Jesus, who had been crucified on a Roman cross and raised from the dead, and so brought true peace on earth through love and reconciliation. To acknowledge Jesus as one's true emperor, then, meant following and obeying him as *kyrios*. If one did not seriously follow him, it was clear that one's loyalty and faith (*pistis*) were not in Jesus, but in the reigning emperor and his system of violence and injustice.[25] From within a social system built on the brutality of slavery, Paul declared that the true *kyrios* was the one who had willingly become a slave for the sake of others and whose name was now above every name, "so that at the name of Jesus every knee should bend . . . and every tongue confess that Jesus Christ is *kyrios*" (Phil 2:10-11). Paul also declares himself a "slave" for Jesus' sake (2 Cor 4:5) and calls his hearers "through love, to become slaves to one another" (Gal 5:13). In Jesus' new reign, Jew and Greek, slaves and free, male and female, are one (Gal 3:28). The radical political implications of all of this are plain to see: Following Jesus, in our time, as in Roman times, involves radical political commitment and opposition to every unjust and oppressive *kyrios* or empire. It is not surprising that Paul was repeatedly arrested and imprisoned and finally executed, and that Jesus' most faithful followers in any time or place are likely to suffer for their commitment to the crucified *kyrios*.

However, because the apostle Paul sometimes contrasts faith and works, faith is sometimes thought to be an experience or attitude devoid of action. This is a grave misunderstanding of the whole biblical tradition, including Paul himself. For Christians, "following" is an integral part of believing in Jesus. And this is in continuity with the Hebrew prophets, for whom knowledge of the holy God is to hear the command to be holy (Lev 19:2). To be liberated from the oppressive power of imperial Egypt and the falsely deified *kyrios* or pharaoh is to become a worshiping, obedient people (Exod 20:2). As we have already seen, to know the just God who delivered them from Egypt was to do justice: "He judged the cause of the poor and needy; then it was well. Is not this to know me?" (Jer 22:16).

In the Gospels and letters of the New Testament also, faith is not only an epistemological and soteriological concept; it is also ethical, having to do with being faith-full. In the Synoptic Gospels, Jesus calls us to take up the cross and follow him (Mt 16:24) and commands us to love God with all our heart, soul, mind, and strength, and our neighbour as ourselves (Lk 10:27, etc.). It is not those who say "Lord! Lord!" who enter the reign of God but "those who do the will of my Father" (Mt 7:21). We are called to "die with Christ" that we may also live with him (Rom 6:11), to walk "according to the Spirit and not according to the flesh," to live in faith, hope, and love, "but the greatest of these is love" (1 Cor 13:13). In the Johannine letters, too, it is clear that anyone who knows

God as love through faith in Christ will also live in love (1 Jn 4:7). One could go on to detail all of this voluminously from scripture, but the point is clear and simple: Faith in Jesus implies following him. Obedience is *not merely a consequence* of believing; it is *part and parcel* of believing. If there is no obeying and following, faith is simply not there.

Justification by faith, for Paul, however, is a radical rejection of mere submission, of a life of abject fear, lived under the law for the sake of reward. In this respect, believing and following Jesus were utterly different from the fearful, abject following of Caesar. Since God's love is utterly free and unconditional and cannot be earned as a reward, Paul can say to the Galatians:

> We know that a person is not justified by works of the law but through faith in Jesus Christ. And we have come to believe in Christ Jesus, so that we might be justified by faith in Christ, and not by doing the works of the law, because no one will be justified by the works of the law. (Gal 2:16)

In the fifth chapter of this same letter Paul is emphatic, however, that the life of faith includes obedience:

> For you are called to freedom . . . ; only do not use your freedom as an opportunity for self-indulgence, but through love become slaves to one another. For the whole law is summed up in a single commandment. "You shall love your neighbour as yourself." (Gal 5:13-14)

The Gospels, too, are replete with Jesus' parables of God's free and gracious love (the lost sheep, the lost coin, the prodigal son, the vineyard, etc.) and yet within this faith in God's free and costly grace come the constant call to discipleship and the command to love—indeed to love radically:

> "You have heard that it was said, 'An eye for an eye and a tooth for a tooth.' But I say to you, 'Do not resist an evildoer. But if anyone strikes you on the right cheek, turn the other also; and if anyone wants to sue you and take your coat give your cloak as well; and if anyone forces you to go one mile, go also the second mile: Give to everyone who begs from you, and do not refuse anyone who wants to borrow from you.' You have heard that it was said, 'You shall love your neighbour and hate your enemy.' But I say to you, 'Love your enemies.'" (Mt 5:38-44)

Such radical generosity is commanded precisely because of God's unmerited grace: "that you may be children of your Father who is in heaven; for he makes his sun rise on the evil and on the good, and sends rain on the righteous and the unrighteous" (Mt 5:45). Following Jesus, then, is not a question of avoiding punishment or seeking a reward. John makes the same point when he declares, "There is no fear in love, but perfect love casts out fear. . . . We love because he first loved us" (1 Jn 4:18-19).

The call to following and discipleship is not, then, an obligation consequent upon believing the good news of God's grace. It is part of the freedom of life under grace. To put it another way, not only justification but also sanctification is God's liberation of human beings from the hold of sin upon us. We are liberated for actual obedience and sanctification (an emphasis not only of contemporary liberation theology but also of the Wesleyan-Methodist tradition).

The life of sanctification, however, must never become a self-righteous self-reliance on one's own goodness or good works. When this happens the liberating dynamic of the gospel is lost, and we are once again imprisoned in a religion of fear. In fact, faith as trust and hope is the only thing that can deliver us from the cynicism and meaninglessness that can sap us of energy. It takes energy to love and to seek justice, to be in solidarity with the weak, to struggle for peace. Mere admonitions to moral obligation only sink us further into despair. "Faith-knowledge" of God as trust and hope and faith as discipleship are inseparable; this is clear whether we read the synoptics or Paul, John, or James. If we imagine that we "know God" by faith without serious commitment to the life of love, we are deluded. But to strive dutifully to be loving without faith and hope is, for most people, exhausting.

> Beloved, let us love one another, because love is from God; everyone who loves is born of God and knows God. Whoever does not love does not know God, for God is love. (1 Jn 4:7-8)

4. Faith as Knowledge

Faith as trust and hope cannot energize us, though, if it is not faith as knowledge. Faith-talk is not a mere language game, and not just morally inspiring rhetoric. We have to believe, seriously, that God's love is real and that the object of our hope is real, if our faith is to make any difference to our lives.

I suggested above that believing in Jesus, or believing in God through Jesus, is trust in a person and, in that sense, a kind of knowledge. But believing in Jesus, unlike believing in another human person, has enormous metaphysical, eschatological, and ethical consequences. It is believing in *someone*, but also believing *something* about reality. Because Jesus reveals *God* to us, faith in him means believing that reality is ultimately trustworthy. Faith as hope means that we expect the hope finally to be fulfilled. That is, faith always involves propositional content; it means *believing that*. . . . Believing in God, for example, obviously implies *believing that* God exists: "Whoever would approach [God] must believe that [God] exists" (Heb 11:6). Paul tells us that, "if we have died with Christ, we believe *that* [my emphasis] we shall also live with him, for we know that Christ being raised from the dead will never die again" (Rom 6:8-9). Note also the words of Peter spoken to Jesus in John's Gospel: "we have believed, and have come to know, that you are the holy One of God" (Jn 6:69). Believing, then, inescapably involves truth claims, not vague and general ones but very particular ones. We claim, by faith, that certain things are actually so and will be so. They are not only true for us, but true for God, and true for everyone. This is not to deny the element of mystery that remains, since our words and concepts of God always inadequately reflect the realities to which they refer. Nevertheless, we believe that we speak the truth insofar as this is humanly possible. When we retreat from the risk of making actual truth claims, then our witness loses all existential significance, and everyone knows we are not serious.

Yet faith is not sight. Faith in the "foolishness of God that is wiser than human wisdom" is vulnerable. "Without risk there is no faith," Kierkegaard insisted.[26] Faith is not a calculation of probabilities but a passionate conviction on which one stakes one's whole life.

Here I am in disagreement with Wolfhart Pannenberg's concept of faith. He is right, I think, to insist that Christian belief includes metaphysical knowledge of reality;[27] that is, it involves a worldview. But for him, "knowledge" in theology has to be founded upon philosophical argument and historical reason. Having arrived at secure beliefs about God and Jesus Christ that are founded on reason, faith, for Pannenberg, is simply the attitude of trust and hope in God's promise, which is inherent in historically established events, primarily the resurrection. Faith, then, for Pannenberg, is "based upon knowledge,"[28] and "knowledge of the ground of faith must, as such, logically precede faith."[29] Pannenberg thinks that any rational person must consent to Christian arguments for the historical reality of the resurrection. Over against this, I suggest that faith is not an attitude that we take up as a result of demonstrated, certain knowledge; rather, faith itself claims to *be* a kind of knowing, which is not based on previous arguments or foundations; that is, it is knowledge in relationship. Faith is risky. Faith is not sight. Faith in the "foolishness of God that is wiser than human wisdom" is vulnerable and intellectually noncoercieve, just as our God is gently noncoercive.

We must turn now to consider the radical difference between faith and human reason.

The Radical Disjunction of Faith and Reason

In our discussion above I have argued that faith is something quite different from a human philosophy or metaphysical system. Though it claims knowledge of God and (as I shall contend) must be positively related to reason, we must acknowledge that Christian faith is radically distinct from human reason as such. As an experience of and relationship to God, as an attitude of trust and commitment of a person's whole life, it is also something far more than a set of intellectual viewpoints or opinions. As a response to revelation that is "given" from beyond ourselves, it is not the product of human speculative or theoretical reason. Moreover, it is not only more than the product of human reason; it often positively contradicts and overturns what seems reasonable to the speculative mind reflecting naturally upon life and the universe. A basic affirmation here is that faith is a gift of the Holy Spirit.

1. Gift of the Spirit

That faith is a gift of the Spirit is basic to Christian theological epistemology and is one way in which Christians have testified to the disjunction of faith and reason. We know that if we have faith it is not our own achievement. We have not reached it simply by some correct operation of our human rational faculties, nor can we take credit for having faith. "For by grace you have been saved through faith, and this is not your own doing; it is the gift of God" (Eph 2:8). The justified, reconciled relationship of trust in which we live is not something we could have accomplished either intellectually or morally. It is not an achievement of the intellectually or ethically sensitive individual. To say that faith is a gift of the Spirit is, again, a way of saying that God cannot be known except by God's own self-disclosure. Not even the "revealed-ness" of a once-upon-a-time revelation suffices to reach us here and now. It is God's *present* activity through the Spirit that reveals God to us now. This statement is itself a confession of faith: "No one can say 'Jesus is Lord' except by the Holy Spirit" (1 Cor 12:3).

The English word "spirit" translates the Hebrew word *ruah* ("wind" or "breath"), which in the Old Testament names God's presence and activity in the world. The metaphor of wind or breath signifies an illusively mysterious and living reality. When the Gospel of John declares that "God is Spirit" (Jn 4:24) and that "the Spirit blows where it chooses," we are being told that God is utterly free and unpredictable. The word "spirit," because of its association with a mindful, purposeful God, also has connotations of personhood. Thus it also came to be used to speak of human beings (e.g., Gen 41:8; Prov 16:18; Lk 8:55; etc.), who, as persons, are also illusive and mysterious, even to themselves. Communication between God and human beings is said to be from Spirit to spirit, as in the statement of Paul, "When we cry '*Abba!* Father!' it is that very Spirit bearing witness with our spirit that we are children of God" (Rom 8:15-16).

As we said above, knowledge of God as faith may then be compared to knowledge of other persons, for the knowledge of a human person is always a gift of human self-revelation. Such a gift can be received only by a kind of "faith," that is, a response of trust in a reciprocated relationship of mutual self-disclosure. An analogy in ordinary human experience is the relationship of marriage, which the Bible calls "one flesh," perhaps the most profound form of human mutual self-revelation and personal knowledge, even of mutual indwelling (see Gen 2:24; Mt 19:6; Eph 5:28, 31). The faith relationship with God is also a mutual one. We believe that God has reached out to communicate with us in Jesus and still continues to do so in the Spirit. What God communicates in Christ through the Spirit may be said to be intimate self-communication, disclosing God's passion for us, God's pain, God's joy. We communicate in return through prayer and worship. The scripture speaks of this relationship too as mutual indwelling: We are "in the Spirit" and the Spirit dwells in us, and this is identical with the indwelling of Christ (Rom 8:9, 11; Gal 2:20). John speaks of the same reality when he has Jesus say, "Abide in me and I in you" (Jn 15:4). John begins to glimpse a trinitarian sense of mutual indwelling, wherein humans are given a share in the triune life of God, "you, Father, are in me, and I in you, that they may also be in us" (Jn 17:21). Both our knowledge of God and our eternal life are, then, a gracious *inclusion* in God's eternal life and love. We detect in Paul what might be called a "mystical" participation in God's self-knowledge.

> These things God has revealed to us through the Spirit; for the Spirit searches everything, even the depths of God. For what human being knows what is truly human except the human spirit that is within? So also no one comprehends what is truly God's except the Spirit of God. Now we have received not the spirit of the world, but the Spirit that is from God, so that we may understand the gifts bestowed on us by God. (1 Cor 2:10-12)

It is clear in all these texts that the Christian knowledge of God as faith is in some respects discontinuous with, and qualitatively different from, other kinds of human knowledge, which might be represented generally by the term "reason." It is something that, if not graciously gifted to us, would be beyond our ken. God never comes under our control. Precisely because God is God, God cannot be demonstrated or proved by ordinary human epistemological procedures. The mysterious holy One, whom we believe we know by faith, is beyond us and all our natural capacities. We are not fitted to know that which is infinitely beyond us. Yet faith affirms that God fits God's very Self, in Jesus, to be knowable by us and, by the Spirit's work, also fits us to respond.

2. The Foolishness of the Cross

That faith is a gift of the Spirit is one classic way of speaking about the disjunction of faith and reason. Another important biblical and theological theme that bespeaks this disjunction is the foolishness of the cross, wherein the gospel is said to be the direct opposite of human wisdom. Paul connects these two in an illuminating way:

I did not come proclaiming the mystery of God to you in lofty words of wisdom. For I decided to know nothing among you except Jesus Christ, and him crucified. And I came to you in weakness and in fear and in much trembling. My speech and my proclamation were not with plausible words of wisdom, but with a demonstration of the Spirit and of power, so that your faith might rest not on human wisdom but on the power of God. (1 Cor 2:1-5)

It is precisely the foolishness of "Christ crucified" that is contrasted with human wisdom. What could be more foolish, what could be better evidence of failure and lack of wisdom than to find yourself tortured to death on a cross? Young people in a confirmation class see the issue clearly, as the young often do.

Conversation

REV. BRIAN: *Remember, last day we were talking about love as the way of Jesus. We were saying Jesus has shown us that the way of love is the way of truth, the way of abundant living. A life of love and caring for others, of service and self-giving, is not a drag. This is life at its best.*

JASON: *Well, OK, but don't you think if we're all that loving and self-sacrificing people will take advantage of us? What's so great about being a sucker all your life?*

MATTHEW: *Yeah, like "nice guys finish last."*

DEBBIE: [Chewing gum as she speaks] *I can see being loving and self-sacrificing to a certain extent. That could give you nice relationships and friendships and all that. But if you carry it too far you could get hurt. I mean, isn't that what happened to Jesus? He was loving and caring and took the side of all the down-and-outs, and look what happened to him. He ended up on a cross.*

REV. BRIAN: *Well yes, Debbie, I'd say there is a place for self-care, or loving yourself. Being radically loving isn't necessarily the same thing as being walked all over. On the other hand, circumstances may arise where you would actually put your life on the line. Think of the people who have gotten involved in political struggles in places like Latin America or Korea or South Africa, and have found themselves imprisoned for long periods of time, or tortured, or shot. Think of the amazing folk who offered themselves as human shields in Baghdad to protect the Iraqi people! Do you really think these people are just dumb, or just suckers? Now that's the foolishness of the cross! You might just consider whether there's a cause that you would actually die for.*

KIM: [After a moment of stunned silence] *Anyway, Debbie, how can you just say he ended up on a cross? He also rose from the dead three days later. Millions of people believe in him as their Lord and Saviour. His religion is the biggest in the world. And he's in heaven with God. Now that's how he ended up!*

REV. BRIAN: *Yes, even secular people say that Jesus is the greatest man who ever lived, that, crucified or not—in fact because he was crucified—he's had more impact on history than any powerful king or politician, or any scientist or philosopher in history. We number our years from his birth. But don't let that fool you. Don't miss the point. His real success was not his fame or his historical influence. His real success was that he went lovingly to the cross!*

MATTHEW: [Puzzled and skeptical] *Yeah, but maybe we've made him a hero because what he said makes us feel good. The stories about him make him seem great, but maybe in real life he was just a failure—maybe a real nice guy, sure, but he ended up dead.*

JASON: *Yeah, and everybody knows he was crucified. But most people don't really believe he was resurrected. That's just faith.*

The conversation brings out the contrast between human "wisdom" of a fairly basic kind and the "foolishness" of the gospel. The message of a loving, suffering God who calls us to walk in love, the message of a reign of God initiated in history by this humble, loving, crucified man, does not seem particularly reasonable in a world like ours. Its truth is not plainly visible or observable. Love and justice certainly do not reign in the world as we know it. The words of the Christmas carol "Joy to the World" seem strangely out of touch with reality:

> He rules the earth
> With truth and grace
> And makes the nations prove
> The glories of his righteousness
> And wonders of his love

In fact, we know that what "rules the earth" is economic, military, and political power. It's money that talks. What works and succeeds is competition, the strong over the weak, the clever over the not so clever. If the church has succeeded in history, so that its Lord is called "the greatest and most influential man who ever lived," even to the point where our years are numbered from his birth, does this not suggest that the church has departed from the message of a lowly, humble man who came to serve, to exalt not himself but to exalt others? We know that Christianity is the "biggest religion in the world," partly because from the fourth century it had the Roman army behind it and, later, from the sixteenth century, the wealth and power of the world's richest, most successful colonial powers. Does the history of Christianity not itself suggest that economic, military, and political power are what counts in history? Has the "triumph of the cross" really been a triumph of lowly service, or has it often been a triumph of religious and cultural imperialism? Since the time of Constantine the success of Christianity in history has been, at the least, a very ambiguous story indeed.[30]

The foolishness of the cross and the minority theological tradition known as "the theology of the cross" precisely affirm the strangeness, the incredibility, and the improbability that Jesus is indeed Lord. It affirms the radical discontinuity of the gospel of Jesus Christ with sweet reasonableness, yet affirms in the face of all human wisdom that the true God is the crucified God, that the eternal truth about the meaning of things is found in suffering love, specifically in the suffer- ing love of Jesus on the cross. Such truth can only be known by faith, that is, by risky response to God's self-revelation. If we choose to live the life of love, we "walk by faith and not by sight," for the success of love in the world is scarcely evident. As the author of *Hebrews* knew very well, the people of faith down through history have found the life of faith a very dangerous one indeed. Having reiterated many success stories of faith, Hebrews also notes that

> Others suffered mocking and flogging and even chains and imprison- ment. They were stoned to death, they were sawn in two, they were killed by the sword; they went about in skins of sheep and goats, desti- tute, persecuted, tormented. (Heb 11:36-37)

The risk of faith is not simply the risk of being wrong in our opinions when we take an epistemological leap into believing. The risk comes when we actually live (even a little, because few of us manage it to any radical degree) as though Jesus is the risen Lord, and as though love is the truth. It is faith as following that is truly risky in a world like ours. Again, as we said earlier, such faith is accom- panied by the insecurity of doubt, in the spirit of the father of the epileptic child: "I believe, help my unbelief!" (Mk 9:24).

Theology of the Cross: Paul. This is why the tradition known as the theology of the cross has always rejected attempts to prove the existence of God or to con- vince people by argument that faith is reasonable in terms of worldly wisdom. Such a natural theology attempts to find epistemological security by building faith upon some indubitable foundation, thus replacing faith by sight. Theology of the cross begins with Paul's stark contrast of God's wisdom with human wisdom:

> For it is written, "I will destroy the wisdom of the wise, and the dis- cernment of the discerning I will thwart." Where is the one who is wise? Where is the scribe? Where is the debater of this age? Has not God made foolish the wisdom of the world? For since, in the wisdom of God, the world did not know God through wisdom, God decided, through the foolishness of our proclamation, to save those who believe. For Jews

demand signs and Greeks desire wisdom, but we proclaim Christ crucified, a stumbling block to Jews and foolishness to Gentiles, but to those
who are called, both Jews and Greeks, Christ the power of God and the
wisdom of God. (1 Cor 1:19-24)

Paul's theology of the cross derives, of course, from reflection upon the life and
death of Jesus. We find a similar theme in the Gospels in words ascribed to Jesus:
"I thank you, Father, Lord of heaven and earth, because you have hidden these
things from the wise and the intelligent and have revealed them to infants" (Lk
10:21). The simplicity, humility, and apparent foolishness of the child, Jesus suggests, gives the child a certain advantage where the knowledge and reign of God
are concerned. Also the poor, the unlearned, and the "sinner" seem to be in a better position than the rich, the scribe, or the "righteous" person, as Jesus saw it.
The latter are self-sufficient, or feel so, in their possessions, their learning, or
their moral achievement, and so they feel no need of God's grace. This disqual-
ifies them for the reign of God, which is a reign of grace, of unconditional,
unmerited love for all. The smart ones tend to be impervious to the gentle Spirit
that reaches out to their hearts and minds. That is why Jesus frequently warned
about the dangers of wealth, made enemies of the rich and powerful, as well as
the theologians and clerics and "the righteous" of his day. "Those who are well
have no need of a physician," he said ironically (Lk 5:31).

The emphasis on foolishness, childlikeness, and Jesus' apparent bias for the
oppressed, poor, and sinners was largely forgotten for centuries. It can be found
in Tertullian and in Francis of Assisi. But much of the theology of the Middle
Ages, even at its zenith in the impressive thought of Thomas Aquinas, sought to
be strong and wise, to be intellectually unassailable. Aquinas, making heavy use
of the philosophy of Aristotle, "proved" the existence of God, together with the
attributes of God, which, he thought, could be known by natural reason.[31]
Aquinas certainly left room for faith, as distinct from reason, but in the high Middle Ages the validity of revelation seemed assured by a magnificent church ruled
over by a hierarchy of glorious, powerful men and by respectable philosophical
arguments with their pedigree in Aristotle.

Luther: Theology of the Cross. It was Martin Luther, near the end of the medieval
period, who first called all this into question in terms of substantial theological
thought. Luther vigorously attacked the powerful and glorious church, its
exploitative practices, its vanity and pomp, its power-mongering. But most significantly he attacked its theology of righteousness and was deeply suspicious of
the alignment of scholastic theology with Aristotle. With characteristic drama and
colour, he declared: "He who wishes to philosophize by using Aristotle without
danger to his soul must first become thoroughly foolish in Christ."[32] So said the
young Luther in the *Heidelberg Disputation* of 1518. He was building of course
upon the theology of Paul, but also upon the teaching of Jesus as he read it in the

Gospels. "According to the gospels," he says, "the Kingdom of heaven is given to children and the humble [Mk 10:14, 16] and Christ loves them."[33] But most especially Luther was building upon the suffering and the cross of Jesus as the revelation of God and God's salvation. In Theses 19-21 of the *Heidelberg Disputation* Luther characterizes "true theology" as "theology of the cross" and the false, dominant theology of the church as "theology of glory":

19) That person does not deserve to be called a theologian who looks upon the invisible things of God as though they were clearly perceptible in those things which have actually happened (Rom 20).
20) He deserves to be called a theologian, however, who comprehends the visible and manifest things of God seen through suffering and the cross.
21) A theologian of glory calls evil good and good evil. A theologian of the cross calls the thing what it actually is.

For Luther, of course, every Christian is called to be a "theologian" (this is a corollary of his doctrine of the priesthood of all believers), and it is not his intention to set up an elitist category of theologians within the church. They "deserve to be called theologians" all the more if they are humble and unlearned, knowing God in the suffering of the cross. Luther's explanation of Thesis 20 is important and deserves to be quoted extensively:

The manifest and visible things of God are placed in opposition to the invisible, namely, his human nature, weakness, foolishness. The Apostle in I Cor. 1 [:25] calls them the weakness and folly of God. Because men misused the knowledge of God through works, God wished again to be recognized in suffering, and to condemn wisdom concerning invisible things by means of wisdom concerning visible things, so that those who did not honour God as manifested in his works should honour him as he is hidden in his suffering. . . . Now it is not sufficient for anyone, and it does him no good to recognize God in his glory and majesty, unless he recognizes him in the shame and glory of his cross. . . . For this reason true theology and recognition of God are in the crucified Christ.[34]

For Luther, theology of the cross has essentially to do with justification by grace alone and faith alone. Pride in one's own good works and the attempt to be justified through them are the very heart of sin and evil. That is why he says:

The friends of the cross say that the cross is good and works are evil, for through the cross works are dethroned and the old Adam, who is especially edified by works, is crucified.

Thus his main statement of Thesis 21, which names and contrasts "theology of glory" and "theology of the cross": "A theology of glory calls evil good and good evil. A theology of the cross calls the thing what it actually is." Evil here is the pride of a person "puffed up by his good works." It is the strength, wisdom, and even goodness of the proud human being who knows God by human wisdom through the things God has made, and who is strong to obey the moral law. However, the paradox of God's foolish wisdom overturns what the wise, strong, and good person knows.

> He who does not know Christ does not know God hidden in suffering. Therefore he prefers works to suffering, glory to the cross, strength to weakness, wisdom to folly, and, in general, good to evil. These are the people whom the apostle calls "enemies of the cross of Christ" [Phil 3:18] for they hate the cross and suffering and love works and the glory of works.[35]

Luther's struggle against the pride of good works moved him to speak rather shocking words: "He is not righteous who does much, but he who, without work, believes much in Christ."[36] This would seem to contradict what we heard from Sobrino about faith as following Jesus (though Sobrino considers that he is doing a *theologia crucis*). Yet Luther does not, as it may seem, deny that the way of love is the way of truth. He explains, "Not that the righteous person does nothing, but that his works do not make him righteous, rather that his righteousness creates works. For grace and faith are infused without our works. After they have been imparted the works follow."[37]

Faith working through love appears all the more foolish to the wisdom of the world. The content of faith itself cannot be demonstrated. That Jesus is risen is not a demonstrable fact to which all rational people must assent. "Blessed are those who have not seen and yet believe" (Jn 20:29). It is "just faith," as is commonly said, for God continues, even in the resurrection, to be hidden to worldly wisdom. God's glory continues, even in the resurrection, to be *abscondita sub contraria* ("hidden under its opposite"). That is, God is revealed in the cross as the opposite of what we would expect—weak and lowly, suffering and humiliated. God wills to be known and loved and obeyed as this suffering and lowly One, indeed as one not acknowledged by the world. That Jesus is risen, that he is the living Lord, must remain something for faith and not for sight. The resurrection is something experienced by the disciples, who were equipped to understand and believe in him, but it is never public fact (as the crucifixion was), never visible to Herod, Pilate, or Caesar. God refuses to be publicly visible in power and majesty, for God will be worshiped only in the shame and suffering of the cross. That is why the resurrection cannot become grounds for a triumphalistic church, glorying in its conquest of the world. Nor can the resurrection rightly become the basis of the church's worldly success, since faith, even in the resurrection of Jesus, offers no epistemological security.

So also the life of discipleship offers no guarantee of success, happiness, or fulfillment. It is true that Jesus promises joy: "Abide in my love. . . . these things I have spoken to you that my joy may be in you and your joy may be full," says the Johannine Jesus (Jn 15:9-11). Yet we soon find him warning, "If the world hates you, know that it hated me before it hated you. . . . the hour is coming when whoever kills you will think he is offering service to God" (Jn 15:8; 16:2). In all of this, the disciple does not accumulate credits toward a reward in heaven, nor enjoy the moral or spiritual security of being on God's side. "The greatest security is the greatest temptation," says Luther.[38] His theology of the cross despises the spiritual security of indulgences and of good works, but also the epistemological security of a theology of glory, which replaces faith in the crucified Christ with the sight of an intellectually secure philosophical theology.

Faith in the God of the cross and following Jesus in the foolishness of love are indeed contrary to all human reason. It is not merely additional to what can be known by human wisdom; rather, it overturns human wisdom. It is truly foolish, truly an affront, an offence, a scandal to human wisdom.

Theology of the Cross, Theodicy, and Rational Theism. Nevertheless, I wish to contend, this very reversal of human wisdom and reasonableness has a certain deep credibility about it. As justification by grace alone is welcome news to one who despairs of one's personal goodness, so also, the foolishness of God revealed in the suffering of the cross is good news to one who despairs of finding meaning or sense in the observable world by the use of philosophical reason. By "credibility" I do not mean coercive verifiability. Credibility has to do with relevance as well as rationality; it has to do with the power to address deep human needs and to grapple with the world's real problems. Whatever arguments for the existence of God there may be, however valid or invalid, cogent or incogent they may be philosophically, they cannot bring us to a vision of ultimate reality as just and compassionate. The God whom such arguments reach could just as easily be Satan or, almost as terrifying, Aristotle's indifferent prime mover. The Supreme Being, or Necessary Being, or the *ens realissimum*, or Moral Lawgiver of moral monotheism are unimaginably far from the God of the cross. Here we join with Tertullian in asking, "What has Athens to do with Jerusalem?" These philosophic versions of deity are the radical contrary of the Son who cries out, "My God, my God, why have you forsaken me?" and the grieving Father, bound to the Son by the life-giving Spirit. The "Supreme Being" etc. are the deities of the theologies of glory, the god who is beyond the vicissitudes of history, the almighty one who "can do anything" (but for some reason will not). Many theologians, both Jewish and Christian,[39] have pointed out the utter difference between the immutable, immortal, impassible god of Greek metaphysics, the god who cannot suffer and cannot die, and the biblical God of Abraham, Isaac, and Jacob, the God of Moses, of the prophets, and of Jesus. This God of the Hebrews longs for the love of the people, weeps over them, repents, and rejoices. This is the God of passion, who, according to Christian faith, has entered fully into human flesh, human joy, human suffering, and human death.

In the latter half of the twentieth century many thoughtful people have found credibility in various aspects of a theology of the cross, stemming from Paul and Luther. It is difficult to add to the depth and breadth of their thought, but in this section I shall gather together some of their best thoughts and discuss how they bear on our methodological concern. All of them have asked with new urgency: In the face of such horrors as war and famine, mental illness and torture, just how does one seriously believe in a loving Father in heaven who sees the little sparrow fall? The disjunction of faith and reason cannot itself justify believing in what is simply nonsense. How does one believe in almighty love, while enslaved and systematically humiliated and degraded in Auschwitz, or in a rat-infested dungeon, where human beings go mad with terror? "If it does not make sense in a concentration camp, it just doesn't make sense," someone has said. The hideous reality of torture, which can go on and on without divine intervention, is itself enough to refute the Almighty Father. "I can forgive God anything but the central nervous system," George Grant once said.[40] And lest we attempt a defence of God by blaming it all on human sin, we must ask how it is possible still to believe in the loving God while trapped in agony, hunger, and thirst for days or even weeks under the rubble of an earthquake, or while one's own beloved child is innocently and miserably dying of some emaciating cancer, events for which no human being's sin can be blamed. Intellectual honesty and any kind of emotional or experiential authenticity would seem to demand that we rebel against any God who perpetrates or allows such things. "The only excuse for God would be for him not to exist," said H. Stendhal.[41] Albert Camus articulates poignantly (what Moltmann calls) "protest atheism"—the inadequacy of all cool intellectual, cosmological, or moral arguments for God. "I rebel, therefore we exist," wrote Camus. Metaphysical rebellion seems the only authentic attitude an honest human being can have in the face of the nonsense and absurdity of the world. Remarkably, Camus, as one who did not believe in the God of the Bible, finds the roots of metaphysical rebellion in scripture: "The history of the rebellion that we experience today is far more that of the descendants of Cain than the pupils of Prometheus. In this sense, it is above all others the God of the Old Testament who sets in motion the energies of rebellion."[42] As an atheist, Camus grasps with remarkable clarity the significance of the suffering of Jesus:

> The night of Golgotha only has so much significance for man because in its darkness the Godhead, visibly renouncing all inherited privileges, endures to the end the anguish of death, including the depths of despair. This is the explanation of the *Lama sabachthani* and Christ's gruesome doubt in agony. The agony would have been easy if it could have been supported by eternal hope. But for God to be a man, he had to despair.[43]

Nevertheless, Camus remained a protest atheist. Moltmann, empathizing with Camus, says it well from a Christian standpoint: "The question of the existence of God is, in itself, a minor issue in the face of the question of [God's] right-eousness in the world."[44]

The question of theodicy (the defence or justification of God in the face of evil and suffering) took on a new poignancy in the twentieth century. Not, I think, because human suffering has been greater in our time than in previous times. Massacres, refined methods of torture, human sacrifice, leprosy and plagues, hurricanes and earthquakes, crucifixions and burnings were long part of human-ity's lot. We in the modern West have been relieved of at least some of these and, through the discovery of anaesthetics, from much of the worst pain of natural ill-ness. But expectations are higher in our time. We no longer accept that life must be a horror. The human wisdom predominant today no longer bows humbly before the will of an omnipotent, inscrutable deity. Humanity "come of age" (as Dietrich Bonhoeffer put it) has less need for the hypothesis of God and less tol-erance for superficial theodicies. Rational theism (belief in God based on argu-ments for the existence of a Supreme Being), for all its apparent reasonableness, has less credibility following the disasters and atrocities of the twentieth century. The imprisoned Bonhoeffer, aware of what was happening to the Jews under the Nazis and awaiting the gallows himself, was the first of the twentieth-century theologians to apply a theology of the cross to the tormenting questions about evil and suffering. Bonhoeffer was not spared the time to articulate Paul's theme of the weakness of God with any thoroughness before he was finally hanged on April 9, 1945. His fragmentary *Letters and Papers from Prison*, collected by a friend after his death, have been endlessly provocative in the decades following his execution. "God lets himself be pushed out of the world onto the cross. He is weak and powerless in the world, and that is precisely the way, the only way, in which he is with us and helps us."[45] Perhaps the credible choices are represented by these two mid-twentieth-century thinkers: Bonhoeffer, the martyred theolo-gian of the suffering God, and Camus, the atheist of metaphysical rebellion. In full view of the absurdity of the world, the latter choice may indeed be a matter of sight, while the former can only be faith and hope against hope.

In the last analysis, though, we may reasonably doubt whether Camus' despair can really be the final truth. Is humanity now to become God? Human-ity, nobly rebelling against injustice and absurdity, may indeed seem godlike. Yet so much of what we have to rebel against is humanity's own cruelty, arrogance, and pettiness. Promethean humanity hardly seems a suitable candidate for our worship, obedience, and trust.

We have to ask also whether despair and meaninglessness are really a cred-ible last word. Whence has come this noble rebellious human creature, longing for meaning and love? How has an utterly absurd universe brought forth this thinking, philosophizing, praying, rebelling human being, crying out for justice? Despite the absurdity and nonsense of life and the world, many of us have intimations of meaning and beauty, even outside of biblical revelation. Most of the world religions testify to a sense of "holy presence" or transcendent mystery that forbids final despair. Particularly in experiences of human love, and indeed in metaphysical rebellion itself, one senses a depth and truth in reality more fundamental than the absurdity and nonsense. C. S. Lewis says it well:

> Atheism turns out to be too simple. If the whole universe has no meaning, we should never have found out that it has no meaning: just as, if there were no light in the universe and therefore no creatures with eyes, we should never know it was dark. Dark would be a word without meaning.[46]

Does this amount to a philosophical argument for God from natural reason? Perhaps, but of course it rests on no indubitable foundation, carries no coercive cogency. I would contend that a valid sort of reasoning of this kind is appropriate; it may open us to faith, but in the last analysis it is only the risk of faith that can give us hope in the face of the world's darkness. For Christians, it is the story of Jesus that puts flesh on these vague intimations of meaning and hope. That such a One has lived and suffered among us cannot be overlooked. That he lived magnificently in faith, that he exhibited such graciousness and courage, that he shared our despair and doubt is precious to us. As crucified and risen, he saves us from meaninglessness and hopelessness and testifies that we are acceptable and beloved despite our own participation in the world's evil. Because of this we confess that in this suffering One we find the presence of Deity. Deity is none other than this suffering, self-giving Love embodied in Jesus, which commands our worship, obedience, and trust.

If the true God is indeed like this, then God will often appear to be silent and powerless in the face of our troubles. As the novelist John Updike puts it,

> The sensation of silence cannot be helped: a loud and evident God would be a bully, an insecure tyrant, an all-crushing datum instead of, as He is, a bottomless encouragement to our faltering and frightened being.[47]

Theology of the cross, then, begins not with strong arguments designed to compel the intellect but with the beauty and weakness of this loving human person and finds Deity there.

Despite the inadequacy of Camus' conclusions (from the point of view of faith), his protest atheism exhibits a nobility of spirit closer to biblical faith than what is often called "rational theism," for that faith itself is a protest against what is, in the name of what God wills to bring about. The God of exodus is a protesting God, against the typical human structure of domination and oppression. The God of Jesus too is the protesting God, standing against the tyranny of law and self-righteousness, fighting against injustice and lovelessness. The God of the gospel entirely identifies with the lowly and oppressed, with sinners, and with the sick and the poor. Here is a God who wills to move the whole of creation and humanity beyond the pattern of survival of the fittest to the deeper and more profound reality of *agapē* love. Such a God is not the buttress and guarantor of the way things are but the lure (as the process theologians say) toward an utterly different reality that Jesus called "reign of God." That reign means ultimately the end of sin and death, the end of all crying and tears (Rev 21:4).

Such ideas are a revolution in the concept of God if we compare them to what is commonly called rational theism. But this revolution is not really new, since it had its foundation in God's own self-disclosure with Moses and the exodus—the self-disclosure of God in solidarity with the oppressed and the poor, the God who is against the way things are. This same God is the One crucified in our humanity on the cross of Golgotha. Not Caesar to the nth degree, not the commander in chief writ large, not the head of a great corporation projected into the heavens, but a strange, gentle, terrifying holiness, a Wholly Other. Jon Sobrino explains:

> God is not simply the one who holds and wields power, as . . . defined by various religions and philosophies. On the cross God does not show up as one who wields power over the negative from outside; rather, on the cross we see God submerged within the negative.[48]

We find in this liberation theologian, then, as in Bonhoeffer, Moltmann, and Hall, the powerful insight of Luther, which he in turn derived from Paul and from the gospel story of Jesus. God is revealed *absconditus sub contraria*, hidden under the opposite of all that we would naturally expect of God. The true God of the cross turns out to be an utter surprise to human wisdom, a direct contradiction to what appears reasonable to natural human thought. Yet for many today this very contradiction carries credibility. For this very reason we have to attempt to understand God more than ever from the death of Jesus. To speak of God for Jesus' sake we must "develop a particular theology within earshot of the dying cry of Jesus."[49]

> The only way past protest atheism is through a theology of the cross which understands God as the suffering God in the suffering of Christ and which cries out with the godforsaken God, "My God, why have you forsaken me?" For this theology, God and suffering are no longer contradictions, as in theism and atheism, but God's being is in suffering and the suffering is in God's being itself, because God is love. It takes the "metaphysical rebellion" up into itself because it recognizes in the cross of Christ a rebellion in metaphysics, or better, a rebellion in God.[50]

In the thought of these contemporary theologians of the cross, the radical disjunction of faith and reason is evident. The gospel of Jesus Christ cannot be reduced to some comfortably reasonable religious philosophy devoid of mystery. Such a reduction renders Christianity banal, uninteresting, superficial, and ultimately incredible.

Although faith in the God of the cross is not derived from human reason, and even contradicts and overturns reason, faith may nevertheless be reasonable. Let us turn to consider what it may mean for a rational person to have faith.

CHAPTER 3

Faith as Rational

The reader may suspect that I am about to contradict all that I said in the previous chapter, where I spoke of a radical disjunction between faith and reason. By that I mean: Christian faith is in no way a product of human reason or of natural human wisdom, cannot be coercively demonstrated by, or to, human reason, and even contradicts natural human reason. Must one then become an irrational human being in order to believe as a Christian? Should we abandon the quest for a rational theological method, which we have been pursuing since the beginning of this inquiry? I think not. Paradoxically, we must continue to seek an understanding of faith that is not only faith-full, acknowledging the radical disjunction of faith and reason, but that is rational as well. Douglas John Hall, who affirms in his own *theologia crucis* the "cognitive priority" of revelation as "point of departure" for Christian theology, can set the tone for our discussion:

> Nothing at all can be gained by an authoritarian, revelation-based religion which gloats over every humiliation of the human mind. The point of the cross is not that the faithful should win arguments, but that the world might know peace. Partly, this peace depends upon the exposition of a theology of revelation which does not humiliate but can fulfill and exalt the quest of the intellect.[1]

I shall argue, then, that faith can be credible to the intelligent mind, and that faith must account for itself in a reasonable manner. Revelation does not merely negate human reason, but informs and illuminates it.

What Is Rationality?

The word "rationality" derives from the Latin *ratio*, "reason"; rationality, broadly speaking, is reasonableness. The term denotes right thinking or the right functioning of the human mind. However, what constitutes rationality, reason-

ableness, or right thinking and how it is to be identified or measured are highly
contentious questions that philosophers have debated endlessly. I shall not propose a universal measuring stick of rationality; all the best minds in the history
of philosophy have failed to reach agreement on this, and there is now a widespread opinion that none such exists.[2] I will offer here only a tentative working
definition and go on later to characterize rationality more fully. My definition no
doubt reflects various contingencies of my personal location and faith orientation, but I do not apologize for this, since no absolute definition is available.

I propose to use the term "rationality" to mean a genuine effort of the human
mind to relate to reality in all its depth and complexity. Rationality occurs above
all in everyday practical life; it is a matter of praxis, in which practical action and
theoretical thought come together. It is also an aspect of every discipline of
thought.[3] Rational thought implies, first of all, an appropriate attention to the
object of inquiry or whatever it is that one seeks to know. It can be described,
then, as receptivity and response to whatever it is that one encounters. It is also
active, in the sense that it calculates how best to achieve practical goals. Rationality, for libertionist/praxis-oriented thought, seeks a reasoned correlation of
theory and practice. It is capable of contemplating and reflecting on what those
goals of practical action should be. When I say "reality in all its depth and complexity," I imply that rational thought is as broad and deep in scope as the whole
vast range of matters about which human beings inquire and which they wish to
accomplish in the world.

A rational person is characterized by an openness not only to that which he
or she seeks to know but also to the rationality of others, and therefore to discussion and persuasion. The rational person possesses an attitude of mind that is
willing to be challenged by relevant evidence and is open to others' viewpoints
or arguments, whether they be logical, experiential, or practical. Obviously the
basic laws of logic, such as the laws of noncontradiction and of logical sequence,
are essential to rationality. Without reason in this sense it is impossible to know
or to argue anything, even the limitations of reason! An extremely irrational person, on the other hand, is easily recognized by others as insane or mentally unbalanced, paranoid, or deluded. A more moderately irrational person is usually seen
by others as closed-minded, rigidly dogmatic, unwilling to consider evidence, or
simply very subjectivist or emotivist in an arbitrary manner. Rationality may be
hindered not only by dogma or emotion but also by ideology or selfish interests.

Rational persons, however, are not necessarily dispassionate or detached in
the process of knowing, or of acting. In some aspects of existence—for example,
sexual love, the appreciation of music, the love of nature, religious devotion, or
political commitment—passion and attachment are appropriate and rational in
the broad sense; indeed, to relate to these dimensions of life dispassionately
would be irrational. Reason and passion, then, are not incompatible. On the contrary, reason is appropriately passionate about certain things. The new father,
perceiving how beautiful and precious his new child is, knows rationally what he

never knew before. The lover, besotted with erotic passion, knows his beloved more truly than he has ever known anyone. The social activist, impassioned with outrage about a brutal war, sees injustice and cruelty with incisive accuracy. Of course, one must recognize the conventional truth as well: passion, whether sexual, aesthetic, or political, *can* obscure rational processes, blinding us to the complexities of the world around us.

Rational persons, however, may disagree with each other, may be believers or unbelievers; Christians, Muslims, Buddhists, or atheists; and conservatives, liberals, or radicals. This implies that rationality and truth have to be distinguished. When I say a person is rational (say, a thoughtful Muslim, Hindu, or atheist) I do not imply that I agree with that person's ideas or beliefs. Out of the givenness of their own experience and resources, they may be functioning very rationally in coming to quite different conclusions from those I reach out of my experience and resources. On the other hand, I may consider a person to be irrational whose basic faith and viewpoints I share (e.g., some Christians or socialists I can think of) if they refuse to be accountable in any way for their beliefs. "To claim that a belief is rational is not the same as to claim that a belief is true."[4] Rationality and truth are by no means identical, yet rational persons are not at all indifferent to truth, for truth is the goal of the rational person. The rational person seeks "truth," that is, needs to be in touch with reality in order to live and to act well in the real world. It is also the case that I may consider someone essentially a rational person and at the same time judge some of his/her views or attitudes to be irrational. Human rationality is fallible, so that, as limited finite creatures, we are rational only to a certain degree. I reluctantly admit that some rational persons would find me to be irrational in some respects.

J. Wentzel Van Huysteen proposes a helpful, broad concept of rationality that coheres with what I am suggesting here. He suggests that "rationality is all about responsibility: the responsibility to pursue clarity, intelligibility, and optimal understanding as ways to cope with ourselves and our world." It is the "intelligent pursuit of epistemic goals, of which intelligibility is the most important." Thus "optimizing our judgment about what we think, do, and value forms the crux of rationality."[5] Rationality also has to do with accountability, that is, a willingness to explain oneself. Within the Christian community, such accountability will draw upon internal Christian criteria, such as Christ, scripture, tradition, and so on. But even when one converses with those outside of faith, accountability is called for. This does not imply submitting oneself to someone else's critieria of truth or making oneself responsible for universal verification of one's truth claims. It does mean an attempt to communicate reasonably by explaining why one thinks and believes as one does.

The broad working concept of rationality that I am suggesting here is useful enough, I think, to proceed with the discussion of faith as rational, though the concept of rationality will have to be filled out as we proceed. I do not wish to prove or establish the content of Christian faith on the basis of some universal standard of human reason, which would be contrary to all that I have said previously about faith as gift of the Spirit and about revelation and theology of the cross. Rather, revelation and human reason must be put into a kind of dialogue. As Hall argues, there is no good reason to suppose that human reason will always be inhospitable to what is meant by revelation.[6] We need to give reason its due, as one of God's good gifts to humanity. Karl Barth is a theologian who eschews all philosophical prolegomena for faith and theology. His comment on reason is instructive:

> Concerning reason, I want to say this: I will have nothing to do with the distrust of reason. I have great trust in reason. I am not a rationalist, but I believe that reason is a good gift of God and that we must make full use of it in theology. This is our praise of God, who has given us this gift to distinguish that two and two equals four instead of five. That is my rationalism! Some people want to make reason the abstract judge of all—and that is unreasonable![7]

Some would suggest that the whole drive for rationality in thought is alien to biblical faith, that it is Greek and not Hebraic. But I suggest that the approach to rationality taken here is in keeping with the kind of rationality we find in the Bible. For example, Jesus as depicted in the Gospels is no mere dogmatist and is often involved in argument and debate (see Mk 8:11; 12:28; Mt 19:1-12, 21, 23-27; 22:15-46; etc.). The apostles, we find, not only preach, teach, and bear witness; they also discuss (Acts 6:9; 9:29), demonstrate (Acts 18:28), and reason (Acts 17:2; 18:19; 19:8-9). The best-known biblical text for the rationality of faith is 1 Peter 3:15: "Always be ready to make your defense (*apologia*) to anyone who demands from you an accounting for the hope that is in you; yet do it with gentleness and reverence." The text does not, I think, call for an elaborate philosophical apologetic in terms of human wisdom; it does encourage open, persuasive, and reasonable communication with people who do not share one's own faith and hope.

The Challenge to Rationality in a Postmodern Context

The attempt to speak of faith as rational finds an important challenge in much of what is called "postmodern" thought. We have frequently spoken of postmodernity and postmodernism without explaining what is meant by these terms. The terms are so widely used by such a wide variety of different thinkers, whether philosophers or theologians, scientists, artists, and others, that they can be very vague. Yet an awareness of the discourse of postmodernity and postmodernism is essential for understanding important developments in contemporary theology.

Is there a Postmodern Context? The periodization of history is not an uncontroversial matter. While most historians of the West would agree, with hindsight, to speak of an ancient world, a medieval world, and a modern world, just when, how, and why these transitions have occurred is ambiguous. Even more unclear, since so far we lack hindsight, is whether, why, or just when we have passed out of modernity into postmodernity; whether what is sometimes called postmodernity is really just a kind of hyper-modernity; and in what postmodernity consists.[8] However, there is quite wide consensus today that in the latter part of the twentieth century, in the Western/Northern world at least, a cultural and intellectual transition has occurred, or has started to occur, which may be called "postmodern context." Even if we do not wish to espouse postmodern*ism*, we may speak of postmodernity, or a postmodern cultural mood or atmosphere which expresses itself in many cultural forms. No doubt its origins lie at least in part in the new technologies that we live with—the computer and the Internet—and all that they mean for cross-cultural communication and in our awareness of living in a much smaller world. It is also not unconnected to what is sometimes referred to as "post-foundationalism." If there are no secure, demonstrable foundations for human knowledge upon which people can agree, then structures of authority begin to break down. Authority figures are questioned in every sphere of practical life, whether in medicine, religion, science, art, or architecture. This is not only because many people are better educated and better able to read, research, and think for themselves. More than that, people have begun to be aware of the uncertain nature of so much of what has been regarded as knowledge. We know, for example, that there is not one medicine for or one agreed upon way of treating various ailments or diseases, and so now more than ever we question our physicians and dare to disagree with them, not only in the details but in their basic presuppositions. Postmodernity has something to do with this new awareness of complexity in every field of inquiry and practice. Clergy and the magisteria of various faith communities carry less automatic authority among people who know that there is no one set of correct answers to their religious questions. Christians, for example, are more aware not only of other religions but also of the great variety of differing traditions and discourses that have existed and still exist within the broad range of Christian faith. Teachers and professors, professionals and experts of all kinds, find themselves questioned more fundamentally than they used to be. Postmodernity has made its presence felt in the arts as well—in painting and architecture, in music, fiction, drama, and movies. It is nothing new, of course, that many very different styles have come and gone, existed and coexisted in all of these media. What may be qualitatively new, some suggest, is an explicit celebration of diversity and pluralism, a deliberate choice for *collage* of styles and materials, or *bricolage,* a "reconfiguration of various traditional objects in order to achieve some contemporary purpose or make an ironic statement."[9] In architecture it may mean an intentional bringing together of old and new and apparently incompatible styles, techniques, and materials. In fiction and film one may speak of the ironic, playful juxtaposing of the real and the fictitious, emphasizing contingency and temporality, throwing doubt on universal truth. In dress, costume, and performance, "correct" and coordinated ways of doing things are defied. Stanley Grenz comments:

> The pop culture of our day reflects the centerless pluralism of postmodernity and gives expression to the antirationalism of postmodernism. As evidenced in the clothes they wear and the music they listen to, postmoderns are no longer convinced that their world has a center or that human reason can perceive any logical structure in the external universe. They live in a world in which the distinction between truth and fiction has evaporated. Consequently they become collectors of experiences, repositories of transitory, fleeting images produced and fostered by the diversity of media forms endemic in postmodern society.[10]

Postmodernity, then, has to do with suspicion of all claims to knowledge and truth, suspicion of the power that is exercised in the name of knowledge and truth, distrust of dominant worldviews and objective ethical values. Key words are "deconstruction," "decentering," and "indeterminacy."[11] While suspicion of authorities and truth claims was also characteristic of early modernity, reason was considered the appropriate arbiter, replacing vested or dogmatic authorities. The postmodern attitude carries this further and doubts even reason and science and their practical results. It is critical, then, not only of doctrines of God and religious moral values but also of scientific progress, technology, and aesthetic standards laid upon individuals by experts.

It would be a mistake to think that postmodernity has entirely taken over society and culture, since in many ways and in many places modernity is very much alive and well. One of the elements of postmodern consciousness is a suspicion of the continuing prestige of modern science and technology, of the domination exercised by international corporations and the governments of great nations through technique, and of the environmental damage wrought by the application of scientific knowledge and technology. Dominance through science has been, unquestionably, one of the major features of modernity since the days of Francis Bacon. That early scientific theorist spoke of "virile minds" extending the power and "empire" of the human race over the universe, conquering nature, "penetrating her, forcing her to give up her secrets."[12] Ecological, especially ecofeminist, theology has done much to raise our awareness that these attitudes are alive and well in the twenty-first century. Early modern technological weaponry was used by Europeans to dominate and exploit vast regions of the world, so that modernity is associated also with the political, economic, and religious imperialism of the ("Christian") white race. But military, political, and economic domination is, more than ever, a dominant feature of our present reality, and religious imperialism is certainly not dead.

Postmodernity as cultural context may be severely critical of religion in some quarters, but may also open people to "spirituality" in a situation that is less confident of human reason and more hospitable to faith and to communities of faith. Faith in God will not be founded upon forceful pretheological arguments of reason by which we seek to impose correct answers on everyone. A more humble faith, however, which knows it is not "sight," may be espoused with passion by postmodern people, for we now know, through reason's own criticism of reason, that "reason does not provide a viable and satisfying alternative to faith, as it once seemed to do."[13] Moreover, typical postmodern critiques of power, hegemony, and domination obviously have much in common with Christian liberationist perspectives.

Some academic philosophers who have warmly embraced the phenomenon of postmodern culture have offered philosophic theory that attempts to account for and support it. It will be useful to consider the work of some major representatives of what is called postmodernist philosophy, in order to consider their significance for theological epistemology.

A Glimpse of Postmodernist Philosophy. We have space here for only the briefest glimpse of the broad phenomenon of postmodernist philosophy, which includes many differing and complex thinkers. The genre of postmodernist thought (though it may be anti-postmodern to speak of genres at all) is extraordinarily diverse, and this should not surprise us, since the celebration of diversity and difference is a central point of all postmodernism. The term is so much in vogue, and so widespread is the concern to dissociate from the "modern" philosophy of the Enlightenment and various aspects of the modern world, that the term *postmodern* (though not necessarily *postmodernist*) is used positively by almost everyone from nihilistic atheists to conservative evangelical theologians!

We have noted already in Kant's response to Hume's skepticism in the late eighteenth century the appearance of cracks in the modern philosophical confidence in human reason, and we saw growing fissures in this confidence in the post-Enlightenment thought of Marx, Nietzsche, and Freud. The philosophers of recent decades who have espoused postmodern*ism* have often drawn substantially upon Marx but also on such hermeneutical figures as Wilhelm Dilthey, Martin Heidegger, and philosophers of language such as Ludwig Wittgenstein and Ferdinand de Saussure, all of whom may be described as post-Enlightenment thinkers, and all of whom, in their various ways, historicized or relativized truth claims about reality and so undermined the modern assurance of certain knowledge. But the postmodernists have especially honoured Nietzsche as their intellectual father, and postmodernism often takes a nihilistic turn. Friedrich Nietzsche (1844-1900) was a virulent critic of Enlightenment reason and also an avowed enemy of Christianity. He was a radical skeptic about human knowledge in general, believing that we live in a constructed world that derives from our own human perspectives. He is contemptuous of the modern "self," which is so prominent in modern thought from Descartes on, as a solid foundation for truth about God and the world. While the problematic of the human subject's knowledge of external objects, whether through rationalism or empiricism, had been laid out in the eighteenth century by both skeptics and idealists, Immanuel Kant had attempted to save human knowledge with his transcendental idealism and practical reason, and Hegel had brought together "reason" and "the real" in his grand system of absolute idealism. But Nietzsche was persuaded by neither Kant nor Hegel, believing that the whole of human so-called knowledge was but a "web of illusion, "[14] constructed by human beings out of their aesthetic gifts for creation and self-creation. Nietzsche himself was a writer of remarkable artistic, poetic flair. Most especially and of most interest to us here was his rejection of all moral and religious claims for "truth." Both ancient Greek philosophy and Christian theology believed that moral truth is objective and "given" in reality. They believed that moral truth is there to be discovered through perception of the eternal, either through reason or through revelation. The moderns, culminating in Kant, thought that autonomous human reason (practical reason) could discern objective moral obligations within the self. Nietzsche attacked this view, arguing that moral values are actually expressions of the human "will to power."[15] Instincts of self-preservation and self-aggrandizement produce the illusions of moral duty and of God. In this respect his thought resembled Marx's theory of "ideology" as "superstructural" to the economic and technological base of the social order, so that religion, philosophy, art, morality, and law all constitute a "false consciousness" serving the interests of the ruling class. Nietzsche's "web of illusion" is also not unlike Freud's view (a generation later) of religion as self-deceptive, illusory wish fulfillment.[16] For all of these thinkers, the relation of God and creation is reversed: It is not that God created the world and people, but that people have created God for their own purposes. Even if we do not accept their accounts of human thought, culture, and religion, we need to acknowledge the critical insight of these thinkers into what is often the self-serving, alienated, and alienating character of religious life.

Nietzsche, more virulently than any of them, attacked the concept of God, announcing the actual "death of God" in Western culture.[17] The concept of God had been useful for human beings for a certain period of time, but all truths are now increasingly seen to be lies and conventions that serve the will to power. Beliefs are not universal or rational; indeed, specifically Christian values of humility and self-abnegation are forms of slave morality, pandering to human weakness and engendering mediocrity. Nietzsche was particularly contemptuous of women, whom he regarded as weak and properly mastered by men: "Man shall be educated for war, and woman for the recreation of the warrior. Everything is folly. . . . Thou goest to women? Remember thy whip!"[18] Christian ethics, he proclaims, is "indecent, dishonest, cowardly, effeminate." Nietzsche believed that Christianity was already essentially dead and that Christian ethics was about to perish:

> Thus Christianity as dogma perished by its own ethics, and in the same
> way Christianity as ethics must perish; we are standing on the threshold
> of this event. . . . Christian truthfulness must now draw its strongest con-
> clusion, the one by which it shall do away with itself.[19]

Nietzsche was particularly contemputous of the Christian notion of "god on the
cross," which he regarded as "the revenge of the oriental slave on Rome." Religion is essentially a "neurosis."[20] He did, however, assert (quite inconsistently)
some metaphysical truths, for example, the figure of the Superhuman (*Über-
mensch*), the strong, free, creative man, liberated from slave moralities, controlling the human and nonhuman world in his own interests; and also, strangely, a
doctrine of "eternal return," according to which all that happens will happen
again and again an infinite number of times.

   Though his thought is important for any critical account of religious life, it is
obvious that Nietzsche's philosophy cannot be espoused by Christians. He asserts
a radical historicism (i.e., the relativization of all notions of good and evil to their
historical contexts); the rejection of all notions of the eternal and all attitudes of
reverence or thanksgiving, asserting instead the primacy of will; and his ideal figure of the Superhuman, promoting the domination and mastery of human and nonhuman nature. George Grant, a virulent critic of modern thought and of the
modern technological world, comments that "there is no escape from Nietzsche
if one is to understand modernity."[21] Nietzsche, says Grant, understands and
theorizes the modern project more clearly than any other author. This raises in
our minds the question of whether Nietzsche (and even his self-avowed postmodernist followers) are really postmodern, or just hyper-modern. Have they
simply drawn the project of modernity to its logical conclusion? Grant points out
that Nietzsche invented the concept of values, which has become universal cur-
rency in modern parlance, indicating the victory in modernity of radical historicism and of the technical mastery of the world. Grant warns that "one should
teach Nietzsche within the understanding that he is a teacher of evil."[22] He is, of
course, the teacher of nihilism: God is dead. Nothing is true. Nothing is good or
evil. He is indeed the quintessential philosopher of despair.

   Perhaps the most famous of the twentieth-century postmodernists, Michel
Foucault (1926-1984), has been called "Nietzsche's truest disciple,"[23] following
him in his radical rejection of Enlightenment reason. Foucault particularly dis-
misses the central concept of modern philosophy, the autonomous self of both
Descartes and Kant, as well as their claims to valid knowledge of the world. He
objects to all alleged knowledge of universals, stressing difference over same-
ness, heterogeneity over homogeneity, denying especially the reality of a single
human nature. He echoes Nietzsche in his contention that all such universal concepts are instruments of power and domination. Claims to knowledge, whether
of religion or of philosophic reason, are to be seen as hegemonic.[24] His attitude
to power is different from that of Nietzsche, who both exposed and celebrated the

will to power and exalted the Superhuman. Foucault's exposure of the hegemony of rational concepts has something in common with Marxist and liberationist concerns (though Foucault is not found valorizing justice or compassion for the poor) in that he obviously dislikes domination. As a lover of poetry and other aesthetic pursuits, rather than rational discourse, he wishes to draw attention to "local, discontinuous, disqualified, illegitimate knowledges against the claims of a unitary body of theory which would filter, hierarchize and order them in the name of some true knowledge."[25]

The Jewish, Algerian-born, French-speaking philosopher Jacques Derrida (b. 1930) follows Nietzsche and resembles Foucault in his rejection of knowledge as corresponding with reality. Focusing on language, especially written language, he throws doubt on its ability to refer to objective reality beyond itself. Influenced by Heidegger's hermeneutical thought, Derrida thinks that, where written texts are concerned, there are no singular meanings; the meanings of texts are infinitely fluid. We must abandon what he calls "logocentrism" as search for objective meaning, either in an author's intention or in a world outside the play of language. "Deconstruction," then, is the important word for Derrida, questioning the correspondence between language and concepts and metaphysical presence or reality. The agenda of deconstruction is congenial, to a degree, to liberation theology's hermeneutics of suspicion and, again, is opposed to the domination that can arise from claims to true interpretation or knowledge of what is real. These words of Derrida disclose both the obscurity of his thought and the political critique of power inherent in his work:

> Deconstruction does not consist in passing from one concept to another, but in overturning and displacing a conceptual order, as well as the non-conceptual order with which the conceptual order is articulated. For example, writing, as a classical concept, carries with it predicates which have been subordinated, excluded, or held in reserve by forces and according to necessities to be analyzed. It is these forces . . . whose force of generality, generalization, and generativity find themselves liberated, grafted onto a "new" concept of writing which also corresponds to whatever always has resisted the former organization of forces.[26]

Jean-Francois Lyotard, a contemporary French philosopher, is one of the more comprehensible postmodernists.[27] He, like the others, opposes the Enlightenment's optimistic project of knowing, on a firm epistemological foundation, the laws and principles of the real world and what he calls the "master narratives" or myths and worldviews that more or less unconsciously undergird and legitimize the central core of values and beliefs in human societies.[28] Modern claims to replace ancient myth with rational postulates, whether the claims of science and technology or of progress, or Christian claims in the religious and ethical field, are criticized as equally illusory. Since the Second World War, not only religious narratives but also the grand narratives of scientific progress have lost credibility. No single scientific enterprise exists; rather, natural scientists themselves are divided about their visions of the real. Various disciplines are seen to be sets of competing, parallel, and incompatible "language games," and questions of truth are now replaced by questions about usefulness and performativity.[29] Recognition of the end of modern rationality, he thinks, assists us in coping with the radical pluralism found both in the various searches for knowledge and in social life. Lyotard comments on contemporary capitalism, which he sees as a great blind system of technical management, subjectless and value free.[30] But we may ask whether, according to his own concepts, his perception is real or illusory. He has no interest in cross-cultural or even philosophical dialogue with those who disagree with him, since usually they are bringing reasonable arguments to bear. He seems to be opposed to totalitarianism and to favour human freedom, but on what grounds? And how should social goals be achieved, according to what criteria? The postmodern idea that people create their world and themselves seems absurd, as Gregory Baum argues, in view of the hard realities that press themselves upon us: "Here our speech is tested and judged when we apply it to the many dangers which threaten humankind at this time: Hunger, we note, is a discourse-transcending reality, so is AIDS, so is torture and assassination by death squads."[31] Baum, as a Christian theologian who defends the emancipatory aspects of the Enlightenment, objects to the postmodernist rejection of a common humanity, of all universal moral truth, and of the value of cross-cultural dialogue. Since they strongly affirm difference, why do the postmodernist philosophers not revel in open dialogue with those who disagree with them? The problem would be that dialogue has to be reasonable in some degree. Baum comments further:

> If . . . the deconstructionist message of the death of the subject were offered to the Blacks of South Africa or Natives in North America, people forcefully excluded from the scene of history, this message would be rejected as an ideology of the Western empire. People identified with the formerly colonized nations argue that poor people cannot afford to be nihilists: nihilism is the privilege of the advantaged.[32]

Most readers, ensconced as we are perhaps in modern presuppositions, do not find the extreme assertions of the postmodernist philosophers particularly convincing. The problem with all kinds of radical historicism and skepticism is that the proponents find themselves, willy-nilly, making statements about the nature of knowledge and the nature of reality, and thus they turn out to be self-defeating. Their usefulness may be their ability to shake loose some of our unconscious assumptions about what we know and what is actually certain. However, it is improbable that any Chrisian believer could adopt the extreme nihilistic views of these postmodernist thinkers. The perspective of faith cannot dispense with the "Other" reality of the holy God impinging upon our consciousness, commanding, promising, transforming. Nor does their thought persuasively rule out or refute such experience. The objectivity of the good creation of God and of the humanity of Christ that we encounter in the experience of faith makes it impossible for Christians to buy into the radical relativism and extreme agnosticism about reality that these authors propose. The convictions that reason is a gift of God to our good humanity, and that love and justice are intensely real, both in the will and nature of God and in human experience, mean that Christians cannot be followers of Nietzsche, Foucault, Derrida, or Lyotard. Christians of liberationist or feminist persuasion certainly share the suspicion of power and of the use of hegemonic discourses and metanarratives to dominate in the world, but these theologies do not depend on the postmodernist philosophers for these insights.[33] Moreover, the postmodernists seldom offer concrete social or cultural analyses that would be useful for human or ecological emancipation. It is impossible, of course, for Christians to set aside the metanarrative of the history of creation and salvation, or to depart from the "center" of all reality revealed in the Christ. Nor have these authors persuaded us that we should! After all, persuasion by rational argument or dialogue is ruled out by them from the beginning. In fact they appear to have further constricted, rather than opened up, the range of possible rational knowing of which human beings are capable and sometimes to have descended into a kind of self-defeating skepticism or solipsism.

The Wide Variety of "Postmodern" Theologies. Contemporary theology and philosophical theology no doubt need to relate to what is called "postmodern context," but this is not the same as adopting the attitudes and approaches of postmodernist philosophy. A host of Christian thinkers, both philosophers and theologians, can be described as postmodern in their attitudes and approaches, and feature in their thought a suspicion of the modern Enlightenment confidence in human reason and the wish to decenter the human self. Some of them, such as Mark C. Taylor and Mark Kline Taylor, two postmodern thinkers, each very different from the other, are happy to identify themselves explicitly as postmodern and to borrow substantially from postmodernist philosophy.[34] Some are perhaps more aptly described as "poststructuralist," such as Mary McClintock Fulkerson.[35]

In sharp contrast, one might cautiously use the term "postmodern" of George Grant, a classically oriented Christian thinker who, in defending classical reason, would vigorously oppose any thought associated with Nietzsche, but who is at the same time a virulent critic of modernity, especially its absorption by technical reason. Douglas John Hall, a Canadian Protestant contextual theologian and appreciative inheritor of neo-orthodox theology, shares much of Grant's antimodernity. Alasdair MacIntyre is another, very different Christian philosopher who could be described as postmodern in a "premodern" way, arguing voluminously and with great erudition that there is not one rationality and not one justice.[36] One could say the same of Thomas Oden, conservative Methodist theologian, and Reformed philosophical theologians like Alvin Plantinga and Nicholas Wolterstorff, who are also sharply critical of modern thought.[37] Then too, the American postliberals (who may be called neo-Barthians) such as Hans Frei, George Lindbeck, Ronald Thiemann, and Stanley Hauerwas, can all be described as postmodern, together with a British thinker congenial with them, John Milbank.[38] The term can be used, then, of theologians who might be described as radically liberal (and perhaps "hyper-modern"?) and others who might be described as quite conservative defenders of Christian traditional orthodoxy. If they have anything in common, it is perhaps their rejection of modern foundationalism or confidence in any universally verifiable basis for theology.

I am both appreciative and critical of these various postmodern thinkers and would like also to be "postmodern" in the sense of rejecting the quest for sure reasonable foundations for knowledge as sought by modernity, but without buying into the antirational rhetoric of many postmodern*ist* authors.

Not Foundationalism

If we are to consider faith as rational, must we opt for some kind of modern foundationalism? That is, must our faith and theology be *founded upon* information (facts) or other well-founded beliefs, that is, premises from which they are logically inferred? "Foundationalism" is the term used (pejoratively) in current debate about epistemology to refer to a typically modernist approach to knowledge, whether in theology or human knowledge in general. Foundationalism is the search for an absolute and indubitable certainty on the basis of which true knowledge can be constructed. For foundationalism, on the basis of first principles, knowledge will be discernible and verifiable to all rational persons.[39] Knowledge is built from the bottom up, then, by deductive (logical) and/or inductive (empirical) methods. Ancient Greek philosophy sought for certain knowledge and ways to demonstrate it, but this was most especially the preoccupation of modern philosophy, especially during the Age of Reason or Enlightenment, when classical notions of reason and knowledge were called into question. In theology, the question is: Do our faith affirmations, to be rational, have to be arrived at, or at least be defensible as, the conclusion of a logical argument?[40] Is it in fact possible to find a general, publicly acceptable intellectual foundation on which faith and theology can be constructed? Certainly there is a long and respectable tradition of arguing rationally for the existence of God reaching back far before modern times. Great medieval Christian thinkers like Augustine, Anselm, and Aquinas tried, from within faith, to demonstrate by reasonable arguments or proofs that God exists. Early modern rationalists, empiricists, and moralists (e.g., Descartes, Locke, Kant) were the true foundationalists, however, trying to argue to the existence of God from outside faith, respectively by various deductive, empirical, or moral premises. In addition, some modern (liberal) theologians have attempted to ground theology firmly in religious experience, while other modern (conservative) theologians have built on the foundation of infallible scriptures.[41] Others try to offer historical foundational premises and deductive arguments for the specific content of the gospel, such as the resurrection of Jesus, Wolfhart Pannenberg being perhaps the ablest and most striking example of this kind of foundationalism. We might first consider briefly the apparent foundationalism of premodern theologians.

The Medievals and Their Successors. Thomas Aquinas, who lived in the thirteenth century, is sometimes regarded as the foundationalist par excellence in his five proofs for the existence of God. According to these somewhat similar, overlapping arguments, the thinker moves from something known—the contingency and orderliness of the world—to something unknown—the existence of a necessary Being, who is first cause and designer of the world. Long before him, older medieval theologians like Augustine and Anselm, although they also offered arguments for God's existence, asserted a more basic epistemological principle: *credo ut intelligam* ("I believe in order that I may understand"): "The believer does not seek to understand that he may believe, but he believes that he may understand."[42] They used arguments to corroborate, and to better understand, what they already believed by faith. Anslem's famous ontological argument for God is really an example of *fides quaerens intellectum* ("faith seeking understanding").[43] Anselm argues: "God is that, than which nothing greater can be conceived. That which can be conceived not to exist is not God." He thus asserts the "necessary" existence of God.[44] It hardly amounts to a coercive demonstration; it assumes already the reality of the God revealed to faith. In fact, Anselm presents his argument in the form of a prayer: "So truly, therefore, dost thou exist, O Lord, my God, that thou canst not be conceived not to exist."[45] However, neither Augustine nor Anselm thought that Christians were required to found their faith on argumentative foundations.[46] Nor did Aquinas, despite his two-step epistemology from sense experience and reason to revelation and faith, think that simple believers were irrational if they did not found their faith on his proofs.[47] He contended "that it is not a mark of levity to assent to the things that are of faith, although they are above reason."[48] For him, the proofs were really corroboration for faith. The great medievals, then, though they offered ontological or cosmological/teleological arguments for God's existence, were not foundationalists in the modern Cartesian sense. They did not in fact arrive at faith on the basis of outside premises and logical inferences. They did not think it was irrational to believe in God without founding that faith upon prior premises or arguments. In fact their proofs are really *a posteriori* (after the fact) confirmation of a credo they already possessed.

In our time thinkers who may be regarded as in some way the successors of Aquinas, such as Karl Rahner, Bernard Lonergan, and David Tracy, offer updated arguments or anthropological reflections in favour of a rational and natural human awareness of divine transcendence. To take Tracy as an example of this mode of thought, the arguments of what he calls "fundamental theology" are offered as prolegomena for theology as public discourse. He asserts that "the fundamental loyalty of the theologian qua theologian is to the morality of scientific knowledge which he shares with his colleagues, the philosophers, historians, and social scientists."[49] Thus, he is interested in offering fundamental theology, or what might be called a kind of "natural theology" or "general revelation" argument for God or transcendence: "Fundamental theologies will be concerned primarily to provide arguments that all reasonable persons, whether 'religiously involved' or not, can recognize as reasonable."[50] Tracy does not speak in terms of proofs and does not imagine that, as arguments, this mode of thought will produce general philosophic assent. Rather, he offers "metaphysical and transcendental reflection"[51]—here he resembles Rahner and others—which he hopes will evoke agreement from people who would otherwise dismiss religious claims. He is not necessarily, then, a foundationalist in the modern sense (which will be discussed below). The evocative arguments of what Tracy calls fundamental theology, have been both criticized and defended ably by philosophers for centuries. There seems to be no agreement among philosophers and logicians as to the validity or force of such arguments, but it would be rare today to find a philosopher who thought they were decisive; obviously they are not universally compelling (and therefore not successfully foundationalist). It is true and significant, though, that some religious believers (some that I know) have found their way to faith, or remained in faith, partly with the help of such arguments.

I am reminded of John Updike's story "Pigeon Feathers," of the boy David Kern, who had his faith knocked out from under him by a vision of the grave in its all cold certainty and inevitability. But coming across a dead pigeon, the pattern of its feathers awesomely beautiful, David found that he simply could not go back on an intuitive conviction that "the God who had lavished such craft upon these worthless pigeons would not destroy His whole creation by refusing to let David live forever."[52]

This mode of discourse, then, should not be dismissed or deplored. Yet many others are quite unmoved by such arguments, feeling there is enough disorder and misery in the universe to counter the so-called evidence or indications of God that these arguments adduce. Reasoned arguments from the world to God cannot in themselves produce faith in Jesus Christ, something which Aquinas knew very well. To communicate the God of exodus, of cross and resurrection, one needs to speak out of a broader rationality about the specific content of faith itself.

The Modern Quest for Certain Knowledge. The dawn of what is called "modernity" following on the Renaissance and Reformation meant that the medieval certainties about faith and knowledge were severely shaken. The Renaissance revived much of the wisdom of the ancient classical philosophy and to some extent fostered a semisecular spirit. The Reformation too stimulated many people to question the traditional faith they had been taught, challenging people to doubt and question authoritative doctrine by checking it with scripture.[53] The old question How do you know? took on new urgency. In some ways this resembled what we today call "postmodern context," a transitionary time of doubt and radical questioning. However, the Enlightenment of the seventeenth and eighteenth centuries can be described as a positive, optimistic effort to find secure, unquestionable foundations for human knowledge, and so to be liberated from both doubt and the tyranny of dogma. Even at its height, though, Enlightenment reason was never unanimous about what the foundations of assured knowledge should be.

The French philosopher René Descartes (1596-1650), a brilliant contributor to mathematics and empirical science in the early seventeenth century, often described as the first major figure of modern philosophy, set out to doubt everything until he reached a rock-bottom certainty that could not be doubted: "I perceived that . . . I had to undertake seriously once in my life to rid myself of all the opinions I had adopted up to then and to begin afresh from the foundations, if I wished to establish something firm and constant."[54] Descartes found that he was capable of doubting the existence of external objects and generally the evidence of his senses, since these sometimes deceived him. What he could not doubt was his own "self," his own existence as a doubting, thinking subject. In this way Descartes arrived at his famous *Cogito ergo sum* ("I think, therefore I am"). He could only be sure of his own existence, however, as long as he was actually thinking. By a circuitous route beginning from his *cogito,* he reached, through a kind of ontological argument like that of Anselm, the conclusion that a perfect God must exist (for he would be imperfect if he did not exist) who is the guarantor of his innate, clear, and distinct ideas. It was, therefore, on the indubitable basis of his own personal existence that he constructed a rational edifice by way of a process of logical deduction. The human subject or self, then, is the center of all knowledge, and God can be seen to exist only inasmuch as the human self needs him as guarantor of human knowledge. Descartes' dream of building all knowledge upon absolutely secure foundations and rational deductive processes did not last long, though his basic intention—to secure a rational foundation for all knowledge—became a major agenda for modern philosophy. Descartes also thought that the human mind or self was a "thinking substance" distinct from the world of matter or "extension," including the human body. This dualism of mind and body isolated the self from other persons and from the world around. Thinking became an abstracted intellectual deductive process cut off not only from any essential relationship to other persons but from practical activity in the real world.[55]

Empiricist philosophers who followed knew that it was not enough to think deductively (though Descartes also knew that to know the real world one has to observe it by means of the physical senses). The Englishman John Locke, for example (1632-1704), questioned Descartes' innate ideas, but optimistically sought his rock-bottom certainty in the mind's perception of sensible objects, the mind being understood as a *tabula rasa,* something like "white paper, void of all characters, without any ideas."[56] This was Locke's way of finding a secure, unquestionable starting point on which to build true knowledge. Locke developed a cosmological argument for God on an empiricist basis and even tried to argue, with a combination of empirical and deductive procedures, for the revelation of God in Christ. Christianity needed, however, to rid itself of mysteries and dogmatic baggage, without which it could be an entirely reasonable religion.

The devout French believer and mathematician Blaise Pascal (1623-1662) was already very skeptical about such uses of reason and held a very low assessment of reason's powers, which, according to him, were purely calculative.[57] Pascal's skepticism about reason, whether deductive or empirical, preceded the highly developed philosophical skepticism of the Scottish philosopher David Hume (1711-1776), however, who threw a good deal of cold water on the cogency of the arguments of both rationalists and empiricists, putting in doubt the validity of both religious and scientific knowledge of the real world as well as the substantial reality of the self. At about the same time the idealist philosopher George Berkeley argued that the only things we really know are the "ideas" that we directly perceive in our minds, with no grounds for thinking that such ideas correspond to external objects.

Immanuel Kant (1724-1804), following upon a century or so of philosophical controversy among rationalists, empiricists, and idealists, called into question all real knowlege of the "thing-in-itself" (the real world as it actually is), postulating in his *Critique of Pure Reason* the imposition of the principles and categories of human understanding upon all perception. In other words, the human mind is emphatically not a *tabula rasa,* as Locke thought, but contributes its own perception of the real. Yet Kant proposed his own kind of rock-bottom starting point for what he called "practical reason" in the self's own inner consciousness of moral obligation. Having in his first *Critique* demolished, he believed, the traditional cosmological and teleological arguments for God, Kant developed in his *Critique of Practical Reason* a moral argument for a God who must exist as the lawgiver of what he thought was surely beyond doubt—our sense of moral duty. This concept of God—and modern philosophic concepts of God generally—tended, then, to be functionalist, in the sense that "God" came to be manipulated for human purposes, designed to fit our specifications, or, as William Placher has argued, modern theology tended to domesticate God.[58] God became a postulate of the human self, which remained the epistemological center and arbiter of knowledge. Out of great confidence in the capacity of the human reasonable self to know the truth, and the necessity of this truth to be useful to our modern projects, modern theology deemphasized the doctrine of the Trinity, played down the theology of grace, and generally disparaged the recognition of God's transcendence and mystery.

A passionate rejection of this whole philosophic endeavour to prove the existence of God came from Denmark in the outpourings of Søren Kierkegaard. His brilliant attacks upon philosophical theology (especially the system of Hegel) asserted the radical givenness of faith and used reason to discredit reason's presumptions to prove or establish the existence of God. He also protested the abstractness of so much Christian philosophy, as in this rather typical snippet of his writing:

> For the rights of understanding to be valid one must venture out into life, out on the sea and lift up one's voice, even though God hears it not, and not stand on the shore and watch others fighting and struggling— only then does understanding acquire its official sanction, for to stand on one leg and prove God's existence is a very different thing from going on one's knees and thanking him.[59]

The point to note here, with a little help from Kierkegaard, is that the modern philosophers and their various rationalist, empiricist, idealist, or moralist successors down to our time have not succeeded in finding universally acceptable foundations for certain knowledge—not of the physical world and certainly not of God. Succeeding generations of philosophers have made us even more aware of the complexity of the question of knowledge. As we noted in chapter 1, the "masters of suspicion"—Marx, Nietzsche, and Freud[60]—and later such figures as Wittgenstein have thrown doubt on the validity of much of our rational thought and its correspondence to reality, not only in theology but in other disciplines as well, and also on the alleged secure foundations of human knowledge.

Nonfoundationalist Science. What may be called the nonfoundationalist character of physical science also came to the fore in the latter half of the twentieth century. That science is not simply a matter of demonstrable facts was evident, for example, to the theoretical physicist C. F. von Weizsacker, a prominent figure in the development of quantum theory, who could speak of scientific knowing as a kind of meditation, pointing to "the process by which consciousness takes possession of a truth in such a way that not only the content but also the structure of consciousness is changed."[61] Similarly, the philosopher of science Michael Polanyi, in his famous epistemological work *Personal Knowledge*, discussed the similarity of new scientific discovery to religious conversion:

> We can now see the great difficulty that may arise in the attempt to persuade others to accept a new idea in science. We have seen that to the extent to which it represents a new way of reasoning, we cannot convince others by formal argument, for so long as we argue within their framework we can never induce them to abandon it. Demonstration must be supplemented, therefore, by forms of persuasion which can

induce a conversion. The refusal to enter on the opponent's way of arguing must be justified by making it appear altogether unreasonable.[62]

The epistemological foundations of physical science have been shaken especially
since the work of Thomas Kuhn on scientific revolutions.[63] A helpful commentator on Kuhn on the significance of philosophy of science for rationality in theology is Van Huysteen in his book *The Shaping of Rationality.* He points out that the
modernist view of science was very positivistic in that scientific knowledge was
thought to be objective, factual, subject to strict verification or falsification,
beyond the need for interpretation, and fixed in meaning.[64] Kuhn explored the
transition in basic scientific paradigms, for example, from Newtonian to Einsteinian, showing that the shift from one vision of the physical world to another
was not strictly based in unambiguous facts that were immediately provable to all
scientists. Many scientific researchers engaged in "normal science" continued for
a long time to work within the assumptions of the old paradigm. The eventual
widespread shift of paradigm has to be seen as a revolution that occurred gradually and resembled for many scientists a kind of conversion.[65] Yet it was not
merely an individualistic shift but a communal one within the scientific community that was seeking the greater holistic intelligibility of certain realities of the
physical universe, which now, through relativity and quantum theory, was seen to
be far more mysterious than had been previously thought. Kuhn and his successors in philosophy of science began to speak of "the undetermination of theory by
evidence or data, and the theory-ladenness of observation."[66] This implies a
breakdown in the sharp distinction that modern thought usually drew between
properly scientific rationality and the rationality of the humanities and social sciences, and even of theology. Rational science is no longer seen to require universal demonstrability. Concepts such as "intuition," "creativity," and "leap," usually
associated with "softer" disciplines, come to be part of scientific discourse. Moreover, the concept of praxis in relation to truth is important here, since practical
interests are highly determinative in the development of scientific theory: "Post-
Kuhnian philosophy of science has explicitly taught us that when scientists
observe, they do so selectively, and these selections are always determined by
both theoretical and practical interests."[67] Since Kuhn, scientists and philosophers
of science have argued that the natural sciences have not achieved a universal
basis for mediating disagreements, that the rules regulating scientific decision are
not universally recognized. While Kuhn had argued for growing consensus among
scientists at the theoretical level, making way for widespread revolutionary agreement about a new paradigm, post-Kuhnian postmodern philosophers of science go
even further than he did, suggesting that rational scientific thought does not necessarily require consensus, but only the openness of scientific researchers and theorists to the evaluation of the relevant scientific community, since there now exist
side by side competing paradigm theories and research traditions. Van Huysteen
cites a number of philosophers of science who have argued that

[i]n order to even begin to understand what rationality in different modes of inquiry is about, it is necessary to see that even in natural science, as arguably our best example of the cognitive dimension of rationality at work, the arguments and value judgments employed by scientists are grounded in historical contexts and social practices, and that there is an essential openness even in the very criteria and norms that guide scientific inquiry.[68]

All of this does not imply surrender to an extreme postmodernist, antirational subjectivism. Rather, it implies that "we never escape the intersubjective and cross-disciplinary obligation to support our rational judgments with the best available reasons and the best possible arguments."[69]

We see, then, that it is not only that scholars of the humanities and social sciences, the philosophers of religion and theologians, whose rationality is complex and less than unanimous; the scientists and philosophers of science, classically seen as the exemplars of truly rational verifiable discourse, also lack absolute foundations and generally accepted methods and theories. What we have is a general breakdown of foundationalism in epistemology, if by foundationalism we mean a universally acceptable standard or starting point of rationality that can be used as a basis for further knowledge. William Placher, as a nonfoundationalist theologian, states the matter cogently:

all this implies a dead end for Descartes' project, and with it of the Enlightenment dream. We cannot find a starting point firmly established on its own, on which we could construct the rest of our system of knowledge.

. . . If theologians try to defend their claims by starting with basic, foundational truths that any rational person would have to believe or observations independent of theory and assumption, they are trying to do something that our best philosophers tell us is impossible—not merely for religious beliefs but for any beliefs whatever.[70]

Having said all this, a cautionary note is called for. To reject foundationalism is not necessarily to reject totally the rationality of the Enlightenment. Humanity passed through some very important learning experiences between the seventeenth and nineteenth centuries, and we cannot merely return to what was, all too often, the authoritarian dogmatism and superstition of premodern times. Nor is it appropriate to revel in the humiliation of the intellect so that people will have to return to a mindless "faith" and submit themselves to ecclesiastical authorities! However, the human intellect may be in fact more capable of certain kinds of knowledge than modernists have usually granted, since, while modern philosophy and theology were very confident of certain kinds of deductive or empirical ways of knowing, they also tended to constrict the range of acceptable reasoning. Perhaps postmodern thought can be both more humble and more positive about faith as a rational way of knowing.

Not Fideism

In speaking in the last chapter of the radical disjunction of faith and reason, I ruled out any kind of rational*istic* approach to faith on the grounds that it is inappropriate to the radical givenness of faith derived from revelation. Our discussion of the failure of foundationalism confirms that even secular thought about human knowledge discounts the possibility of a secure rational ground on which all knowledge can be constructed. How, then, should we construe the nature of knowledge and, in particular, theological knowledge of God?

I wish to argue that the alternative to this need not be an irrational or anti-intellectual *fideism* (faith-ism) which renounces or disparages the responsible use of the rational mind. Beyond foundationalism there remain important and better ways to be rational, in human knowing generally and specifically in theology. To be fair, the fideist at his or her best is so overtaken by the wonder of what has been revealed, that s/he thinks that the critical intellect, or use of human reason, has little or no role in understanding or defending the revelation. Fideists may actually be highly intelligent individuals who use their rational minds to disparage rationality. At his or her worst, however, the fideist is simply mindless and intellectually lazy and makes of this a spiritual virtue. But the controversy is not by any means limited to academics. A common sort of conversation along these lines might go something like this at a church study group of adults, sitting comfortably in someone's living room.

Conversation

TED: *Well, I guess I should say right off the bat that I have a lot of trouble believing in God at all. I don't know if I'm an atheist or not; well, I guess maybe I am. The fact is, I just can't imagine a loving God standing behind all the pain and suffering in the world. Especially since Becky died. But it's not just that. I know we're not the first parents to lose a daughter, but . . . I'd like to believe in a good and loving Father in heaven but I just can't get my head around it. I actually feel like a bit of a hypocrite going to church, singing the hymns and all that, when actually most of it doesn't make much sense to me. But I'd like to be talked into it. I mean, I'd love to be a believer, if I could do it with intellectual integrity.*

MIMI: *[Smiling sweetly] Oh Ted, why worry so much about it? If you want to believe, just believe. Take it on faith like I do. I find a lot of comfort in my religion because I just don't let those kinds of questions bother me.*

TED: *I'm glad you do, but I can't just shut my eyes and believe. I need to hear a good argument before I believe something. Why not believe the moon is purple, or the Red Sox are going to win the pennant? It has to be reasonable or I can't believe it. Look, I'm in business. I don't just believe any cockeyed story anybody tells me. If I did I'd be bankrupt overnight. And the same with politics. You can't just believe everything every politician tells you. They'll take you for a fool every time. As far as I'm concerned, it's exactly the same with religion. How can I base my life on something that seems so irrational? If you expect me to believe it, sell me on it.*

REV. BRIAN: *Well, I'm with you, Ted. If you were going to throw out your rational faculties every time you talked about religion, you'd be wide open to every kind of religious charlatan who came your way. Mind you, it depends what you mean by "reasonable."*

JANE: *Yes, that's the key thing, isn't it? What do we mean by "reasonable"? I don't believe everything in the Bible, or just anything the minister says. It has to make sense somehow. But religion can't be reasonable the same way as businss or politics is, or science, say. Aren't there different ways of being reasonable about different things?*

REV. BRIAN: *Absolutely, Jane, you're onto something there.*

JANE: *For one thing, I know I can't believe literally in both creation stories in the book of Genesis. They actually contradict each other. But I feel that those old stories have something really important to say to us.*

TED: *Keeping in mind that those old stories have been refuted for a long time by evolutionary science!*

REV. BRIAN: *That's why it's reasonable to read them as poetry rather than as science or history. Then you read them for wisdom rather than historical or scientific facts. We'll have to go further into that later. And then too, there's a whole different kind of reasoning, say, for interpreting poetry, or studying history, or economics, or for personal relationships. Ted, as for the suffering of the world, you make a very good point. Lots of people don't believe in God precisely for that reason, and I sympathize with them. I know what you went through when Becky died. But maybe we have to rethink our whole concept of God so that what we believe is credible and makes some kind of sense to a thinking person.*

MIMI: *Well, I guess I'm just not a thinking person then, and don't care to be either. As far as I'm concerned, I was brought up to believe in the Bible and I'm very comfortable with that. If the Bible seems to contradict itself I'm sure God has some good reason and we'll understand it all some day. But if we're going to come here and pull apart the Bible maybe I should stay home. I'll just believe what I like, thank you very much.*

This kind of conversation occurs often among Christians and their friends. Ted's position leans toward rationalism, Mimi's is fideism of the less admirable sort. Jane's or Rev. Brian's attitude, insofar as we've observed it, is approximately what I would call "rational faith." Rational*ism* (or rational*istic* theology) imagines that Christian faith can be a secure intellectual system built upon prior premises and foolproof intellectual foundations. Some rationalists think that it's possible to argue people into fully traditional Christian belief with compelling logical force. Others of rationalist inclination are inclined to reduce or dilute the content of faith to the point where it is palatable to reason. Fideism, on the other hand, tends to abandon rational processes and simply assert the right to believe anything at all: "I'll believe whatever I like." The queen in *Alice in Wonderland* could believe in "as many as six impossible things before breakfast." Or fideism of a more sophisticated kind may tend to keep to itself and evade the critical questions of skeptics. In arguing for the disjunction of faith and reason I have clearly rejected rationalism, but have not defended fideism.

Mindless Fideism. Fideists can be extreme and mindless, becoming exasperated with the Teds of this world. But some highly intelligent, sophisticated thinkers can tend toward fideism. The great church father Tertullian, a brilliant mind and generally a rational person, is famous for his fideistic statements: "What has Athens to do with Jerusalem?" That is, What has reason to do with faith? Or, "The Son of God died: absurd, and therefore utterly credible. He was buried and rose again: impossible, and therefore a fact."[71]

The wisdom of God in the cross of Christ may appear foolish to human understanding, but it is not mere nonsense. What I am calling mindless fideism refuses to be accountable for its path to knowledge. The attitude of extreme fideism could justify believing in alchemy or astrology or that the world is flat. It could mean that the two accounts of creation in Genesis 1 and 2 are both literally true or ruling out *a priori* the theory of evolution or any other empirically based information or theory because it seems to contradict the Bible. It could mean insisting that the four Gospel accounts of the resurrection events are all factually accurate (though they contradict each other) or, in the face of feminist criticism, denying the patriarchal character of much biblical literature. It could mean refusing to consider the findings of form or redaction criticism, or refusing to listen at all to the criticisms of religion that have arisen from thinkers like Marx and Freud, a refusal to listen and be challenged, a mere closed-minded repression of doubt, rooted in fear and usually ending in fanaticism. The Russian theologian Shestov reportedly held that "one can attain religious truth only by rejecting the proposition that $2 + 2 = 4$ and accepting instead $2 + 2 = 5$."[72] Such attitudes as these are emphatically not defended here. Human reason, even if it cannot itself discover the truth of God, is nevertheless (according to faith) the gift of God and must be given its due.

Luther. We have to be grateful for the penetrating insight of Martin Luther's theology of the cross, which we considered in the last chapter. He insisted on not rationalizing and domesticating the "foolishness of God" in the cross of Christ. A brilliant and courageous man, Luther was also a bellicose, larger-than-life character who lived in a time of religious turmoil with constant danger to his life. So it is perhaps not surprising that his language could at times become magnificently excessive. His intense distaste for Aristotle and scholastic theology was part of his insistence that salvation does not come by works, and certainly not works of the intellect. The apostles of Jesus, he insisted, were not doctors of philosophy but humble fishermen and tax collectors. That is why "the wise" of this world condemn faith: "When God speaks, reason judges his word as heresy and the word of the devil, for it seems so absurd."[73] This being the case, Luther declares,

> Faith slaughters reason. . . . So all the godly who enter with Abraham into the darkness of faith, kill reason and say: "Reason, thou art foolish, you do not understand the things which belong to God: therefore speak not against me but be quiet; judge not, but hear the word of God and believe it. . . . The evening sacrifice is to kill reason; the morning sacrifice is to glorify God."[74]

We should not be misled by such dramatic overstatement to the view that Luther was a mindless, irrational fideist. He constantly demonstrated an ability for orderly, logically coherent thought. The most famous example was his early debate with John Eck at Worms, when he argued that popes and councils sometimes contradict each other (thereby proving that they cannot both be absolutely right) and pushed for the authority of scripture in the church—but scripture interpreted in a reasonable fashion: "Unless I am convinced by scripture and plain reason, I will not . . . recant."[75] If taken at face value, all "antireason" is self-defeating, vanquishing its own arguments, and Luther's antireason diatribes can be dangerous if they make theology an enemy of all the rational sciences and give honest human beings the impression that to be Christian they must lose their intellectual integrity.[76]

The Postliberals. This is a contemporary movement of scholars and theologians whose thought in some respects tends to move toward a subtle form of fideism. The late Hans Frei of Yale, being concerned not to dilute or revise the content of Christian faith by correlating it to universal, cultural/religious quests for meaning, speaks of Christian theology as "Christian self-description," that is, an internal discipline of the believing community.[77] This is valid enough in itself. This is the same Anselmian/Barthian tradition that I have been utilizing here in making the point that reflection on theological method proceeds *a posteriori*; that is, it lays out the ways in which conversation and debate typically occur among Christians and explores the internal logic and interconnectedness of faith statements. This is a form of rational discourse. In theology, according to Frei, we spell out and articulate the content of actual Christian faith and we do so descriptively, not allowing this to be distorted by apologetic concerns or submitting to alien rational criticism from other disciplines or from outside the faith community. As an interpreter of the Bible, Frei proposes that biblical stories have to be read as "realistic narrative," rather like a novel (and here he does use literary studies to analyze the character of biblical narrative).[78] The stories, especially in the Gospels, "render an agent," identifying Jesus Christ as the risen Saviour and Lord, inviting and enabling faith. This hermeneutic is, I think, very illuminating, a helpful way of characterizing and interpreting biblical narrative, and Frei is surely right that faith as response to revelation is response to a story. Frei is concerned to point out that the meanings of the biblical narratives do not depend on their historical accuracy or reference, certainly not the historical factuality of all the details, and he is surely right in this. In this way he avoids the mindless fideism of literalism or fundamentalism.

But Frei's utterances are sometimes rather ambiguous on the question of reference and truth claims, as though he is retreating from any need to espouse or defend them at all. While at times it seems clear that, as a Christian theologian, he is claiming certain things to be so, for example, that Christ is risen,[79] at other times, he argues that biblical narratives do not "mean" by referring either to historical facts or to ontological realities.[80] William Placher, a friendly critic, comments on Frei that he "sometimes leaves what he wants to say about their truth a bit unclear." Trevor Hart, too, while appreciating Frei's contributions, insists that, "realistic narrative" or not, questions of truth "will not go away."[81] Frei's approach can be seen as a postmodern nonfoundationalist move—a local, internal, or communal hermeneutic. His concern about the internal integrity of Christian faith leads him to refuse to become involved in open-minded discussion as to truth claims. For example, his insistence that it is "impossible not to believe" the resurrection of Jesus[82] would not be helpful to ordinary thoughtful Christians who know themselves more than capable of doubt. In addition, his refusal to discuss questions concerning the historical Jesus (questions about historical reference) give us a whiff of fideism, but of a subtle kind: truth claims of faith are the internal language of the faith community and cannot be questioned or evaluated from outside. One must read scripture and do theology "intratextually"; that is, the text is not to be correlated with the context of the world but rather "absorbs the world." The world is interpreted in light of the text; the text is not interpreted in light of the world. It is difficult to avoid the impression that Frei is simply retreating from the challenges of historical scholarship, that this is a protective strategy designed to make faith immune to rational challenge from any quarter.

George Lindbeck, also of Yale, is closely associated with Frei in his emphasis on doctrine as "Christian self-description." Lindbeck becomes more explicit in his deemphasis on, if not denial of, the significance of ontological truth claims (an approach that owes much to the philosophy of Wittgenstein). Lindbeck too is motivated to uphold the internal integrity of Christian faith, to resist any dilution of the content of faith by methods of correlation with context or contemporary questions. He wishes to resist any compromise or negotiation with rival truth claims in other religions, and to oppose the idea of a common core among the world religions. In *The Nature of Doctrine,* he argues that the various religions, including Christianity, must be understood as distinct "language games," with their own "communally authoritative rules of discourse, attitude, and action."[83] The study of doctrine is the study of regulative theory within a faith community. Thus,

> a religion can be viewed as a kind of cultural and/or linguistic frame-work or medium that shapes the entirety of life and thought. It functions somewhat like a Kantian a priori, although in this case the a priori is a set of acquired skills that could be different. It is not primarily an array of beliefs about the true and the good (though it may involve these).[84]

Doctrine, then, regulates faith statements within the faith community and resembles rules like "Drive on the left" and "Drive on the right."[85] Later writings by Lindbeck seem not to have departed from this general approach. He speaks of the Christian "idiosyncratic journey," of the exclusivity of the elect community and its "incommensurable, untranslatable frameworks."[86] This, again, can be identified as a form of postmodern nonfoundationalism, but one immediately suspects a fideistic retreat. Lindbeck appears to have collapsed faith commitment into a postmodern theory of many rationalities, conceptual structures that function only in terms of their own internal logic. Van Huysteen, commenting on another postliberal author, sees this move as a kind of "disciplinary closure and intellectual autonomy."[87]

Yet Lindbeck's own stance about rationality is ambiguous. Toward the end of his book we find a few paragraphs in which he opens out to a broad and non-fideist notion of rational discourse that appears very helpful. Defending his nonfoundationalist, intratextual approach, he points out that standards of rationality vary from field to field and from age to age, making the discovery of universal foundations for knowledge, either within or across disciplines, unlikely. Citing Wittgenstein and Thomas Kuhn, Lindbeck argues that "the norms of reasonableness are too rich and subtle to be adequately specified in any general theory of reason or knowledge." Nevertheless, a kind of "reasonableness" is appropriate:

> Thus reasonableness in religion and theology, as in other domains, has something of that aesthetic character, that quality of unformalizable skill, which we usually associate with the artist or the linguistically competent. If so, basic religious and theological positions, like Kuhn's

scientific paradigms, are invulnerable to definitive refutation (as well as confirmation) but can nevertheless be tested and argued about in various ways, and these tests and arguments in the long run make a difference. Reason places constraints on religious, as well as on scientific options, even though these constraints are too flexible and informal to be spelled out in either foundational theology or a general theory of science. . . . Thus, although a religion is not subject to decisive disproof, it is subject . . . to rational testing procedures not wholly unlike those that apply to general scientific theories or paradigms.[88]

These thoughts approach closely to the kind of rational faith and rational theological discourse that I am defending here. However, they remain marginal to Lindbeck's main thrust. In defence of his cultural-linguistic theory of doctrine, he argues at length against what he identifies as a common alternative approach in modern liberal theology, the "experiential/expressivist approach," in which doctrinal statements are reinterpreted as "noninformative and nondiscursive symbols of inner feelings, attitudes, or existential orientations."[89] Here one suspects that he has described certain authors unfairly in a rather pejorative way. In Wittgensteinian fashion, he argues that, since it is language that permits and shapes experience, and not vice-versa, the internal language of a religious tradition determines the kind of religious experience people will have within that tradition. This too is interesting, but continues to beg the question of truth claims about reality. Of particular interest here is Lindbeck's opposition to what he calls the "cognitive/propositional" approach, which understands doctrinal statements as "informative propositions or truth claims about objective realities."[90] Lindbeck tends to dismiss this approach rather swiftly as something naive and passé, characterizing it simplistically, as though theologians of this stripe have thought they were "describing objective realities" in some permanently valid, unchangeable way. But of course so-called cognitive/propositional theologians have always known that their theological formulations are analogical and inadequate to describe the divine mystery. Great theological minds, like Augustine, Anselm, Aquinas, Luther, Calvin, and Barth, knowing the inadequacy and tentativeness of their theological language, nevertheless believed that their theological statements corresponded, imperfectly yet truly, to the divine reality, and this precisely because of God's self-revelation. Further, contextual theologians today also know very well that they are not offering *theologia eterna,*[91] that perspectives, emphases, and even truth claims will shift in theology. Yet this does not imply the withdrawal of propositions about the true and the good. But then Lindbeck, in rather confusing manner, does not rule out truth claims as part of the cultural/linguistic approach,[92] and can say later in the book: "modified or historicized propositional theories seem no less capable of admitting historical change and diversity than is a rule theory."[93]

Another dimension of the thought of Lindbeck and other postliberal theologians is their failure to grapple with context. Wishing to do theology intratextually, they emphasize the internal logic and coherence of scripture and tradition, insisting that theology must not be absorbed by situations or contexts but rather should "absorb the universe into the biblical world."[94] Here they exhibit a characteristic of postmodern thought generally, in that they emphasize the particularity of Christian communal rules of discourse, but theirs is (as Mark Kline Taylor suggests) a "postmodernism of reaction,"[95] in that they disdain to be in serious dialogue with the pluralities around them and fail to struggle with the concerns raised within their own American context by black or feminist theologies.[96]

Other representatives of this movement—Stanley Hauerwas, Kathryn Tanner, David Kelsey, and John Milbank (not to suggest that this is a monolithic group)—also make important contributions, emphasizing the internal faith of the community and scripture as canon, constitutive for the life of the church. The work of this group is helpful in maintaining Christian identity and the integrity of faith. Yet there remains a suspicion that the deemphasis on truth claims that one detects in some of their work amounts to a retreat into relativism or ontological agnosticism. In their neglect of a positive approach to the rational, postliberal theology leans toward a highly intellectual form of fideism.[97] Lindbeck especially seems to imply that we should not be in dialogue with non-Christians about truth claims; rather we should simply continue to believe, worship, and be the church. The credibility of the church, he argues, will derive from the authenticity of its practical life and not from any rational defence of its truth claims.[98] In fact it is unclear whether he thinks Christians should make any truth claims at all. In turning aside from the absolute, demonstrable certainty of modern foundationalism, he seems to opt for the opposite error—a kind of relativism or agnosticism.[99] This approach may have a certain charm in academic circles but would be scandalous to most ordinary faithful Christians; for their faith it is crucial and indispensable that the claims of the gospel about God, Jesus Christ, salvation, and so on, are true. We may ask, with Kathryn Tanner, "What would be the point of doing theology if one were not really talking about God?"[100] Does God actually hear our prayers? Is God actually there, and does God truly love us, as the Christ revelation tells us? If not, why pray, however correct our internal language game may be? Is God's Spirit actually at work among us, healing, supporting, inspiring, striving for the reign of justice, peace, and wholeness? Does God truly forgive and accept us in Christ and offer eternal life? At a time of crisis, or at a funeral, a pastor's words must be seriously meant to correspond to reality. Engaged in social struggle, Christians build upon the assurance that God's reign is real and that the Spirit who leads and inspires is *really there.* Otherwise prayer and proclamation are a sham. Language games are inimical to serious faith and undermine the power of faith to motivate, inspire, or console the believer. If this is not what the postliberals intended, they at least leave themselves open to this kind of interpretation and criticism. As I have been arguing here, one need not choose between modern foundationalism and ontological agnosticism. Faith may be both rational and epistemologically risky. A rational person may, with good reasons, take the risk of faith by taking up a form of faith that is more credible than its alternatives.

Theology as a Rational Discipline

I have spoken (in chapter 2) of the "radical disjunction of faith and reason," but also (in this chapter) of "faith as rational." By so saying, I am suggesting that Christian faith and theology are both continuous and discontinuous with general human knowledge and reason.[101] Faith lives out of the radical givenness of God's revelation and so does not derive from human reason as such. The truth of the gospel comes as sheer gift from beyond us, truth that we cannot tell ourselves but which is itself "gift" for human reason, having the power to redeem and renew our rational faculties. Yet at the same time faith lives in a positive relationship to reason, which is also God's good gift. Faith and rationality, then, live within a relationship of tension. Moreover, the need to communicate the gospel as public discourse demands that faith be communicated rationally, making contact with and honouring the rational faculties of those with whom we speak.

A Broader and Deeper Concept of the Rational. At the beginning of the chapter I began to suggest a broad concept of rationality as a genuine effort of the human person to be in relation with reality in all its depth and complexity. Borrowing from Van Huysteen, I further characterized rationality as the pursuit of "clarity, intelligibility, and optimal understanding as ways to cope with ourselves and our world." It is very practical in that it has to do with living well, for both individuals and societies, and in this respect it is of great interest to liberationist theologies, for which praxis, as an interaction of theory and action, is a crucial concern. Faith in the liberating God is closely associated not only with receiving divine revelation but also with the rationality of the social analyses and the practical experience of social struggle.[102] Liberation theologies must utilize reason rigorously if they are to help people discern God's presence and activity in situations of poverty and oppression.

However, these references to "coping" and practicality should not be misunderstood to indicate a reduction of rationality to what has come to be called "instrumental reason." Reason is not merely the means to obtaining ends about which reason is irrelevant. Nor is it limited, as in modern logical empiricism, to the gathering of verifiable facts that are useful for obtaining desired goals. George Grant protested against the concept of human beings as simply "clever beasts with a facility for mathematics."[103] Sometimes religious people have surrendered reason to its purely instrumental or calculative function. Blaise Pascal is an example of this, limiting reason to truths of fact and mathematical relations, and locating faith not in the mind but in the heart: "The heart has reasons, of which reason is ignorant."[104]

One finds persuasive protests against merely calculative or instrumental reason also in the neo-Marxist thought of the Frankfurt school[105] and in the thought of the philosopher Charles Taylor. The latter writes insightfully about the "atomism" or individualism and associated relativism of modern life, wherein the individual self must invent his or her own values, and where it is in bad taste to question anyone else's values, since everyone has the right to seek one's own fulfillment. This individualism and relativism may be seen as part and parcel of an untamed capitalist system operating according to market mechanisms with little government or democratic supervision. Society being so fragmented, it is difficult for the individual to identify with his or her community or nation, which also becomes instrumental to individualistic economic goals. The right to advance one's own interests is assumed; but historical communities and environmental well-being are dismissed as irrelevant, and more vulnerable individuals simply withdraw into themselves. Choices of one's lifestyle become trivialized and privatized. Faith and religious opinions are a merely private matter, perhaps a kind of hobby, and certainly beyond the rational.[106]

As we have seen, in ancient biblical sources one already finds a range of rational, meditative, and contemplative thought far richer than that to which modern rational thought is constricted. The believer thinks in a relationship of prayer, in response to what is given in God's revelatory Word. As we noted above, we find in the reported teachings of Jesus and in the discourse of apostolic texts a persuasive style of rational argumentation, which reaches far beyond the narrow confines of logical empiricism or instrumental reason. Also, as a reading of George Grant suggests, theology may find corrective, broadening concepts of *ratio* in both biblical and Greek philosophical traditions. For the ancients, whether of Jerusalem or of Athens, thought was receptivity; it arose out of a passion of astonishment. For Plato, reason had to do with the discernment of the good; its proper realm was the ethical and the aesthetic. The Augustinian tradition, which contextualized Christian faith to Hellenistic culture, borrowed this broad range of the *ratio*.[107] This contrasts with the moderns, for whom, according to Grant, thought is mainly about hypotheses and experimentation, for the sake of controlling the world.

> The belief that reason and tradition are at loggerheads is only a product of modern thought. . . . The traditions that came to us from Athens and Jerusalem claim to be, in the main, reasonable, but what was handed over in them is now accepted, if accepted at all, less and less as thought-filled because it is so assailed by the modern account of reason, and all of us are increasingly enclosed in that modern account.[108]

Some thirty years after Grant wrote these words, the modern account of reason is broadly questioned and found to be inadequate in a world that is increasingly postmodern. While we see growing skepticism about rational foundationalism in the sense of thought based in indubitable premises, we also find an unwillingness to limit human thought to the narrow range of the logical and empirical. All of this helps to create a situation of opportunity for faith and theology, which, we hope, will not fly off into postmodernist irrationality or fideism, but rather reclaim its own proper mode of rationality.

We need, then, a concept of faith as rational, and of theology as a rational discipline that is not merely esoteric and that sees theology in continuity with other spheres of rational human thought. Rather than retreat into fideism, theology needs to recognize the "fiduciary" (faith-like) character of all significant human inquiry. We have seen that faith experience has much in common with and overlaps with ethical, aesthetic, and social dimensions of reality and that theology as the thought dimension of faith therefore has much in common with the disciplines that consider ends as well as means, the beautiful, and the evaluative dimensions of the social. The humanities and social sciences too are rational, even if they do not achieve universal agreement and even if their findings are without utilitarian value. But more than that, we have seen that the natural and physical scientific disciplines, at their more profound levels, are also selective, intuitive, and committed—that is, "fiduciary" in character.[109] Theology, then, may not hive off into a private corner and refuse to engage in open, interdisciplinary conversation with other realms of thought. While not abandoning its own autonomy, it must open itself to the critical thought of other disciplines and bring critical perspectives to bear on them as well.

Modes of Rationality in Various Disciplines. At the same time, theology, like other disciplines, must recognize its own unique character and the specific methods that are proper to its unique object of inquiry. While it is true, we may say, that human reason is one, there are nevertheless many quite different modes of rationality. As a discipline of faith, and of a particular faith, Christian theology (like other disciplines) does operate *a posteriori* out of its own peculiar sources and carries its own distinct mode of rationality. The mode of inquiry in every discipline is determined by its object, that is, by that which it seeks to know. There is not, then, one mode of rationality that can adjudicate among all disciplines or, more narrowly, among various religious truth claims or philosophies. There are many very different kinds of realities which present themselves to us, a multitude of different objects of inquiry. It is not possible, therefore, to prescribe *a priori* for any kind of inquiry the appropriate way to knowledge, for each reality prescribes the mode of inquiry by which it can be known. In fact, it is only when we already know something about an object of knowledge that we know how to learn more about it. A mathematician or logician, for example, knows how to use methods of deductive reasoning to increase awareness of the intricacies of number or to analyze the structure of arguments. But empirical scientists must be rational in a very different way. Geologists, metallurgists, and chemists, for example, know how to force information out of physical objects in a laboratory;

because they already know something about the properties and behaviour of metals, gases, and chemicals, they know how to learn more and indeed how to apply the information obtained to technological purposes. The historian, on the other hand, must pursue the realities or objects of the past (historical events and the interpretation of their meaning and interconnections) in yet another way. Written records and manuscripts must be consulted. The testimonies of people who lived through a war, through an election, or through a scientific revolution must be gathered, carefully heard, compared, and weighed, if these events are to be understood—a quite different form of reason and very different method from that found in mathematics or chemistry. Only when an historian has actually learned something about the past can s/he know how such an inquiry should be pursued. It would be irrational, even absurd, for the historian to use the methods of chemists, or chemists the methods of logicians.

It is possible to use the term "scientific" very broadly for all such *a posteriori* methods of rational inquiry (as the medievals used the term *scientia* to mean any disciplined pursuit of truth). T. F. Torrance stated the matter clearly many years ago:

> In all scientific knowledge, we let the nature of what we know prescribe for us the specific mode of rationality we adopt toward it. That is why in every science we operate with a distinctive form of inquiry proper to the nature of the object we investigate in it.[110]

It may not be useful today to use the word "scientific" in this broad way, since it might suggest to people that all inquiries should follow the methods and processes of verification found in the natural sciences. It is important to recognize that modes of verification also vary in relation to the many kinds of realities we seek to know and understand. We test our results in metallurgy quite differently from the way we test, or defend, our conclusions in history. The kind of agreement or consensus one hopes for among inquiries varies also. There may be easy and general agreement among metallurgists about which application of heat and chemicals should be used to obtain copper from ore, or among astronomers about the day and hour of the appearance of Halley's comet. There may be less agreement among historians about the factors that led to the eruption of World War I. Two very intelligent, learned, and rational historians may disagree profoundly, even passionately, about the factors that have brought about the collapse of Communism in Eastern Europe. No doubt they will share and agree about certain facts, but they may gather and select different sets of data, weigh and evaluate matters quite differently, and reach opposing conclusions. In the social sciences too, economists, political scientists, and sociologists may study the same phenomena using rigorous and meticulous methods of research and reach startlingly different conclusions about inflation, unemployment, labour and management relations.[111] I do not imply that the truth cannot be reached or at least approximated in these areas. However, the more complex the object of inquiry, the more difficult for rational inquirers to prove or verify their conclusions to others. When we move to areas such as human and social psychology, literary analysis, philosophy of law, art criticism, or musicology, we find it even more difficult to test, verify, or find consensus. One may say that the fiduciary dimension of the rational increases as one moves into the areas of the human, the social, the aesthetic, and the ethical. Nevertheless, evaluative thought, as distinct from the empirical factuality and logical analysis of mathematics, may be rational. For example, I, for one, am unwilling to admit that "Mary Had a Little Lamb" is as beautiful or valuable as a Mozart concerto. I may have difficulty verifying this to a little child, but rational perception, I insist, is nevertheless at work. The musicologist may be able to throw light on what constitutes one a trite ditty and the other magnificent artistry. I maintain that literary theory and musicology, aesthetics and ethics, sociology and history are every bit as rational as geology and astronomy, if they pursue their inquiries in a manner appropriate to the realities they seek to know and understand.

All this means that the rationality of a discipline cannot be measured simply by its potential for universal verification and agreement. The activity of literary, artistic, and philosophic disciplines may find it difficult to reach consensus, but cannot for that reason be dismissed as irrational or as mere opinion. Nor would I agree that they should be diminished as nonrational. This would be an intolerable diminution of the powers and depths of the human mind. Nor would I agree that informed viewpoints in these areas are merely the expression of subjective preferences, even if subjective or personal elements come into play. I suggest that rational discernment occurs and that rational conversation is possible when, for example, ethicists debate the right and wrong of sexual behaviour, or the proper goals of a social and economic system. We have seen that at a theoretical level, the thought of physical scientists too can move very close to the thought of theologians and philosophers. But this too is rational thought in its creative, intuitive dimensions.

Again, one must distinguish between rationality and truth, even though the rational person, by definition, seeks truth, that is, seeks to relate with reality in all its depth and complexity. Rational persons may disagree, while remaining rational. The rational, I am saying, must be recognized far beyond the realm of the so-called hard sciences, those disciplines where universal assent is more or less obtainable. Universal verifiability, then, cannot be the measure of rationality.

I may add briefly here, since this point was made earlier, that rationality occurs not only in academic disciplines of thought but perhaps more importantly in ordinary life, wherein one negotiates the ways and means but also discerns the ends and goals of practical existence. This applies also in the realm of personal relationships. We know persons rationally (appropriately) in relationship and most deeply in relationships of trust and love. Here more than anywhere we see the continuity of the rationality of faith and theology with other forms of the rational.

When all is said and done, we have to speak also of discontinuity. This is because God—the object of inquiry in theology—is utterly incomparable, ultimately mysterious, far beyond any possibility of human comprehension. As with other objects of inquiry, we can only know how to seek the knowledge of God when God is already known. The question is: How do we actually know God? The knowledge of God, for Christians at least, is more like personal knowledge than any other. It is not first or essentially an academic discipline at all; it is knowledge in relationship, knowledge by self-revelation. Speaking *a posteriori* (after the fact), Christians have always said: We know God in God's own personal self-disclosure in Jesus the Christ.

The Word Made Flesh: Object of Inquiry. Knowing God is, of course, an utterly unique mode of knowing, which we call faith. As I have said in the previous chapter, knowledge of the God of the cross is radically "given," a gift of the Holy Spirit, quite discontinuous with other kinds of knowledge, even contradicting and overturning the natural wisdom of speculative human reason. This is an encounter with Otherness infinitely greater than ourselves. This Other is presented to our apprehension, yet, in profound mystery, is utterly beyond our comprehension. This Other is not available to our manipulation, but, unlike any other "object,"[112] calls forth adoration.

That God speaks a Word to human beings is the fundamental conviction of Israel and the church. Yahweh spoke the *dabar* to Israel through the mediation of the prophets, who interpreted events of history as God's liberating presence and activity. The people heard the Word in its own persuasive power, its own convincing, converting capacity to command and promise, to judge, inspire, and console. The prophets of Israel never argued, like foundationalists, from premises to conclusions about God's reality, presence, or will. Rather, the *dabar* of God came upon them with power, the power of God's *ruah* (Spirit). Not that there was never confusion or disagreement about what was truly God's Word and the work of God's Spirit. According to Jeremiah, speaking of those he regarded as false prophets, "The prophets are nothing but wind, for the Word is not in them" (Jer 5:13). A process of discernment was necessary on the part of those who lived within a community and a tradition, and rationality played its part in that process of discernment. The prophetic discernment was often a startling one, speaking against the community's general understanding of God, and it was recognized only much later as truly a Word from God.[113]

It is John's Gospel that explicitly identifies Jesus of Nazareth, crucified and risen, as God's Word made flesh. John is utilizing a highly rational Greek concept—*logos*—to address his Hellenistic context, that is, the Stoic concept of God's mind and reason. Yet John is also very much in continuity with the whole Hebraic tradition of God's *dabar*. The Word of God, says John, is God's own self. It is God's own mind and reason, God's own eternally self-communicating Being. Just as, when you or I speak in a self-revealing way, it is my very self, or your very self, that is given and communicated to others. My word is my very self going forth from myself. So also, "In the beginning was the Word, and the Word was with God and the Word was God" (Jn 1:1). God's Word, God's very self, goes forth from God, creates, and redeems: "All things were made by [the Word] and without [the Word] nothing was made that was made. In [the Word] was life and that life was the light of human beings" (Jn 1:2-3). John goes on to say that God's Word, which had been spoken hitherto by the prophets, now took human form. God now communicated in full identity with a human person, namely, Jesus of Nazareth: "And the Word became flesh and we beheld his glory, glory as of the only begotten of the Father, full of grace and truth" (Jn 1:14). To know and recognize God's "glory" is, again, not arrived at on the basis of premises and arguments. In him we were confronted by "grace and truth." John is talking about a kind of direct perception. To "behold his glory" is to be struck with awe, with worship and trust. It is to be met by something that—or rather *Someone who*—grasps heart and soul, mind and strength, by the sheer power of self-giving love. I am reminded again, as mentioned earlier, of the man who said he tried to dismiss the Jesus story as a hoax or a delusion, or as pure legend or myth. But in the end the "glory" of Jesus would not go away. The story was too powerful and compelling, and, try as he might, he could not reasonably dispose of Jesus or explain him away.

In the Word made flesh, then, the life, death, and resurrection of Jesus Christ, God becomes uniquely visible and audible as an object of inquiry. God gives Godself to be known in this humble way, in the raising to life of this good and free human being, who died courageously in love. It is the whole Christ, Christ "clothed in his gospel," Christ the teacher and healer, the human one of compassion and courage, crucified and risen, present with us by the power of the Spirit, who confronts us as the object of our inquiry, making it possible for us to know who God is. Again, Torrance states it clearly:

> Hence in Jesus Himself, word and deed, language and event, were inextricably interwoven in His revealing activity. His words were done as well as spoken and His deeds spoke as much as His words, for in Him God's word has become physical, historical event, while the very fact and existence of Jesus was itself Word of God.[114]

To know God rationally, then, is in this respect rather like knowing anything or anyone rationally. All objects of knowledge and all subjects or persons must be known in a manner appropriate to their nature. As knowledge of persons is knowledge in relationship, so also knowledge of God is knowledge in relationship, but in this unique instance, this specific relationship of faith, it is one of loving worship, obedience, and trust.

PART II

The Christological Criterion

CHAPTER 4

Is It Founded in Jesus Christ?

This is the first proposed criterion of theological adequacy: A Christian theology must be founded and centered in Jesus Christ. The "Christic center" means that Jesus Christ is our primary norm. Our premise, of course, is that Jesus reveals God, and knowledge of true deity is the goal of all theological inquiry. To say that, for Christians, all theological proposals must be defensible christologically is to say that they must be shown to be congruent with our best understanding of Jesus Christ.

But this is exactly the rub. How do we reach this best understanding? Since Christ is understood in so many ways in so many different times and places, according to such different readings of scripture, and in accordance with so many differing interests and concerns, which Christ is normative for us? As I suggested in chapter 1, this criterion must be understood dialectically with the praxis criterion: Is it life-giving and liberating? Jesus Christ is foundational for us precisely because he gives life and liberty. Thus, in faithfulness to Jesus himself, we need a christology that is life-giving and liberating. Our best understanding of Jesus Christ will be rooted and founded in the biblical testimony to him, since the Bible is our primary source of information and testimony about Jesus and must involve discussion of historical/critical questions about those texts. Moreover, the praxis question implies that christology must be pursued in a contemporary and contextual way. Further, the reality of Christian life in community implies that our christology must be ecclesial, taking tradition and the ecumenical Christian community into account. These considerations, while they complicate the christological norm, do not undercut its basic correctness. First let us explore how we have reached the conclusion that all good theology, at least for Christians, must be founded in Jesus Christ.

Not *A Priori*

That Jesus Christ is our primary norm and that Christian life and thought must be christologically based are not things that can be known *a priori*. That is why we have to begin by speaking descriptively. As the primary canon or rule of theological thought, the christological criterion arises out of the faith of the Christian community. It is only after the fact, *a posteriori,* that is, from within faith, that we are able to speak both descriptively and prescriptively about theological method. It is a question of the inner necessity, the internal rationality or grammar of Christian faith itself. Similarly, historians may not prescribe *a priori* to physicists how they will pursue their science; nor may chemists impose methods on sociologists. In each case, their objects of inquiry prescribe the mode in which they can be known. One must already know some history, some physics, or some sociology in order to discern (*a posteriori*) appropriate methods in each of those disciplines. To draw a different kind of analogy, Christians may not prescribe to Buddhists how they should think as Buddhists. From outside the Buddhist community it is not possible to say how Buddhists should handle their scriptures, their traditions, and their meditative practice, or how these function as criteria of truth and wisdom for Buddhists. Nor may Hindus prescribe to Muslims the inner rationality of Islam concerning the relation of Muhammad, the Qurʾan, and the Hadith. It is only from within these traditions that their inner rationality and ways of knowing can be determined.

The point is this: Christians confess and proclaim that Jesus is *kyrios* (Lord or sovereign). The early Christians knew and rejoiced that Caesar was not *kyrios*; today we know that no political leader or ideology, not even capital or the market, is *kyrios.* None of these evokes our ultimate loyalty. Christians believe that they have encountered "deity" in Jesus, that the true God is revealed in Jesus. They have found salvation, liberation, and life in Jesus. That is, in the crucified and risen Jesus, they believe they have met One who is worthy of worship, trust, and final loyalty. That is why we may say that our life is "centered" in Jesus Christ. He becomes the focus of meaning and hope, and so also the focus or center of both our action and our thought. As *kyrios* he reigns over all our thinking about God, about humanity, salvation and sin, creation and death, not to mention our ethical thinking about personal life, our work, our sexuality, as well as technology, the environment, and politics. If we deny that he rightly reigns over all of our life and thought, we have effectively denied that he is our *kyrios* and have confessed that we have other lords or truths that are in some respects above him and his truth. Perhaps no more eloquent statement of the centrality of Jesus Christ exists than that of the Barmen Declaration of 1934, by the German Confessing Church in opposition to the Nazi takeover of the church: "We reject the false doctrine, as though there were areas of our life in which we would not belong to Jesus Christ, but to other lords—areas in which we would not need justification and sanctification through him."[1]

Thus, the discipline of Christian life and thought is precisely to be disciples of Jesus Christ in everything and therefore to be centered in him. For those who confess Jesus as Lord, to depart from Christ-centeredness is to lose bearings, to fall into a kind of incoherence; it is precisely to become arbitrary in word and deed.

What it means in practice is this: If we are discussing among ourselves as Christians what our course of action should be in a particular circumstance (ethics), or what we are called to do as church at a particular time and place (mission), or what we should or should not do when we gather for worship (liturgy), or how we should understand and teach some aspect of our faith (doctrine), the most fundamental question of adequacy we must put to any proposal is a christological one: Is it congruent with our best understanding of Jesus Christ? To ask Is it biblical? is also essential (as we shall discuss in a later chapter) but this in itself does not go deep enough, leaving us with an array of critical questions about interpretation and about the relative weight and emphasis we give to various books or passages of scripture. Unless the scripture is read christologically it can become destructive and oppressive. This is why I suggest that it is not scripture but Christ himself who is *norma normans non normata* (the norming norm which is not itself normed by any higher or deeper norm).[2] Nor is it enough to ask, Does it suit the times? or Does it fit our context? (though these are also valuable questions). In themselves these leave us wide open to fads and ideological takeover and negate the lordship of Jesus. Nor is it appropriate to ask first: Is it in accordance with tradition, or with the majority of the ecclesia? (also a useful question in itelf). An overemphasis on tradition would leave us stuck in the past, perhaps in accumulated, outmoded, or erroneous concepts and practices, leaving us without a living Word for our own time and place. Merely to make an ecclesial majority the primary measure of truth would equate *vox populi* with *vox dei,* thereby enthroning whatever is popular in the church at a particular time.

Could the Holy Spirit be our foundation and center? Because the Spirit is God's own presence among and within us, she must certainly not be subordinated to Jesus Christ. But it is mistaken to think of the Spirit apart from Jesus, since it is through the concrete visibility of Jesus that we can discern the presence and work of the Spirit. Speaking epistemologically and methodologically, then, the Spirit cannot be the center and foundation, even though it is the Spirit who draws us to Jesus and unites us to him. As we shall see in our discussion of the triune God in the next chapter, for Christians, to be "in Christ" and to be "in the Spirit" are one and the same, since Christ and the Spirit are one.

Speaking descriptively, we note that Christians live and think out of the concreteness of Jesus, commonly asking themselves: What would Jesus do? (the famous WWJD!). Perhaps it is not farfetched even to ask, What would Jesus drive? in this age of smog. Would Jesus favour this war? Would Jesus give his backing to capital punishment? Would Jesus favour this building project? We may ask: What is the will of Christ for today? Or: How do we meet Christ and celebrate his presence? Or: How should we discern what Christ is doing in the world today, and join him in it? It is not a simple matter to answer these questions, but to ask the question is important. To be centered or oriented in this way is to know where we are, where we stand, which way to move. The center provides a vantage point from which to look in all directions. If we are unclear about our center, we may find ourselves confused by conflicting claims to truth and authority. To use the metaphor of construction, we may say that Jesus Christ is the foundation (1 Cor 3:11). It is a case of building our house upon a rock (Mt 7:24). The foundation is a firm place to stand. As the questions just mentioned indicate, christology cannot be divorced from practical questions, nor, if we are Christians, can our consideration of practical matters be divorced from christology. Our social analysis and vision, our political commitments and strategies, must also be congruent with Jesus. Our personal relationships, family commitments, our relationship to the natural order—all of these things must be congruent with our best understanding of Jesus. Similarly, at the level of theology and doctrine, we hear Christians say, "the doctrine of God you are expressing does not fit with my understanding of Christ"; or "we need this doctrine of the Trinity if we are to make sense of the Lordship of Jesus"; or "this understanding of the work of the Holy Spirit is congruent with what I believe about Jesus Christ." In other words, among Christians, a basic test of adequacy for any practical or theological proposal is this: Is it christologically founded? And a test of adequacy for any whole or systematic theology is much the same: Is it Christ-centered? In a theological debate among Christians, whether a doctrinal/theoretical one—the nature of God, the way of salvation, the nature of creation, and so on—or a practical ethical or missiological one, those who admit they are not "with Christ" have surrendered the most important ground of theological discourse and debate within the Christian community. One could not hope to persuade a church magisterium, the synod or council of a national church, or even a local congregation to adopt a course of action that was not seen to be congruent with our best understanding of Jesus Christ. Jesus is not simply the exemplar of values, commitments, or ideologies that we already hold independently of him. Rather, as "revelation of God," as liberating and life-giving *kyrios,* Jesus Christ is rock bottom for our life, our worship, our thought.

The Whole Christ

When we speak of Jesus Christ as primary norm, center, and foundation, we need to be clear that we mean the whole Christ. We do not refer, for example, *only* to the "Jesus of history," or "Jesus of Nazareth" prior to the events of the cross and resurrection. Nor we do mean some abstract Christ cut apart from the Jesus of history. The center and foundation of Christian faith is Jesus of Nazareth, the Christ, crucified and risen, and present with us now in the power of the Spirit.[3]

It is possible and valid to draw a distinction between (while not separating) the Jesus of history and the Christ of faith, or the pre-Easter and post-Easter Jesus, as this has been developed by the long quest for the historical Jesus in its various phases. The distinction has legitimacy and value.[4] Clearly, the story of Jesus of Nazareth prior to the resurrection is told with hindsight in light of the resurrection. To cite just one example among many, we may note that many, perhaps most, New Testaments scholars agree that the "I am" sayings of Jesus in the Gospel of John are not likely to be from the mouth of Jesus of Nazareth himself. The Johannine Jesus is so different from the Synoptic Jesus and John's christology appears to be so far developed by the postresurrection church that we may indeed see these sayings as inspired early-church reflection on Jesus in light of the resurrection.

The scriptural value of these texts does not, at any rate, depend on their having come from the lips of Jesus himself. They are canonical because they were regarded as faithful postresurrection testimony to Jesus. Nor do we believe in Jesus' divinity because Jesus himself taught it. We need to recognize that the whole of the New Testament, including the testimonies of the Synoptic Gospels about the pre-crucifixion Jesus, is postresurrection early-church proclamation of the risen Lord. Christian faith is a response to this whole Christ.

Where historical-Jesus scholarship is concerned, surely it is good for Christians to know as much as possible about the historical Jesus, insofar as this may be discernible through historical investigations into his context and through comparative detective work on the Gospels by such scholars as John Dominic Crossan, Richard A. Horsley, Marcus Borg, and N. T. Wright.[5] We would be mistaken, I think, to try to ban or to dismiss such inquiries, which in recent years have been very rich and fruitful. Jesus, after all, is a gigantic figure in human history, of great interest to and in some degree accessible even to secular historians. Christian faith is rooted in historical events and must have nothing to fear in the investigation of these events, insofar as such investigation is possible. Moreover, any theological concentration upon Pauline and Johannine christology, barring questions about or neglecting the Synoptic testimony to the man of flesh, Jesus of Nazareth, runs the danger of docetism (denying the true historical humanity of Jesus). One must keep in mind, however, the limitations of such investigations, utterly dependent as they are on the New Testament sources, which are testimonies of faith. We also need to be cautious about the philosophical presuppositions of modern historical scholars about what is or is not possible.[6] In fact, the history of the historical Jesus is not by any means a precise science, and it has been difficult for historical inquirers to find unanimity on many questions.[7]

Christian faith, while it may distinguish the pre-Easter Jesus from the risen Christ and may (given differences among the Gospel witnesses) take note of possible or probable differences between the Jesus of history himself and the church's testimony about him, cannot simply separate the two. It is basic and essential to the Christian confession that the rabbi of Nazareth *is* the Christ. The Christ *is* this one who resisted the structures of imperial Rome in his native

Palestine; who taught in parables and proclaimed the reign of God; who healed the sick, stood in solidarity with the poor and outcaste, and forgave sins and taught love above all else. The risen Christ is not some metaphysical principle, some abstract divine presence, but *is this one* who was crucified for political crimes under Pontius Pilate. The crucified Jesus *is* the one who was raised, and the risen Christ is none other than the crucified one. This means that the Christ to whom we respond in faith is not simply a historical Jesus, perhaps some minimal, verifiable Jesus and his *ipsissima verba et facta* (his very words and deeds) that the critical scholars can agree upon. Such a Jesus would not account for the rise of faith itself or the continuing faith of the church. Paul is saying something like this when he declares, "even though we once knew Christ from a human point of view, we know him no longer in that way" (2 Cor 5:16). It is *the whole Christ*, crucified and risen, "Christ clothed in the gospel," who is central and foundational for us and to whom we respond in faith. Jesus in his whole life, teaching, and deeds, and in his death and resurrection, and present with us now by the Spirit, is the *kyrios* of Christian faith.

The Christ-centeredness
of Christian Worship and Life

Lex Orandi, Lex Credendi. The law of prayer is the law of belief. This old adage of Prosper of Aquitaine (c. 390–c. 463) from the early Middle Ages means that theology can never be dissociated from the worship of the community. Worship expresses the faith and theology of the community, but also helps to form it.[8] Doctrines grow out of people's actual life of prayer and worship, that is, their actual relationship with God. This insight coheres with our argument that theological method operates *a posteriori*, not *a priori*. Let us speak descriptively for a moment, then, about the worship and prayer of the ecumenical Christian community. The actual Christ-centeredness of Christian faith is nowhere more evident. The liturgical year—the calendar and lectionaries—revolves around Christ's advent, birth, and epiphany; his suffering and death; his resurrection and ascension; and his continuing presence by the Spirit. The worship of a Christian congregation often opens with a salutation: "The grace of the Lord Jesus Christ be with you." Hymns of praise and thanksgiving extol not only the majesty and goodness of God the Creator but also the love of Jesus, our crucified and risen Saviour, present with us by the power of the Holy Spirit and expected to come again in glory. Confession of sin and forgiveness are sought "through Jesus Christ our Lord," and pardon is assured on the basis of "the grace of our Lord Jesus." Readings from scripture always include Gospel readings, which are explicitly about Jesus Christ himself, often followed by the versicle, "Praise be to you, O Christ!" The sermon proclaims God's Word, and the Word made flesh is understood to be Jesus Christ himself. The sacraments too are focused on

Jesus: We are baptized into his death and resurrection; in the Lord's Supper we hear of and receive "my body broken for you . . . my blood shed for you." Prayers are offered in Christ's name and are sometimes addressed to Christ himself. Benedictions, like Christian worship as a whole, are usually trinitarian, lifting up "the grace of our Lord Jesus Christ" to the same divine level as "the love of God" and "the fellowship of the Holy Spirit." Christian worship, whether Reformed, Roman Catholic, Baptist, Eastern Orthodox, Anglican, Lutheran, Mennonite, Methodist, or Pentecostal, is Christ-centered and trinitarian in structure and content. The indications we have from the New Testament, if we look at Paul's letters or the book of Acts, are that the church's worship has been Christ-centered in this way from the beginning.

It is evident from a reading of the earliest strands of the New Testament that the first Christians were focused on Jesus as the Christ. They testified that they had met him risen and alive and that, through the Holy Spirit, he continued to be present in their midst. They related to him in an attitude of praise and thanksgiving. They related to him as the Messiah/Christ, as the one who had inaugurated God's reign decisively in human history. In Jesus' life and death and resurrection, God's reign had broken in upon them and changed their lives utterly. It is evident that very soon they related to Jesus Christ as to God, because he was the one who had saved or delivered them from the powers of sin and death. They trusted in him as their Jewish forebears had trusted only in God. In one sense, their worship reflected their belief, but in another way, their relationship to Jesus in prayer and worship pushed them to articulate certain beliefs about him, about his identity and mission. If we praise and thank him, if we trust and hope in him, Who is he?

Does this prove anything about appropriate theological method or about christology? Could this not be an argument for a merely conservative status quo in Christian theology and worship? Indeed, this description of the grammar of Christian worship does not itself prove that Christian thought must be christologically based. Conceivably the church should cease to worship in this way. Perhaps Christ should be removed from the center of Christian worship. Paul Newman, a pluralist theologian, has argued that Christian faith and theology should become theocentric (God-centered) rather than christocentric/trinitarian. He suggested that the worship of the churches, its songs and rituals, should gradually move away from its excessive focus on Jesus. He regrets that "[i]t is and has been Christian liturgies that, by addressing prayers and confessions to Jesus and not only through Jesus, make him equivalent to God in religious practice."[9] He is surely quite right about this. Simply to describe Christian worship as traditionally Christ-centered does not immediately prove that this is appropriate, since tradition as such is not our primary norm, and no doubt there have been all kinds of abuses and wrong directions in Christian liturgy over the centuries. Nor does it prove that theology should move in the same direction. Yet the long-standing fact of the Christ-centeredness of Christian worship cannot be ignored theologically. Our worship reflects actual Christian consciousness and experience from the beginning and up to the present. While Paul Newman deplores the theological impact of Christ-centered worship, I rejoice in it. A liturgical scholar has pointed out quite rightly that "theological study becomes abstract and highly speculative if it is not grounded in the worship life of a faith community."[10] The dictum *lex orandi, lex credendi* suggests that *worship is primary, theology is secondary.* The developed, articulated doctrine of the ancient church followed upon long years of Christian worship centered in Christ. Long-standing, even ancient and primitive practices and prayers put us in touch with our historic roots and identity as Christians and with our continuing personal and community experience of Christ as Life-Giver and Liberator. Most Christians feel that when liturgical life is not Christ-centered, or when Christ is reduced to a sideline in the worship of the church, it is getting off course. It seems to follow that, if we are going to worship christocentrically, our theology, preaching, teaching, and ethics must also be rigorously christocentric.

Lex Sequendi, Lex Credendi. The law of following is the law of belief. We may go on to note how not only liturgy but Christian life, ethics, and mission are also, *de facto*, centered in Jesus Christ and that (as Jon Sobrino frequently insists) following Jesus is a source for understanding him.[11] We speak of following and obeying him. Our practical commitments to justice and peace, to the oppressed and the poor, are seen to be part of our discipleship of Jesus. Debates about violence, about human relationships, about racism or sexism, inevitably make reference to Jesus, his teaching, and the implications of his cross and resurrection. When ethical discussion ceases to make reference to Jesus Christ, it ceases to be coherently Christian, becomes confused and unfocused, and fails to be persuasive in the church. Similarly, our mission is said to be (at least in part) "to proclaim Jesus, crucified and risen, our judge and our hope," but also to "seek justice and resist evil, to live with respect in creation,"[12] because we believe that the Christian mission is nothing else but our participation in Christ's own ongoing mission in the power of the Spirit.

The concept of *lex sequendi, lex credendi* suggests that Christian doctrines about Jesus Christ arose in part out of the experience of following him. Christians found themselves in a relationship of following and obedience to Jesus Christ and found *life* within this relationship. But if we follow and obey him, Who is he? This liberationist insight is entirely congruent with our basic methodological stance: that liberative praxis and the christological foundation are a dual bottom line for theology. It is not Jesus Christ in the abstract who is normative but the life-giving, liberating Christ. Here I draw insight, but also differ from, Clodovis Boff, in his massive, meticulous study of the epistemology of Latin American liberation theology. Boff argues for "praxis as criterion of truth," and "the primacy of praxis over theory," contending that "it is praxis that gets theory going . . . that leads the way in the dialectical method in question, standing at the beginning point and end point of this movement."[13] If we consider christology as theological "theory," it is surely true that our theological affirmations about Christ flow (at least in part) from the experience of following him. Boff is right about this. Unfortunately, when he speaks of "theological criteriology" he does not speak explicitly of Christ or scripture (though these seem to be implicit or assumed), and therefore his treatment of criteria is insufficiently dialectical. The praxis criterion has insufficient dialogue with the christological criterion. If praxis is the criterion of truth, we have to ask, What is the criterion of praxis?[14] That believing flows out of following underscores the necessity that theology, like Christian life itself, must be Christ-centered.

Again, why do I bother to describe what is so obvious and well known? Does the fact that we follow Jesus prove anything about theological method? This description of Christian ethical life and the grammar of ethical reflection does not in itself prove that Christian thought must be christologically based. Conceivably the church should cease to think in this way. Perhaps we should find other equivalent, more up-to-date and relevant models of ethical life. Why should we not find equally helpful models or guides in Gandhi, Martin Luther King, Mother Teresa, and Jean Vanier? Perhaps we have personal moral and spiritual heroes—mothers or grandmothers, teachers, pastors, friends, leaders, co-workers—who will never be famous but who are an inspiration to us. These and others like them of our own time, whether famous or not, may surely be more relevant as moral and spiritual teachers and examples for contemporary life. But in fact it is not any of these, or others like them, that we follow. Quite clearly, for Christians, Jesus is far more than moral teacher or example of spiritual life. He is unsubstitutable as the one to be followed, obeyed, and trusted. As the one crucified and risen, it is he who has blazed the path, even for these admirable people of our own time. Again, the practice of following him implies something about his identity. The articulated doctrine of the ancient church followed upon long years of following Jesus, so that not only prayer and worship but action too has shaped doctrine. Gustavo Gutiérrez made the point clearly about both *lex orandi* and *lex sequendi* when he declared: "The first phase of theological work is the lived faith that finds expression in prayer and commitment. . . . The second act of theology, that of reflection in the proper sense of the term, has for its purpose to read this complex praxis in light of God's word."[15]

One thing must be faced: If we decide theologically that we should be centered somewhere else than in Jesus Christ, if we conclude that our norm for Christian theology is to be found elsewhere, then indeed our language of worship and Christian life must change drastically. A decentered Christ, understood in terms of a reduced christology, must cease to be so prominent, both in our worship and in our ethical reflection or practice. Hymns of praise to Jesus must cease. Our trinitarian worship and prayer must be eradicated. We must no longer speak of obeying or following Jesus. To continue as we do in prayer and hymnody, sacrament and preaching, following and obedience would be sheer idolatry!

Can We Be Cosmocentric
or Centered in Creation?

Two major alternatives to a theology founded and centered in Jesus Christ are the pluralist theocentric or soteriocentric theologies, which are concerned with the relationship of Christians to the world religions (to be considered in chapter 6), and the creation-centered or cosmocentric theologies, which are motivated by environmental/ecological concerns. Sometimes these are linked, in that some theologies of interreligous dialogue are also ecologically oriented, and vice-versa. We may consider the cosmocentric theologies briefly in order to clarify what it may or may not mean for a Christian theology of creation to be founded in Christ.

Ecological theologies have grown out of an intense awareness of global climate change, the vast destruction of forests and the expansion of deserts, the disappearance of thousands of biological species, the depletion of the ozone layer, and the threat to human health through polluted air and water. Their goal is to awaken our sense of kinship with the Earth and all living beings, to deepen our gratitude and love for all creatures, and therefore also for God as Creator. We should note that not all ecological theologies are cosmocentric. A wide spectrum exists, including on the one hand Evangelicals for Social Action,[16] and on the other hand the proponents of "creation-centered spirituality."[17] The spectrum includes also substantial christologically centered trinitarian theologies such as those of Jürgen Moltmann in his ecological doctrine of creation, as well as his messianic christology; Leonardo Boff, in his Latin American trinitarian, liberationist/ecological, and pro-feminist theology; Douglas John Hall, in his strongly biblically based contextual theology of stewardship.[18] Major contributors and pioneers in this area are the ecofeminists who may or may not be "Christ-centered" (among whom Rosemary Radford Ruether was a trailblazer nearly thirty years ago),[19] who emphasize the connection between the domination of nature and the domination of women. Elizabeth Johnson is an ecofeminist who unites ecological theology to a trinitarian wisdom christology, emphasizing the Creator Spirit.[20]

Some ecological theologians explicitly decenter the Christ, and Thomas Berry would be a good example of this. Berry can be called a cosmocentric theologian in that he considers the universe, the solar system, and planet Earth as "the primary revelation of that ultimate mystery whence all things emerge into being."[21] Berry can say that, since God is now speaking to us through the universe, we should set aside the Bible for twenty years and listen to God in nature.[22] One hesitates to be critical of an author who is doing so much to raise consciousness in North America about environmental destruction; his work is provocative, inspirational, and prophetic, especially in his analyses of the connection between the ecological crisis and the profiteering of the capitalist sys-tem.[23] However, I suggest that it is impossible for most Christians to agree that the universe is the "primary revelation" of God. It is true that "the heavens are telling the glory of God and the firmament proclaims God's handiwork" (Ps 19:1), that the mystery and majesty of creation, both in its immense and its microscopic dimensions, do indeed speak to us of the greatness and mystery of the Creator. Yet the creation in and of itself does not show us the gracious God whom we find disclosed in the story of Israel, and in Jesus. It was only the lib-erating event of the exodus and the presence of the holy One with the Israelites in exile that led the ancient Hebrews to believe in the universal Creator of a good creation (Gen 1:31). It is only because of the Jewish Jesus that Gentile Christians have come to know the God of grace as the Creator of all. It is not observation of the world but our knowledge of God founded in Christ that assures us that cre-ation is good and that it will ultimately be brought to a glorious completion and fulfillment.

Sallie McFague, a major ecofeminist contributor to ecological theology, is another important and challenging thinker in whose theological work Jesus Christ plays a major role. But McFague describes herself not as christocentric, but as theocentric and especially as cosmocentric.[24]

McFague argues that Jesus' command to love God and one's neighbour as oneself should be extended to nature: We must also love the animals and birds, insects and plants, the soil and the seas, mountains and rivers *as neighbours.* We should love and care for them not only because our very survival depends on all of them, but in and for themselves as precious and valuable in themselves, as God's creatures. McFague thinks that Jesus' ministry, while it obviously far pre-cedes in time our contemporary concerns about the well-being of the natural environment, is implicitly pro-nature. Jesus overturned existing hierarchies of rich over poor, righteous over unrighteous, powerful over weak. It makes sense in our time, she argues, to extend this attitude and to overturn the hierarchy of human over nonhuman.[25] Further, in his healing acts, Jesus exhibited love and care not only for souls but also for bodies, embedded in the physical, natural world. Jesus' practices of feeding the hungry, eating with outcast people, promis-ing an eschatological banquet again emphasize Jesus' affirmation of the natural and the physical.[26] McFague is surely right about these things.

Through the lens of our present ecological difficulties we may notice other things too about Jesus' relation to nature. We hear that, when Jesus retreated to the desert to face temptation, he was "with the wild beasts" (Mk 1:13), surely an allusion to his redemptive significance for the beasts. Jesus speaks of a God who cares for sparrows (Mt 10:29), who adorns the lilies of the field (Mt 6:28). Nat-ural creatures—yeast, mustard seeds, mother hens—bear witness to God's reign and God's maternal loving care. Jesus, as we meet him in the pages of the New Testament, evinces a definite admiration and affection for the world of nature.

Jesus' vision of God's coming rule is not a heavenly kingdom somewhere else but a this-worldly transformation of the earth. It is evident that Jesus cherished God's good creation and expected its transformation and salvation.

What McFague omits to mention in this regard is the bodily resurrection of Jesus. Surely this is a central New Testament witness to the significance of the natural and the physical in God's scheme of things. Bodies are not merely expendable shells that temporarily house the all-important souls of human beings. On the contrary, the bodily raising of Jesus, however strange and incomprehensible this may be (we shall discuss it again in the next chapter), is the basis for the Christian hope for our own bodily resurrection (1 Cor 15) and for a "new heaven and new earth" (Rev 21:1). These eschatological hopes are also very strange and beyond comprehension. But the resurrection of Jesus (as we shall discuss in the next chapter) is our glimpse into that eternal realm.

The incarnation of God in Jesus Christ is also, of course, a prime reason for Christians to take the physical world seriously as the sphere of God's care and activity. We are told that God's Word became *flesh* in Jesus (Jn 1:14) demonstrating God's love and care for all flesh (not only human beings), honouring and giving dignity to flesh as a medium of the divine presence and activity. But McFague's handling of the incarnation is also problematic. She can speak of the Word made flesh in Jesus, of Jesus as incarnation of God, but she has reinterpreted this drastically as one instance or paradigm within a generalized incarnation of God in the world. In her earlier work *The Body of God,* she proposed that the primary Christian belief in incarnation should be "radicalized beyond Jesus of Nazareth to include all matter. God is incarnated in the world."[27] Thus she wishes to "relativize the incarnation in relation to Jesus of Nazarth, and . . . maximize it in relation to the cosmos. Jesus is paradigmatic of what we find everywhere: everything that is is the sacrament of God (the universe as God's body)."[28] According to McFague, then, God is incarnated not only in Jesus but in the universe as a whole. Jesus is the clue, and a paradigm or example of the pattern of God's presence and activity in the world in the service of love and justice, but there are other special irruptions of the divine presence in persons or events. "Jesus is one such place for Christians, but there are other paradigmatic persons and events."[29]

McFague names her vision of God's relation to the world as "panentheistic": *All things are in God, and God is in all things.* She protests that, traditionally, Christians have separated God from the creation and have allowed for the divine presence in the world only in the incarnation in Jesus, thus rendering the natural world profane and open for abuse and exploitation.[30] I think she is partly right about this; Christianity has a long history of profaning the created order, desacralizing it by separating it radically from the Creator, encouraging human beings to "subdue" and "have dominion" over other creatures (as in Gen 1:28). In recent years the Christian traditon has been accused, with some justification, of sponsoring the domination of nature, leading all too often to its rape and desecration.[31] This argument must be heeded by Christians, and the domination of nature must be seen as a distortion of the Christian message, a heresy about God and creation. However, McFague has overstated her charge that the Christian theological tradition has removed God from the physical world except for the divine presence in Jesus. Most obviously, the catholic sacramental tradition (including not only Roman Catholics, but, in their different ways, Anglicans, Lutherans, Calvinists, and Wesleyans) has always affirmed the real presence of God/Christ in the Eucharist. Beyond that, traditional doctrines of God have always included the divine omnipresence in all creation. One of the clearest statements of this tradition is found in the words of Luther:

> God in his essence is present everywhere, in and through the whole cre-
> ation, in all its parts and in all places, and so the world is full of God,
> and he fills it all, yet he is not limited or subscribed by it, but is at the
> same time beyond and above the whole creation.[32]

It is true, however, that this traditional doctrine has been insufficiently empha-sized and that Christians, especially in the modern era, have seen the world as merely profane, available for our masterful technological control. A number of ecological theologians (e.g., Moltmann, Leonardo Boff, Elizabeth Johnson) have offered major panentheistic treatments of the doctrines of God and creation, inspired in part by our present context of ecological destruction. They were able to do this without diminishing the specificity and uniqueness of the incarnation of God in Jesus Christ.

And why is it inadmissible for Christian theology to transfer the doctrine of incarnation from Jesus Christ to the universe as a whole? I would argue that this basically misunderstands the roots and raison d'être of the doctrine in Christian faith. Jesus is said to be the incarnation of the divine Wisdom and Word not because he exemplifies, as paradigm, a moral ideal of justice and compassion, and therefore of divine presence, but because his life, death, and resurrection are acknowledged as the eschatological event of salvation. The early Christians wor-shiped and praised Jesus, and Christians do so still, not because he was an extra-ordinarily good man but because he reconciles us to God, overcomes the power of death, and ushers in decisively the eschatological reign of God. For these rea-sons Christians relate to him as to God, in worship, trust, and obedience. But the created order as such cannot incarnate God, cannot be for us the object of wor-ship, because it does not save or liberate us. In fact, the divine disclosure in Jesus stands in contradiction to the world as we know it, in which typically the strong dominate the weak. The gospel of cross and resurrection *contradicts* the realm of "nature red in tooth and claw," because Christ has "brought down the powerful from their thrones and lifted up the lowly; he has filled the hungry with good things and sent the rich away empty" (Lk 1:52-53). The cosmos as we know it does not incarnate or reveal the gracious God, though God loves it and is intimately present and at work within it; rather the cosmos itself stands in need of redemption from its own horror, conflict, pain, and death. The apostle Paul says that the whole creation "groans inwardly" while we wait for the redemption of our bodies (Rom 8:19-23). Thus it is not the whole creation that incarnates God, but the crucified Jew, tortured, executed, and risen from the dead. It is only in him that the Christian church finds the glory of God incarnate.

Thus, the universe as "God's body" is not, as McFague suggests, a radicalization of the doctrine of the incarnation, but a deradicalization, a domestication of the incarnation. Its great danger is that it tends to divinize and romanticize the creation—a move that has, in the long run, conservative implications, in that it tends to bless whatever is so. This is contrary, of course, to McFague's intention, but we must ask: If the world is God's body, can we strive to change it radically? Does the God of Israel, the God of hope and promise, not protest and challenge the world as it exists—not only the world of human sin but also the whole creaturely realm of violence, sickness, decay, and death?[33] The New Testament proclaims Jesus as both Creator and Saviour not only of human souls but of whole persons, and indeed of the whole created order of which human bodies are a part.[34] Echoing the Hebrew and Greek wisdom literature concerning the divine mediator of creation, the apostle Paul speaks of Jesus Christ as the one "through whom are all things and through whom we exist" (1 Cor 8:6). John also speaks of Jesus as the divine *logos* who was with God and was God from the beginning, the one "through whom all things came into being," in whom was light and life (Jn 1:1-4). Colossians sees Jesus as a Cosmic Christ, Creator and Saviour not only of human beings, but of *ta panta,* all things!

> . . . in [Christ] all things in heaven and earth were created, things visible and invisible . . . all things have been created in him and for him. He is before all things and in him all things hold together. . . . For in him all the fullness of God was pleased to dwell, and through him God was pleased to reconcile to himself all things, whether on earth or in heaven, making peace by the blood of his cross. (Col 1:19-20)

The Christian relationship to Jesus, one of gratitude and praise, worship and following, implies that the creation as such, of which we ourselves are a part, cannot function for Christians as the "incarnation of God." It is evident also that our christological norm rules out cosmocentrism, but it is ruled out also by scripture and tradition. The contextual requirements of the ecological crisis do indeed call for new directions in theology for our time; we urgently need a widespread appropriation of ecological theology among Christian people. We need to see, in light of our christological center, that the *dominium* of Christ implies that human dominion in the world is nothing else but a service of loving stewardship and loving service to the other creatures that share planet Earth with us.[35] The christological center does not hinder, but enhances such an appropriation, deepens it, and renders it more credible to the Christian ecclesia.

The Variety of Christocentric Theologies

It is important to realize that Christ-centeredness does not imply that there exists a single, correct theology for all Chistians. Many different but more or less compatible Christ-centered theologies can coexist peacefully (in an atmosphere of vigorous debate) within the church. It seems useful at this point to note the widespread agreement with the church's *de facto* christocentrism by gathering together a diverse group of theologians and to hear their statements on this matter. Let us listen, for example, to a Swiss Reformed theologian, a Roman Catholic Peruvian liberationist, a Presbyterian feminist from the United States, a Canadian United Church contextual theologian, and an American Methodist process theologian: Barth, Gutiérrez, Russell, Hall, and Cobb. Although all of them call for theology to be Christ-centered, their theologies differ from one another in major ways, and in these differences they may, or may not, be in disagreement; they may differ mainly in emphasis or contextual location, or may differ in important doctrinal ways.

Karl Barth (1886-1968) was unquestionably the greatest champion of Christ-centered theological method in the twentieth century. As we have mentioned, he was one of the main leaders of the German Confessing Church resistance to Hitler, the main author of the Barmen Declaration, a lifelong democratic socialist, and a vigorous opponent of the nuclear arms race. He is generally regarded as the most powerful leader of the movement commonly called in North America "neo-orthodox."[36] It was precisely the accommodation of the earlier liberal theology, in which he had been raised and educated, to the imperialistic and warlike world of late modernity that moved him to question the solidity and depth of that theology and convinced him to take seriously what he called the "strange new world of the Bible." In the Bible, and more specifically in Christ, he found firm ground on the basis of which to resist Nazism: "Jesus Christ is the one Word of God whom we have to hear and believe in life and in death," said the Barmen Declaration. Consistent with this commitment, in his mature *Church Dogmatics* Barth constructed every doctrine upon an explicit christological foundation. There he insists,

> Theology must begin with Jesus Christ and not with general principles, however better, or, at any rate, more relevant and illuminating, they may appear to be. . . . Against all imaginations and errors in which we seem to be so hopelessly entangled when we try to speak of God, God will indeed maintain Himself if we will only allow the name of Jesus Christ

to be maintained in our thinking as the beginning and end of all our thoughts.[37]

Gustavo Gutiérrez is an example of a Christ-centered theologian who represents another, quite different school of thought and writes out of a very different time and place—late twentieth-century Latin America. He has often been accused (unjustly) of having been co-opted by a political, specifically Marxist, ideology. In fact, although Gutiérrez has sometimes utilized a Marxist social analysis, he is also clearly and explicitly Christ-centered. His intention is a liberative political theology, articulating a vision of Christian faith that will help to free and uplift the poor of Latin America. He declares a clear political/theological agenda at the outset of his first major book:

> This book is an attempt at reflection, based on the gospel and the experiences of men and women committed to the process of liberation in the oppressed and exploited land of Latin America.[38]

That theology is based on both the gospel and the experience of struggle in a specific context makes clear that this is intentionally a contextual theology. To describe his context as "oppressed and exploited" is already to operate with a thought-out social analysis and consciously to allow this social analysis to have a bearing on his reading of scripture. In this explicit, intentional contextuality, he differs methodologically from Barth. Yet this contextuality does not compromise his Christ-centeredness, for he can often be heard to say, "The basis and foundation of all theological reasoning is Jesus Christ."[39] A close reading of his theology demonstrates that this is no hollow claim. In a later book, Gutiérrez wrote:

> The primordial, and in a certain sense unique, source of revealed truth is Jesus the Christ. The announcement of the kingdom must be made to persons living in a particular historical and cultural situation, but it takes on its full meaning only when connected with Jesus. . . . The good news is Jesus Christ himself. Any reflection on the truths of Christianity and on the language needed for communicating them must start from him who is the truth.[40]

Gutiérrez is certainly not alone among liberationists in this respect. He is found together with Leonardo Boff, José Míguez Bonino, Jon Sobrino, and many others.

Among feminist theologians there is great diversity on the question of centeredness in Christ. Within the wide spectrum of feminist theologies there are many who would certainly put Jesus Christ off center and to the side; some adopt a theocentric (God-centered), or "survival" or "life-centered" approach.[41] For some, the maleness of Jesus is a problem, and for some, what appears to be the

Western origin of Christ-centered theology is objectionable. Some would simply make women's experience the theological foundation, or make the Spirit more primary and central than Jesus Christ. Here one would have to mention major figures such as Rosemary Radford Ruether, Elisabeth Schüssler Fiorenza, Sallie McFague, Carter Heyward. Others, such as Elizabeth Johnson, while not speaking of christocentrism, operate out of a high, trinitarian christology and may be described as Spirit-centered.[42] Other feminist theologians who may be described as Christ-centered are the American Roman Catholic Catherine Mowry LaCugna, the womanist theologian Jacquelyn Grant, the Latin American Maria Clara Bingemer, and the West African, Mercy Amba Oduyoye. The Canadian feminist theologian Pamela Dickey Young, while not espousing a high christology, would be an example of one who supports the idea of Christ as "central symbol."[43]

Letty Russell is most notable perhaps as a substantial, biblical feminist theologian, a professor at Yale whose theology has grown also out of many years of pastoral ministry with the urban poor. Feminist ecclesiology, calling the church to be a "house of freedom," has been perhaps her most important contribution. For her "the authority of experience," and especially women's experience, is a very important and necessary element for theology in its attempt to articulate faith in contemporary terms. She is keenly aware of what she calls "standpoint dependency," and of the various aspects of our contexts and personal life experience which shape the character of faith for individuals and groups. She is affirmative also of the legitimate influence of black experience on black people's theology.[44] Yet it is also clear to her that,

> The self-revelation of God in Jesus Christ and through the Spirit is the source of authority in our lives as Christians. . . . In the Christian faith there is a *center* (commitment to Jesus Christ) and a circle (a hermeneutical circle). Every theological interpretation affects every other, so that we continue to move around the circle trying to create metaphors and models that are faithful to the center of our commitment.[45]

Russell is quite insistent about this center, even though she has been criticized by some feminists for this. She contends that a group that wishes to assert the liberative character of the church "ultimately finds authority in God's action in Christ." Traditions in the church, she says, should be afforded weight only if they are "authoritative or life-giving."[46] Russell distinguishes tradition, traditions, and Tradition. But "*the* Tradition" (the one handed over by God) is Christ himself. For her, Christ is essentially an eschatological figure, providing us a fore-view of the future that God intends for the world. Thus she argues:

> Although some feminists would question that the story of Christ has special privilege as a witness of God's intention to create a new house-

hold, I myself consider that the biblical witness to this action still makes sense of my existence and that the witness of the church continues to be . . . a "transforming memory of the future."[47]

Douglas John Hall, to speak again of a theologian very different from those above, is the "contextual" theologian par excellence. A Canadian concerned to promote a theology that is acutely both contemporary and contextual, addressing the pressing needs and concerns of North American Christians, Hall has spelled out perhaps more thoroughly than anyone the meaning of contextual method.[48] His approach to contextuality is to do theology within a holistic vision of his age and culture (late twentieth-century, early twenty-first-century North America) rather than in relation to a specific group or specific concerns. He is especially notable as a theologian who has thought deeply about suffering and evil, and as an ecological theologian.[49] Hall finds a Pauline/Lutheran theology of the cross helpful for this task. It is with the eyes of *theologia crucis* that he views and critiques the "officially optimistic" outlook of North American life, disclosing the "covert despair" that lies beneath.[50] It is clear to Hall that a theology of the cross that gives true rather than false hope in a time of despair implies christocentrism:

> Revelation in the Christian understanding of it is mediated through historical events, the decisive event being the one in which Jesus as the Christ is center.
>
> In some respects this is the most difficult aspect of the Christian view of revelation because here the presence is identified explicitly with a historical person. The particularism of this identification seems, among other things, to make dialogue with other faiths impossible, or at least difficult.
>
> As was demonstrated during the period of theological liberalism, however, there is no escaping the fact that Christians are bound to a revelational religion which is christocentric.[51]

Again in a later work Hall speaks of "Jesus Christ and him crucified" as the "foundation and core of the whole Christian profession of belief." Jesus the Christ, he argues, is the perceptual foundation through which Christians gain insight and foresight by which to make sense of existence: "A theology is Christian if and when it finds in Jesus as the Christ the meditative core in and around which it intends to weave its reflections about 'everything.'"[52]

John Cobb, one of the leaders of the process theology movement, is again a very different kind of theologian, particularly interested in framing Christian doctrines in ways that correspond to contemporary scientific understandings of the physical world and the evolutionary process; he is notable also for his interest in interfaith theology. In response to pluralist theologies which displace Christ from the center of faith and theology, Cobb denies that theology can begin with a perspective shaped neutrally by all the religious ways of the world rather than by one of them in particular: "I protest against the implicit relativization and even negation of basic Christian commitments."[53] Cobb proposes a wisdom christology, affirming Jesus Christ as the incarnate Wisdom of God, recognizing at the same time the universal presence of God's Wisdom in the whole world and among all people. He argues for an inclusive christology, recognizing the value and truth in other religious traditions while maintaining the specificity of Christian claims about Jesus Christ:

> As a Christian theologian I commend all efforts to break Christianity out of its parochial limits and epecially out of its implicitly or explicitly negative relationship to the other great ways of humankind. But I am troubled by the dominant proposals for carrying out this task. I do not believe these proposals will commend themelves to the most sensitive and committed representatives of some of the other great ways. I do not believe they commend themselves to Christians. Hence I am calling for a different approach—for Christians, a Christocentric catholic one.[54]

Cobb is notable for his respectful openness to other religious "ways," and wishes to go beyond pluralism to an openness to others based precisely in Christ:

> Centering on Jesus or Christ often functions as a form of closure, as an insistence that nothing more needs to be learned. . . . The deeper question is whether centering ourselves on Jesus or on Christ truly has this effect of closure or whether this itself is a misunderstanding of the meaning of Christocentrism. . . . It is my conviction that Christocentrism provides the deepest and fullest reason for openness to others.[55]

This brief glance at a few selected Christ-centered theologians illustrates that it would be a mistake to think that christocentrism locks Christian theology into a single straitjacket. It would be a mistake also to characterize the Christic center in theological method as merely conservative, or merely orthodox in some stultifying sense. In fact it is shared by many who wish to conserve the center of the historic faith while exhibiting an acute awareness of contemporary human crises and radical commitment to addressing them theologically.

A Note on Method for Christology

Christology, of course, is controversial and does not constitute a simple measuring stick for theology, even for theologians such as those mentioned above who understand their theologies as Christ-centered. Since most Christian theologies, including those that do not claim to be Christ-centered, will claim that they are in some sense congruent with their best understanding of Jesus Christ, we must ask: What criteria do we use to measure and assess the primary criterion? All of our best understandings of Christ also have to be criticized and assessed for their adequacy. If Jesus Christ himself is our solid foundation, how do we put content into Jesus Christ? To reiterate, the praxis question—Is it life-giving and liberating?—is basic here, but this in itself needs to be informed by other criteria of adequacy—scripture, context, ecclesia.

We have, of course, a kind of dialectic, and a number of hermeneutical circles here. We interpret scripture in light of Christ, our primary norm, but scripture, which must be read in view of contemporary critical scholarship, is obviously our incomparable source of information and of the original testimony about Christ. Further, we interpet and assess our present cultural, social/political, and economic context out of our center in Christ, yet our context, which we understand also with the help of social science and social analysis, has an undeniable role in our perception of Christ himself, in that we see and hear him through some contextual lens. In faithfulness to him, we deliberately choose to interpet him through the lens of the underside and thereby intentionally adopt a liberationist hermeneutic of christological texts. Similarly, we evaluate traditions and community perspectives through Christ, our primary norm (as attested in scripture); and yet traditions, understood through historical study, together with the faith of the worldwide community, constitute another kind of lens which is indispensable to our interpretation of Christ himself. Christology is done dialectically, then, having all our criteria in mind; it is done out of our faith experience, which is rooted in scripture, experience that is never a-cultural or a-contextual, and never merely individualistic or a-communal.

What we will say in later chapters about all of these criteria in theological method will also pertain to christology. In what I shall say in the next chapter about Jesus Christ, the reader will observe all these criteria in operation: I shall speak out of scripture, with an eye to historical/critical hermeneutical considerations, viewing Christ through the lens of contemporary and contextual experience and drawing upon the wisdom of tradition and ecumenical perspectives. Without pretending to do christology at all thoroughly here, I shall suggest a number of reasons for the foundational place of Jesus Christ in the minds and hearts of Christian people, and so his centrality for theological method.

CHAPTER 5

Apologia for
the Christic Center
The Mission and Identity of Jesus Christ

I have been contending that theological method should be centered and founded not in creation or experience as such, nor in life or liberation, nor even in God, abstractly considered, but concretely in the liberating, life-giving Jesus, the Christ. As Christians, we are centered in God through Jesus. We need to clarify more substantially, then, just why Jesus is foundational for Christian worship, life, faith, and theology. What justifies this centering upon a human being? Just what was it, what is it still, that accounts for this extravagant praise and thanksgiving to Jesus, this following, this hoping in Jesus? To answer this we must enter, however briefly, into the content of christology. As we have seen already in our discussion of revelation and faith, we cannot think clearly about method in theology without delving substantially into its substance. Method and content in any discipline of thought are mutually dependent and circular, first in that the object of inquiry prescribes the way in which it can be known; that is, content always determines the way of knowing, while at the same time appropriate methods of inquiry illuminate and discipline the articulation of content. That is why, in this book on the Christic center, we cannot avoid substantial christological reflection.

Moreover, since Christ-centered theology operates out of a trinitarian theology of Jesus Chist as divine and human, we have to consider whether such a christology can be both liberative and defensible in rational terms. We have seen that the Christic center has been called into question in a number of influential theologies. A kind of apologetic is appropriate here: If we are committed to justice and peace, equality and ecological sustainability, and if we are rational people, alert to what is going on in the world around us, can we still hold to a trinitarian christology and the Christic center for our worship, our life of discipleship, and our theology? What follows in this chapter, however, is not a fulsome christology but a particular methodological slant on christology; that is, we are asking specifically what it is about Jesus Christ that makes him foundation and center in theological method.

Another dialectic pertains in that within christological reflection questions of Jesus' identity and mission, or person and work, are also mutually dependent and circular. Jesus is foundational for us both because of who he is, and because of what he does. We know *who he is* on the basis of *what he does*—his saving, liberating work or mission. On the other hand, his mission can be made intelligible only in terms of *who he is*.[1] I propose that the appropriate starting point for any understanding of the saving significance of Jesus and of his foundational place in theology can be nothing else but his resurrection.

1. The crucified Jesus is raised from the dead and so established as the Christ, who brings God's reign of justice and peace.

Jesus is foundational for us and acknowledged as the Messiah or Christ, because he was raised from the dead. Though crucified, dead, and buried, he is no longer among the dead but among the living. As the just victor over the power of death he is Messiah, the sure sign of the victory of God's reign of righteousness and truth. Because justice, peace, and power come together in him, he is indeed life-giving and liberating.

The resurrection of Jesus himself is sine qua non. Everything is at stake for Christian faith in the resurrection of Jesus. If he had not been raised up from death, he would not be foundational for us. If he was not raised, we would have no good news and no final ground of hope for ourselves or for the world. He would not be Messiah, but at the most would be another admirable prophet and martyr, crushed for the cause of righteousness. If we had heard of him at all, he would not be the Christ but would perhaps be a great teacher and moral hero. Because he is raised up from death he is *kyrios*, both of the dead and of the living, and given "a name that is above every name, that every knee should bend" (Phil 2:10). Scripture attests this foundational character of the resurrection in the words of Paul:

> If Christ has not been raised, then our proclamation has been in vain. We are even found to be misrepresenting God, because we testified of God that he raised Christ. . . . If Christ has not been raised, your faith is futile and you are still in your sins. Then those also who have died in Christ have perished. If for this life only we have hoped in Christ, we are of all people most to be pitied. (1 Cor 15:14-18)

We must begin by recognizing that the event of Jesus' resurrection was profoundly mysterious, since we do not know exactly what resurrection means. The event is utterly without analogies and so deeply hidden and beyond description that the Gospel accounts maintain a respectful silence and do not attempt to depict the event of rising iself. An event of a rising from the dead is in itself so strange and improbable that it is understandable that alternative accounts should arise. At the same time, it is easy to point out discrepancies in the stories and to throw doubt on their authenticity.

Yet I contend that the resurrection should not for these reasons be regarded as a myth. Rudolf Bultmann was famous in the mid-twentieth century for his argument that vertical divine interventions can no longer be credited by modern scientific people and that mythological narratives, such as that of the resurrection, should be demythologized. The stories are important and meaningful, he thought, but they speak to us not of an actual literal raising of Jesus from death, but of the "rise of faith" in the disciples, who came to see the redemptive significance of his death.[2] The resurrection, then, according to Bultmann, was not really about something that happened to Jesus but something that happened to his followers after his death—a new awareness, a new, more authentic quality of life. There are various versions of this approach to the resurrection. Those who would decenter the Christ, whether pluralist or cosmocentric theologians, usually presuppose some such reduced theology of resurrection. By no means, however, has most of the Christian world accepted this interpretation. Faith in the actual raising up of Jesus himself has remained strong within the ecumenical church, even among well-educated and discerning persons for whom a closed, modern scientific worldview of what is and is not possible is too limited.[3]

The question of the nature of the resurrection texts is crucial. Are they, in fact, mythical in character? Mircea Eliade, the great scholar of mythical religion, tells us that myths of dying and rising gods were common in the ancient world. These divinities, often "sons of gods," had a close connection with the cycles of vegetation, of the return of the seasons, and so their deaths and resurrections were repeated every year and celebrated ritually.[4] Eliade believes that the ancient Hebrews broke through to a different, noncyclical or linear concept of time wherein events of history are seen as unique and meaningful. The story of the event of the resurrection of Jesus is not told mythically; rather, it is "played out once, once for all, in a concrete and irreplaceable time, which is that of history and life."[5] This does not prove that the event of the resurrection actually happened. It means that the narrators intended the story in a factual, historical sense. Hans Frei, a theologian who utilizes the work of specialized literary analysts for the interpretation of scripture,[6] also insists that the resurrection narratives cannot be regarded as mythical. Jesus is a unique, unsubstitutable historical individual, at a very particular time and place in history, who cannot be regarded as a symbolic figure:

The story of Jesus' resurrection . . . does not function like a myth in the gospel narratives. Unsubstitutable identity gained in unsubstitutable circumstances is simply not the stuff of mythological tales. . . . Myths are stories in which character and action are not irreducibly themselves. Instead, they are representatives of broader and not directly representable psychic or cosmic states—states transcending the scene of finite and particular events subject to causal explanation. . . . Myths are true or convincing by virtue of their embodiment or echoing of universal experience.[7]

Frei argues that the literary character of the Gospel narratives is more like that of the fictional novel or "realistic narrative"; that is, they are not symbolic, but history-like, depicting a common public world, and, unlike myths and allegories, "they literally mean what they say."[8] These do not, like mythical texts, render a symbolic account of the human condition or convey general truths about God and the world; they do not belong to that genre of mythical narratives that sees reality in cyclical terms. Jesus is obviously not a dying and rising god linked to the seasons of the weather and vegetation. In fact these texts cannot be demythologized, in the sense of drawing abstract truths out of them. "We cannot have what the story is about . . . without the stories themselves."[9]

Again, Frei is not saying that this proves the factuality of the resurrection event. Nor does he insist that all the details of the story must be accurate. It is obvious that the four Gospels contradict one another in many details. We need not deny that there are legendary or even mythical elements in the story, as, for example, the earthquake, the curtain of the temple torn in two, and the tombs of the saints opening so that "many bodies of the saints who had fallen asleep were raised. After his resurrection they came out of the tombs and entered the holy city and appeared to many" (Mt 27:51-53). These are indeed symbolic tales, presumably the product of the devout imagination in the early days of the church. We recognize too that the resurrection stories expand with more and more detail in each successive Gospel. None of this, however, changes the basic message, without which these accretions would never have appeared: Jesus is risen and alive. Frei is right that we cannot have the meaning without the central event itself. The resurrection of Jesus was the sign and promise of the resurrection of the martyred saints. It meant the tearing down of the curtain of alienation between God and humanity. It was earthshaking indeed. The resurrection is proclaimed in the New Testament as the vindication and victory of Jesus himself, not merely a new insight or new awareness in the minds of the disciples.[10] If Jesus himself is not raised, however, there has been, in fact, no victory over sin, oppression, and death. If Jesus himself is not raised, the murderers have remained victorious over their innocent victims, and there is no hope of justice for the dead. All the faithful martyrs, not only of ancient times but of the struggles of our own time, are merely lost and defeated, if Christ himself is not raised. Nor are we assured of God's inexhaustible grace and pardon if Christ is not raised (or, as Paul says, "we are still in our sins"). If we are to continue to proclaim good news, then, the resurrection cannot be reduced to a concept, an idea, a myth, or a symbol. We may, of course, doubt that it happened at all. Though it is not a myth, it could be simply a delusion or a lie, a fiction. But if it did not happen, it can have no significance. If Jesus himself is not risen and alive, then, as Paul says, Christians have misrepresented God and the story of his resurrection is false and can symbolize nothing. The resurrection of Jesus himself is *sine qua non.*

Moreover, we need to understand the resurrection of Jesus as a bodily event. Again, we do not know exactly what this means. We do not know just what it is that Paul struggles to express when he speaks of a "spiritual body" (1 Cor 15) or what it meant to touch Jesus or not to touch him, as he appeared to Thomas or to Mary (Jn 20:17, 27). To encounter the risen Jesus was, for Paul, like a vision of blinding light[11] (Acts 9:3). And yet, strangely, he could be among his disciples incognito, unrecognized (Lk 24:16). The narratives no doubt include legendary elements, and all the conflicting details of the Gospel accounts cannot be taken as factual; but the New Testament authors loudly and clearly insist that it was the whole Jesus who was raised up. It was not merely his soul. He was not a "ghost," Luke insists (Lk 24:39), and certainly his resurrection was not merely the power of his ideas or his influence. If there was any resurrection at all, it was the personal objectivity of Jesus himself, transformed, not "in the flesh" in the ordinary sense but nevertheless, strangely, in bodily form. Elizabeth Johnson brings out the significance of his risen body: "Faith in the resurrection affirms that God has the last word for this executed victim of state injustice and that word, blessedly, is life. Jesus in all his physical and spiritual historicity is raised into glory by the power of the Spirit."[12] To assert Jesus' bodily resurrection affirms the importance of bodies and of matter. Of this Johnson declares:

> There can be no dichotomy between matter and spirit or prizing of one over the other, but matter itself is a treasure related to God. Resurrection announces that this will always be so, for the body itself is glorified in the power of Wisdom's spirit, not discarded. Furthermore it is the tortured and executed body of Jesus that is raised. This grounds Christian hope for a future for all the dead and explicitly for all those who are raped, tortured, and unjustly destroyed in the continuing torment of history.[13]

Without the resurrection, then, there is no final hope either for the dead or for the living. But, because he is risen in his body, we expect also (incomprehensibly) our own resurrection to eternal life. Not only that. In the bodily resurrection of the crucified Jesus, the whole fleshly material world is lifted up, blessed, and dignified.[14] The world of matter, of flesh, of earth, of animals and fish, and of soil, skies, and seas cannot be discarded or callously desecrated as unimporant in the eternal scheme of things, for bodies and all creation have an eternal future!

The event of Easter was a hidden, noncoercive event that can be known only in the relationship of faith and following. We may ask: Is the resurrection of Jesus so foundational for us because we worship power and success? Why could we not worship the purity of his love and suffering on the cross without resurrection? The worship of success has certainly entered into our Christian history, in that the resurrection has indeed been used in a triumphalistic way, setting up Christ as the king of an imperial Christendom. But this has been an absurd distortion, readily visible in our post-Christendom culture. In fact, from the point of view of the world, we worship a failure, a crucified king, someone who ended up on a cross. His raising was an event that cannot be proved, a victory that cannot be demonstrated or verified.[15] This event can only be believed in the vulnerability of faith.[16] Jesus did not appear to Pilate, Caiaphas, Herod, or Caesar to frighten them into submission. He appeared first to women, whose testimony could not even be credited in a court of law. He appeared then in quietness and gentleness to his male disciples, who were overwrought with grief. Even then, "some of them doubted" (Mt 28:16). Celsus, critic of the church in the third century, made plain the vulnerability of the resurrection message: The risen Jesus had appeared, allegedly, only to a "hysterical woman and a deluded disciple," while he "ought to have appeared to the very men who treated him despitefully and to the man who condemned him, and to everyone everywhere."[17] The disciples were left to proclaim a risen Lord who had gone away and could not be produced as evidence! The resurrection of Jesus, then, was not simply a reversal of the crucifixion, and it is not available as the basis for Christian triumphalism. Because the event is noncoercive, it can be known only in the costly relationship of faith and following.[18] God does not offer us overbearing evidence, will not force us, even by facts or logic, to believe and to follow. Nor can we, then, impose this on others, even by the power of argument. Believing it, we dare to trust the witnesses.

Indeed the credibility of the witnesses—their transformation, their dedication, and their commitment—may carry some persuasive, apologetic value. Critical scholar E. P. Sanders asks: "Without the resurrection, would his disciples have endured longer than did John the Baptist's? We can only guess, but I would guess not."[19] N. T. Wright also argues learnedly that in the case of the deaths of a host of other visionary or glorious leaders of the ancient world, not once did their followers claim that their leader was alive again in any sense.[20] Rational people may decide, with good reason, to trust the witnesses. Other reasonable people may, understandably, dismiss the whole story as a delusion. No one can say, definitively, which of these approaches are right.

Emphatically, I am not suggesting that the resurrection should be believed as probable. To one who does not respond in faith, the resurrection stories remain "absurd," as Kierkegaard would say. Kierkegaard's ironic wit helps us to see the unviability of belief by probability:

> Suppose a man wishes to acquire faith; let the comedy begin. He wishes to have faith, but he wishes also to safeguard himself by means of an objective inquiry and its approximation-process. What happens? . . . it becomes probable, it becomes increasingly probable, it becomes extremely and emphatically probable. Now he is ready to believe it, and he ventures to claim for himself that he does not believe as shoemakers and tailors and simple folk believe, but only after long deliberation. Now he is ready to believe it; and lo, now it has become precisely impossible to believe it. Anything that is almost probable, or probable, or extremely and emphatically probable, is something he can almost know, or as good as know, or extremely and emphatically almost *know*—but it is impossible to *believe*. For the absurd is the object of faith, and the only object that can be believed.

In the last analysis, believing it, we go out on a limb. As Kierkegaard would say, we rush to believe in the risen Jesus with passion and joy. To believe in it and to live in the light of it are more than having an opinion about a strange event in the past; it is a commitment to the risky, joyful life of following Jesus.

The message and practice of Jesus of Nazareth was centered on the reign of God, which was for him a revolutionary alternative social vision. In the event of Easter we see the vindication of righteous martyrs and of all the victims of history. Jesus was undoubtedly a prophet of the reign of God.[21] Critical scholars of the historical Jesus in every phase of that scholarly movement seem to have agreed at least about this: that the *basileia* (the reign, rule, or kingdom) of God was the primary concern of Jesus of Nazareth himself,[22] and this is evident also to any *prima facie* reading of the Synoptic Gospels. According to Mark, Jesus initiated his preaching ministry with this announcement: "The time is fulfilled and the kingdom of God has come near; repent, and believe in the good news" (Mark 1:15). "I must proclaim the good news of the kingdom of God in the other cities also," he says, "for I was sent for this purpose" (Lk 4:43). He sends out his disciples to "proclaim the kingdom of God and to heal" (Lk 9:2). His preaching and parables are full of God's *basileia*, God's rule of peace and justice, love and wholeness. The reign of God is precious and ardently to be sought after, like a treasure hid in a field (Mt 13:44) or a pearl of great price (Mt 13:45). We are to seek God's reign above all other things (Mt 6:33) and pray for God's reign and for God's will to be done on earth (Mt 6:10). In this way Jesus' disciples are called to be stewards of God's reign, contributing to its growth in the world (Mt 25:14-31). We are to sow seeds of God's reign (Mt 3:3-23), and the reign will grow in the world from something tiny like a mustard seed to something great like a tree (Mt 13:31-32), from something small and hidden into something powerful, like the yeast leavening in flour (Mt 13:33).

Jesus' healing works are seen to be the work of the Spirit in him overcoming evil forces and a sign that the reign of God "has come to you" (Mt 12:28; Lk 11:20). But his healings are not without their social and political significance. Possession of unclean spirits, often taking the form of self-destructive and mad behaviour, was part of the general social/spiritual condition of being under the control of Roman imperial forces but was understood in terms of superhuman demonic forces. Richard Horsley suggests:

> On the widely accepted assumption that Jesus did indeed perform healings of various kinds, we must imagine dozens of individual healings and healing stories. . . . The stories that survived the winnowing process of repeated oral performances would have been ones that "spoke to" the general malaise of the people who heard them. Thus not only was the original healing (to which we have no direct access) both a healing of a particular person and embedded in social relationships, but each healing story was both a healing of a particular person and a continuing "healing" of the social "body" of subsequent communities of hearers.[23]

The reign was already breaking in, then, in Jesus' own life and ministry. When asked whether he is the one to come, he answers, according to Luke: "the blind receive their sight, the lame walk, the lepers are cleansed, the deaf hear, the dead are raised, the poor have good news brought to them. And blessed is anyone who takes no offence at me" (Lk 7:22-23). According to Mark 9:1, Jesus promised that before the death of some of his contemporaries, the kingdom of God would have come "with power." There is debate among scholars as to whether or not Jesus was an apocalyptic prophet, expecting a sudden, imminent inbreaking of God's final kingdom[24]—a debate we cannot resolve here. But certainly the early church expected Jesus' own imminent return in the power of the kingdom, which was still to be consummated (see, e.g., Mt 24:29-31; 1 Thess 4:16; 1 Cor 15:24; etc.). They saw his whole life, and most especially his resurrection, as the sign of the inbreaking of God's reign, and they expected more to come.

It is sometimes argued that Jesus of Nazareth, the pre-Easter Jesus, was theo-centric, or God-centered. Obviously he was not Christ-centered as Christians were after the resurrection. But it would seem more accurate to say that Jesus was centered in God's reign. It is the most certain historical datum we have about Jesus of Nazareth, derived from all the sources: His work and his passion were not simply to serve God, but specifically to serve God's reign. Jesus preached the kingdom of God and not himself; that is, he himself is not the focus of his own message.[25] This reign of God is not merely a personal inward thing (though this is not excluded) but has to do with the transformation of this world, of its structures and relationships. It has to do, above all, with the liberation of people from all injustice and brokenness. This is evident in the announcement at Nazareth: "The Spirit of the Lord is upon me because he has anointed me to preach good news to the poor. He has sent me to proclaim release to the captives and recovery of sight to the blind, to let the oppressed go free, to proclaim the year of the Lord's favour" (Lk 4:18-19). To say that the Spirit of God is upon him is to identify him as the expected messianic one upon whom (as in prophetic hope) the Spirit would rest. The reign of God that the anointed one brings into the world is precisely "good news for the poor," which means not something merely inward and spiritual, nor merely heavenly, but something this-worldly, something economic and political. The reign of God is about God's will being done in this world: "Thy Kingdom come, thy will be done on earth" (Mt 6:10). His actual personal solidarity with all the poor, the disabled, the sick, and the socially rejected was the way in which he lived out his own preaching and teaching. So also he calls his followers to love unflinchingly, to love God and to love their neighbours as themselves (Mk 12:31; Mt 22:39; Lk 10:27) and even to love their enemies (Mt 5:43), which is dramatized most notably in the parable of the Good Samaritan (Lk 10). In this way they will participate already in God's reign of love. Matthew proclaims Jesus as the Servant in whom God's Spirit is at work: "he will proclaim justice to the Gentiles . . . until he brings justice to victory" (Mt 12:18-20, referring to Is 42:1-4).

Studies of the historical Jesus, reading the Gospels with cognizance of his social and political milieu, offer even more persuasive evidence that Jesus did indeed present an alternative social vision to his nation. John Dominic Crossan, for example, describes the deeply cruel and corrupt patronage system of Roman-dominated society, its steeply hierarchical system of honor and shame. An example of Jesus' resistance to this was his "open commensality"—eating together with those who were socially despised, shamed, and dishonored. Crossan writes: "Open commensality was . . . a strategy for building or rebuilding peasant community on radically different principles from those of honor and shame patronage and clientage. It was based on egalitarian sharing of spiritual and material power at the most grassroots level."[26]

His unflinching service of God's reign through the service of the poor and the afflicted, his denunciation and resistance to the privileged and powerful who oppress the lowly and serve the anti-reign, led to his death, and his willingness to die must also be seen as Jesus' willingness to serve God's reign to the end.

The reign of God, so central for Jesus, must also be central for his followers, first in terms of practical action, but also primary for any theology of liberation and particularly for any christology.[27] Other christological concepts or categories will be distorted if they are abstracted from Jesus' central service to the reign. Belief in Jesus as Messiah will be misunderstood and abused, turned into a kind of Christian arrogance, if dissociated from Jesus' passion for God's reign of justice and love. The reign of God can really only be understood rightly, and for that matter can really only be believed in, properly speaking, from within our own activity of practical service. Thus Sobrino speaks of the "hermeneutic value of praxis—praxis as a means of grasping the nature of the Reign of God, in such wise that, conversely, without praxis an understanding of the Reign of God would be crippled and diminished."[28]

That is why the reign of God must be interpreted through the "option for the poor."[29] If our following of Jesus is not "good news for the poor" (Lk 4:16), then it is not true service to God's reign and does not truly express faith in Jesus or love of God. So also resurrection, if interpreted separately from Jesus' commitment to God's reign, "can and does feed an individualism without a people, a hope without a praxis, an enthusiasm without a following of Jesus—in sum, a transcendence without a history."[30] The resurrection of Jesus must be understood in terms of the reign of God to which Jesus was devoted. His resurrection was not his victory alone, but the victory of the reign.

The victory of that practical, worldly—yes, economic, political—reign of God becomes a reality and a hope, however, only through that resurrection. The risen Jesus constitutes for us a prolepsis, a "presentness of the future"[31] of God's final reign. In it we are given a glimpse ahead of time of the victory of life over death, of liberty over enslavement and oppression.[32] In light of the resurrection, we look for victory not only over evil in some abstract sense, but the victory over concrete evils—hunger, poverty, war, imprisonment, illness, and even death. The messianic hope of the Hebrew prophets was for one who would come from God in the power of God's Spirit to bring the reign of peace and justice (e.g., Is 11; 61). Although Jesus' life, deeds, and comportment may have indicated to his disciples that he was the expected anointed one, or Messiah (e.g., Mt 16:16), his death would have been more than enough to dash these hopes. "We had hoped," they said on the Emmaus road, "that he was the one to redeem Israel" (Lk 24:21). It is unimaginable that, without the resurrection, the dead Jesus would have been acknowledged by the earliest church as the Messiah, the Christ.[33]

Ironically and tragically, this very recognition of the messianic victory over oppression and injustice, shamefully distorted by Christians, has led to great misery, especially for Jesus' own people, the Jews. In the twentieth century, Christians became intensely aware of the danger implicit in the concept of Jesus the Messiah. The long history of the persecution of the Jewish people, culminating in the Holocaust of the Jews in Nazi Germany, cannot be dissociated from Christian concepts of Jesus as Messiah. Because of a bad theology of Messiah and accompanying Christian triumphalism, Judaism was thought to be entirely superseded, and the Jews were depicted as a stubborn, perverse people who had killed their divine messenger.[34] Jesus as Messiah was dissociated from the reign of justice to which he was devoted, and the kingdom of God became an otherworldly "kingdom of Heaven." Christians were seen as the privileged ones who, having accepted the Messiah, would benefit from his heavenly salvation. Not that Christianity itself was directly, unambiguously responsible for the Holocaust; it was the ghastly technological achievement of the modern world and of certain currents in modern thought. Yet Christian anti-Semitism, the long centuries of pogroms, of the scapegoating and victimizing of Jews in Christendom, bears some responsibility for this catastrophe. The Western world had been well trained in anti-Semitism by old Christendom.

Following upon Jewish–Christian dialogue, a number of post-Holocaust Christian theologians have emphasized the unfinished character of the redemption offered in Jesus.[35] While the salvation accomplished in the life and death and resurrection of Christ is decisive and irrevocable for the whole world, it is at the same time anticipatory, as evil and death continue to be rampant in God's creation. One of the great evils has been Christian (and other) religious imperialism, most dramatically against the Jews. The praxis outcome of an exclusivist Christianity is theologically unacceptable and drives us to the scriptures for a more faithful reading of Christ's messianic person. Jürgen Moltmann is among those who have written helpfully about this, insisting that

> all "fulfilment" enthusiasm must be banished from the christology of the church as it exists in the world of history. Jesus of Nazareth, the messiah who has come, is the suffering Servant of God, who heals through his wounds and is victorious through his sufferings. He is not yet the Christ of the parousia, who comes in the glory of God and redeems the world, so that it becomes the kingdom. . . . What has already come into the world through the Christ who has come and is present, is the justification of the godless and the reconciliation of enemies. What has not yet come is the redemption of the world, the overcoming of all enmity, the resurrection of the dead, and the new creation. . . . But just because men and women "now already" have peace with God through Christ, they are "no longer" prepared to make terms with this peace-less world. Because they are reconciled with God, they suffer from this "unredeemed world" and "sigh" with the whole enslaved creation (Rom 8) for the coming glory of God.[36]

The similar post-Auschwitz thought of Gregory Baum moves him to declare that "room remains in world history for many religions, for other ways of grace, and in particular for the other biblical faith, for Judaism."[37] In God's providence, and in the freedom of God's Spirit, the Jews and indeed many other religions remain. This means that Christianity, while holding fast to the inbreaking of God's reign in Christ, must deabsolutize itself and recognize that others, too, particularly the Jews, have truth and wisdom. We must recognize that the Jews remain God's special covenant people, and we must stand together with them, looking still for the fulfillment of the promises of God.

We should note that the resurrection of Jesus, the raising up of a righteous martyr, was an eschatological sign (a sign of the decisive inbreaking of God's reign) for the first Jewish Christians. Hope for resurrection had arisen among the Jews rather late, only at the time of Daniel (second century B.C.E.), a time of foreign oppression and dreadful suffering, including the deaths of many of Israel's most righteous and faithful people (Dan 12:1-4).[38] The resurrection of the dead would come at an end-time (an apocalypse, a revelation), the time of the victory of God's rule. Without resurrection, there could never be justice for these victims. Thus, the first Christians saw the victory of Jesus' raising as an inbreaking and inauguration of God's rule of justice, when righteous martyrs would be vindicated. The prophetic expectation was not, however, for the raising of just one person. The risen martyr Jesus was seen by Paul, for example, as "the first fruits from the dead" (1 Cor 15:20). In keeping with the Danielic expectation, Jesus was also given the title Son of Man, signifying that Jesus' coming is the coming of God's reign and the beginning of the end of the rule of evil and death.

2. Jesus is Emmanuel, the presence of the vulnerable God with us, truly God and truly human.

Jesus is foundational for us also because he is *one with God,* and God is *one with us* in Jesus' humanity. It is evident that, if this is so, Jesus himself cannot be relativized or decentered in Christian life, worship, or thought.

That Jesus is "God with us" is an assessment based not on his moral character but on his saving and liberating work. For believers in one God, whether Jews, Christians, or Muslims in the family of Abraham, only God gives life and liberty. Only God is "Saviour." Jesus, then, if he is our Saviour, is "God with us." But Jesus is life-giving and liberating also because he is one with us as human, demonstrating God's amazing grace and love toward us from within our own vulnerable humanity.[39]

If Jesus were not "God with us," truly God and Saviour, he would not be central and foundational for Christian worship and life. We would not praise and thank him, follow and obey him, trust and hope in him, if he were not truly God. Christian worship at Christmastime is most especially premised on this doctrine of the incarnation, as we pray it, preach it, sing it: "God of God, light of light . . . , very God, begotten not created, O come let us adore him." To be so centered on a prophet, a moral example, a messenger or representative from God would be impossible. Such adoration of a mere human being would be the most shocking idolatry if it were not true that he is Emmanuel, God with us. So also, ultimately it is only God who can be obeyed or followed. If Jesus were not true God, he could not be addressed as *kyrios* (Lord, or Sovereign), for he would have no final authority for us.

At the same time, if Jesus were not fully human and one of us, he would not be central and foundational for us. We love and follow him because in him God has identified with us completely in our finite humanity. We are devoted to him because in him God has suffered as we suffer and knows intimately our human joys, human temptations, our weakness, our misery, and our death. Moreover, it is in his humanity that he is raised up, lifting up the humanity of us all to a share in the eternal life of God.

That Jesus was a person of great love and courage is certainly true and essential to his unity with God. That it was *this* man, who exhibited solidarity with the poor and outcast, with women, with the disabled, the blind, and the lepers, that it was *this one* who was raised up from death is of utmost importance. The manner of his life, his tenderness toward sinners, and at the same time his resistance to oppressors and anger with the self-righteous are indispensable to his disclosure of the God who is love. Yet it is not his personal moral character as such, or by itself, that leads to the extravagant conclusion that he is "God with us." Mere enthusiasm and hero worship about a wonderful person cannot, in themselves, justify the elevation of a human being to the status of deity.

The doctrine of the divinity, or incarnation of God in Jesus, arose out of the relationship of the first Christians to him as risen Lord. *Lex orandi, lex credendi:* The law of prayer is the law of belief. They found themselves in a relationship of praise and thanksgiving with him. But also, *lex sequendi, lex credendi:* They found themselves in a relationship with him of following and obedience. He had turned their lives around, and had overcome the power of death. His life and ministry prior to his death had to be seen and understood in light of the eschatological event (that is, the inbreaking of God's reign) in his resurrection. His coming was the coming of God, and so the immediate presence of the eternal. His overcoming of death was *God's* overcoming of death. His compassionate healing of the sick and disabled was therefore *God's own* compassion to all who suffer, and a sign of God's final overcoming of all suffering and misery. His forgiveness of sins was *God's own* forgiveness and the sign of God's reconciliation of a broken, sinful world. His authority to forgive and to command was *God's own* authority, and a sign of God's ultimate and effective rule.

The true divinity of the human Jesus is a profound mystery, incomprehensible but not unintelligible. Those who question the centrality of Jesus generally discount belief in the unique divinity of Jesus as something unworthy of a rational modern mind. The idea is thought to be not only incomprehensible, and probably mythical, but simply unintelligible. However, if we take what seems to be the obvious step and demythologize the incarnation, treating it as a metaphor or symbol, there is no good reason to continue to be founded and centered in Jesus; the general truth that he symbolizes would relativize him personally.

But can the incarnation be taken seriously as a reality? Those who knew Jesus in the flesh knew that he was really human like us, and it is obvious to us today that Jesus was *flesh,* with all the limitations and vulnerability of *flesh.* Can a human being really be God? Is this not a nonsensical statement, a sheer impossibility? Can such an assertion make sense, let alone be demonstrated?[40] It is not, of course, demonstrable in the sense that one could prove it to every questioner with coercive logic or evidence, nor is it comprehensible, in the sense that we can ever fully grasp it or master it intellectually. An intelligent person, obviously, can doubt this, and it has been questioned since the time of the Ebionites in the early church. Christians, however, believe it because they are confronted with the mystery of a human being who is Saviour. Theology's task is not so much to defend it as to elucidate it. An *apologia* here can only be a clarification. The point is not to prove or even explain the incarnation, but to elucidate what it does and does not mean. One can only encounter him, "behold his glory," and respond. Yet, for both believers and for others, the question persists: Is talk about Jesus as divine and human intelligible at all? Do we know what we are saying when we say it? Or is it simply double-talk, "bagglegab," nonsense?

The possibility lies not, of course, in the capacity of a human being to be God, but in the possibility of God being human. If we begin our reflections on the divinity and humanity of Jesus with a preconceived notion of God, especially a philosophical concept of God as immutable and impassible (unchangeable and incapable of suffering), the suggestion that God has become human may well appear to be nonsense. According to this conceptuality, God cannot "become," for God is already perfect. And God, as in-finite, cannot become finite without ceasing to be God. This was the difficulty that the Alexandrian theologian Arius had in the early fourth century, when he insisted that the *logos* which became flesh in Jesus could not be fully God, coeternal with the Father, for God the eternal Creator could not become so enmeshed with a creature while maintaining deity. The *logos* incarnate in Jesus, then, according to Arius, must have been an intermediate being, *homoi-ousios* (of *like* substance) but not the same substance as the Father. But in light of the biblical story, and especially in light of Jesus, this philosophical concept of God is rather limited. This God is unable to suffer, unable to be deeply engaged with creation, and therefore unable to love.[41] But if God is unable to suffer and to love, God is less than us and unworthy of our worship. Gregory of Nyssa in the late fourth century already made this point: God's power is displayed not so much in the vastness of the heavens and the orderly arrangement of the world as in the divine freedom to share in the weakness of our human nature.[42]

If we set aside preconceived notions of God, if we allow our concept of God to be shaped instead by the mystery of Jesus and by the experience of salvation experienced in Jesus, that whole concept must change. Perhaps God is free to be God in more than one way. Perhaps God as Spirit, *Ruah,* like the wind or breath, the God known to the Hebrew people in exodus and exile, is not bound to any one place or space, or even to one mode of being. We are told that the God of Israel went into exile with the people, sharing their misery and humiliation.[43] Isaiah tells us that "in their afflictions, [God] was afflicted" (Is 63:9). God, who is so unimaginably great that all the heavens and earth cannot contain him, nevertheless dwelt among them, they believed, in particular places, such as the temple (1 Kgs 8:27). As Spirit, as free, unpredictable, and uncontained as a mighty Wind, she could be beyond and above the world and yet also alive within the world and within human beings, even particular human beings (e.g., Ezek 36:27). If God were a finite being, limited in time and space, confined to one place and one mode of being, we could not begin to say intelligently that God became human in Jesus. This would be rather like saying "Sam became an oak tree." This would be sheer nonsense. But the Hebrew experience of the saving God among them and within them, and the Christian experience of "God with us" in Jesus, and within us by the Spirit, demanded a revolution in the concept of God.[44] This revolution began long ago with the Hebrews when God, as "the God of Abraham, the God of Isaac, and the God of Jacob" addressed Moses (Exod 3:6), that is, the God present in history. The concept of God underwent profound transformation again, but in the same direction, when Christians began to see that "God was in Christ, reconciling the world" (2 Cor 5:19). It all became very explicit when, under the leadership of Athanasius, the Council of Nicaea (325 C.E.) proclaimed that Jesus Christ, the eternal Son and *logos* of God, was indeed *homo-ousios* (of one substance) with the Father. This God, who is deeply engaged with human beings in their history and even lives in intimate unity with a particular human being—this is a very different sort of God. That Jesus was human, and fully human (*homoousios* also with our humanity), need not compromise his true divinity. God as Spirit is free and capable of "self-emptying" (*kenōsis*) (Phil 2:7), free to be both present and beyond,[45] free to be human, free to be servant as well as Lord, free to be lowly and obedient as well as majestic and commanding, free to suffer, free to enter into the mortality of a creature, while yet remaining God.[46]

As we have seen, the fathers of Nicaea stated the mystery of Jesus in terms of the Greek concept of *ousia,* "being," which was translated into Latin as *substantia,* "substance." These concepts, though not biblical, helped to contextualize Christian faith in Hellenistic culture. They were rather static metaphysical concepts that served well in their time, but today, with our awareness of the fluid, processive, relational, and interactive character of all realities, these concepts are less useful. If we try to think of the possibility of divine substance and human substance coming together, it is difficult not to imagine a mixture—something like that of salt and water, or water and oil. With the first, we would have neither true, undiluted water nor pure unadulterated salt, but salty water. With the other, we would have a separation, oil floating on top, with no real unity of the two. These are the alternatives that the Council of Chalcedon (in 451 C.E.) admirably rejected merely by doggedly asserting the inexplicable mystery. They insisted on the enigma that confronted them: a human being who is Saviour, who commands, forgives, overcomes death, reveals God, and reconciles us to God! Therefore, the council declared, Jesus is one person in two natures, truly God and truly human, without change or confusion, without division or separation.[47] By this they meant to say that Jesus' humanity was real humanity, identical with ours, uncompromised by his unity with God, and that his divinity was also real, undiminished by his unity with humanity. We cannot comprehend such a reality. We can only respond with astonishment.

Strangely enough, ancient biblical categories seem more relevant and intelligible to us today than ancient Greek philosophical ones. I refer, for example, to the concept of "indwelling." As we have seen, the God of the Hebrews was free to be above and beyond the world yet also within it, and to be particularly present in specific places and to live within people, and particular people. The author of the Gospel of John, reflecting on the mystery of the saving God in Jesus, and of Jesus in God, thought of their unity not in substantial but in relational terms, especially as mutual indwelling:

> The Father and I are one. (Jn 10:30)
> The Father is in me and I am in the Father. (Jn 10:38)
> As you, Father, are in me, and I in you, may they also be in us.
> (Jn 17:21)

We need not think, necessarily, that these are the words of the historical Jesus himself. Although Jesus of Nazareth may have experienced an intimate unity with his *Abba* (and these words may express truly something of what he experienced), we need not suppose that he had thought through what we now call "christology." These words do express the early Christians' encounter with God in Jesus and God's unity with Jesus.

There is something not only mysterious, but mystical about the unity of Jesus with God. When we speak of God in Jesus and Jesus in God, the preposition "in" becomes a kind of metaphor; God is not "in" Jesus the way that tea is in a teapot. The word "in" expresses intimate unity. Other, less perfect instances of mystical, mutual indwelling may help us to apprehend what is meant by this unity. If we can grasp (but not comprehend) what it means to speak of the Spirit of God dwelling in us, and we in God, we have a glimpse (but only a glimpse) of what it means for God to be in Jesus, and Jesus in God.[48] So also, if we can speak meaningfully of the unity of Christ and the church (which the Letter to the Ephesians [5:31-32] compares to the unity of husband and wife) and of members of the church as "members one of another" (Rom 12:5), then we have a glimmer of what incarnation may mean. I suggest that mutual indwelling, and relationality as such, is conceptually more useful and intelligible to us than "being" or "substance." If we can speak experientially of the mystery of the oneness of husband and wife, or of lovers, in the intimate unity of "one flesh" (Gen 2:24; Mt 19:5), we again have a glimpse (but only a glimpse) of what the unity of Jesus with God may be. It is possible for people to live "in and through" each other, so that, while they remain two, they are deeply one. We may say that *we are who we are* in and through our relationships. Jesus is Mary's son, the brother of

James, friend of his disciples, and so on. Most significantly, *he is who he is* in his unique relation with his *Abba*.

When we ask, concerning the identity of a person, Who is he, or she? what are we asking? Catherine LaCugna (utilizing the philosophy of John Macmurray) suggests that a person cannot be understood as an isolated entity, but only as a "being-in-relation-to-another." "Mutuality," she writes, "is the hallmark of personal identity. . . . 'I' am constituted as a person only in relation to 'You.'"[49] Elizabeth Johnson speaks similarly when she says that Jesus' person, as one with the divine Wisdom (*Sophia*) and one with humanity, is "constituted by these two fundamental relations."[50] Theologians a few centuries after Chalcedon (such as John of Damascus [c. 655-750]) developed a concept of *perichōrēsis* (circling round, or mutual indwelling)[51] to articulate especially the doctrine of the Trinity, concerning the oneness, distinction, mutual interaction, and inseparability of the persons of the Trinity. The concept is helpful also for understanding (glimpsing, but never comprehending) the mystery of the divinity of Jesus. Gregory of Nazianzus suggested, even before the Council of Chalcedon, that the divinity and humanity of Jesus should be thought of as a *perichōrēsis*.[52] This dynamic unity in differentiation, this "perichoretic" presence of God in Jesus, and of God's saving work in and through Jesus is so compelling that God's presence in him has to be seen as utter identification, a total, inseparable oneness. This is so much so that we can say that in Jesus, God lived a human life! And, more astounding still, a human being shared in the eternal life of God! From within our humanity—the humanity of Jesus Emmanuel—God reached out to us as one of us. This, we believe, was more than empathy. We can say, in a spirit of wonder and adoration, that God knows intimately, firsthand, the joy and misery of human living and human dying.

That Jesus was truly divine did not compromise his true humanity. The mystery that confronts us in Jesus is that of a real human being like ourselves, who inaugurates God's reign, overcomes the power of evil and death, and saves or liberates us for our own true humanity. We know his divinity through his saving work. And yet his real humanity is beyond doubt. It is true that in the ancient church some believers were so convinced of his divinity that they doubted whether he was really human at all. They were commonly called "docetists" (from the Greek *dokeō*, "to appear") in that they thought Jesus only appeared to be human. That group of people prominent in the second and third centuries known as "gnostics" (people supposedly of special *gnōsis*, or "knowledge") were docetic, doubting whether Jesus was really a human being of flesh, questioning whether he really suffered and died. Today no one, as far as I know, defends this kind of docetism, though the idea still lingers in the minds of many devout people.

That Jesus was really flesh (Jn 1:14) implies that he experienced all the limitations, joys, and vulnerability of creaturely flesh. He lived and died at a particular time and place, belonged to a particular people, spoke a particular language (or languages) and possessed a particular gender. He was a sexual being. He knew the creaturely needs as well as satisfactions and pleasures that accompany our bodily existence. He enjoyed eating and drinking, had personal friends, and apparently loved partying with his friends (Mt 11:19). Even if he had special insight or knowledge of God, his knowledge was nevertheless limited; he knew nothing of the English language, nothing about nuclear physics or the solar systems and galaxies.

The Council of Chalcedon, as we mentioned above, insisted that the one person of Jesus Christ existed in "two natures," fully divine and fully human. The divinity and humanity were "without separation or division, without confusion or change."[53] This formula of words did not by any means explain the mystery of the unity of the human Jesus with God; to explain would be to dissolve away the mystery. Jesus was not *partly divine* and *partly human* (as a centaur is half man, half horse!). Despite his *kenosis* (self-emptying), God in the lowliness of Jesus remains God. Nor did Jesus' divinity subsume or cancel out his humanity. As we have seen, the substance language of the ancient world renders this almost unintelligible. The more fluid, interpersonal language of scripture, however, can still make sense to us in our time. If God dwells in us, by the Holy Spirit, we are not for that reason less, but more fully human. So also, by dwelling in us, God does not become less than God. If we as human beings dwell in one another (*perichōrēsis*) in relationships of deep love and unity, our distinct identities are not diminished but enhanced. So also, God's utter unity with the human Jesus and his utter unity with God do not compromise either his divinity or his humanity.

That God in Christ is united to our whole human nature, body, mind, and spirit, is important for the theology of salvation. Gregory of Nazianzus, in the late fourth century, had argued: "that which [God] has not assumed he has not healed."[54] That is, if God was not incarnate in the whole of Jesus, body, mind, and spirit, then our whole humanity has not been redeemed and given a share in God's eternity.

An important point to remember about this in our time is that the humanity of Jesus was the humanity of us all, male and female. As both men and women, both girls and boys, are created in God's image, so also God has blessed, dignified, and lifted up the humanity of all, of both genders and of all races, ages, and conditions. The New Testament—and for that matter also the early church councils and creeds—never emphasizes the maleness of Jesus. Though it is obvious that Jesus had to be one sex or the other, and was indeed male—this was part of his limited, finite humanity—we are never told that God has become male. In the Latin translation of the Nicene Creed we do not read *vir factus est*, but that God has become human—*homo factus est*. His maleness is incidental to his salvific significance.[55] Although the maleness of Jesus is a problem for some feminist Christians,[56] it is not a problem for all of them. Elizabeth Johnson, a Roman Catholic feminist, for example, deplores "a certain leakage of Jesus' human maleness into the divine nature," but insists that "gender is not constitutive of the

Christian doctrine of the Incarnation." To make it so, as the Roman Catholic Church does in its doctrine of priesthood (refusing ordination to women because they do not resemble Jesus in his maleness), is heresy and blasphemous, she writes.[57] Nor does Rosemary Radford Ruether have difficulty with the maleness of Jesus. His solidarity with the marginalized, including women, and his foot-washing stance as humble servant consist in a "kenosis [self-emptying] of patriarchy," so that his renunciation of hierarchy would have been less significant or remarkable had Jesus been a woman.[58] His tender giving of self offers us a vision of what humanity, even male humanity, can be.

The true humanity of Jesus is liberating for us in that we can identify with him as one of us. This is especially so in the case of oppressed and poor people. God, by becoming human in Jesus, became, specifically, a poor person—born in a stable, we are told, the child of obscure, pushed-around little people in a conquered, occupied country. In his death he was one, specifically, with the condemned and the rejected, those wrongfully accused and executed, the innocent victims of history. That God is incarnate in such a person is good news for the poor and the conquered everywhere. This was precious to black slaves in America, who in their prayers and songs identified Jesus with God and took Jesus as their true master in circumstances of unimaginable brutality.[59]

We are told, too, that he was tempted to sin (Mt 4:1-11; Lk 4:1-13), yet also that he was "without sin" (Heb 4:15). What it means to be without sin is indeed strange to us. It is not something that could possibly have been observed by those who knew him; though they may have known him as incomparably loving and compassionate, courageous and truthful, they could not have known all of his deeds or inner thoughts. The doctrine of his sinlessness is a corollary of his divinity or oneness with God. It also implies that sin is not, properly speaking, part of our true humanity as God intends it to be, but a distortion or spoiling of our humanity. This means that, if Jesus is "without sin," he is not less, but more genuinely human than we are. He did not, however, possess merely an ideal, unfallen humanity, utterly unlike our own. A number of biblical texts imply a certain qualification to Jesus' sinlessness. Paul speaks of Jesus as "born of a woman, born under the law" (Gal 4:4) and sent "in the likeness of sinful flesh" (Rom 8:3). Presumably the sinlessness of Jesus does not mean a life of complete moral flawlessness,[60] without the need for moral or spiritual growth, which would certainly compromise his genuine humanity. He "grew in wisdom and in stature and in divine and human favour" (Lk 2:52) and "learned obedience through what he suffered" (Heb 5:8). We should not try to imagine Jesus as a perfect little boy, devoid of mischief or quarrels, or as a teenager with no fond glances in the direction of the opposite sex. Moreover, however faithful to God he was, he lived within a corrupt and oppressive society and, like the rest of us, was inevitably implicated in its structures and systems. What we can say is that his humanity was as whole as it could be within the conditions of a fallen world. He was a human being with and for God, and with and for others. He was a human person

"led by the Spirit" (Mt 4:1) and so empowered for the wholeness of his humanity. He is life-giving and liberating in that he gives us a vision of what true life
can be, liberating us from false life, triviality, and meaninglessness.

The risen Jesus too remains truly human. He has not ceased to be who he is,
transformed and glorified beyond the limitations of space and time as we know
it. He "ascended into heaven," as we are told in legendary fashion in Acts 1:9
(and as the Apostles' Creed attests). Thus Jesus gives us a glimpse of what God
intends for our humanity beyond death. Part of the good news is that a human
being like us is, speaking metaphorically, "seated at the right hand of the Father,"
and so we too may hope to share, with him, in God's eternal life.

3. Jesus, as Saviour, meets us in our sin and guilt, offering forgiveness and reconciliation, undermining our self-righteousness, and inspiring a life of gratitude.

Jesus is foundational for us because he meets us in our deepest need, which
is our alienation from God, from one another, and from the created order around
us. If Jesus were not pertinent to our human brokenness, he would offer us no
hope, could not be foundational for us, or central to our worship, life, and
thought. Because God, in Jesus, reaches out to us as sinners, we have hope for
ourselves and our world. Yet that "Jesus died for us" is a difficult concept today.
Many find it impossible to affirm the centrality of Jesus Christ because talk of
atonement through his death is simply meaningless, even reprehensible. In what
sense can we appropriate this message today?

*The New Testament testimony that "Jesus died for us" reflects the Hebrew aware-
ness of the depth of human sin and the costliness of reconciliation with God.* If we
were willing simply to accommodate our faith and theology to the contemporary
mood, we might well neglect this whole theme. The language of sin is very
unpopular in our time. Secular folk, and even some church members, tend to smile
at the word sin as at something quaint. When I worked as a pastoral minister,
church members complained from time to time about having to say prayers of
confession, feeling that, while they may have had a few faults, they were hardly
sinners! The good news that we are forgiven and accepted by an unconditional
gracious love is not often received with enthusiasm by people who feel no great
need for any such grace. It is true, as Paul Tillich said half a century ago, that modern people have little anxiety of guilt, but suffer rather from an anxiety of emptiness, meaninglessness, and despair.[61] Or is that awareness of brokenness and
alienation often repressed in our time? In fact, while some have little awareness
of being in the wrong, others carry an overwhelming weight of guilt, either about
their personal sins or about the systemic inequities in which they are implicated.
The anxiety of guilt, or of repressed guilt, is surely a dimension of the anxiety of
meaninglessness and despair. Our estrangement from God, and therefore from any

sense of ultimate meaning, may render us cynical or hopeless about ourselves. However, the gospel message that "Jesus died for our sins," which should free us from these anxieties, is a message that few people today are able to appropriate as life-giving, liberating grace. An exploration of the roots of a Christian doctrine of sin in the faith of our Hebrew forebears may help us to grapple with what has become a widespread crisis in the theology of sin and grace.

The ancient Hebrews knew that the holy One who led them out of slavery in Egypt called them to be a holy people, living in justice under God's command-ments. The prophets were painfully aware of the idolatry and unfaithfulness of their own people, worshiping false gods and oppressing one another. From the golden calf in the time of Moses (Exod 32) to the human-made idols in the time of the prophets (Jer 10) they bowed down and worshiped deities of fertility or of prosperity, rather than the holy liberating Lord of the exodus. In this they failed to know God and were unable to trust or love God. The prophets saw that the worship of false gods led to cruelty toward one another: "they sell the righteous for silver, and the needy for a pair of sandals . . . , trample the head of the poor into the dust of the earth, and push the afflicted out of the way" (Amos 3:6-7). The mythical tale of the disobedience of Adam and Eve, symbolic of all humankind, reflects an awareness that humanity as a whole, and not only the covenant people, is deeply alienated from the Creator, seeking to be "as God" knowing good and evil for themselves (Gen 3:5). In the story of the tower of Babel, proud humanity seeks to invent itself, rather than to receive its life from the Creator, striving arrogantly to build "a tower with its top in the heavens" (Gen 11:4). This mythical wisdom is strangely relevant in our time in that ambi-tious technological humanity brings destruction upon itself. The sin of humanity, as the Christian theological tradition has long said, is most fundamentally pride, the desire to be ourselves absolute, to define ourselves according to our own free decision, setting aside all restraint and limitations that come from beyond us. The author of Genesis depicts the resulting estrangement of the man and the woman, and of both from the creatures around them (Gen 3:12-19) as the man and woman both refuse to take responsibility, accusing one another and then the serpent. According to the Genesis saga, violence and murder follow in the next genera-tion, when Cain murders his brother Abel. Today we are painfully aware of the triviality, the banality, and the pettiness and meanness that so often characterize human relationships, even when they do not spiral into anything as dramatic as murder. We realize that sin is often omission, or sloth, rather than proud or vio-lent commission. Moreover, we who live at the opening of the twenty-first cen-tury are perhaps more poignantly aware than ever of the macro level of human corruption. From the time of World War I, through economic depression, fascist and communist regimes of terror and oppression, the Second World War, the nuclear arms race, the increasing poverty of the third world, the ecological cri-sis, and so on, humanity has learned that greed and hatred have not diminished through the spread of Enlightenment reason, science, or education. Rather, new scientific knowledge and technological power have enabled vastly greater, more subtle, and more ghastly atrocities than ever before.

Consciousness of the broken, corrupted state of humanity was basic to ancient religions. The sacrificial system in Israel (not unlike many systems of sacrifice in many religions, including ancient European and African) is an indication of humanity's awareness that sin cannot be shrugged away, that forgiveness and reconciliation are costly.[62] In the book of Leviticus, the ritual of the Day of Atonement lay the sins of the people symbolically on the head of a goat, which was driven into the wilderness bearing the sins of the people (Lev 16:20-22). Blood sacrifices of oxen, lambs, or goats were presented as propitiation or expiation—appeasement or cleansing away of sins,[63] for "the life of the flesh is in the blood; and I have given it to you for making atonement" (Lev 17:11). One sacrifices the life of living creatures for the sake of reconciled life with God. Yet they knew that they themselves could not effect their reconciliation, for, as in the story of Abraham and Isaac, God provides the sacrifice (Gen 22:14).

Beyond the sacrificial system itself, the belief that innocent human suffering and death could bring reconciliation is reflected in the words of the Servant Song of Isaiah 52-53. The prophet speaks of a righteous one who "was wounded for our transgressions, bruised for our iniquities" (Is 53:12). The idea that reconciliation is costly and demands a price was expressed again centuries later in 4 Maccabees, a Jewish writing approximately contemporary with Jesus and the apostle Paul (first century C.E.).[64] An example of this is the noble prayer of a dying martyr: "Be merciful to your people and let our punishment be a satisfaction on their behalf, make my blood their purification and take my life as a ransom for theirs" (4 Macc 6:28).[65]

A grasp of this Hebraic/Jewish background in sacrifice and vicarous suffering is helpful for an understanding of the New Testament teaching that "Jesus died for us." Christians believed that Jesus had died "once and for all" and had canceled the need for any further sacrifices. Perhaps for this reason, many centuries after the abolition of animal and human sacrifice in our culture, the mentality of sacrifice now seems to us strange and remote, merely primitive. However, the insight and wisdom that lay behind centuries, even millennia, of sacrifice in many religions were the seriousness of sin and the costliness of reconciliation. Modern people who, because of their Christian history, no longer offer sacrifices but also do not believe in the sacrifice of Christ may tend to wink away human guilt.

Modern Christians may often rather casually assume that God easily forgives anything. The attitude is humorously expressed by a character of W. H. Auden: "I like committing crimes. God likes forgiving them. Really the world is admirably arranged."[66] It is what Dietrich Bonhoeffer called "cheap grace." But this fails to take sin and guilt seriously; the wrath and love of God are trivialized or sentimentalized, and therefore "grace" offers no profound response to the human need for reconciliation.

I suggest that, despite its strangeness to us, we need to open our minds to the alien wisdom contained in the proclamation that "Jesus died for us," which is so constantly taught in the New Testament. How did the first Christians reach this conclusion about Jesus' death? Out of the Easter experience of Jesus risen, the first Christians reflected back on his death in the light of his resurrection. The resurrection opened their eyes to see that his death must have had redemptive significance. But it was to their own Hebrew scriptures that they turned for the conceptual equipment by which his death could be understood. According to Paul, he "died for us" and "for our sins" (Rom 5:8; 1 Cor 15:3). God, like Abraham, "did not withhold his Son, but gave him up for us all" (Rom 8:32). For Mark, Jesus is the (Danielic) Son of Man who (like the Suffering Servant of Isaiah, or the martyr of Maccabees) came to "give his life a ransom for many" (Mk 10:45). For John he is the sacrificial "lamb of God who takes away the sin of the world" (Jn 1:29). The sacrifical theme is most thoroughly developed in the Letter to the Hebrews, where Jesus is "the merciful high priest in the service of God who made atonement for our sins" (Heb 2:17). As the blood of sacrifices offered life for the sake of life reconciled to God, now the blood of Jesus, the willing victim, affords life to all. Just as Jesus, seen from the perspective of the resurrection, was interpreted as Messiah out of the Hebrew tradition of hope, so also he was interpreted as priest and sacrificial victim.

No Christian doctrine of atonement has ever been officially promulgated by an ecumenical council, but doctrines of substitutionary atonement have been predominant through most of Christian history. Nevertheless, the idea that the God of the Hebrews requires blood sacrifice and death for the forgiveness of sin and reconciliation is questioned within the Hebrew canon itself, in historical Christian theology, and especially in contemporary theology. Can a doctrine of sacrificial, substitutionary atonement still be viable for us today?

The God of grace whom we encounter in Jesus Christ does not demand to be paid in blood and suffering for the forgiveness of sins. To suggest that God demands to be paid in blood for our sins is unimaginable and meaningless to most contemporary people; it also totally negates the gospel of grace and constitutes a block to genuine love for God. The Hebrew prophets already declared, many centuries before Jesus, that God does not demand sacrifice. The prophet Hosea proclaimed the "Word of the Lord" (Hos 4:1; 6:6): "I desire steadfast love and not sacrifice, the knowledge of God rather than burnt offerings." Jeremiah also declared on God's behalf: "in the day that I brought your ancestors out of the land of Egypt, I did not speak to them or command them concerning burnt offerings and sacrifices" (Jer 7:22). Isaiah too spoke for God: "What to me is the multitude of your sacrifices? says the Lord; I have had enough of burnt offerings of rams and the fat of fed beasts; I do not delight in the blood of bulls, or of lambs, or of goats" (Is 1:11).[67] The prophets called rather for justice and mercy toward the poor. It is debated whether the prophets seriously demanded the abolition of the sacrificial system or whether their intention was to ethicize sacrificial practices.[68] Whatever the case may have been so many centuries ago, we may well hear these texts today as encouragement to question whether we should think of God as having required propitiatory sacrifice, and therefore as good reason also to question whether God required the sacrificial death of Jesus. We note first our christological grounds for this view.

Jesus himself, as he is depicted in the Gospels, never claims that God commands ritual sacrifice. In Matthew Jesus refers favourably to the prophetic denunciation of sacrifice: "Go and learn what this means: I desire mercy, not sacrifice" (Mt 9:13). The most famous of his parables depicts God as a loving father who waits eagerly for the return of his son, falls upon him with embraces even before his words of repentance, and receives him home with overwhelming generosity. This is how Jesus thinks of his *Abba* God. Moreover, Jesus himself enacts radically gracious acceptance of sinners without reference to any required sacrificial payment. He announces in the same text: "I have come to call not the righteous but sinners." We see him reaching out in friendship to "tax collectors and sinners" and even eating and drinking with them (Lk 5:30; 7:34)—what Crossan calls "commensality"—in Jesus' time an act of extraordinary solidarity with marginalized and disreputable people.[69] He befriends the corrupt tax collector Zacchaeus and turns his life around (Lk 19), rescues the woman caught in adultery (Jn 8), and defends the "sinful woman" who anoints his feet in the home of a Pharisee (Lk 7). Repentance and change of life are called for, but forgiveness and acceptance precede any such repentance and are entirely free and cannot be paid for, ritually or in any other way. All of this leads us to the conclusion that the God about whom Jesus teaches us requires no payment of any kind for the forgiveness of sins.

That God the Father required, or willed, the torture and death of Jesus his Son as the price for forgiveness is a dangerous and destructive doctrine that has tragically damaged the faith of countless souls. Can we seriously love and worship such an almighty tyrant? How could such a monstrous deity seriously inspire us to free, gracious, and forgiving love toward one another, if God, God-self, requires such a brutal payment? Yet something like this has been the regular teaching of the church for centuries. For example, the classic teaching of Anselm of Canterbury (1033–1109) held that God was like the greatest of all feudal lords. When a lord is disobeyed, restoration of his honour was required in a way satisfactory to himself. The lord must be satisfied by suitable payment or punishment. The greater the lord and the greater the offence, the greater the required payment. Since God's lordship is infinitely high, any offence against his honour could be paid only by an infinite being. Thus "only a God-man can make the satisfaction by which man is saved."[70] This, according to Anselm, was why God became human (*Cur Deus homo*). God has shown love toward humanity in that God the Son "died voluntarily" for us.[71] Since we no longer live in a feudal system, this theology of atonement is very unconvincing to us today. Moreover, it seems to divide God into an angry Father and a compassionate Son, negating not only the love but the unity of God.

Very soon afterwards, Peter Abelard (1079–1142) of Paris, Anselm's younger contemporary, objected strenuously to Anselm's "satisfaction" theology of atonement:

> How cruel and wicked it seems that anyone should demand the blood of an innocent person as the price of anything, or that it should in any way please him that an innocent man should be slain. Still less that God should consider the death of his Son so agreeable that by it he should be reconciled to the whole world![72]

Nevertheless, sacrificial, substitutionary atonement has been preached and taught right up to our own century. Feminist theologians especially have pressed home powerfully a point similar to that of Abelard. Elizabeth Johnson says it eloquently:

> Feminist theology repudiates an interpretation of the death of Jesus as required by God in repayment for sin. Such a view today is virtually inseparable from an underlying image of God as an angry, bloodthirsty, violent and sadistic father, reflecting the very worst kind of male behavior.[73]

Dorothee Soelle also points out the danger of sado-masochistic pathology in a doctrine that glorifies suffering, so encouraging women and other people to put up with abuse.[74]

These considerations—biblical, traditional, and contemporary—lead us to abandon the language of "sacrifice to God" as it relates to christology. The God of Jesus does not demand retribution or payment of any kind, neither ritual sacrifice nor a brutal spilling of blood in exchange for the forgiveness of sins. It is unworthy to think of God sulking until sufficient torture and misery have occurred to "satisfy" his honour.[75] We need, then, to understand differently what it can mean to say that "Jesus died for us."

Jesus died a political death as a result of his faithfulness to God and his political solidarity with the poor and sinners. In this death, God, in Jesus, suffers the judgment and bears the cost of reconciliation. It is important that the single death of Jesus be seen in these two dimensions. Our New Testament sources show us that it was the political martyrdom of a prophetic figure who was aligned with the oppressed and poor, but also an event of God's compassionate solidarity and grace toward sinners. In a truly life-giving theology, these two dimensions must be understood together, as of a piece with each other.

The liberation theologies of the latter part of the twentieth century have pressed upon us an obvious truth that most of historical theology has overlooked: that the death of Jesus was indeed a political death. Jesus died because of the way he lived. He was "condemned as a political agitator," Jon Sobrino tells us.[76] His friendship and eating with all the outcasts of his day, his questioning of the rigid legalism and hypocrisy of those who held power in his nation, made him an affront and a challenge to their authority. His "alternative to the Roman imperial order," both spoken and acted out, made him dangerous indeed. Richard Horsley, out of his knowledge of Jesus' social/political context, paints a persuasive and poignant picture of Jesus working in village communities, where he "launched a mission not only to heal the debilitating effects of Roman military violence and economic exploitation, but also to revitalize and rebuild the people's cultural spirit and communal vitality."[77] Drawing on the rich resources of the covenantal tradition of Israel, Jesus called the people to solidarity and mutual assistance, asking them to set aside mutual blaming and to opt instead for radical forgiveness, love of neighbours, and the practice of radical generosity. Horsley writes:

> The renewed covenantal community that Jesus advocated and enacted also forms a striking contrast with frequent modern interpretation of his teachings. In the context of covenant renewal, "love" refers not to a feeling or an attitude, but to concrete economic practices in village community, such as canceling debts and generous mutual sharing of resources. In Jesus' program, and the underlying Mosaic covenantal tradition, there is far less of a sense of or emphasis on private property and far more of a sense of commonality in claims on and uses of economic resources than in modern capitalist society.[78]

To the religious ruling classes of his own people he appeared to call into question the law of Moses, the very law of God, on the basis of which they claimed their own social power and control. At the same time he fearlessly defended poor and disreputable women and kept the company of lepers (who were considered sinners and cursed by God) and the despised tax collectors, collaborators with Rome. He was not himself in collusion with the Romans, though he was capable of befriending and seeing good in them (Mt 8:10; Lk 7:9). The Sadducees, the wealthy priestly class, ruled the temple and held sway in cooperation with and with the permission of the occupying Roman forces. His attack on the temple trade as a "den of robbers" (Lk 19:46) was directly an attack on the influential Sadducees and, indirectly, upon their sponsors, the Romans. It was done in defence of God's honour and of the little people who were being cheated there and was perhaps the decisive public event that brought down upon him the wrath both of his powerful countrymen and the imperial power. The Roman governor, Pontius Pilate, had the reputation of being a brutal tyrant; he had crucified great numbers of people and would do anything necessary to keep order and control his province. Crossan makes a strong case for laying responsibility for the death of Jesus mainly at the feet of the Romans, and he charges the church with anti-Semitism in its accusation of the Jews.[79] At any rate, according to New Testament accounts, it was finally the Roman governor who condemned Jesus to die on a Roman cross. He died, then, as the enemy of both religious and political authorities, in a situation where politics and religion were not clearly distinguished. He died as a prophet and a political martyr, not unlike the righteous martyrs who were tortured to death at the hands of a foreign power in the time of the Maccabees. The charge against Jesus, posted on the cross over his head, was a political one, even if it was derisive in intention: "Jesus of Nazareth, King of the Jews" (Jn 19:19). It places Jesus together with many people of our own time who have "disappeared" and died miserably in the struggle for justice in Latin America, and many who were maimed, tortured, and murdered ignominiously in the South African struggle against apartheid. His execution is entirely understandable and historically common at the political level. None of this, however, justifies our centering on him in worship, in life, or in thought. A political death as such does not constitute him our Saviour. That he died *for us* is another level of reflection entirely.

The question about what Jesus understood about his death, whether he went to the cross with the intention of offering himself as a sacrifice for sin (as the Maccabean martyrs did) is difficult indeed. We are always on tenuous grounds when we imagine we can get inside the mind of the historical Jesus on the basis of the New Testament testimonies about him, which are postresurrection testimonies of the believing community. The debate between Marcus Borg and N. T. Wright is a good example of how two learned scholars can disagree on this matter.[80] Whereas Borg is convinced that the interpretation of Jesus' death as salvific is entirely a postresurrection understanding of the early church, Wright thinks that Jesus, knowing well the Maccabean as well as the Suffering Servant texts, would have had no difficulty imagining his death as having redemptive meaning.[81] Certainly such meaning is found on Jesus' lips in a number of Gospel texts (e.g., Mk 10:45; Mt 26:28), yet Borg may be right that these are projections back upon Jesus, reflecting the faith of the first Christians. While the biblical testimonies give us good reason to believe that Jesus went to his death willingly, speculation about how he understood it is perhaps not helpful. It was surely only after the resurrection that a salvific significance of the death could come clear to the first Christians.

In light of his resurrection, Jesus' death took on new redemptive meaning, since from hindsight, in view of the resurrection, the death itself was seen as a victory. Through the Spirit, Hebrews tells us, he was empowered to offer himself "without blemish" (Heb 9:14). As John sees it, his death in utter faithfulness, his refusal to bow to the powers of evil, was his true victory. According to John, as Jesus died on the cross he cried out, "It is finished" or "It is accomplished" (Jn

19:31).[82] John sees Jesus' "lifting up" on the cross as his true glory, which will draw all people to him (Jn 12:32-33).

But if we leave behind the notion that Jesus died as a sacrificial payment to God for the forgiveness of sins, how are we to understand the meaning of his death for us? It is impossible, if we take the scriptural witness seriously, to conclude that the cross had nothing at all to do with God's grace and pardon. It would be an impoverishment of the church to strip away the eucharistic words: "My body broken for you . . . , my blood shed for you." There is something precious here, not to be lost.

The key to any understanding of Jesus' death as an event for us must be the confession that he is "God with us," truly God and truly human. If we read the texts about Jesus' death for us in light of God's incarnation in him, we begin to see Jesus' suffering and death as *God's own suffering and death*, or as "death in God."[83] "God was in Christ reconciling the world," says Paul (2 Cor 5:19), that is, both pardoning and setting the world right. Christ cannot be separated from God, who is utterly one with him in his vulnerable humanity. The sacrificial "lamb of God who takes away the sin of the world" (Jn 1:29) is not, then, some poor creature whom God singles out for victimization, but the very Word of God who, according to the same chapter of John, was with God and was God and was in the beginning with God (Jn 1:1-2) and who became flesh in Jesus (1:14). Thus, God's giving of the "only Son" out of great love for the world (Jn 3:16) was nothing else but God's own agapeic *self*-giving. To say that Jesus is Saviour implies that Jesus is the embodiment of the liberating God of exodus, the enfleshment of God's own creating and saving Wisdom. We have seen that the theology of God's incarnation in Jesus flows from the experience of salvation through him. So also, in circular fashion, the theology of salvation by God's grace in Christ has to be understood in terms of incarnation.

But we still need to ask: Wherein lies the *necessity* for the suffering of Jesus? Even if his suffering was God's own suffering, do we still say that it was God's requirement, God's will? Is this a sovereign divine decision, meeting a need within God for judgment and punishment to be carried out? If so, are we not returning, willy-nilly, to a wrathful, vengeful God who is now not only sadistic but masochistic as well?

I suggest that this is where we need to keep together the two dimensions of Jesus' death—that it was a political death yet at the same time a reconciling and redemptive death, through which God brought the victory of resurrection. This political death then became the instrument through which God reached out to humanity in love and grace. It seems unhelpful to become involved in old debates about whether God foreordained or only foreknew the death of Jesus, whether the death of Jesus was "planned" by God. I suggest that it is an unworthy, overly anthropomorphic, and amoral concept of God that imagines God planning and willing the death of Jesus in such physical and spiritual agony. This would be incongruent with the compassionate God whom we encounter in Jesus. Rather, we must see God's activity in regard to the cross in historical/political terms, for the God of the Bible acts in freedom, taking initiative as well as responding to the contingencies of human activity. We may say, with hindsight, that the death of Jesus was inevitable or "necessary," given the reality of human fear and cruelty. Alienated humanity could not stand his strong freedom, his courageous challenge to hypocrisy and injustice, his holy innocence. Like the "just man" of Plato's *Republic*, it was inevitable and predictable that he would be crushed. This is why the first Christians understood Jesus' death as foretold by the prophets, as an event "according to the scriptures" (1 Cor 15:3). We may say, if rather anthropomorphically, that the death of Jesus "did not take God by surprise." We may say that his death was, in this sense, both predictable and a "necessity." The New Testament tells us that Jesus himself was not taken by surprise, but predicted his death (e.g., Mt 16:21). Perhaps it was with hindsight that the disciples understood the necessity of the cross: "Was it not necessary that the Messiah should suffer these things and then enter into his glory?" (Lk 24:26). But it is not the "necessity" of God's will for punishment and satisfaction (as in Anselm's account), but a necessity within the contingency of sinful human history. Jesus came calling the people to repentance and to God's reign of peace and love; he declared his gracious, forgiving *Abba,* offering free, unconditional love and pardon. The challenge was too great. This grace was an overwhelming affront to human pride. Powerful forces of his own society and of the imperial power joined together to be rid of him. He died asking his *Abba* to "forgive them, for they do not know what they are doing" (Lk 23:24). The response of sinful human beings to such a one was almost necessarily murderous.

We may say, with Jon Sobrino, that "the cross is the outcome of an incarnation situated in a world of sin."[84] To say "incarnation" is to say "cross." But was it pleasing, was it satisfying to God that human cruelty and cowardice nailed Jesus to the cross? Was God pleased to accept this substitute as a sacrifice for our sins? The suggestion is blasphemous. We need to stop preaching this destructive message, which destroys the love and worship of God. What was pleasing to God was Jesus' utter dedication and fidelity to God's reign, even unto death.[85] What was satisfying to God was a human being totally committed not only to his *Abba,* but to his sisters and brothers, especially the most oppressed and poor among them. His death was the necessary and predictable outcome of this very faithfulness, which was, in itself, a true victory.

And what of the judgment of God? Was judgment carried out on the cross? If we affirm this, we must do so very carefully. There is a great deal about judgment in the Bible, including the New Testament. Even the teaching of Jesus, as we have it in the New Testament, contains much of God's anger and judgment. Those who fail to be good stewards of God's reign are judged harshly, with the warning of "weeping and gnashing of teeth" (Mt 25:14-30). God is depicted as

full of wrath toward human lovelessness and unfaithfulness. In the story of
Lazarus and the rich man (Lk 16:19-31), the latter finds himself after death in the
agony of the flames of hell because he refused to care for the poor man at his
gate. Those who do not care for those in need are judged severely also in Jesus'
parable of the sheep and the goats:

> "You that are accursed, depart from me into the eternal fire prepared for
> the devil and his angels; for I was hungry and you gave me no food, I
> was thirsty and you gave me nothing to drink, I was a stranger and you
> did not welcome me, naked and you did not give me clothing, sick and
> in prison and you did not visit me. . . . Truly I tell you, just as you did
> not do it to one of the least of these, you did not do it to me." And these
> will go away into eternal punishment, but the righteous into eternal life.
> (Mt 25:41-46)

These texts must be heard in all their stark demand and urgent warning. In our
time we must see it as a demand not only for charitable deeds for the needy but
for social-justice action for structural and systemic change that addresses the
causes of poverty—something much more difficult. Yet read by themselves, they
throw us all into despair, for who among us can ever say that we have done
enough for the "least of these"? We all know very well that we have not. These
and other texts of judgment, read by themselves, carry no message of grace or
forgiveness for weak human beings and actually imply that we must earn our
way to God's love and favour. If we are to hear "good news" in relation to our
sin and guilt, these texts must be read together with texts of grace, such as the
parables of the lost sheep, the lost coin, and the lost son and forgiving father (Lk
15). They must also be read in light of the cross and resurrection and in the light
of the message of grace and forgiveness that we find throughout the theology of
the Synoptics, of Paul, of Hebrews, and of John. The texts of God's free pardoning grace do not simply negate the texts of God's wrath; rather, they proclaim
that God's pain in the face of our sin and God's wrath and judgment have fallen
upon Jesus and, in him, upon God's very self. That Jesus is the "lamb of God"
and the "ransom for many" tells us that God has not shrugged off our sinfulness.
The consequences of sin—condemnation, death, and hell—have fallen *upon
God,* in Jesus: "For our sake [God] made him to be sin who knew no sin, so that
in him we might become the righteousness of God" (2 Cor 5:21). Again, "Jesus
was handed over to death for our trespasses and was raised for our justification"
(Rom 4:25). For 1 Peter, "He himself bore our sins in his body on the cross, so
that, free from sins, we might live for righteousness; by his wounds you have
been healed" (1 Pet 2:24).

Can we take these texts of judgment and grace seriously without falling back
into an unacceptable theology of satisfaction? I suggest that, while the texts grow

out of sacrificial language, they need to be understood in terms of God's painful outreach for the sake of our reconciliation.[86] God, in Christ, comes near to us, offering love and pardon, calling us to repentance and reconciliation. But reconciliation is always costly, as we know from our ordinary experience of human relationships. When grave offence and deep hurt have occurred among people, whether among individuals, races, nations, or classes, reconciliation is never easy or cheap. The overcoming of alienation usually involves painful confrontation and honest communication, but the one who forgives does not get "paid." Rather, the one who forgives pays the price and bears the cost. We are told that "God was in Christ reconciling the world" (2 Cor 5:19). The cost of reconciliation, then, falls upon God, in Christ. Through the human faithfulness of Jesus, with whom God is utterly one, *God bears the judgment,* and "the Judge is judged in our place."[87] William Placher states the matter nicely:

> Christ stands with us in our place of sin, and therefore it is no longer a place separated from God. . . . We were running away from God looking for a place to hide, and we found that God was running beside us, sharing our fear and shame. The sense that we had irreparably damaged our relation with God disappears, and we can stop running away.[88]

That Christ, God with us, stands with us in the place of sin does not mean that God willed the atrocious event of his terrible death, for the gracious *Abba* of Jesus does not will that human beings should be vicious and hateful or that anyone should suffer the degradation and despair that Jesus endured on the cross. That Jesus cried out "My God, my God, why have you forsaken me?" shows Jesus' human experience of forsakenness and abandonment, the very pit of human desolation and despair. It does not mean that God demanded a sacrifice, but that God, at one with Jesus, shared that desolation and despair with us.[89] The event of God's self-giving in Jesus' life and death was the exact opposite, then, of payment or retribution. Retribution is entirely set aside by the freedom of grace, and no one is punished as a substitute for others. Yet the pain and cruelty of sin fall upon Jesus and, in him, upon God, with whom he is wholly one.

It is all the more evident, then, why Jesus Christ is central and foundational for us: Crucified and risen, Jesus, God with us, reconciles us to God and so meets us in the deepest need of our brokenness and alienation.

There is so much more of the theology of salvation for which we have no space here: justification and sanctification, judgment and repentance. The grace discovered in Jesus means, existentially, that the struggle to live in righteousness, to follow Jesus in a life of compassion and courage, is not an onerous duty but a response of gratitude. It is life not under law but under grace. That we are loved for ourselves and not for our good works is life-giving, liberating us for a life of gratitude. Suffice it to say here that the theology of the reconciliation of the whole world with God through God's sharing in our universal humanity gives us hope that all God's children will ultimately say yes to God's outreaching grace, that none will finally be lost, and that "the earth will be full of the knowledge of the Lord, as the waters cover the sea" (Is 11:9).

4. Jesus reveals the triune God, the eternal communion of love, ground of our hope.

Jesus is foundational for us because in him, and only in him, we know God as the eternal communion of love. The distinctive Christian doctrine of God as Trinity and the peculiar trinitarian character of Christian worship and prayer to God—through Christ, in the Spirit—depend entirely on the revelation of God in Jesus Christ.

The doctrine of the Trinity is rooted initially in the trinitarian pattern of the Gospel story, which reflects the identity of Jesus as the Son who reveals the Father in the power of the Spirit. We know God in the way that we do because in Jesus we encounter true God in his true humanity. Yet Jesus is never apart from the Spirit who fills and empowers him and the *Abba* who sent him. In this way Jesus, in his twofold relation with the Spirit and the Father, is foundational for our specifically trinitarian knowledge of God.

To reiterate briefly our earlier discussion of the concept of revelation, we said that revelation implies something radically given that we otherwise could not know. Revelation did not occur for the first time with Jesus of Nazareth, who must be understood in terms of the tradition of revelation that preceded him. Revelation reached the people of Israel through remarkable liberative, life-giving events, and through inspired, courageous, prophetic voices who spoke God's Word. God also acted into the world by the Spirit. The Wind or Spirit of God is at work in the events of creation (Gen 1:2; Ps 104:30), exodus (15:21), military struggle (e.g., throughout Judges, 1 Samuel), prophetic inspiration (e.g., Ezek 2:2; Mic 3:8). The messianic hope of the prophets looked forward to one who would come in the power of the Spirit (e.g., Is 11:1; 61:1). But the long history of God speaking and acting in the Hebrew tradition culminates, for Christians, in the self-disclosure of God's own Word made flesh, Jesus the Christ, who comes in the Spirit's presence and power. The trinitarian pattern emerges in narrative form first in the event of Jesus' baptism. The Spirit is said to descend upon him, accompanied by the Father's voice: "This is my Son, the beloved, with whom I am well pleased" (Mt 3:17; Lk 3:22). The Spirit is with Jesus to overcome the power of temptation (Mt 4:1; Lk 4:1) and is upon him to fulfill his role as Servant and Messiah (Lk 4:18; Mt 12:18) and to do his work of healing (Mt 12:28). So convinced are the early Christians that Jesus is the unique bearer of the Spirit, that Matthew and Luke proclaim that he was conceived by the Spirit and born of a virgin (Mt 1:18; Lk 1:35).[90]

As we noted in our previous discussion, there is something new here where revelation is concerned. Jesus is not one more inspired prophetic leader and teacher, but the unique messianic bearer of the Spirit. Because he is raised from the dead and brings God's reign decisively into the world; because he liberates, saves, gives life by reconciling us to God, Jesus is perceived as more than a prophet. He does not merely *speak* God's Word; he *is* God's Word. He does not only *bring* God's light, but *is* God's light. He does not simply proclaim and interpret a salvific event; he himself, in his life, death, and resurrection, *is* the saving event. The first Christians related to him as to God, prayed to him and through him, praised and thanked him, obeyed and followed him, as we still do today. The incarnation of God in Jesus Christ, within the trinitarian pattern of the Gospel narrative, is, then, the root of the doctrine of the Trinity.

However, when we say that Jesus as true God reveals God, we do not say simply that Jesus is God. Such a simple equation is too bald and misleading, as though the equation could be turned around to say "God is Jesus." Most emphatically, Christians have never said that God is Jesus. Certainly Jesus of Nazareth does not exhaust the infinite, eternal reality of God, Creator of the universe! Christian faith has always avoided a christomonism (Christ-only-ism), in which Christ supersedes or even eclipses the Spirit of God, or God the Father. It would be more than absurd, of course, for the human Jesus to subordinate either the Spirit who empowered him or his *Abba,* who sent him. We have to say, then, that of course Jesus is not more central or more foundational than God! We are theocentric by being christocentric. When we speak of Jesus as central, we mean that he is *epistemologically* central. It is through him that we *know* God. If we wish to speak of the *ontological* center of all things, we must speak not of Jesus alone but of the triune God, for Jesus is truly God only in relation to the *Abba* and the Spirit.

Early, implicitly trinitarian texts disclose that Trinity language was part of the scene at least as early as the 50s C.E., e.g., the benediction still used universally in the churches—2 Corinthians 13:13: "The grace of the Lord Jesus Christ, the love of God, and the communion of the Holy Spirit be with all of you." In addition, perhaps two or three decades later, we have the almost universal baptismal formula of the churches found in Matthew 28:19: "baptizing them in the name of the Father and of the Son and of the Holy Spirit." Again, we need not think that these are the *ipsissima verba* (the very words) of Jesus himself. Most commentators today would think it unlikely that Jesus himself had worked out a doctrine of the Trinity or spoke in an explicitly trinitarian manner. We may believe that he lived a relationship of intimate unity with his *Abba* and the Spirit, but it is unlikely that even the risen Jesus spoke in trinitarian doctrinal language, as Christians did years later after a long struggle to understand. To insist that he did would amount to a kind of docetism—that he did not share the limitations of our human knowledge. What interests us here, though, is that Christians were expressing their faith in God in this trinitarian way from a very early date.

The doctrine of the Trinity, of course, is a postresurrection ecclesial understanding. Critical scholarship has helped us to see particularly that much of the "Father and Son" language of the New Testament is postresurrection, early-church confessional language. For example, the use of "Father" to refer to God increases from the earlier to the later Gospels, appearing four times in Mark, fifteen in Luke, forty-nine in Matthew, and 109 in John. "Father" in the mouth of Jesus is even more interesting: Mark, 1; Q (common source of Matthew and Luke), 1; special in Matthew, 1; special in Luke, 2; John 73![91] The much later and very different Gospel, John, usually thought to reflect a later period of Christian reflection, makes much of the term "Father," and evidently places it on the lips of Jesus. *Abba* (the Aramaic "father" as distinct from the much more common Greek *patēr*) occurs in the mouth of Jesus only once, Mark 14:36, where Jesus prays in the garden of Gethsemane prior to his death. It occurs also twice in the letters of Paul: Galatians 4:6 is quite an early trinitarian expression: "God has sent the Spirit of his Son into our hearts, crying, 'Abba, Father!'" This seems to indicate an early trinitarian usage of *Abba* among Aramaic-speaking Christians, who may be following the Aramaic usage of Jesus himself. The other usage in Paul is in Romans 8:15: "When we cry, 'Abba! Father!' it is that very Spirit bearing witness with our spirit that we are children of God." We see developing here an early trinitarian tradition (keeping in mind that the letters of Paul are earlier than the Gospels) in which Christ, the Spirit, and the *Abba* are mentioned together. This indication that Jesus may not have used the term "Father" overwhelmingly does not necessarily imply that he did not use it at all; probably he did use it, and the texts reflect this. The prayer that Jesus taught beginning "our Father" (Mt 6:9; Lk 11:2) may very well reflect a vividly remembered usage. In his parable of the loving father and the delinquent son, Jesus teaches us to think of God as a loving Father. It would seem to make "Father" an important metaphor that Jesus used in speaking of God. The use of "Father" should not be rejected, then, but an analysis of its New Testament usage does relativize its theological significance to some degree. Evidently, the name "Father" for God and its use in trinitarian theology were especially the usage of the postresurrection church. Only after the resurrection, looking back on Jesus' life and death in light of it, could Christians begin to understand Jesus as "Son of the Father," and to begin to formulate a concept of God as triune. Both memory of Jesus and post-resurrection faith in Jesus seem to be reflected in Matthew 11:27: "no one knows the Son except the Father, and no one knows the Father except the Son." So also John 10:30: "The Father and I are one," and 14:8: "Whoever has seen me has seen the Father." These texts speak of a remembered intimacy of Jesus with God his *Abba,* about whose love he spoke so vividly.

Quite apart from words ascribed to Jesus, we find nascently trinitarian concepts and expressions cropping up quite early, especially concerning the relation of Jesus to God: for example, 1 Corinthians 8:6: "for us there is one God, the Father, from whom are all things and for whom we exist, and one Lord, Jesus

Christ, through whom are all things and through whom we exist." Paul speaks of Jesus as "our wisdom" (1 Cor 1:30). These texts resonate with the wisdom literature of late pre-Christian Judaism in which *Hokmah/Sophia,* the female, maternal divine presence, is said to be the divine agency through which God creates (e.g., Prov 8:22-31). In these Pauline texts the divine Wisdom, through whom God created all things and through whom God is universally at work in the world, is identified with Jesus—that is, Jesus *is* God's Wisdom among us. A similar high christology, also suggestive of Wisdom and nascently trinitarian, appears in Colossians 1:16: "in him all things in heaven and on earth were created, things visible and invisible . . . all things have been created through him and for him." The prologue to John's Gospel, probably much later, also sees Jesus as the Word who was with God and was God from the beginning, the one through whom all things were created. The Word, the source of life and light, comes to God's people but is rejected by them. This too resembles the *Hokmah/Sophia* of Hebrew wisdom and Greek apocryphal literature (see Prov 8; Wis 7).[92] Given the feminine character of Wisdom, these texts encourage us to consider whether exclusive usage of the Father/Son language is strictly necessary for trinitarian thought.

The masculine Father/Son language is not essential to trinitarian faith. A major problem has arisen in the past few decades about the language of Father and Son. Christian women have pointed out that a deity who is two-thirds masculine, Father and Son, will not do. In fact the Spirit too has usually been referred to as "he," depicting a totally male deity. Mary Daly put it starkly: "If God is male, then the male is God."[93] She and many others like her have simply left Christianity behind as a hopelessly androcentric male religion, worshiping a male God, led by male priests and often espousing male values. Others have set aside or downplayed the Trinity as a patriarchal doctrine. Virtually all feminist and pro-feminist theologians, male and female, including those who have remained steadfastly within the church, have added their voices to this protest against male imagery for God. Elizabeth Johnson, for example, when she writes about the Trinity, speaks of "freeing the symbol from literalness." We recognize, as all classical theology has recognized, that all our language about God speaks analogically or metaphorically of the divine mystery and falls short of the true glory and majesty of God.[94] Thus, we know that when we speak of God as Father we should not imagine that God is literally a male progenitor. When Jesus speaks of his Father, he invites us to think of God as a strong and loving parent, but unless we seriously think of God as male, the exclusive use of the male paternal metaphor is both unnecessary and unhelpful. While Jesus apparently spoke of God as Father, he probably did not do so as exclusively or overwhelmingly as the Gospel of John suggests. According to Luke, Jesus also likened God to a woman sweeping her house for a lost coin (Lk 15:8-10); and, according to Matthew 23:27, Jesus likened himself to a mother hen! Jesus stands here in a long Hebrew tradition of using many varied metaphors and images of the divine reality, including female and especially maternal ones. Deuteronomy can speak of God giving birth to Israel (32:18); Hosea compares God to a mother bear defending her cubs (13:8); Isaiah speaks of God as "like a woman in labour" who will cry out and "gasp and pant" (chaps. 13-14); and Israel is described as having been born from God's "womb" (Is 46:3).

As many feminist theologians have pointed out, it is simply idolatrous to insist overwhelmingly on one metaphor of the divine reality, such as Father, elevating this one limited human concept to absoluteness as *the revealed name of God.*[95] "Father" is obviously a term that pertains primarily to human male progenitors. The outcome of such exclusive naming is the legitimization of male/paternal superiority, since religious language powerfully shapes human relationships and social systems.[96] It also overlooks the ineffability of God and the culturally conditioned nature of biblical testimony. Since Jesus probably addressed God as Father and spoke of God as like a father, it is certainly not a term to be banned, and it still carries great value, providing for boys and men the image of a gentle, loving, and self-giving father, a model for true human maleness and fatherhood.[97] Yet it is rightly balanced by other names and metaphors. In a time such as ours, when both women and men are aware of the fully equal dignity and capabilites of female and male persons, we have become aware of the appropriateness of speaking of God also as Mother. As Johnson has pointed out so well, we can also speak of the divine reality in Jesus as other than "Son." Although "Son" seems to fit well with the male humanity of Jesus and is important in trinitarian discourse, it is not the only way to speak of the divinity of Jesus. The term "Word" (*logos*), also grammatically masculine in Greek, is a biblical alternative, but we can just as properly speak of Jesus as the incarnation of the divine Wisdom (*sophia*), a feminine noun in Greek that calls to mind the maternal imagery of the divine presence found in Hebrew and Greek Jewish scripture.[98]

The Spirit, who is the Spirit of Christ and truly God, reveals Jesus, who is the Christ of the Spirit. The relation of Jesus to his *Abba* would seem to yield only a *binity,* and, true enough, it took longer for the church to be clear about the divinity of the Spirit as a distinct "person" of the triune God. As we have seen, however, Spirit language is also present from the beginning, and the recognition of the unique identity of Jesus is seen to be dependent on the working of the Spirit.[99] The *Ruah* (also a metaphor, Wind, Breath) of the Hebrew scriptures, at work in the exodus and prophetic inspiration, is the same Spirit who is now at work in the life, death, and resurrection of Jesus. Jesus, as we have seen, is said to be conceived by the Spirit, baptized by the Spirit, filled with the Spirit (Lk 4:1). He is anointed by the Spirit for his liberative work, performs works of power and authority by the Spirit, and, according to Hebrews, offers himself in death by the power of the eternal Spirit (Heb 9:14). According to Paul, through the Spirit the crucified Jesus is raised to new life (Rom 8:11). The Spirit, then, is seen to be accompanying Jesus at every stage of his life, death, and resurrection. If the Spirit is to be called "Spirit of Christ," then Jesus should be called "the Christ of the Spirit."[100]

At the same time, the Spirit of God, or Holy Spirit, is also seen to be the Spirit of Christ, or Spirit of the Son (Gal 4:6; Phil 1:19). Romans 8:9-11 shows how the language of Spirit is linked very early to the language of God and of Christ:

> You are not in the flesh; you are in the Spirit, since the Spirit of God dwells in you. Anyone who does not have the Spirit of Christ does not belong to him. But if Christ is in you, though the body is dead because of sin, the Spirit is life because of righteousness. If the Spirit of him who raised Jesus from the dead dwells in you, he who raised Christ from the dead will give life to your mortal bodies also through his Spirit that dwells in you.

We note that the Spirit is the "Spirit of God" who indwells believers, and this same Spirit is identified also as "Christ in you" and "the Spirit of Christ." The unity of Jesus Christ with the Spirit is stated even more sharply in 1 Corinthians 15:45, where Jesus is called a "life-giving Spirit." Again in 2 Corinthians 3:17 we hear the conviction that the Holy Spirit, present with us here and now, is the continuing presence of the risen Christ: "Now the Lord [*kyrios*, i.e., Jesus] is the Spirit, and where the Spirit of the Lord is, there is freedom." All of these ways of speaking about the Spirit are used interchangeably in a way that moves Christian God-talk in a trinitarian direction. God, Christ, and Spirit are one, yet distinguishable. They live within us and within each other. This manner of speaking reflects the Christian experience that God is encountered in this threefold way. "God" and "Father" tend to be used more or less interchangeably in New Testament literature, yet it is clear that the Son and Spirit are no less God, since they also, as one with the Father, also overcome the power of death, and bring us life and salvation. After much controversy about the question of the divinity of the Holy Spirit, the Council of Constantinople (381 C.E.), under the influence especially of the Cappadocian father Basil of Caesarea, affirmed the divinity of the Spirit, "who proceeds from the Father, who with the Father and the Son is worshiped and glorified, who spoke by the prophets."[101]

Paul speaks of the Spirit in a strikingly epistemological way in his first letter to the Corinthians, where he writes about the "foolishness of God which is wiser than human wisdom, and God's weakness which is stronger than human strength" (1 Cor 1:25). This is the scandalous, surprising character of revelation, as radically given—not a human hypothesis or theory, not something that wise human beings would find convincing. Revelation gives us something that "no eye has seen, nor ear heard, nor the human heart conceived" (1 Cor 2:9). Paul

sees the gift of the Spirit as a share in God's own self-knowledge: "no one comprehends what is truly God's except the Spirit of God. Now we have received not
the spirit of the world, but the Spirit that is from God" (1 Cor 2:11-12). The
astonishing claim here is that, through faith in Christ, and by the gift of the Spirit,
we know God "from the inside," as it were. God is known by participation in the
divine life, that is, by dwelling "in Christ" and "in the Spirit." This Pauline statement coheres with the Johannine belief that those who believe and live in Jesus
already have eternal life (Jn 3:36; 6:40, 47, 54). John states that Jesus asks the
Father to send the Spirit of truth: "You know him because he abides in you" (Jn
14:17-18). Because Jesus lives in his Father, and his disciples in him and he in
them (Jn 14:20), they have a share in the relationship of the Son to the Father (Jn
17:21). We may see this as a kind of pneumatic/christomysticism which arose in
the early church. God is known—in worship and prayer, faith and following—in
relationship, which is possible only because God shares God's life, through
Christ and Spirit, with human beings!

*The "economic Trinity" reveals the "immanent Trinity," disclosing the Triune
God as an eternal communion of love.* We could not know anything of this, of
course, without our epistemological foundation in Jesus Christ. In Jesus we
encounter One who is truly God in relation to his *Abba* and in relation to the
Spirit. As we have seen, in the earliest Christian language of worship and testimony, the three are frequently spoken of together as one, and always in a relation that may be spoken of as *perichōrēsis,* mutual indwelling. There are not, of
course, two trinities. The "economic Trinity"—the three-in-oneness of God as
we meet God through Christ and Spirit—reveals the "immanent Trinity"—God's
eternal triunity. The point of the immanent Trinity is that God does not merely
appear to us to be triune but *is truly* an eternal communion of love. The distinction is important. Presumably God could be God without creation and without
relation to us, for the sovereign Creator, Lord of exodus and resurrection, does
not depend on us for her own being and existence. Our confidence in God
depends on God's *aseity*—God is *ab sola,* from Godself alone, absolute. God's
eternal reality as triune does not depend on us. God is not exhausted by, or
defined in terms of her triune relation to us. Yet, if God's revelation is authentically *self*-revelation, then it reveals *Who God really is.* What God is in self-
revelation, God is antecedently in Godself (Barth).[102] Catherine LaCugna has
stated the matter clearly: "The identity of the economic and immanent Trinity
means that what God has revealed and given in Christ and Spirit *is* the reality of
God as God from all eternity."[103] That is, if the way in which we know God as
three-in-one does not reveal the triune way in which God actually is, then God
has not revealed God's own self, and a hidden God remains unknown behind the
revealed God.[104] This is inadmissible if God is to be trusted, loved, and worshiped.

This was essentially the problem with the suggestion of Sabellius, who proposed in the third century a view of the Trinity that came to be known as Sabellianism or modalism. He argued that God is a singular monarchical Being, who, however, manifests himself in three ways, as Father, as Son, as Spirit—that is, as Creator, as Redeemer, as Life-giver. It is as if I, as a single human person, were at the same time husband, father, and teacher. I have these three "modes" of operation and relationality, sometimes acting as husband, sometimes as father, sometimes as teacher, but I am singular in myself. But there is no good reason to stop at three, since in various relationships and tasks I also function as son, as brother, as friend, as writer, as builder, as swimmer, as wood cutter, and so on. There is also no good reason, within a modalist view of the Trinity, to stop at three. The singular Deity is not only Creator, Redeemer, Life-giver, but also Ruler, Lawgiver, Judge, and so on. According to the modalist scheme, *Who God is*, in Godself, is forever hidden behind God's appearances, the masks or modes of the one unitary Being. The concept is thus called modalism, in that it denies that there are three interrelating "Persons" within the unity of God but only modes or functions of operation. Existentially, it would mean that when we relate to God as Christ, as *Abba,* and as Spirit, we are not directly in fellowship with God as God actually is. It would no longer make sense to speak of being "in God" by being "in Christ" and "in the Spirit." The other, related problem with modalism is that it does not take into account the relationality of Christ with his Father and the Spirit. What we are confronted with in the Gospel story is not a singular monadic Person relating to us in three ways, but something—Someone—much more profound and mysterious: God in relation to God! To dismiss the immanent Trinity, or God's own eternal triunity, misses the relationality of God in Godself, which is part of the Gospel narrative.

Karl Rahner offered an illuminating and now famous statement: "The economic Trinity is the immanent Trinity, and the immanent Trinity is the economic Trinity, and vice-versa."[105] Thus, the Trinity is not to be thought of as someone or something back behind God's self-revelation. God in God's self-revelation is Godself. This is precisely the glorious thing that was insisted upon at Nicaea and Constantinople, in opposition to Arianism. In Christ we are in touch with God's very self. In the Spirit God herself dwells within us and we in God. God does not merely touch us with a long pole or send messengers or delegates. If the economic Trinity is the immanent Trinity, and the immanent Trinity is the economic Trinity, then the Trinity is not a hidden Someone behind the self-revealing God, but the self-revealing God *herself!* When we behold Jesus in relation to his *Abba,* empowered by the Spirit, this *is* the Trinity.

The rejection of modalism and the insistence on the eternal reality of the three within God always run the risk of tritheism. A multiplicity of gods is completely contrary to the very heart of the Hebrew tradition out of which Jesus came, and Jesus himself is cited by the Gospel of Mark as proclaiming the traditional Jewish *Shema:* "Hear O Israel: the Lord our God, the Lord is one" (Mk 12:29). For the Jews, and for Christians too, there is no other God than the one who brought Israel out of Egypt, and for Christians, it is the same holy One who raised Jesus from the dead. Moreover, a multiplicity of gods would mean ontological chaos! It is often pointed out that the doctrine of the Trinity was formulated precisely to avoid tritheism. Since Christ, his Father, and the Spirit are each divine, they must be thought as one. We cannot enter here into the long complex debates of the ancient fathers about the Father and his "two hands"—Son and Spirit (Irenaeus)—or the three persons of one substance or being (Tertullian, Origen). The Christian tradition has generally understood that God is one, in that the Son and Spirit proceed from the one Father. Various church fathers proposed that the one God is like the sun, which shines forth multiple rays of sunshine, which are truly the presence of the sun with us.[106] God as Spirit, as Light, is not contained in one place or space, or even one Person. Yet, insisting on the oneness of God, the Cappadocian fathers taught that the three Persons have no independent existence; they live entirely within one another and never act apart from one another. When God acts toward creation, it is the Father who acts in the Son, through the Spirit. Augustine, following them, thought of the one God existing as three in a community of eternal love, but understood the oneness in terms of a psychological analogy, comparing the three persons to faculties of one human person.[107] Of particular interest to us here is the later trinitarian theology of John of Damascus. Following a strain of thought already present in the Cappadocians, he spoke of an eternal *perichōrēsis,* or mutual indwelling, wherein the Father exists in the Son and the Son in the Father, and both of them in the Spirit, in such a way that the Spirit exists also in the Father and the Son. They dwell in one another within a dynamic circulation of life and love. While the three are distinct from one another and are truly in relation, they are not three different individuals who first exist separately and then come together, but a perfect oneness whose very being consists in relationality.[108] All this is rooted, of course, in the Synoptic Gospel story of the Spirit with Jesus and the Father, the Pauline and Johannine christologies and pneumatologies, and confirmed by the doctrinal decisions of the councils of Nicaea, Constantinople, and Chalcedon.

The theology of the immanent Trinity and the perichoretic relations of the three Persons should not be taken to mean that the mystery of God's triunity is entirely known to us. God as Trinity remains mystery, both as immanent and as economic Trinity, though it is in the economic Trinity that we are confronted with the mystery of God's triunity. We encounter unfathomable mystery. When we speak of the Father begetting the Son, and of the Spirit proceeding from the Father, and of the three mutually indwelling one another, we speak biblically, or at least in a manner congruent with the Bible—but we do not know exactly what we say! A healthy dose of "apophaticism," or *via negativa,* is required when we speak of God as Trinity. We know our words fall short; they point to realities beyond our comprehension. Elizabeth Johnson states the matter humorously:

"Clear and distinct trinitarian terms give the impression that theology has God sighted through a high-powered telescope, with descriptions of the interactions between three persons intended to be taken in some literal sense."[109]

We may ask, then, whether it is important to speak of the mystery of the immanent Trinity at all. Have we moved beyond our ability to know? Further, does this have any practical significance for Christian discipleship? I have already suggested that it has significance for our sense of truly knowing God as God is, and it is therefore important for our love and worship of God. Though aware of the limitations of our knowledge, we are not agnostics about God. We believe we really do know God, not because we are naturally capable of it but because God has gifted us with a share in God's own self-knowledge. This knowledge is basic to confident faith and hope, essential to confident preaching, to heartfelt worship, and to committed following.

But modern liberal thought generally has tended to dismiss the Trinity as irrelevant to practical life. Immanuel Kant, for example, argued that the Trinity has "no practical relevance at all. . . . Whether we are to worship three or ten persons in the Divinity makes no difference."[110] For Kant the whole point of religion and God is to inspire good behaviour, promising rewards or punishments on moral grounds; and it is understandable that he thought the Trinity irrelevant. But this merely pragmatic moral monotheism seems impoverishing, leaving us nothing of wonder, offering us nothing profound for our contemplation.[111] This modern moralism offers law, with much concern for knowledge as power, but little of knowledge as awe and adoration, and less of grace. We cannot agree to reduce faith and worship to moral pragmatism. On the other hand, it could well be that the way we think of God may in the long term carry great practical significance for the way we live, as individuals and as communities of people. The feminists have pointed out the destructiveness of thinking about God as male. So also, to think of God as a monolithic, solitary ego may also carry long-term negative consequences at a practical and political level. The contemporary theologians of the "Social Trinity" believe that serious attention to the immanent Trinity is the best way to a vision of God that is life-giving and liberating.

Jürgen Moltmann was the major proponent and initiator in the late twentieth century of the theology of the Social Trinity, and his approach and emphases have been picked up by a number of liberation and feminist theologians, most notably Leonardo Boff and Elizabeth Johnson. Their view also has much in common with the Eastern Orthodox trinitarian thought of John Zizioulas.[112]

Monarchical monotheism, or modalism, Moltmann argued, has been more or less operative in western Christendom for most of its history. Though the immanent Trinity has been correctly acknowledged, the effective operative theology as been essentially monotheistic, by which he means, pejoratively, a doctrine of God that begins with and focuses on God's unity, with the Trinity added on. This stress on the one God went hand in hand with the "classical theism" or "monotheism" of God as omnipotent, omniscient, immutable, and impassible.

The triune God, on the other hand, is the God of the cross, the vulnerable God. A God who cannot suffer cannot love, says Moltmann. But the triune God, who in Christ enters into misery and death with and for human beings, who cries out "My God, my God, why have you forsaken me?" is the God who loves and who can be loved. This is because "God's being is in suffering and the suffering is in God's being itself, because God is love."[113] A theology of the cross needs to be a trinitarian theology in which the Son's suffering and death and the Father's grief at the loss of the Son come together in the unity of the Spirit. The cross, then, is an event within the life of God: "What happened on the cross was an event between God and God."[114]

Such reflection, especially such an emphasis on God's suffering, has been mostly absent from the older theological tradition. It would not have served the interests of a dominant Christendom as this began to take shape in the early Constantinian era, which had an ideological interest in the singularity of an omnipotent ruling deity. The emphasis on the unity of God and the neglect of the triune God's self-differentiation had political implications, Moltmann argues. The emperor Constantine saw value in Christianity for cementing together his empire under one God; the end of polytheism would mean the end of a multiplicity of nations and the universal reign of the *pax Romana*. Eusebius of Caesarea, closely associated with Constantine, articulated the matter well: "The one God, the one heavenly king and the one sovereign nomos [law] and logos [Word or rationality] corresponds to the one king on earth."[115] Thus, Moltmann points out, "The idea of unity in God therefore provokes both the idea of the universal, unified church, and the idea of the universal, unified state: one God–one emperor–one church–one empire."[116] Monarchical monotheism as a vision of God, then, tends to legitimize monarchy, domination, and inequality. But God as Trinity must be the vulnerable God who enters into human misery and death with us and for us. If the mutual indwelling, mutual love, and equality of the three are taken quite seriously, the Trinity "can be seen as a model for any just, egalitarian . . . social organization. On the basis of their faith in the triune God, Christians postulate a society that can be the image and likeness of the Trinity."[117] The social order that would best correspond to the perichoretic Trinity would be some form of genuine democracy and some kind of socialism.[118] "The Trinity is our social program," Boff declares.[119]

Johnson, from her feminist perspective, sounds a similar note. For her, the triunity of God signifies that "relatedness" as love, rather than "solitary ego," is the essential thing to be said about God.

> The ontological priority of relation in the idea of the triune God has a powerful affinity with women's ownership of relationality as a way of being in the world. It furthermore challenges classical theism's typical concentration on singleness in God that has been so consistently reprised in a patriarchal sense. Since the persons are constituted by their

relationships to each other, each is unintelligible except as connected
with the others. Relation is the very principle of their being. . . . At the
heart of holy mystery is not monarchy but community; not an absolute
ruler, but a threefold *koinonia.*[120]

The theology of Social Trinity, in which Moltmann, Johnson, Boff, and others
build on the Cappadocians and John of Damascus, articulates the unity of God
mainly in the doctrine of *perichōrēsis,* emphasizing the relationality of three who
are "other" to one another, yet one. This approach is controversial among trinitarian theologians.[121] Moltmann has been accused, by such authors as Walter
Kasper and George Hunsinger, of flirting dangerously with tritheism, for so
emphasizing the relationality and the threeness of God.[122] Yet it seems odd that
they wish to affirm the immanent Trinity but have so much difficulty with the
relationality and interpersonal intersubjectivity of the three. Moltmann's argument seems decisive:

If there is no "Thou" within the Trinity, then there is not really any
mutual love between the Father and the Son within the Trinity either. . . .
But if, in order to avoid "the danger of tritheism," we are not permitted
to think of mutual love between the Father and the Son within the Trinity, then it is impossible to say, either, that the Holy Spirit proceeds from
the love of the Father and the Son, and constitutes "the bond of love"
between the Father and the Son.[123]

It is not that we need a less relational view of the triune God as an eternal communion of love; rather, we need a less individualistic and more relational view of
human personhood as intimate interdependence and mutuality. This is a more
life-giving and liberating doctrine of God, more congenial to both feminist and
postmodern sensitivities, and, I suggest, closer to the biblical witness to Jesus,
one with his *Abba* and the Spirit.

This theology of the Social Trinity, based as it is in the Gospel narrative of
Jesus with the Spirit and the *Abba,* affords us a different perspective on human
relations and human societies but also opens us up to a different vision of the created order as a whole. Two such diverse theologians as the Greek Orthodox John
Zizioulas and the Latin American liberationist Leonardo Boff make a major point
of this. For Zizioulas, the whole creation exhibits signs of the communion of the
triune God. The fundamental truth about all of reality is communion. In view of
the Trinity, says Zizioulas, "Being means life, and being means *communion*" for
"being is constituted as communion." "*To be* and *to be in relation* becomes identical. For something or someone to *be,* two things are simultaneously needed:
being itself (*hypostasis*) and *being in relation.*"[124] Zizioulas goes on to develop
illuminating theologies of church, Eucharist, and ministry.

In a similar vein, Boff, in his *Cry of the Earth, Cry of the Poor,* is particularly eloquent concerning the ecological significance of the Trinity: "If God is communion and relationship," he argues, "then the entire universe lives in relationship, and all is in communion with all at all points and at all moments." The Trinity, he believes, is perfectly in tune with contemporary cosmology, which critiques all ideas of reality as closed systems, emphasizing "open and processive reality."[125] Boff writes:

> the Trinity helps us to delve deeper into our understanding of our common theme, planet Earth, the universe and its future, because we are all woven of the most intricate and open relationships, in the likeness of the Trinity. The Blessed Trinity constitutes the common sphere of all beings and entities: the theosphere.[126]

It is through the risen, living Jesus, in the power of the Spirit, that we reach this life-giving vision of God, who as eternal communion of love, destines all of creation to reflect this love. Jesus is foundational for us, for our life and discipleship, and for our vision of the earth, because he reveals the triune God.

❦

We began this chapter by asking what it is about Jesus Christ that makes him central and foundational for Christian life and worship, faith and theology. It was impossible to answer this question without substantial discussion about Jesus Christ himself, about his mission and his identity. I have argued that it is *what he does* and *who he is* and our consequent relationship with him in worship and action that place him at the center of all our theological thought.

We have seen that it was soteriology that shaped christology and still shapes it. Jesus, in his life, death, and resurrection, brings God's reign decisively, offering God's unconditional grace, overcoming evil powers, and finally vanquishing the power of death itself. Thus, the disciples find themselves in a relationship of praise, thanksgiving, obedience, and hope with the risen and living Christ. We have seen the logic of *lex orandi, lex credendi*. In prayer and worship, Christians relate to the liberating Jesus as to God, and doctrine follows. Similarly, we have seen the logic of *lex sequendi, lex credendi*. Christians relate to the life-giving Jesus as to God in the practical life of discipleship, and doctrine follows. Theology is about the knowledge of God, and it is none other than Jesus, one with God in all his fleshly humanity, who reveals God. For these reasons, I contend, Jesus the Christ is indeed center and foundation, the *norma normans non normata* for all of our life and worship, faith and theology.

The Christic center, however, is challenged, as we shall see in the next chapter, by the pluralist theologies.

CHAPTER 6

The Challenge
of the Pluralist Theologies

Besides the cosmocentric or creation-centered theologies referred to in chapter 4, a significant number of theologians have appeared in recent decades who seem to be exceptions to the wide agreement that Christian theological understanding should be christologically centered. It is in large part because of their concern for communication with people of other faiths that those who describe themselves as pluralists have in common a proposal to decenter Jesus Christ in Christian theology, calling rather for a theocentric (God-centered) or soteriocentric (salvation-centered) approach. Some prefer to speak of "Reality-centered" or "survival-centered" theology.[1] It is fair to say, I think, that they are motivated by a praxis criterion. They believe that Christ-centered theology is not life-giving and liberating but destructive of the unity of humanity and therefore untenable in our time. We cannot become engaged here in a substantial discussion of the vast literature of the theology of religions and interreligious dialogue, since our focus here is on the centeredness of Christian theology in Jesus Christ as primary norm. Still, the question of christocentrism is intimately connected with the theology of religions. The question is whether Christ-centered theology is a serious barrier to interreligious dialogue, and so also to human understanding and cooperation. Do the Christian centering on Christ and the accompanying high christology imply arrogance and religious imperialism toward people of other religious traditions? Does it imply that other religions are worthless and idolatrous? The answer probably is that christocentrism, as practiced by some, *may be* closed-minded, imperialistic, and out of touch with our pluralist, multifaith world—but not necessarily. It is also possible that an honest christocentrism (for Christians) allows for maximum openness, generosity, and respect for others.

Working Distinctions (and Their Limitations)

In discussions of the theology of religions, or of interreligious dialogue, a distinction is often made among exclusivists, inclusivists, and pluralists,[2] though some alternative concepts have been proposed.[3] Not everyone is enthusiastic about these categories. So-called pluralists, who generally use and approve these concepts, are inclined to think that inclusivists are closet exclusivists, and some who may be dubbed inclusivists suspect that pluralists are closet exclusivists of their own kind.[4] Exclusivists are often unhappy about being so labeled, since the term seems to be used synonymously with narrow-minded bigotry![5] In fact, it is difficult to describe or define a position other than one's own without slipping into pejorative terms, describing the theological "other" in terms that he or she would dislike. For example, pluralists intensely dislike being described as relativists. Nevertheless, the distinctions seem useful as a starting point (and difficult to replace) for a discussion of various possible stances in the theology of religions, and since the concepts are so much part of the existing literature, we cannot ignore them. We should note that, while we are using these terms to distinguish among Christian thinkers, it is possible to extend the distinctions to thinkers of other religious traditions too, since members of all religious traditions take up some attitude or other to the religious "others." For example, one might speak (cautiously) of the pluralism or inclusivism of Hindus or of Buddhists, of the exclusivism or inclusivism of Muslims, and so on.[6]

The *exclusivists,* or those who are so named by others (at least in Christian terms), believe that Jesus Christ is the one, incomparable revelation of the triune God, the unique incarnation of God's own Word, and that God's grace and salvation have come to the world exclusively in him. For exclusivists, the world religions are to be regarded as false and idolatrous, and syncretism (blending of religions) of every kind is to be avoided. There are, of course, shades of opinion within what may be called exclusivism. At one end of that spectrum some would say that all non-Christians are damned and without hope and that there is "no salvation outside the church." At the other end of the same spectrum are those who hope and believe that all will be brought to salvation ultimately through Jesus Christ.[7] These latter might well object to the label "exclusivist" and may actually slide into the inclusivist camp.

The *pluralists,* who have usually identified themselves as such, are on the opposite side of the debate. "Plural," of course, means "many." Pluralists generally think that there are many more or less equivalent ways of salvation, that the truth is mysterious and multifaceted, beyond all of our particular religious traditions and expressions, and that all of the great, enduring religious traditions express and manifest this transcendent truth in equally valid ways. According to most pluralists, there is a common essence to all religions, and each religion manifests this in specific ways arising out of its particular culture and history. This approach usually moves away from any high christology or claims to the finality of Jesus Christ and has the effect of radically relativizing all particular truth claims, not only of Christianity but of every other particular religious tradition. Most Christian pluralists, however, object to being labeled as relativists and insist that they are committed to Christ and to sharing Christ through dialogue.[8] There are, of course, different kinds of pluralists (as we shall see below), who understand their stance in various ways,[9] some of whom may slide in an inclusivist direction.

The *inclusivists*, or those so-named according to this schema, generally affirm that Jesus Christ, in his life, death, and resurrection, is God's unique, definitive, unsurpassable event of salvation for the whole world. In this respect, inclusivists are like exclusivists. However, inclusivists also recognize the presence of truth, wisdom, and salvation in other religions. They may speak of other "revelations," which are in some sense partial. Some inclusivists believe that all religions will finally find their completion or fulfillment in Christ, while others are more positive about the permanent value and significance of the religions in God's salvific, providential design. Inclusivists generally believe that they discern the presence of Christ's saving work, and the presence of the Holy Spirit, in the other religious traditions, and honour the works of grace manifested in the lives of believers in other religions. They are like pluralists in that they expect, through interreligious dialogue with others, to learn something of value from what God has taught others; that is, their Christian faith may be enriched by dialogue with the others. In this way, some inclusivists may slide in a pluralist direction.[10]

Much debate has occurred in recent years among Roman Catholics about the official teaching of the Second Vatican Council (1962–1965), which opened up in an inclusivist direction toward the truth, wisdom, and even saving significance of the world religions.[11] In 2000 a document of Cardinal Joseph Ratzinger, president of the Congregation for the Doctrine of the Faith, set forth what has been called a "severe document,"[12] *Dominus Jesus,* in which he emphasized the unicity and universal salvific significance of Jesus Christ and the church, criticized the "ideology of dialogue," and called for dialogue that is oriented toward evangelization.[13] This is a good example of a stance at the exclusivist end of the inclusivist spectrum.

Both exclusivists and inclusivists may be described as Christ-centered, taking Jesus as their primary norm and foundation (though some exclusivists may incline to be scripture-centered, taking the Bible as their primary norm). Readers will probably notice that this author falls somewhere within the spectrum of inclusivism, perhaps leaning in a pluralist direction, while recognizing the limitations and dangers of these labels. We need to avoid the condescension of including people who do not wish to be included. We seek rather, as Douglas

John Hall has suggested, a more humble, welcoming, and hospitable attitude to the others.[14] But it is the pluralists that particularly interest us here, as challengers to the Christ-centered method proposed in this book.

The pluralist theologians challenge us to help put an end to the interreligious strife and religious imperialism that have so terribly plagued human history, especially from the Christian side. Their goals are surely admirable. Theologies that promote arrogance, oppression, and persecution need to be criticized, precisely from within the christological norm. Followers of Jesus who seek to love their neighbours as themselves must surely affirm the value of dialogue, in the sense of genuine listening and honest communication with others. This is an appeal that must be taken seriously for anyone concerned for life and liberation. Generally the pluralists believe that the urgent need for peace and understanding among the world's peoples requires the end of any kind of religious absolutism or imperialism. Here too, Christ-centered Christians must agree, for followers of Jesus must be committed to peace and reconciliation among human beings. Most pluralists, however, hold that Christ-centered theologies, operating with high christologies of a unique and unsurpassable Jesus as incarnation of God, stand in the way of any significant rapprochement. They also contend that their pluralist theologies have advantages in terms of intelligibility and credibility in our time; they claim to be more rational and acceptable to contemporary sensibilities, and claim support in contemporary scholarship of the New Testament concerning the historical Jesus. Since the thesis of this book obviously stands in opposition to any decentering of Christ in Christian faith and theology, I shall offer both critical and appreciative comment on the work of some of the most prominent pluralist theologians, attempting to take seriously the important challenge they present to the contemporary church. Among the vast array of authors who may be described as pluralists, three stand out as pioneers and leaders, who have articulated their views in many published articles and substantial books. To limit this potentially huge discussion, I focus here on John Hick, Wilfred Cantwell Smith, and Paul Knitter.[15]

John Hick

John Hick was perhaps the first of the late-twentieth-century theologians to propose a theocentric theology (that is, theocentric as opposed to christocentric). In the early 1970s, this British Presbyterian minister/professor, philosopher, and theologian became keenly aware of people of other religions who increasingly populated his city of Birmingham. He was impressed by their spirituality and moral integrity and took seriously their claims to various kinds of revelation. In the face of the reality of the genuine faith of these others, Hick rethought what had been his conservative evangelical theology and soon called for a "Copernican revolution" and a "paradigm shift" from a Jesus-centered to a God-centered Christianity.[16] All the religions, he believed, grew out of essentially the same religious experience of God or "the Transcendent." The various religions, though they appear to be saying very different things, are all speaking in their different ways and ascribing different names to the same noumenal (deeply mysterious and unknown) divine Being.[17] Using Kant's distinction of *noumenon* and *phenomenon,* Hick believes that the actual being of the divine reality (the *noumenon*) is so shrouded in mystery that we, in our various religious traditions, have access only to "phenomenal," cultural manifestations of religious consciousness. The great religious traditions are all, he thought, more or less equally effective in nurturing the moral and spiritual life of their adherents.[18]

A few years later, having heard much criticism of his theocentrism, Hick realized that "God" was not quite the universal concept he had thought (since, after all, Buddhists generally do not think in terms of a God). Hick's God had tended to look rather like a liberal Protestant God, perhaps a unitarian one, and therefore could not well serve as the neutral common ground for interreligious dialogue. God too, then, had to be decentered. Hick therefore proposed instead a "Reality-centered" theology. The Real (or the "Really Real") is that divine Other to which the symbols of all the religions point. When religious people worship and obey "the Real" they move from being self-centered to being Other-centered or Reality-centered.[19] To be Christ-centered, he thinks, is too narrow and out of touch with our awareness of the religious others, whose morality and spirituality are not inferior to those of Christians.

Of particular interest to us here is Hick's view of Jesus Christ. Inevitably, this theocentric or Reality-centered theology would have to operate out of a reduced christology, and in *The Myth of God Incarnate*, Hick and other authors argued that the doctrine of the incarnation of God in Jesus Christ should not be taken literally, any more than we take the Genesis creation stories literally.[20] It must be seen as a myth expressing the truth that in Jesus we have a symbol pointing to the divine Reality. Jesus will continue to be very important for the faith, piety, and worship of Christians, but they will recognize that there are other equally valid "revelations" of the divine in other religious traditions. As a myth, then, and one myth among many others, Christ must be decentered. Later, Hick wrote a christological volume entitled *The Metaphor of God Incarnate.* This is an impressively and powerfully argued book, in which Hick uses philosophical argument as well as biblical scholarship to throw doubt on the traditional Christian doctrine of the incarnation. First, the resurrection of Jesus should not be taken as a real, historical event. Rather, for Hick,

> The term "resurrection" has been used throughout Christian history to refer to the transitional event or events in virtue of which the Jesus Movement survived the death of its founder, withstood persecution, flourished, and went on to become the religion of the Roman empire and so of the Western world and its colonial extensions. Precisely what this transitional event was we cannot now discern with confidence.[21]

The resurrection, then, which I have suggested here is foundational for christol-ogy, is not taken seriously as a real event. Moreover, Jesus, he argues, never taught his own divinity; Jesus himself was centered in God. The doctrine of the Councils of Nicaea and Chalcedon of the two natures of Christ as fully God and fully human has never, he thinks, been adequately explained and is simply unin-telligible and unbelievable to most contemporary people.[22] Hick proposes that the incarnation should be regarded not as an actual assertion about the divinity and humanity of Jesus, but as the language of poetry and symbolism. Specifi-cally, he thinks the doctrine is a metaphor:

> What I shall recommend is acceptance of the idea of divine incarnation as a metaphorical idea. We see in Jesus a human being extraordinarily open to God's influence and thus living to an extraordinary extent as God's agent on earth. . . . He thus embodied within the circumstances of his time and place the ideal of humanity living in openness and response to God, and in doing so he "incarnated" a love that reflects the divine love. . . . It can be liberated from the network of theories—about Incarnation, Trinity, Atonement—which served once to focus but now serve only to obscure its significance, that lived teaching can continue to be a major source of inspiration for human life.[23]

In using the concept of metaphor, Hick has not rejected his previous term "myth," for a myth is "a much extended metaphor."[24]

If this is what incarnation means, then, Hick argues, there is no reason to sup-pose that there need be only one such incarnation. He is not proposing, like the cosmocentrists, that the whole universe is God's incarnation. Rather, we might say, for example, that the divine Logos was also incarnated in Gautama Sid-dhartha, the Buddha.[25] To move away from an absolutely unique Christ as the incarnation of God will also help Christianity to move away from its long history of arrogance and superiority toward other religions, for we can no longer consider that Christianity is the only religion to have been founded by "God in person."[26]

Hick's challenge to classical christology is important and no doubt reflects the opinions of many people in our liberal Protestant (and even Catholic) churches. The reader can assess whether, in the previous chapter on christology, I have presented a tenable case for taking seriously the incarnation of God in Jesus Christ as an intelligible truth claim. What we need to note here is that his departure from christocentrism is a logical correlate to what might be called his "low christology." It is logical enough that, if God did not actually live a human life in the flesh of Jesus of Nazareth, and if in fact Jesus was not really raised from the dead, there is no good reason to be "centered" in him, or to make him, in his life, death, and resurrection, foundational for Christian life and thought. Rather, says Hick, we should center ourselves in "the Real," the "Transcendent," which is known under many names to the many religious traditions of the world.

We should note that Hick does not really think that *all* religions are equally true and valuable. He knows that the history of religions includes all kinds of horrors (and Christianity is no exception). We find human sacrifice, the burning of widows, clitoridectomy, crusades, inquisitions, mass suicide, and on and on. He knows that religion as such is not necessarily a good thing. He proposes an ethical criterion between good and bad religion (not entirely unlike our question: Is it life-giving and liberating?). In *An Interpretation of Religion,* Hick makes this clear, asking: Does it promote love and compassion, a self-sacrificing concern for the good of others? Does it foster "a voluntary renunciation of ego-centeredness and a self-giving to, or self-losing in, the Real . . . ?"[27] He believes that all the great living religious traditions of the world, at their best, meet this standard.

Hick certainly has many allies among academic theologians and clergy. Pluralism is so popular in some departments of religious studies and some seminaries that in some contexts it appears almost to be a new orthodoxy. What shall we say to Hick's challenge to christocentrism?

One could ask initially whether, if so little of the New Testament message about Jesus is to be credited, the Christian faith is worth salvaging. Should Hick not conclude that the Christian project has been a grave mistake and that perhaps one should take up one of the other great religious traditions, or perhaps frankly avow agnosticism? Would not a kind of ethical humanism, or perhaps unitarian humanistic theism, be more serviceable than a drastically revamped Christianity? If Chistianity is to go among the world religions having shed its dearest and most central tenets, will anyone take it seriously for more than a generation or two? However that may be, we may focus especially on his Reality-centered method and its value for interreligious dialogue. The importance of honest, open dialogue with religious others and love and respect for them is, after all, the main point of "Reality-centrism."

Many Christians immediately feel that it would be pointless to enter into dialogue with say, a Hindu or a Buddhist, with so few truth claims on the table. If the religions are so much the same in essence that all can be described as Reality-centered, what is there left to dialogue about? Hick's "Real" is so vague and amorphous that it seems able to accommodate any and every image of the Divine. But can such an empty concept serve as the common ground on the basis of which believers are in dialogue? Further, if we do not expect to find real and important disagreement, but only different religio/cultural ways of expressing the same universal truth, can dialogue really happen at all? If Christians so reduce Christian truth claims about God/Christ/Trinity, and creation, salvation, and so on, do they not then expect dialogue partners to reduce their specific claims also? Must Hindus relativize karma and reincarnation and their monistic vision of the Divine? Must Muslims drop their claims that the Qurʾan is the Word of Allah, and that Muhammad is the last and greatest of the prophets? Hick deplores exclusive truth claims when made by Christians and thinks that they must be renounced in order that dialogue may proceed. This would seem, then, to be required of all other dialogue partners. If the unique divinity of Jesus and the Trinity are off limits, presumably karma and the Qur'an are off limits as well. This would amount to very liberal modern Christians talking to very liberal modern Hindus and Muslims. In fact, most historic religious communities do make universal truth claims. They passionately believe that all people and the whole world stand in need of their Truth. If those with exclusive (or inclusive) truth claims are barred from the table, significant dialogue between actual existing communities will never happen. We may doubt, then, whether "Reality-centered" theology will actually facilitate mutual understanding among the religions.

Perhaps the modernity of Hick is at the heart of the problem. As is evident from a previous chapter, by "modern" I do not mean "up-to-date" or "contemporary," since most people today think that we have entered a postmodern era. By "modern" in this case I mean especially that mode of life and thought known as the Enlightenment, especially of eighteenth-century Europe, with its great confidence in human reason, its distrust of mystery and miracle, and its reduction of religion to morality. The modern Enlightenment wanted (quite rightly I think) to get past religious wars and the authoritarian dogmatism of the churches, which tended to stifle new scientific knowledge. Religions (at that time mainly the various conflicting Christian confessions) needed to be neutralized, both to avoid social conflict and to free the way for rational bourgeois, rather than divinely ordained, aristocratic rule. As Christians, we may indeed still have much sympathy for the emancipatory drive of the Enlightenment. But looking back on that foundational movement of modernity, we may also see its blind spots, among them, its overconfidence in reason and science, its rationalization of European imperial power, and its impoverishment of spiritual or religious consciousness. For Immanuel Kant, perhaps the great culminating thinker of the late *Aufklärung* in Germany, the human mind could have no contact with the Divine reality except in a practical moral sense. We must remain agnostic about God as a *ding-an-sich* (or God as God is in God-self). We can never really know anything about God, but "religion within the limits of reason alone," for Kant, was simply instrumental to morality. Religion provides the norms, rewards, and punishments for the moral life. A contemporary Catholic author, Gavin D'Costa, points out that John Hick's mythical/metaphorical approach to Christian doctrine is moral in this Kantian way. For Hick, the point of the myths of the various religions is to foster unselfishness rather than egocentrism. Hick's Reality-centrism is nothing but this: religion as an elaborate instrument of human moralization. Of course, most deeply religious people know that their spiritual traditions are far more than this. While the ethical is a central dimension of almost all religious traditions, they also have to do (in their various ways) with reverence, awe and worship, peace and serenity, grace and hope. D'Costa contends:

> Hick's "pluralism" masks the advocation of liberal modernity's "god,"
> in this case a form of ethical agnosticism. If ethical agnostics were to

suggest that the conflict between religions would be best dealt with by everyone becoming an ethical agnostic, not only would this fail to deal with plurality, in so much as it fails to take plurality seriously, it would also fail to take religious cultures seriously by dissolving them into instrumental mythical configurations best understood within modernity's mastercode.[28]

Thus, a number of critics accuse Hick of a kind of subtle modern Western imperialism. The pluralists seem to function as missionaries, not of Christianity or any of the traditional religions, but of modern pluralism itself. They claim to stand above all the religious traditions and to see them more truly than they see themselves.

This attitude of pluralism of rising above all the religious traditions is particularly evident in Hick's assumption that there is just one religious end in all the religions.[29] It is a common, popular pluralist idea that "we are all going to heaven in different boats." Hick is aware, of course, that the religions do not agree about what the goal of religious or spiritual life should be, either in this life or beyond. He knows that *nirvana, sunyata,* the reign of God, and so on are quite different, and even contradictory eschatological ends. He is also aware that finally some of these may turn out to be true and others false.[30] For now, no one can know which are true and which are false, but at any rate Hick does not think that these differences are significant. He believes that, despite various conceptions of it, one salvific process is taking place in all the great religious traditions. But then "salvation" becomes a highly abstract, merely formal concept, and the various differing and even contradictory ways of salvation become irrelevant. At the same time, however, Hick thinks that the cultivation of love and compassion, as opposed to ego-centeredness, is the universal moral indication of this salvific process. At first sight this appears to be a universalization of liberal Protestant values. But, especially in his later work, it is clear that the values of love and compassion are given no particular concrete content or norms (such as Christians acknowledge in Jesus or Buddhists in the Buddha), and so these too remain rather vague, lacking any specific concept of the religious end in view. S. Mark Heim presses this argument in *Salvations:*

> The challenge Hick set himself is to provide a religious account of religion which is compatible with affirming a substantial common cognitive truth and a single common soteriological result in all the religions. [But] . . . the attempt to do this is, perhaps necessarily, required to be compatible with so many states of affairs that real cognitive content evaporates.[31]

Thus, in claiming to offer a neutral account of all the religions as more or less equivalently true and valuable, and in this way to foster humility and respect among people of differing religions for each other, Hick actually undercuts the particular visions and truth claims of all these traditions, rendering them all cognitively empty. One suspects that passionate believers in these various religious ways would find it intolerable to suggest that their various ways are optional or irrelevant, that one way is as good as another. Would these people feel that they had been loved, respected, or taken seriously? It appears that, by neutralizing all the great religions, he has in fact set forth his own specific truth claims, even, one might say, his own new modern religion: Pluralism.

Wilfred Cantwell Smith

Wilfred Cantwell Smith, the late historian of religions and theocentric theologian, began his professional life as an ordained minister of the United Church of Canada and a missionary teacher in a Christian college in what is now part of Pakistan. However, he became so impressed with the people whom he was supposed to evangelize, and so distressed about interreligious conflict in that part of the world, that he became a scholar of religions, especially Islam, and an active advocate of religious tolerance and mutual respect. As a professor at major universities in North America, Smith articulated his views in a great many books and articles; these views cannot easily be stated in brief form. While Hick's emphasis is philosophical, Smith's approach is more historical. Like others of the theocentric school of thought, he urges Christians to recognize that they and their faith, rituals, and theologies are part of a single religious history of humankind: "Those who believe in the unity of humankind, and those who believe in the unity of God, should be prepared, therefore, to discover a unity of humankind's religious history."[32]

Out of an impressive erudition in the history of religions, and his evidently wide firsthand awareness of most of the world's great religious traditions, Smith insists that the religious history of humankind is a "global continuum,"[33] and offers many convincing stories and illustrations to evoke in his readers an awareness of this. He believes that "God," or "transcendent reality," or "the Divine," is actively involved in all of past and present human history, reaching out "after all men and women everywhere in compassion and yearning; who delights in a sinner's repentance, who delights to save."[34] Thus, Smith often speaks in a manifestly Christian way, and we may doubt whether all or most Hindus, Buddhists, Confucianists, or Muslims would agree with his conception of what God is doing to save them. At times one suspects that Smith speaks more as a certain kind of inclusivist than as a pluralist, since he appears to read Christian content into the concepts of other religions.

Nevertheless, his respect and reverence for other peoples' faith is instructive and cannot lightly be set aside. What he says about the universality of God's salvific presence in the world is surely to be affirmed from a biblical and Christian perspective. We sense in Smith's work (and in the work of other pluralist theologians also) a generosity of spirit and a loving openness to neighbours that is consistent with the love and freedom of Jesus. Our christological criterion itself prescribes such generosity and openness. Smith's long-standing personal friendship with many Muslims, for example, is evident in *Towards a World Theology,* when he explains what he means when he speaks admirably of Muslims being "saved":

> Saved from nihilism, from alienation, anomie, despair; from the bleak despondency of meaninglessness. Saved from unfreedom; from being the victim of one's own whims within, or of pressures without; saved from being merely an organism reacting to its environment. . . . I note that in fact Muslims derive their courage, their dignity, their capacity to suffer without disintegrating and to succeed without gloating, their sense of belonging to a community, of accepting and being accepted, their ability to trust and to be trusted, to discipline themselves. . . . they derive all this from, and nurture it through, a participation in an Islamic context for their lives. They have derived it from reading the Qur'an, from revering the law, from praying in a Mosque.[35]

Smith has a strong sense of the dynamic power of faith in the lives of real people. He dislikes the term "religion," which he thinks reifies the rich fluidity and dynamism of actual religious faith and practice.[36] There is no such thing as Hinduism, for example; there are only Hindus.[37] He operates out of a major distinction between faith and belief. What really matters is faith, by which he means a genuine response to truth or transcendence. In *Faith and Belief,* he writes that faith is "serenity and courage and loyalty and service: a quiet confidence and joy which enables one to feel at home in the universe and to find meaning in the world and in one's own life, a meaning that is profound and ultimate."[38] Smith, then, seems to operate with an *a priori* positive theology of religions. Religious faith as such seems to be a good thing. Human religious endeavours, rather than God, seem to be the object of praise.[39] Faith, for Smith, is a quality of life, not a set of ideas or concepts. Beliefs, however, are intellectualizations about faith. Beliefs—particular doctrines, ethics, rituals—are incidental, not constitutive of faith as such. They are highly contingent, depending on where and when we were born. But the broad continuum of religious life is about the universal quality of humanity that we call faith.[40]

Smith may be right that there is a common quality of human life that may be called faith and that this is manifest in many religions. But faith in what or in whom? Faith here seems to be contentless, not unlike John Hick's Real. But for religious people, the object of faith is not a matter of indifference. Most Christians would say, I think, that for them, faith is specifically faith in Jesus the Christ, and in God through this same Jesus, and in the Holy Spirit. Christians would generally wish to deny any "seed of conscience in human ontology that renders God's act in Christ materially unnecessary."[41] Islamic faith would surely object to anything that relativized the Qur'an or made it appear optional or replaceable by other religious sources. Hindu, Buddhist, Daoist, and Confucianist faith are very different indeed, both from Semitic monotheisms and from each other. Smith is at least consistent when he speaks of the implications of this. He is convinced that the whole of human religious history should now become the data for a world theology. He writes:

> the history of religion, my studies have increasingly pushed me to hold, is the one true basis for theology. . . . in the next phase of world thought, the basis for theology must now be the history of religion. To speak truly about God means henceforth to interpret accurately the history of religious life on earth.
>
> . . . the true historian of religion and the authentic theologian are in the final analysis identical.[42]

Some of Smith's friendly critics (and I would count myself among them), for example, the Hindu scholar Kana Mitra, have wondered aloud whether this rather "grandiose" plan of constructing a world theology from all of religious history is practicable.[43] Certainly what Smith is saying is drastically different from what is being argued in this book. For him, the questions Is it founded in Jesus Christ? and Is it biblical? are obviously far too narrow. But should we now regard all the scriptures of the world as our own holy scriptures?[44] Should all theological proposals, worship, preaching, and mission be tested by questions about their congruence with, at the same time, the Bible, the Qur'an, the Upanishads, the *Bhagavad-Gita,* and the sayings of Confucius? Is this even imaginable as a coherent mode of thought? Is Smith recommending the dissolution of Christianity and of all religions into a universal homogenous world faith? All this seems implied in much of what he says about a world theology, but he assures us that this is not his intention:

> I do not mean that Christians will cease to be Christian, or Muslims Muslim. What I mean is that Christians will participate, as Christians, in the religious history of humankind; Muslims will participate in it as Muslims, Jews as Jews, Hindus as Hindus, Buddhists as Buddhists. . . . I participate as a deliberate though modified Calvinist in the Christian community, and the Christian process. In much the same way, I choose to participate as a Christian in the world process of religious convergence. For, ultimately, the only community there is, the one to which I know that I truly belong, is the community, world-wide and history-long, of humankind.[45]

Yet Smith would rather not speak of "Christian theology," preferring "a Christian attempt at theology"; nor of "Christian faith," preferring "faith in its Christian form."[46] If we are not to have specifically Christian faith and Christian theology (or specifically Muslim faith or Islamic theology), it is difficult to see how the Christian community (or Islamic community or any other) can continue to exist with any degree of cohesion or identity.

We have to ask whether Smith has taken seriously enough the great differences, even clearly contradictory truth claims, between the great religions.[47] Can justification by grace through faith really be held together with the Hindu law of karma? Can the passionate monotheism of Islam truly be synthesized with the nontheistic attitude of Theravada Buddhists? Smith would argue that such truth claims are only a matter of belief and not of faith. But we may question whether these can be separated so neatly. Surely, to harmonize such beliefs in a world theology would mean redefining them beyond recognition. Perhaps he would deny that synthesis or harmonization is his goal. Yet if it is not, then the project of a world theology built out of the data of the whole of the history of religion becomes incoherent.

What of our criterion "Is it founded in Jesus Christ?" Smith would perhaps agree that in some sense Jesus Christ is normative for a "Christian attempt at theology." At times he himself speaks in that way. For him the significance of Christ is that he revealed the Father. But he would never agree to be christocentric: "my proposal is unabashedly theocentric . . . if Christians insist that Christ is the centre of their lives, it is time we rediscovered that God is the centre of the universe."[48]

But nowhere does Smith offer a substantial christology. Sometimes he speaks of Jesus as divine and as the incarnation of God, and he could even say, in an earlier book, that "in Christ, God dies for us men and our salvation, and that through faith in him we are saved."[49] Yet in other places it is clear that, for Smith, Jesus Christ is one of many symbols of the divine presence in the world. To say that in Christ God came into the world in human form has been a Western way of saying, symbolically, that "every day, every year, transcendence entered its life anew."[50]

Much of the criticism aimed at John Hick would apply to Smith as well. We find here a not so subtle form of modern Western, religious imperialism—as usual in the guise of benevolence, liberality, and tolerance. One finds in Smith a kind of moral sternness and indignation toward those who do not share his modern pluralist faith. As Heim puts it, we notice here a "mixture of humility and hauteur."[51] While adopting a highly apophatic, even mystical stance about divine reality, Smith seems to claim to have seen all the religions from above, as God sees them, sees them better than they see themselves. Is pluralism, then, the new true religion? Smith's missionary zeal for pluralism as such often looks and sounds like religious devotion. Yet this is a purely modern faith, not a postmodern one. Heim states the matter well:

This totalizing approach really surpasses past exclusivist accounts. Such accounts subsumed various religions within one large system they believed to be true. . . . Smith's vision annihilates every other with a supersystem which recognizes no alternatives and can hardly be questioned because it is "ours"—and "ours" is all inclusive. As Smith puts it, there is no point in trying to speak theologically unless you are trying to speak on behalf of everyone. This liberal rational confidence in articulating a universal system grounds Smith's whole approach.[52]

I suggest, then, that Smith's approach to interreligious dialogue will not serve a Christian theology that seeks to be life-giving and liberating. In not honouring differences sufficiently, it will not facilitate true communication and respect among genuine Buddhists, Christians, Hindus, Jews, Muslims, and so on.

An Interreligious Conversation

We may see the connection of methodological and christological issues clearly in the following (fictional) conversation, which takes place at a large house party in one corner of someone's living room. It is a kind of interreligious dialogue—not a sophisticated or formal one, but of the kind that happens frequently in social situations. Although it is a fictional conversation, it does resemble a number of actual conversations that I have been part of, including one involving a Hindu swami. There are many differing nuanced stances that may be labeled exclusivist, inclusivist, or pluralist. I do not claim that the swami in this dialogue represents the views of all Hindus. Nor do the other participants perfectly represent types of Christians. We have just one non-Christian here in order to see how various kinds of Christian theological stances may relate to the religious "other."

Elizabeth is a relatively conservative, middle-aged Anglican laywoman, very active in her church, a well-educated and articulate homemaker and mother of a grown family.

David is a young lawyer and active member of a large mainline Protestant church.

The swami is an elderly and venerable Hindu spiritual leader, slight and bespectacled, dressed in saffron robe and hat. Originally from India, he has served for many years as spiritual leader of Hindu people in a large North American city.

Eduardo is a young Roman Catholic priest from Venezuela who is doing postgraduate studies in theology.

Our brief account of their conversation begins somewhere in the middle:

SWAMI: *Well, it is lovely to meet two devoutly religious Christians. You know, we Hindus value and respect all religion. We believe that all religious people are seeking after the same divine truth, and that all the great religions are one.*

DAVID: [Smiling genially] *I agree entirely. As a Christian, I view Christianity as one religion alongside others that are equally valid. And Jesus, of course, is one of the great moral and spiritual teachers of humanity.*

SWAMI: *I am so glad to hear you say that, David. Christianity has traditionally been, if you will forgive me for saying so, a rather dogmatic and exclusivist religion. This has unfortunately made it rather aggressive and arrogant toward other religious traditions. Of course we Hindus acknowledge Christ as more than a spiritual teacher, but as one of the great manifestations of the divine. We are all on the same spiritual journey, though traveling by different routes. If only all religious people would recognize this, there would be so much less conflict and hatred in the world.*

ELIZABETH: [Frowning and cool] *Well, excuse me, but I find this rather difficult. We Christians don't believe that Jesus is just one of many great religious teachers or manifestations of the divine. I'm used to reciting the creed at Eucharist each Sunday, and I wouldn't say it if I didn't believe it. We say that our Lord was "crucified for us under Pontius Pilate," and "on the third day he rose again from the dead." We say that he's the only-begotten Son of God, "of one being with the Father." I don't wish to be rude, but I would certainly not say any of these things about Muhammad or the Buddha.*

DAVID: *Really? Then you and I are different on that score, Elizabeth. Personally, I'm rather skeptical about Jesus having got up and walked around after he was dead, and all this about Jesus as "the only-begotten Son of God" doesn't make any sense to me. After all, what can it mean for God to have a Son? The older I get the more incredible it all becomes. Especially when I meet people of other religions and realize they're just as moral and just as spiritual and serious about their religion as we are. I have no trouble saying that Muhammad and the Buddha are just as much divine and sons of God as Jesus is. Don't you think it's rather arrogant of us Christians to go on thinking we have all the truth and the others have none and they're all damned to hell?*

ELIZABETH: *I didn't say that we have all the truth and the others have none. And I certainly don't think they're damned to hell. It just happens to be important to me that Jesus Christ is God Incarnate and our Saviour. To me it's obvious that that's quite different from what Muslims say about Muhammad or what Buddhists say about the Buddha.*

SWAMI: [With a kindly smile] *Yes, the Muslims say Muhammad was a prophet, and the Buddhists say that the Buddha was "the enlightened one." But don't you see, Elizabeth, that, whatever the Muslims or Buddhists say, their founders were in fact incarnations of the divine, just as Jesus was? In fact we Hindus believe that there have been countless divine incarnations.*

ELIZABETH: [Not smiling] *Then you obviously mean something quite different by "incarnation" than I do. I am saying that Jesus is uniquely one with God, truly divine and truly human. If he isn't truly divine, he cannot be our Saviour. Don't you see that Muslims—they especially—and maybe Buddhists too would be deeply offended that you call their founders "incarnations of God"? Muslims vigorously disapprove of any notion of incarnation. And the Buddhists I've met would be very annoyed to be told that their Buddha is the incarnation of a God! And besides, Muslims that I've known are very disapproving of the Buddhists because they're usually not interested in a God at all!*

SWAMI: *I'm glad to see you have some learning about the world religions.*

ELIZABETH: *Oh, I don't claim to have learning. I've only taken one university course on world religions, and of course I've met members of other religions from time to time.*

SWAMI: *But from your studies, don't you think that if they could all get beyond their particularistic dogmas, that beneath it all they are all talking of the same divine truth—of the unity of all things in the divine order, of the essential kinship of all humanity and the need for us all to love and respect each other?*

DAVID: *Yes, you're right on there, Swami. Religion has been at the root of so many horrible wars down through history. We have to get beyond these things and emphasize the things we have in common. What really counts is doing unto others as we would have them do unto us. Love thy neighbour. Right?*

SWAMI: *Yes. You see, Elizabeth, it's our dogmas that get in the way of the unity and peace of humanity. We Hindus don't have dogmas as other religions do. We recognize the fundamental truth that underlies all dogmas!*

ELIZABETH: [Smiling now] *Well pardon me, but I think I'm hearing plenty of dogma right here and now in this conversation. You have your own dogma about the unity of all religion and all religious founders. There are lots of intelligent, well-informed people in the world who don't share this dogma. I dare say, Swami, that as a Hindu you have some other dogmas, about karma and reincarnation, haven't you?*

DAVID: *I myself find reincarnation a very appealing idea. It seems to correct some of the inequalities of this life. Why shouldn't we learn some good ideas from other religions? Who really knows the truth about these things anyway?*

ELIZABETH: *I don't doubt that Hindus and others have spiritual insight to share with us. But the law of karma, as I understand it, directly contradicts what I believe as a Christian about salvation. I believe that through the death and res-*

urrection of Jesus Christ we are saved by God's grace. It's not something we deserve or earn. We cannot progress through many lives to a higher stage of spiritual acceptability. In Jesus Christ we are already acceptable and loved by God. You see, my spirituality is centered in the Eucharist. I could not partake every week of the Eucharist if I did not believe in Christ as God and Saviour. I don't have to worry about getting through thousands of lives. My sins are forgiven and I hope for eternal life with God.

EDUARDO: *Excuse me, I could not help overhearing your conversation.* [Offering his hand] *I am Eduardo. I am a Catholic priest from Venezuela. I am a student of theology, so naturally I'm interested in what you're talking about.*

SWAMI: *Wonderful! And what aspect of theology are you studying?*

EDUARDO: *I'm doing a doctoral thesis in liberation theology, on the theologian Jon Sobrino.*

DAVID: *Oh, I've never heard of him.*

EDUARDO: *I agree so much with what you are saying, Swami. As a Christian of Latin America I am painfully aware of the harm of religious exclusivism, and especially of the imperialism of my own Christianity in our part of the world, especially since I am partly indigenous by blood. Christians from Spain came into our region of the world about five hundred years ago, invading, conquering, enslaving, and destroying our people. Our indigenous religion was gentle and peaceful and made us very close to the natural world around us. We lived in harmony with the sea, the land, and the sky.*

ELIZABETH: [With a smile] *Is it possible that you are idealizing and romanticizing your indigenous religion just a little? No doubt it is true that Christian people were very unjust and cruel, and we should never condone this, but didn't the indigenous religions practice human sacrifice? Did your peoples really never fight among themselves?*

EDUARDO: *Oh, possibly yes. But the Christians' certainty that their religion was the one and only truth was closely associated with their belief in their own cultural superiority as well. They thought that, since they could conquer our peoples, their religion must be true. Their God gave them the victory. Their success convinced them that their religion was absolutely superior. Their one true religion legitimized all kinds of unspeakable cruelties and injustice, including massive massacres, the slaying of hundreds of thousands! Human sacrifice indeed!*

DAVID: *So I'm very interested why you remain within this religion, and are even a priest!*

EDUARDO: *Oh yes, because I love my faith. I love the church, and I love Jesus. You see, I think that what Christians did on the South American continent was so unfaithful to Jesus. There were some faithful Christians, including priests like Bartolome de las Casas, who loved and defended the indigenous people in the name of God and of Jesus. I wish to stand in his tradition. I also think that our Christian faith can be combined in some way, "syncretized," if you like, with the best wisdom of our indigenous traditions.*

DAVID: *So you think it's possible to be a Christian and borrow things from other religions?*

EDUARDO: *Yes, there are many new voices in Latin American theology who think that Christians can blend and borrow from other religious traditions, including Afro-Latin American, as well as ancient indigenous South American spiritualities. There is no such thing as pure Christianity. It's always inculturated within some culture or other, and cultures include religion. I am convinced that we can do this with integrity, without losing our center in Jesus.*[53]

ELIZABETH: *I see, Eduardo. I hope this may be true. But as a Catholic priest, presumably you say the creeds, and celebrate Mass. You must surely believe that God was incarnate in Jesus and that he suffered for us, and was raised?*

EDUARDO: *Oh yes indeed I do! To those of us in Latin America who espouse liberation theology, it is very precious that Jesus Christ is the incarnation of God. We believe he is God with us, Emmanuel, sharing in all our human experience, our pain, our misery, our joy.*

ELIZABETH: *Oh yes, absolutely!*

EDUARDO: [Speaking passionately now] *Especially our social and political oppression, and even death by torture and execution. You see, we are still very much a suffering and exploited people. We are poor. Our infants and children die by the millions. So many millions of our children are homeless in the streets. Our people die young, many of malnutrition or starvation. So many of our best people have been tortured and murdered. It's so important to us that Jesus was executed because of his resistance to empire! Jesus hanging upon the cross is not just another good man dying as a martyr. He is God on the cross, sharing our situation as victims of oppression! This is the only kind of God I could love and worship!*

ELIZABETH: *I agree entirely, though I would not have put it that way.*

DAVID: *You certainly have a fresh and interesting angle on it all.*

EDUARDO: *Yes, but not altogether new, sir. Liberation theology has been around now for nearly forty years or so, and most of what it is saying can be found somewhere further back in the theological tradition—especially in the Bible!* [He laughs.] *But you are right, this way of thinking about Jesus Christ has not been the dominant one in the history of Christendom. Our emphasis is on a suffering*

God, a God who strives and struggles with the people. God is present and immersed in the evil of the world, just as we are, and overcomes suffering and evil from within the situation. As I said, I think this is profoundly biblical. Jesus shows us God's hatred of evil and suffering and God's protest and struggle against it. Jesus, God's Son incarnate, is also a political revolutionary who wants human societies turned upside down. That means that, to be with God, we too have to struggle for a radically new world. Of course, it is because of the poverty and oppression of our context that we notice and emphasize this aspect of the biblical story, which has been ignored and neglected through most of Christian history.

DAVID: *So God doesn't send suffering as a trial or temptation?*

EDUARDO: [Shocked] *Oh indeed no! The God of the Bible, the God and Father of our Lord Jesus Christ, is the God of life, not death! God wants wholeness and healing, peace and justice. God is opposed to evil and suffers under it, and finally will overcome it. The resurrection of Jesus is the sign of God's final victory over all evil and sin, oppression, and death.*

SWAMI: [Speaking quietly and calmly] *You see, as a Hindu I would see it quite differently. What may appear as evil to us is not necessarily evil to God. The divine encompasses all. All that happens is within the divine order. If someone suffers pain or sickness or early death, we can accept that with serenity, for it is part of his karma. Someone was asking me just yesterday about a child born blind. She wanted to know why God permitted this. I explained that, if a child is born blind, we must accept this as part of a greater good. It has come upon her because of what she has done, how she has lived in a previous life, because she needs this suffering as part of her spiritual pilgrimage, which spans many reincarnations. This may seem evil to us now, but from the perspective of eternity, it is a good and necessary thing.*

EDUARDO: [Speaking gravely now] *With respect, sir, I could not agree that a child born blind is a good and necessary thing. I know of many such instances in my own country. I know some of our Christian priests also teach that such suffering is God's will, but it gives me no comfort to think of this as part of a divine plan. I believe God weeps over a child born blind. I see this view of God's will as a religious ideology, which is used to justify an evil and unjust situation. Most children who are born blind are born to mothers who have suffered poverty, malnutrition, or even violence during their pregnancy. This is a human-made situation of social oppression that should not be ascribed to the divine order. We should not blame God for human injustice. Such religious ideas serve the interests of the ruling class.*

SWAMI: *No, no, no! I could never accept such an interpretation. Young man, one day when you have lived longer and grown in awareness, you will see all these things as part of the divine goodness, and your spirit will not be so anxious and restless. Remember what Lord Jesus said: Do not be anxious. Take no thought for the morrow. Consider the lilies of the field!*

ELIZABETH: [Smiling now] *It seems to me that we have a genuine clash of dogmas here!*

DAVID: *Yes, and not only between the religions, but also within Christianity. Eduardo's version of Christianity doesn't sound remotely like what I was brought up on, or what I hear from the pulpit on Sundays. I was taught as a child that bad things that happen to you are "acts of God"! Not that I actually believe that!*

ELIZABETH: *But Eduardo, it will take a good deal to convince me that Jesus was a political revolutionary!*

DAVID: *But it would take an awful lot of convincing to persuade me that Jesus is God!*

The conversation was getting a little tense, and our participants one by one excused themselves to refill their glasses and slipped into other lighter conversations in other parts of the house. This is the kind of interreligious dialogue that can happen spontaneously in a pluralistic society. Yet it is obvious that both the *inter-* and *intra*-faith dialogues occurring here could be carried much further and deeper. What might we learn from the conversation?

Elizabeth made it clear, and spoke for most Christians perhaps, when she said that the identity of Jesus is central to her faith. The particularities of her truth claims about Jesus are essential to her—to her confidence in salvation and to her worship and spirituality. She has not been deeply engaged in interreligious dialogue, but is open to learning more about these things and is probably identifiable as approximately inclusivist (but on the exclusivist side of the inclusivist spectrum).

The identity and mission of Jesus are also central and determinative for Eduardo. He is deeply committed to his faith in God through the suffering and risen Jesus, but, rejecting attitudes of religious superiority, he is open to the truth and wisdom of other religious traditions and to the possibility of a syncretic blending of religious insights from different sources, especially from the traditions of his own indigenous people. He is another kind of inclusivist, leaning more in a pluralist direction. His hopeful commitment to change the world contrasts sharply with each of the others.

David exhibits a kind of freewheeling agnosticism about all these things and represents the kind of casual, not-well-informed pluralism, even relativism, that is common among people in the liberal churches. Like the pluralist theologians, he is skeptical about resurrection and incarnation and defines the latter concept so broadly as to include many within it. Essentially he has reduced the significance of religion to morality (in typical Kantian/modernist fashion). It is only fair to say that his views as expressed here do not fairly represent the more subtle, nuanced positions of the pluralist theologians.

As noted above, the swami does not by any means represent all Hindus. But we notice that the swami has his own passionate commitments to the unity of humanity and of all religion and also to certain specific truth claims of his own tradition, which are basic to his sense of the goodness and meaningfulness of life. His pluralism may be expressive of a premodern Hindu pluralism, but may also reflect a modern Hinduism that has been influenced by the western Enlightenment.[54] He believes religious truth and wisdom are found plentifully beyond his own religion, but, in inclusivist fashion, he holds firmly to specific truth claims of his own.

Paul F. Knitter

Paul Knitter is an American Roman Catholic pluralist whose work is, in some respects, highly congenial to a theology that seeks to be life-giving and liberating, and who at the same time gives a good deal of attention to christology. In his later work he shows evidence of having heard some of the criticisms of pluralism that we have mentioned above.

In the autobiographical introduction to a two-volume work, Knitter speaks of his "Dialogical Odyssey," from his beginning as an exclusivist priest of the Divine Word missionaries, through the inclusivist, christocentric approach of Karl Rahner, to a pluralist theocentric stance like that of the early John Hick, and on from there. His exposure to the beauties and depths of Hinduism and Zen Buddhism, and a personal friendship with a devout Muslim, had convinced him that a classical trinitarian theology of Christ as the only Saviour of the world was no longer tenable. In 1985, in his first book, *No Other Name?* Knitter called for a pluralist "non-normative theocentric" approach emphasizing by the term "non-normative" the need for an egalitarian attitude in which no dialogue partner claims superiority, or the right, *a priori*, to provide the norm by which to judge all religions.[55] The book attracted much attention and praise, but also much criticism, similar to that aimed at Hick and Smith. "Chastened" by his theological critics, but also by new experiences, Knitter shifted his position from theocentrism to soteriocentrism. He had left the priesthood and married and had also become deeply involved in various forms of social-justice action, especially the Sanctuary Movement for Central American refugees. Newly sensitized now, not only to the religious "other" but also to the suffering "other," Knitter took a new interest in liberation theologies, and later ecological theologies as well, and came to be convinced that theology of religion and eco-liberation theology must be practiced together. In the first volume of his two-volume work, *One Earth Many Religions*, Knitter set forth a "multi-normed, soteriocentric (salvation centered) approach to dialogue."[56] The second volume, *Jesus and the Other Names,* spelled

out the implications of his soteriocentrism for christology and mission.[57] Knitter
is particularly admirable in his ability to hear his critics, and this is especially
evident in a volume of essays entitled *The Uniqueness of Jesus,* in which he is in
dialogue with other Christian theologians about christology, and in his *Introducing Theologies of Religions,* in which he attempts to assess the strengths and
weaknesses of various approaches to the theology of religions.[58] It is notable that
in this latter book Knitter, while not having significantly changed his mind, is
able to state clearly the objections to his own pluralism (which he now prefers to
call "mutualism" or the "Mutuality Model"). Pursuing our interest in center and
norm, we should consider Knitter's multinormed, correlational soteriocentrism,
which combines theology of religions with liberation and ecological theologies
for global responsibility.

Dialogue, says Knitter, must be multinormed, in that people of many traditions, with their various particular norms, will be brought to the table, and no one
will claim to hold all the cards. Nevertheless, he wants to allow for people to hold
fast to their specific religious commitments and truth claims, to defend them and
to state disagreements vigorously. Differences are not to be boiled away into a
"common religious soup." Dialogue must be "correlational" in that, while differences will remain, complementarity and mutual transformation are expected
and hoped for.

To all of this, a person of inclusivist inclinations might agree. A Christ-
centered Christian, normed by Christ and Scripture, will not necessarily claim to
hold all the cards, will stand fast with his/her specific truth claims and also be
hopeful and open to complementarity, mutual learning, and transformation. The
same could be said, for example, of a Qurʾan-centered Muslim, normed by the
Qurʾan. The pluralist, I suggest, has no monopoly on open-mindedness and open-
heartedness. Pluralists should not blandly assume that those who do not share
their approach are arrogant, or bent on religious domination. Knitter seems to
have heard his critics' charges that pluralism displays its own kind of religious
imperialism.

> In affirming the reality and the incorrigibility of differences between the
> religions, the correlational model agrees with the postmodern reminder
> that there simply does not exist any universal (or "meta-religious")
> standpoint from which one can stand outside the different religions in
> order to look down and evaluate them all. There's no one mountain top
> to which all religions lead and from which one can understand and
> assess them all.[59]

He is also in agreement with most Christ-centered inclusivists when he rejects
any "cultural linguistic prison" (an apparent reference to the approach of George
Lindbeck), which would leave all religious standpoints isolated in incommensu-

rable language games, unable to communicate with others. To all of this, most Christ-centered biblically normed Christians would agree.

But what does it mean for a pluralist theology to be soteriocentric, centered in salvation? Knitter explains that, rather than searching for a common God or any other kind of common core for all religious experiences (e.g., the Real for Hick, or faith for Smith), he will hold up salvation or the well-being of humans and the Earth as the starting point and common ground for interreligious dialogue.[60] Basic to this approach is our common human need and suffering, as well as our common dependence on a suffering and damaged Earth. Religous people of many traditions have at least these things in common, and all share as well a common concern for salvation in the broadest sense. While the different traditions interpret human need and suffering differently and prescribe different remedies or salvations, we can surely come together to share these perspectives and insights and cooperate together in order to diminish suffering and oppose the devastation of the ecosystems on which we all depend. Thus Knitter attempts to coalesce the concerns and insights of liberation and ecological theologies with interreligious dialogue, recommending

> that religious persons seek to understand and speak with each other on the basis of a common commitment to human and ecological well-being. Global responsibility therefore includes the notion of liberation intended by traditional liberation theologians but goes beyond it in seeking not just social justice but eco-human justice and well-being; it does so aware that such a project, in order truly to attend to the needs of all the globe, must be an effort by the entire globe and all its nations and religions.[61]

There is nothing to object to here. His goal is a theology and a religious attitude that are life-giving and liberating in the broadest sense. But Knitter displays a hard edge of judgment when he proposes to evaluate all religions according to their salvific efficacy, that is, how well they serve the "kingdom" of justice, peace, and ecological well-being. He is not interested in merely exchanging ideas and cooperating on practical projects. He wants dialogue to be about seeking truth together. For him, as a praxis-oriented liberationst, the truth is to be found precisely in the saving efficacy of all efforts for justice, peace, and wholeness. He had argued this already in his article in *The Myth of Christian Uniqueness*: "From their ethical, soteriological fruits you shall know them—we shall be able to judge whether and how much other religious paths and their mediators are salvific."[62] Even more strongly, Knitter declares that we should choose not to dialogue with religions or religious viewpoints that "deny any relationship between the transformation of this world and personal salvation or enlightenment."[63] To help remove the suffering of the world is the central goal and point of true religion. Eight years later, in *One Earth, Many Religions,* Knitter makes the same point: People of all the major religions can agree, he thinks, that "whatever else their experience of truth or of the Divine or of Enlightenment may bring about, it must always promote greater eco-human well being and help remove the sufferings of our world." Most significantly, this will be "the shared reference point from which to affirm or criticize each other's claims."[64] Religions will be assessed and valued as salvific according to this moral test. Again, this criterion is very close to our own test question for Christian theologies: Is it life-giving and liberating? What is different is that Knitter does not explicitly relate his criterion dialectically to Christ. His moral criterion appears to stand on its own as self-evident and is to be applied to all the religions. Here, like Hick, Knitter has basically followed the modern Kantian interpretation of religion as morality.[65] Religion exists to serve the moral imperative. At this point, Knitter's soterio-centrism becomes frankly exclusivist and missionary in character!

Again, the Christ-centered praxis-oriented theologian would heartily agree with his liberative and ecological goals and enthusiastically agree that this subject matter would be a desirable agenda for interreligious dialogue, but might find Knitter's stern pluralist exclusivism rather uncomfortable. The Christ-centered liberationist would bring these social-justice and environmental concerns to the interreligious table, but would do so frankly on the basis of Christ and the reign of God, as attested in the scriptures. Believers of other traditions, bringing other bases and norms, may share this ethical agenda, or may not do so. Some Buddhists, for example, may immediately see such a standard of judgment as Western and Christian in origin. They may opt instead for personal "enlightenment" as more truly salvific than struggle for social change (and here, incidentally, they would resemble some evangelical Christians). Knitter's definition of justice might be recognized as culturally constructed, the result of a long history of Marxist and other critical social thought in the West. For the modern, Western Christian of "the left," the gentle rehabilitation of criminals and efforts to transform social systems in order to prevent crime may seem like justice; for some Muslims, deeply rooted in their own norms, justice for criminals may imply dismemberment, and political action for social change may take an entirely different, perhaps theocratic direction.[66] It would presumably be salutary for Christians and Muslims to be in dialogue about such things, with the hope of mutual complementarity and transformation. But it would be the height of Western presumption for pluralist Christians to assume they hold all the cards and have only to convince Buddhists or Muslims to adopt their higher moral standpoint.

Asking the test question: Is it founded in Jesus Christ? and the accompanying question, Is it biblical?, the Christ-centered Christian might very well take up the same practical goals as Knitter does: One would opt for an eco-liberationist ethic of global responsibility. But one would not claim that this is an obvious, universal norm to which all human beings must be subject. If one wished to be seriously in dialogue with others who see things differently, one would need to recognize that there are other quite different value systems in the world, and then to share viewpoints with them in open dialogue. The basis for Christian ethical commitment is Jesus Christ. To understand Knitter's stance, we need to turn to his christology.

Knitter speaks of Jesus with great love and devotion. He affirms that Christianity has its "foundation and focus" in "Jesus the Christ."[67] He asserts that all formulations about Jesus, if they are to be "orthodox," "must flow from and nurture saving experience of and commitment to Jesus (devotion and prayer) and a resolute following of him in the world (discipleship and practice)." If they don't do this they are "heretical."[68] He develops admirably a christology that is in many respects congenial to liberationist theologies, utilizing such concepts as option for the poor, service of God's reign, and the primacy of following: *lex sequendi, lex credendi.* Orthopraxis is as important as orthodoxy. We believe in Jesus because, through following him, we find life and liberation. Moreover, Knitter speaks readily of Jesus as unique, universal, decisive, and indispensable. All of this integrates with the ethical, globally responsible eco-liberationist approach to interreligious dialogue, which would be entirely congenial to the Christ-centered liberationist.

However, as a pluralist, Knitter argues that, while Jesus is unique as Saviour and revelation of God, he is not the only unique saviour or revealer. While he is universal, decisive, and indispensable, this may be said of others as well.[69] Knitter can even speak of Jesus as incarnation of God, but he asserts that God may "be incarnated in other human natures besides that of Jesus."[70] Not only can there be other revelations, but other revelations at the same level; that is, Jesus can be placed within a "community of equals with other revealers."[71] Exclusive language about Jesus in the New Testament, such as "only Son," "only begotten," "once and for all," and so on, must be reinterpreted as love language (such as one might speak exclusively to one's spouse) or as performative, action language, expressing one's intention of following Jesus. Again, in "Five Theses on the Uniqueness of Jesus," Knitter contends: *"The uniqueness of Jesus' salvific role can be reinterpreted in terms of truly but not only."*[72] Uniqueness is affirmed of Jesus, but not exclusivity. He argues that there is no logical or experiential ground on which Christians can claim that Jesus is definitive or unsurpassable, no grounds for claiming that God could not be incarnated and act salvifically through others as well as through Jesus.

Knitter goes out of his way to meet the objections of his critics on the question of incarnation. He goes as far as to agree that Jesus can be called *totus Deus,* totally divine, but not *totum Dei,* the totality of the Deity.[73] Colossians 2:9, when it declares that "the whole fullness of Deity dwells bodily" in Jesus, cannot mean that the whole fullness of God's Deity is exhausted or restricted to Jesus.[74] But Knitter has set up a straw man here, since classical trinitarian christology has never claimed simply that Jesus is God and that God is Jesus! In a trinitarian theology, Jesus Christ is true God, and God has given God's own self utterly and without reserve in Jesus, but Jesus is never thought to exhaust the divine reality. Knitter has said a great deal, however, in claiming that Jesus is *totus Dei*, "totally divine." Again, in "Five Theses," he asserts that "Jesus is truly Son of God and universal Savior. . . . Jesus' divinity remains integral and essential to a pluralist christology." We encounter Jesus as "God's sacrament—as the embodiment, the historical reality, the symbol, the story that makes God real and effective for me." He can say that "Jesus is utterly at one with God . . . truly divine." He can even say that "God has acted in and as Jesus."[75]

It is extraordinary that all this can be said of Jesus, but of other revelatory, saving figures as well. It would indeed be startling and objectionable to the Muslim, the Buddhist, or the Confucianist if such things were said of Muhammad, the Buddha, or Confucius! We have to ask: Who are these others of whom these things can also be said? Who are Knitter's other candidates for divinity? Surely they should be identified so that we can proclaim them, follow, worship, and hope in them also? Or are there perhaps innumerable incarnations of the divine, like the innumerable avatars of Hinduism? Knitter leaves all of this rather vague.

We might ask also: What is the "unique" revelation or salvation that Jesus brings? In what sense is Jesus life-giving and liberating, according to Knitter? In *Jesus and the Other Names,* he spells out his preferred concepts for understanding Jesus. They are: spirit person, teacher of wisdom, social prophet, and movement founder. He adds, to sum them up: "mystic and social prophet."[76] In all of these ways Jesus is one of many, but any person of this kind will be "unique," in that he or she is distinctive. Jesus is distinctive, for Knitter, in the way he teaches about the reign of God, and this reign is one of love and justice. He explains: "Today, the uniqueness of Jesus can be found in his insistence that salvation or the Reign of God must be realized in this world through human actions of love and justice."[77] Jesus is unique, then, in what he insists upon, that is, in the message that he brings. But this would seem to make the great Hebrew prophets also unique, since they also insisted on worldly love and justice. Are they then also incarnations of God? Knitter goes on to argue that an appropriate christocentrism should not replace "kingdom-centrism," because Jesus would want us to focus not on him but on the kingdom.

It is obvious that this is a revised christology, not new or strange to liberal Protestantism, resembling the social-gospel theologies of the early twentieth century, but with a distinct contemporary liberationist and dialogical dimension. Though he is willing to use the language of incarnation, it is clear that he does not mean what Christians have usually meant by it, or what liberationists today (e.g., Gutiérrez, Boff, or Sobrino) mean by it. Jesus is essentially one who brings a message from God, that is, a prophet. He may be said to embody or incarnate the message (as other prophets might). He may even say that God is present and active in Jesus. But Jesus is not the Word of God made flesh in the full trinitarian sense in which Christians have usually proclaimed it. That is, as Knitter makes clear in *Jesus and the Other Names,* Jesus (among others) *represents* God's revealing and saving activity, but *is not* the triune God's own self-revealing self-gift.[78] Jesus, like many others, is representative of God's love, but is not *constitutive* of God's own self-giving. Jesus represents and signifies something that is generally true prior to and aside from Jesus.[79]

Not only is "incarnation" redefined drastically, but we notice that the concept of "Christ" is undeveloped. That "Christ" means "Messiah," the "anointed one," is ignored by Knitter. The matter is indeed a sensitive one in Jewish-Christian dialogue, in that, as we have seen, the designation of Jesus as Messiah has been implicated in the long history of Christian anti-Semitism. At the same time, political and liberation theologians have been at pains in recent years to point out the radical political and liberative significance of the Messiah as one who brings God's kingdom of justice and peace.[80] At any rate, the New Testament does not proclaim that Jesus merely preaches about the kingdom or admonishes people to be part of it, but that he decisively inaugurates or initiates the kingdom. The reign of God is said to have decisively broken through in Jesus, in his life, death, and resurrection. To say that he is the Messiah, the Christ, is far more than to say that he is a social prophet. It is to say that in him an eschatological event has occurred. God's reign of justice and peace has appeared and is decisively victorious in Jesus. The reign of God has come in Jesus, is coming here and now in the power of the Spirit, and is yet to come. If Jesus is merely another social prophet who calls people to obey God, there is no gospel and no grounds for Christian "Hallelujahs."

What we also notice about Knitter's christology is a notable deemphasis, indeed almost total neglect, of the cross and the resurrection of Jesus. It is strange that we find remarkably little about the cross in Knitter's writings. Though even within his perspective he could have spoken extensively about Jesus as martyr who died because of his radical commitment to God, even this is not emphasized. The scandal of the cross is canceled out, for we no longer hear of God's own self-giving on the cross, of God entering into death, with us and for us on the cross. We no longer here of the "foolishness and weakness of God" (1 Cor 1), for Knitter cannot say, with Jon Sobrino, for example, that "God suffered on Jesus' cross," and "God is crucified."[81] The theology of reconciliation is also abandoned, and so we hear little of grace or forgiveness of sins. That "God so loved the world" as to give "the only Son" (Jn 3:16) is not mentioned. Thus what we have in Knitter's theology is not a message of love and grace for sinners but a challenge for moral heroes.[82]

We also find few references to resurrection, but when we do hear of it the resurrection is spoken of in a very qualified way. For example, he speaks of "the experience his followers came to call the resurrection."[83] He also speaks ambiguously of "the power of his vision as it lives on in the community after his death."[84] As I have argued in the previous chapter, the actual resurrection of the crucified Christ is basic to the development of classical christology. Without the resurrection, there would have been no grounds for the apostles' conclusion that he was the Messiah. We would not be speaking of him as "the Christ," because without the resurrection there would have been no victorious inbreaking of God's reign. Moreover, as I have argued, without the resurrection no theology of incarnation would have developed. Knitter appears to want to affirm the language without the substance or the grounds on the basis of which the language appeared in the first place.

In view of this much-reduced understanding of the identity of Jesus Christ, it is quite logical that Knitter, like the other pluralists, wishes to move him out of the center and to speak of theocentrism, Reality-centrism, or soteriocentrism. As he explains in a footnote, Jesus is not *norma normans non normata,* a norm that norms all others but is not normed itself. Rather, for Knitter, Jesus is *norma normans et normata*, a norm that norms others, but can also be normed itself.[85] Jesus, then, is not primary norm. There is something more normative than Jesus Christ. That something is not some other great revelatory figure (e.g., the Buddha or Muhammad) since that would create another unacceptable, exclusive norm. The higher norm is nothing else but Knitter's own moral sense as a modern Western eco-liberationist. "The Enlightenment ghost," says Gavin D'Costa, "drives his christological project." His pluralism is "a strong form of Kantian exclusivist modernity."[86]

ॐ
ૐ

The pluralist theologians are to be appreciated for having pushed and challenged us to take the world religions seriously, to question the blatant or implicit imperialism in much of Christian theology and practice. They seek to express a generosity of spirit and respectful openness toward others that are consistent with the love and freedom of Jesus. Our christological canon itself prescribes such generosity and openness. What they say about the divine universality in the world is surely to be affirmed from a biblical and Christian perspective.

But, as I have suggested, the pluralists have no monopoly on a dialogical attitude or openness of mind and heart toward others. What shall we say to the claim that the pluralist decentering of Jesus is more respectful of the world religions and is therefore more life-giving and liberating? We have seen that, in the case of these three major pluralist authors, the claim is fallacious indeed. The religions are radically reinterpreted from within a liberal modernist perspective. Their primary norms, whether Jesus Christ, the Qur'an, the Buddha, or another, are relativized in terms of modern moral principles. Their particular truth claims are mythologized and/or relativized; their differing visions of salvation, their differing ways, are subordinated to a particular Western vision of moral progress. In this way the pluralists have set themselves up as the adjudicators of what the religions really mean, or should mean. While they intend to be evenhanded and to value all the great religions equally, they evidently operate out of a certain version of modern Western liberal Christianity, even if this is radicalized ethically in liberationist and ecological terms. What kind of dialogue will this promote? Perhaps a very comfortable dialogue of the devotees of modernity within the existing traditions. This is dramatically evident in a statement of Wilfred Cantwell Smith about his conversations with Muslims about scripture:

> I am more at ease with, feel more at home with, several of my Muslim friends (liberal intellectuals like me) as we consider together the meaning of scripture in the modern world . . . than I do with certain fellow Christians, as we speak together about the Bible."[87]

This may be all very well for liberal intellectuals, but will it really bring mainstream Christians or mainstream Muslims together in mutual understanding and mutual transformation? Presumably a Muslim, speaking with a Christian, is interested in hearing about the Trinity, salvation by grace, and, yes, the reign of God that has come, is present now, and is yet to come. Perhaps the Muslim would like to understand better what Christians mean by the suffering of God. The Christian, in turn, believing in the omnipresence and freedom of the Holy Spirit, may well be interested in hearing what the Muslim can share about the sovereignty and unity of God and about the disciplined life of prayer and fasting.

Something we must recognize about interreligious dialogue, if we are to be true to be the best insights of postmodernity, is just this: No one can hear truths that are utterly alien to his or her own formation. We are unlikely to be influenced or persuaded by ideas or concepts that are utterly strange, and we are likely to identify insights and wisdom in other religions if they already dovetail with our own. This is the nature of finite minds. Paul Knitter recognizes this. He remains a pluralist, though he now prefers to be labeled a "mutualist." He has not gone over (back across the Rubicon) to the inclusivist or what he now calls the "fulfillment" camp, but he is admirably aware of the pitfalls of his own stance. Acknowledging there the critical acumen of his critics, Knitter declares in *Introducing Theologies of Religions:* "We are all inclusivists." Inclusivism is the name for those who affirm the beauty and truth of other religions but assess them according to their own criteria, perhaps enlarging or deepening their own vision by learning from the religious other, perhaps also inviting the other to be fulfilled by taking up one's own fuller vision of the truth. But, says Knitter, "no matter how open-minded or liberal we might be, this is what—at least to some extent—we are always doing." This applies also to the pluralist or mutualist:

> When a mutualist theologian identifies something in another religion as "challenging" or as a "powerfully new insight," what's the basis for reaching such a conclusion? It's because what the theologian finds in the other traditon relates to, or fits into, what she/he already knows and affirms in his/her own religion.[88]

All of us, then, are always inclusivists in this sense.[89] When we fail to recognize this, we fall into the danger of religious or intellectual imperialism and arrogance. It is important to recognize that our faith stance is just that: faith and not sight. Faith by its very nature is vulnerable, fragile, and essentially humble. It has no power to coerce by powerful arguments and therefore can never take the attitude that it holds all the cards. Rather, it takes up an attitude of genuine friendliness and hospitality in which friends listen to each other and share their different stories. I suggest that we avoid arrogance and imperialism in relation to the religious other not by relativizing or reducing our truth claims (thereby implying that others should do the same) but by simply recognizing our own vulnerability in faith. This is especially appropriate if we are centered in Jesus Christ, the crucified one. We worship not a forceful, domineering deity but a gentle, suffering God who brings life through death and liberates through love.

PART III

Other Indispensable Criteria of Theological Adequacy

CHAPTER 7

Is It Biblical?

We seek a life-giving and liberating approach to the Bible and its normative status. We have already said a good deal about the authority and interpretation of scripture in the chapter on revelation and faith, but we need now to explore further what it means for the scripture to be normative. Speaking descriptively, for Christians an adequate theology or a defensible theological stance on any particular matter must be biblical. This is not the most fundamental of theological norms, however, since the Bible is not in and of itself the Word of God and not persistently liberating. It must therefore be read both reverently and critically if it is to give life. I have already argued that the question Is it founded in Jesus Christ? is a more basic criterion of theological adequacy for Christians. There is a sense in which, as Karl Barth said, "theology begins and ends with Jesus Christ," in that he is, as Jon Sobrino has said, *norma normans non normata* (the norm which norms other norms and is not normed by any higher norm).[1] While Christians have most often given scripture this status,[2] I would contend (with many others) that not the Bible, but Christ, is rock bottom for a liberative Christian theology. Scripture has secondary normative status for us as Christians precisely because the Bible is our primary witness to Jesus Christ, who is *himself*, in his life, death, and resurrection, the revelation and Word of God made flesh (Jn 1:14). Scripture is, or better, *becomes again and again*, Word of God by the Spirit's power, in that it witnesses to the decisive events of God's revelation. At the same time we have to recognize that the Bible is our first *tangible* source for theology, in that we know Jesus Christ in and through it. Those who argue for scripture as the *norma normans* have this on their side: that in a certain practical sense, we begin concretely with the Bible.

We might initially consider what the scripture itself says about scripture. No Hebrew term translated specifically as scripture is ever used in the Hebrew Bible by its own authors, though we sometimes hear of "scrolls" (e.g., Jer 36:2; Ezra 6:2) and frequently of "the book," especially the "book of Moses," the "book of the law," or the "book of the covenant" (e.g., Deut 29:21; 31:26; 2 Kgs 23:21;

2 Chr 25:4; Ezra 6:18; Neh 13:1; etc.). New Testament texts, of course, do not refer to themselves as "scriptures" since they were not written *as* scripture. But they do refer frequently to the Hebrew scriptures (*graphai*) and to the "book" (*biblia,* from which the term "Bible" comes, especially, again, "book of Moses," "book of the law," and "book of the prophet," e.g., Mk 12:26; Gal 3:10; Lk 4:17), books that came to be regarded by Christians as the "Old Testament." Prophetic texts are cited (whether or not the word "scripture" is used) as foretelling aspects of Jesus' life in order to identify him as the expected anointed one (e.g., Mt 1:22-23; Lk 24:27; 1 Cor 15:3). Very frequently the term "scripture(s)" is found in the New Testament on the lips of Jesus, and there is every reason to believe that Jesus knew the scriptures intimately and cited them often (e.g., Mk 12:10; Mt 21:42; Lk 24:45; Jn 5:39). Even more numerous are the instances of the word "written" in both testaments. In the story of Jesus' temptation (Mt 4; Lk 4) he repeatedly replies to Satan: "it is written. . . ." Evidently, Jesus and his disciples, and the whole religious milieu of the time, lived out of the scriptures and regarded them with great reverence as communicating God's will and truth to the people. With reference to the Hebrew scriptures, we find in the Second Epistle of Timothy a doctrine of scriptural inspiration: "All scripture is inspired by God and is useful for teaching, for reproof, for correction, and for training in righteousness" (2 Tim 3:16). On the other hand, Jesus sometimes relativizes the written word: "You have heard that it was said to those of ancient times. . . . But I say to you . . ." (Mt 5:21-22; etc.). Here the texts place the authority of Jesus above that of the scriptures. Jesus himself becomes the *norma normans.* According to Mark 11:28-29, Jesus refuses to provide scriptural authority for what he is doing. Sometimes, "human traditions" or "traditions of the elders" are referred to, suggesting that some of the details of the law, as interpreted by the Pharisees, are human and not divine in origin (e.g., Mk 7:8; Mt 15:2, 6). The first Christians, after the resurrection, still quoted the Hebrew scriptures constantly, yet with a certain freedom in relation to them. Paul, for example, tells the Christians at Corinth that they themselves are "a letter of Christ . . . written not with ink but with the Spirit of the living God, not on tablets of stone but on tablets of human hearts." He goes on to say, using a play on words, that "the letter kills, but the Spirit gives life" (2 Cor 3:2-3, 6). Jesus and his first followers, then, refused to give ultimate authority to written words, even words of scripture, or to long-held traditions, for final authority belongs only to the living God.[3]

A Posteriori

That Christian theology must be biblical, and that the Bible is a secondary norm, is not an *a priori* principle or axiom. As we said in the case of christology, it would be impossible to say, in the abstract, prior to any engagement with Christian faith or theology, how theology should proceed, just as it would be impossible to say, *a priori*, how geology, history, physics, or sociology should proceed prior to some engagement with these disciplines and their objects of inquiry.[4] Rather, to say that theology must be biblical is to state an *a posteriori* methodological precept. It is an after-the-fact observation about actual Christian theological discourse. Not that this is a simple matter of observing any theological discussion and making normative whatever is going on, since, no doubt, theological discussion often proceeds in inappropriate ways. There is a difference between descriptive and normative discussion. Yet it is only from within actual engagement with Christian faith and theology that it becomes evident that Christian theology is *appropriately and properly* biblical. While it is true that we need to be ready to explain to anyone in a reasonable manner, either within or without the faith community, why and in what sense the Bible has normative status for us, the rationality we seek is not some external rationality imposed from outside of faith. What we need to understand is the inner necessity that Christian theology should be biblical.[5]

A methodological precept we identified in relation to christology is relevant here too: *Lex orandi, lex credendi.* The law of prayer is the law of belief. Or, a little more broadly, the law of worship is the law of belief. Always and everywhere Christians read the Bible when they gather for worship. They pray that they will hear God's Word from the words of these scriptures. That the Old and New Testaments have unique status in the church is reflected in the fact that throughout the Christian ecumenical world only these texts are read out as "scripture," seeking God's Spirit in order that God's Word of truth may be heard from them. Yet the reading of the Bible is accompanied by prayer that the Spirit will truly speak through this book, for it is not the book in and of itself that gives life, light, and wisdom. Moreover, the liturgical reading of scripture is normally followed by interpretive preaching. Interpretation and preaching are required because the Word we seek is not an old and dead word but a living Word for here and now. Scripture's place in worship, then, and therefore in Christian faith and life, establishes and reflects its normative character for theology. We may recall once again here the precept that is especially congenial to the liberation theologies: *Lex sequendi, lex credendi.* The law of following is the law of belief. We saw, in the case of christology, that our efforts to follow Jesus in practical life, and the life and liberty that this affords, establish his authority for our theological thought. So also with scripture: we live our lives and carry out the work of discipleship and mission under the guidance of these scriptures. The Bible is indispensable to Christian *praxis* and therefore also to our theological thinking; without it, the life that Christ offers could not have reached us.

In actual theological discussion among Christians it is normal (if not quite universal) for people to defend their theological stances by arguing that they are biblical. "What I am saying," they will contend, "is from the Bible" (that is, those texts that we read out every Sunday when we gather for worship). Or, "what I am *doing* is based in the Bible," or "in harmony with or congruent with the Bible," or "derives from the Bible at its best" (that is, those texts from which we hear of God's reign of justice and peace, those texts that teach us about grace, love, and hope).

Though most Christians will feel it is essential to be biblical *in some sense*, both for their own theological integrity and for the purpose of recommending their theological viewpoints to others in the church, it is not a simple matter to decide in what being biblical consists. In theological debate among Christians, when they discuss courses of action, or doctrine, or ethics, or worship, everyone (or almost everyone) knows that the biblical ground cannot be surrendered. In theological debate, whether about practices of discipleship, political ethics, ordination, mission, the Trinity, christology, or baptismal or eucharistic practice, to admit that your position is unbiblical is to admit that it is indefensible in the faith community. The authority of the scripture for all theological thinking is, in this way, *a posteriori*: after the fact.

Not Oppressive Biblicism

But let us consider more closely why and in what sense theology must be biblical. It is not enough to describe this as a *fait accompli* without appreciating its inner rationale. Is this perhaps a piece of superstition, as though the Bible is some supernatural phenomenon, fallen from the skies, a book "with all the answers to all our problems" (as I was once told in Sunday School)? Is it because the Bible is the inspired Word of God from which "God's own words" can therefore be quoted to resolve any disagreement?

There are great voices of the Christian tradition which assume a very high doctrine of scriptural inspiration. Calvin, the founding systematic theologian of the Reformed tradition, could say of scripture that "God is its author,"[6] and he could even say that it is "dictated by the Holy Spirit."[7] The great Methodist patriarch John Wesley also, truly a life-giving preacher and leader of his day, could speak of the Holy Spirit as the "author of Scripture," and in this he was not out of line with Augustine, Aquinas, and even Luther.[8] For Wesley, "the written Word of God" is "the only and sufficient rule, both of Christian faith and practice."[9] He could say that Protestants "believe whatsoever God has declared. By this they will abide, and no other."[10] Although these authors were not entirely unaware of the humanity and fallibility of the scriptures, it was the character of scripture as "inspired" and its powerful, liberating influence in their own lives and in the life of their churches that most impressed them.

In spite of our great respect for these authors of our theological tradition, no such biblicism will be defended here. A simple application of the logical law of noncontradiction rules out any such supernaturalist notion of the Bible. A mere comparison of the creation texts in Genesis 1 and 2, or the differing stories of Paul's conversion (Acts 9:7; 22:9) or the divergent reports concerning the resurrection of Jesus in the four Gospels, makes it immediately evident that this is a human and fallible book. Presumably, if God had written it, God could have done better. And even a casual reading of the Bible makes it plain to contemporary people that this collection of ancient books of stories, laws, poetry, letters, and so on is culturally conditioned, finitely located as to its worldviews and ethical precepts, and even theologically diverse in its understandings of God, humanity, sin, and salvation. Karl Barth, who among twentieth-century theologians placed the authority and "miracle" of scripture very high indeed, pointed out that the Bible is fallible, not only historically and scientifically, but theologically as well.[11] It is easy for anyone of intelligence to tear the Bible apart; indeed, as William Placher puts it, "You need not deconstruct these texts. They fall apart in your hands."[12] Any dictation theory of biblical inspiration is plainly untenable to reasonable people.

Moreover, with heightened modern and postmodern consciousness, we realize now that the Bible can be quoted and used to defend all kinds of destructive opinions, attitudes, and actions, or, as some church people are wont to say, "You can use the Bible to defend anything!" Or, as Shakespeare put into the mouth of one his characters: "The devil can cite scripture for his purpose."[13] This is not only because the Bible is badly interpreted; many texts are in themselves potentially destructive, raising questions in the minds of many faithful people about their status as "inspired" Word of God.

Imagine an encounter between three women, Jenny, Kathy, and Brenda, in a church study group on peace and violence in the Bible. They have been looking at parts of the Old Testament, including 1 Samuel 15.

Conversation

JENNY: *What do you make of this part in 1 Samuel 15:3, where God tells them to kill all their enemies? It says: "Now go and smite Amalek, and utterly destroy all that they have; do not spare them, but kill both man and woman, infant and suckling, ox and sheep, camel and donkey." I don't believe God ever commanded such a horrible thing! One thing for sure, it doesn't sound like Jesus!*

BRENDA: *You know I heard a preacher on TV using one of these kinds of texts, saying that this shows how God's people—and by that he seemed to mean the United States—sometimes have to kill their enemies ruthlessly. He was actually using the Bible to back up the president on the Iraq war! I have to say, I really doubt whether this text is the Word of God.*

KATHY: [Shocked and annoyed] *Oh, get off your anti-American kick! Laugh at these preachers if you like, but at least they're not watering anything down. They're not picking and choosing, taking from the Bible what they like and throwing the rest out! I still say the Bible is the Word of God, the whole Bible, and not just a couple of verses you like!*

JENNY: *Yes, but what do we mean by the Word of God? I can't really think of it that way. To me the Bible is a kind of religious classic. Like other great classics of religious literature. It has a lot of deep, inspiring thoughts, but a lot of primitive and really dreadful stuff as well. And besides, there are lots of other inspiring books besides the Bible with deep inspiring thoughts. I get more out of the Bhagavad-Gita than I do from 1 Samuel, let me tell you. The book of Leviticus never did much for me, or parts of the New Testament, for that matter. I love Kahlil Gibran. You know,* The Prophet? *Now there's an inspiring author. He's so humane, so wise, and he's not even a Christian! This bit about God commanding a massacre without mercy just seems to be a piece of power politics. Imagine reading this out in church? It would be dangerous in case there was some unbalanced individual who might take it seriously.*

KATHY: *Well, if I thought the way you do I'd be so confused I wouldn't know what I believed. My faith is important to me, but if I can't trust the Bible, how can I believe in God at all?*

BRENDA: *I know what you mean, Kathy. There's no way I could start reading all the holy books of all the religions of the world. Let's face it, I haven't got the time, and I've got enough trouble just understanding the Bible. But I must admit, there are other spiritual writings that I find much more inspirational than most parts of the Bible. Sometimes I think that maybe we should add on to the Bible some of the really good writings from later times. Like Christian writers of our own time who seem to be in touch with the world as it is now. Recently I picked up Dietrich Bonhoeffer's* Letters and Papers from Prison. *Found it in the church library. Now there is a deep thinker. I found what he had to say really moving. I felt when I was reading Bonhoeffer that God was speaking straight to me. I can't believe God stopped revealing himself with Jesus.*

JENNY: *So you think other books besides the Bible are inspired as well?*

BRENDA: [Hesitantly] *Yes, I guess so.*

KATHY: *Well, I'm sorry, but as far as I'm concerned, the Bible is the Bible, and nothing can take its place. Last Sunday in church, what did we read? The Bible, and nothing but the Bible. Nobody got up and read from the Koran or Gibran or Bonhoeffer. If we went by what you two are saying, we'd be reading from who knows what! Before long everything would be the Word of God! But it doesn't make sense!*

All of these women are making good points. "The Bible has done so much damage in the world!" a liberal church member said to me once. We see the need to defend ourselves theologically by means of "hermeneutical suspicion" against those who would quote the Bible for destructive or oppressive purposes. In our time it has been especially the feminists who have pointed out the potential of the

Bible to do damage, since it has so often been used as a weapon against women, for example, texts that blame women for the sin of the world and place them in subjection to men (e.g., Gen 3:16; Jud 11; Eph 5:22; 1 Tim 2:11-15). But beyond this, the authority of the Bible has been used to suppress the freedom of the mind to think and research in the physical and biological sciences. It is still used to defend creationism and other forms of anti-intellectualism. Parts of the Bible have been used to uphold the violence and domination of oppressive rulers over their subjects (e.g., Rom 13:1-7) and authorize the discrimination or abuse of homosexual people by heterosexual people (Lev 20:13); of disabled people by those who are well (Lev 21:18-20); of conquering peoples over the vanquished (Deut. 7:1-5; 1 Sam. 15:3); of the natural order by humanity (Gen. 1:28). Of late some folk have been taking very seriously the text from Proverbs 13:24: "Those who spare the rod hate their children . . . ," and shocking the Children's Aid Societies by beating their little ones. The authority of the Bible for Christian faith and life can no longer be this kind of authority. For example, rules for the regulation of relationships cannot be read simplistically out of the Bible. Few today will agree that wives should obey their husbands or slaves obey their masters! (Eph 5:22; 6:5). The Bible is simply not a rule book, and attempts to use it as such have lost credibility to reasonable people in our time. Yet, on the other side of the argument, the Bible has to be taken seriously as "scripture," and therefore indispensable to faith and theology.

"Canon" of "Inspired" Scripture

Having recognized the human and flawed character of the Bible, we need to acknowledge and understand its unique place as "canonical scripture" in the life of the church and its indispensable and incomparable place in theological method. It has been considerations such as those mentioned above that have pushed so many people in our churches, quite understandably, to adopt another kind of extreme in their attitude to the Bible. If one extreme is a dictation theory of inspiration and an oppressive biblicism by which the words of the Bible become the very Words of God available for the support of our prejudices, there is another extreme that sees the Bible not as holy scripture at all but as just one of many sources of truth and inspiration in the church—a kind of religious classic. It is surely true that scriptural texts such as 1 Samuel 15 and many others have to be read critically in light of our primary norm, Jesus Christ. We believe we know God most fully in Christ, that he *is* God's revelation and Word made flesh. The gentle, compassionate, and suffering God whom we meet in Christ seems to pass judgment on the concept of God found, for example, in 1 Samuel 15 or 1 Timothy 2. Surely it is true that God is free to "speak" to us beyond the words of the Bible, so that we may indeed feel that God is speaking to us through the scriptures of other religions or through other later Christian writings, whether devotional or theological. God speaks through sermons, and even through movies and novels. To say that the Bible is uniquely holy and scriptural is not to say that God is tied down to communicating with us through the Bible only. Yet scripture does have a special and unique place in the church's life and worship. Just what is really special about the Bible that makes it holy scripture? Why do we read only these texts in the context of worship? It is interesting that even many liberal members of the church feel that they must show that their theological stances and practical proposals for decisions in the church are biblical, and that their protagonists' viewpoints are not biblical enough.

Wherein lies, then, the Bible's unique place in the life of the church? It is derived, first, from the historical character of the church's foundational events. A peculiarity of what Christians believe concerning God is God's historicity. Christians (defined very loosely for the moment in terms of belief) are those who claim that the ultimate truth, and the meaning and destiny of humanity and of all things, is found in the holy One disclosed in the history of the people Israel and in the Jew from Nazareth, Jesus the Christ, who was crucified, is risen, and is present with us by God's Spirit. A few people, like the nineteenth-century philosopher G. E. Lessing, have tried to argue that "the logical truths of reason have nothing to do with the accidental truths of history"[14]—that is, that Christian truth is a general metaphysical and moral truth, independent of any historical events. But Christians have usually recognized that their actual faith in God is tied irrevocably to the events of Israel's history (such as exodus, covenant, Sinai, the prophets, exile, restoration) and finally to the events of the life, death, and resurrection of Jesus Christ. Without these foundational events Christian faith as such would certainly not exist. This does not mean that God's self-disclosure ended with Jesus' resurrection. It does mean that all subsequent self-revelation of God, as far as Christians are concerned, has reference back to Jesus within the history of Israel. What we know of God there, in the biblical testimony to that history, has become normative, or as we say, "canonical" for what we know of God here and now. Fresh revelation, through the Holy Spirit, of the love of God and of God's will for us, is evaluated, or discerned, by reference to the decisive past events of God's self-disclosure and liberating work.

This very historicity of God in Israel and in Jesus Christ implies the necessity of scripture. Since God has given God's very self to us in an extraordinary manner at a particular time and place, those of us in another time and place can only know of this by the "narrative of the things which have been accomplished among us by those who from the beginning were eyewitnesses" (Lk 1:1-2). What we have in the Old and New Testaments is testimony to particular, unique, unrepeatable events. The exodus, for example, was a specific historical, liberative event. Even if the story is told in legendary fashion and the actual events prove difficult to reconstruct, even if the vision of God we find there falls short of what we find in Jesus, this event still became and remains formative for all subsequent Jewish faith, and for Christian faith as well. Jesus too, was a very specific, datable human being, whose person and work were of a particular character. The biblical material does not consist of philosophical reflection about deity. It is not a verbally inspired message dictated from on high. Nor is it profound human religious thought. Rather, it consists (mainly) of imperfect but nevertheless solid testimonies to historical events, and faith-full interpretation of those events.

It is common language among Christians to speak of scripture as "inspired by God" and this has a long history among the great theologians of the church. Having noted the palpably human and fallible character of the scripture, it is obvious that this cannot mean word-for-word inspiration in the sense of dictation, as though God whispered the words of the Bible verbatim into its authors' ears. That is why it is impossible simply to equate the Bible with the Word of God. We may think of the inspiration of the Bible in this way: The biblical books were written by people who were inspired—enlightened, empowered—by experiences of God's presence in the life and history of their community. To say that the writers were inspired is to say that the Spirit of God "breathed into" them (*inspired*) a way of seeing and understanding certain persons and events. This occurred, of course, not "out of the blue" but within the context of a faith community and tradition and within a relationship of faith and prayer. It is evident that this process of inspiration did not in any sense take over their minds or personalities, or negate the limitations of their time and place. Yet we may say that God's self-disclosing and saving initiative lies behind these writings and still works through them. When we read them, we too may be inspired—that is, we are drawn into those revelatory events and share in them by what Calvin called "the inward testimony of the Holy Spirit."[15] They become "Word of God" for us again and again by the breathing of God's Spirit in and through them, and by the Spirit's work within us, opening mind and heart to be receptive to what God communicates. This is why we typically pray before reading scripture, asking that the Spirit will speak to us here and now through the mediation of the scripture.

If we take the Holy Spirit seriously as God's present activity within us and among us, then later, extrascriptural writings by wise, inspired teachers or leaders may be just as inspired and inspiring as the Bible is. Though certain revelatory events of the past are "once and for all" and decisive in their significance, the work of the Holy Spirit here and now is not less revealing than the revelatory events of the past. (To think otherwise has sometimes been called the heresy of subordinating the Spirit to the Son, or the Spirit to the Word.) Thus, the work of devotional writers, spiritual leaders, teachers, theologians such as Dietrich Bonhoeffer in our discussion above, and countless others may be a means through which God's Word and Spirit reach us now. It should not be surprising that such writings from times and circumstances closer to our own are often experienced as more inspiring or moving than the ancient scriptural documents. Moreover, last Sunday's sermon, based in the scriptural witness, spoken aloud by the living voice, was also, we hope, the Word of God for us, and it may be in some way better or more inspired than some parts of the Bible. The proclamation of the Word too, after all, is truly the Word of God, by the power of the Holy Spirit.[16] Scripture, as we have said, requires interpretation for every new time and place, in order that a "living Word" may be spoken. Preaching and verbal witness are human and fallible, of course, but so also is the scripture. God speaks and the Spirit works through "earthen vessels," that is, faulty human documents and flawed human minds.

Nevertheless, later inspired or inspiring writings and present witness and preaching cannot replace or fulfill the same function as the original testimonies to those decisive and foundational events. The specialness of scripture is not that it is qualitatively better than all other writing or witness. What makes scripture incomparable and irreplaceable is not that it is more inspired or more the Word of God, but its historical and spatial proximity to original, decisive revelatory events. That is why present-day proclamation of the Word depends on and is based in the scriptural testimony.

When we consider the Old Testament specifically, we must keep in mind that these were the original Christian scriptures. As we already noted above, when the New Testament speaks of "scripture," it refers to the Bible of Israel. It is impossible to imagine the existence of a Gospel of Christ apart from this Hebrew witness, since everything that is said in the Gospel is said about a certain Jew, who stood in the tradition of exodus and the prophets, who is proclaimed as Israel's Messiah, Servant of God, and Son of Man. With beautiful circularity, the first Christians interpreted Jesus through the Bible of Israel and then interpreted that Bible itself through Jesus. Thus, as Robert Jenson puts it, Israel's scripture is "antecedently constitutive for the apostles' relation to their Lord and so for the existence of the church."[17]

This spatial and temporal proximity of the scriptural witness to revelatory events is not all that needs to be said about the special status of scripture. Where New Testament scripture is concerned, books gained their canonical status because the church believed them to be "apostolic." With the death of the apostles it became necessary to have some authentic and authorized compendium of their message. The New Testament is spoken of as "apostolic witness"—not that all or most of its books were written by the apostles themselves but that they gained their authority as faithful record of the apostles' own preaching and teaching. While Christ himself is our ultimate authority, we have access to him, in his life, death, and resurrection, only through the witness of the apostles. We may, through scholarly detective work, try to go behind the apostolic witness as we have it in the New Testament, to the true "Jesus of history." This project has a certain validity, since Jesus is a verifiable figure in world history, subject to the inquiry even of secular historians. But even this is impossible without the scriptural documents themselves. If we affirm faith in Jesus Christ, we are totally dependent on the apostles' witness, since, as Jenson put it so well: "if the apostles did not get it right, no one ever did. And when we arrive at the apostles, we have no place else to go, for . . . there can be no witness in any sense between them and the resurrection."[18]

Closely related to this, of course, is the unique place of the Bible as "the book of the Church," recognized (with minor variations) as *canonical* (the standard, or rule of faith) by the whole universal church. If biblical texts speak life and liberty to us, we may indeed see the process of canonization also as a work of the Spirit. It was the early church, through a long experience of constant usage and gradual consensus, which put together the New Testament canon, though the church was never without a canon of holy writings, for it always recognized what we now call the Old Testament as scripture. The Bible, constituted more or less as we know it, was in place in the church by approximately the middle of the second century, and the term "canon" was applied to the biblical writings to indicate their status as sacred scriptures for the first time about the middle of the fourth century.[19] That the Christian community acknowledged these books and not others does not mean that the church had authority over scripture or gave authority to scriptures that they did not already have. Calvin, as a theological leader of the Reformation, made this point vigorously in his *Institutes* over against teachings of the Roman Catholic Church, wishing to insist that the church does not have authority over scripture but rather is under the authority of the Word, as found in scripture.[20] Rather, the church acknowledged these books (and not others) because it believed that they were apostolic and that they had been received from God. That is, through its lengthy process of ecclesial discernment, the church acknowledged these books because of their own inherent life-giving authority and because of the inspiration of the Spirit.[21]

Although the distinction between scripture and tradition is important, there is a sense in which the distinction is not absolute (something still to be discussed in a later chapter) in that scripture is the earliest, ecclesially authorized tradition (from *tradeo*, that which has been handed on). Because it is the earliest, and because it was by a process of consensus acknowledged by the whole church, it has become uniquely authoritative for us, not in an individualistic sense but as a community of faith. The individual does not lightly or arrogantly assert his or her own preferences over against the whole church about the makeup of the canon. However, this does not mean that the acknowledgment of these books as canonical by the church is guaranteed as absolutely correct. On the contrary, as Barth teaches, the setting of the canon involved fallible human decision, so that the question of the canon cannot be regarded as necessarily closed. It is not impossible that some ancient books hitherto rejected could gain canonical authority by a responsible ecumenical church council. We cannot say, *a priori,* for example, that other ancient Gospels—say, the *Gospel of Thomas,* or the *Gospel of Mary*—should not be canonized (though a close reading of them may give us a good idea why they were set aside by the early church). We have no guarantee that other ancient books may not yet be discovered that could be acknowledged as rightly canonical or even that a responsible church body could decide to decanonize certain texts. We know that the makeup of the canon was controversial in the early church, and again in the time of the Reformation, and that the canons of Roman Catholics and Protestants are somewhat different. "We cannot . . . then say to individuals in the Church—as though Luther and Calvin had never had any doubts on the question—that in certain Scriptures . . . they will hear in equal measure the Word of God."[22] Yet a radical questioning of the makeup of the canon would place one's whole faith in jeopardy. Jenson makes the point: "Perhaps the canon is a disastrously bad list. . . . Then the church must have been irretrievably astray since the middle of the third century at the latest. Belief that the gospel is still extant includes the belief that the canon is adequate."[23] By honouring and listening to scripture, we acknowledge the dependence of our faith upon it and at the same time honour our original forebears of Hebrew and Christian faith as well as the worldwide ecumenical community. This is an additional reason why, in theological debate, especially in worship and preaching, and in decision-making courts of the church, scripture has incomparable status and authority.

Other Scriptures

But what about all the other scriptures of the world? Is it not arrogant and rather unrealistic to give so much weight to our scriptures and to disregard all the others? Other people are just as convinced about the validity of their scriptures as we are of ours. This is an important question in our time, part of that vast field of interfaith dialogue and theology of religion that this book does not deal with substantially. But I shall attempt one or two clarifications here.

What is meant by scripture or sacred writings in other religions can throw light on the specific character of Christian scripture. We should first note that "scripture" is a Christian term for which there is not always a corresponding concept in other religious cultures. In his major study of the general concept of scripture, Wilfred Cantwell Smith makes it clear that what we Christians mean by scripture (and even among Christians there is great variety) may be quite different from what people of other religious traditions understand about their sacred books. For some Asian peoples our concept of "classics" is perhaps closer to their concept, that is, collections, sometimes huge, of wise and ancient writings. For Buddhists, for example, holy books amount to a thousand times or more the length of our Bible![24] Though they include records of the Buddha and his life story, there is no clearly defined canon relating to a particular ancient time or decisive revelatory events, so that they include also vast sapiential reflections deriving from the religious life of many centuries. The holy books would include, then, writings comparable to those of the Christian church fathers and many theological and devotional writers of numerous schools of thought down through the centuries. The Hindu *Vedas,* also, are not made up mainly of historical witness to unique revelatory events, but offer rather "knowledge," since *veda* means essentially transcendental insight or spiritual awareness.[25] Some parallel to them may be found in the wisdom literature of the Bible—Proverbs, Ecclesiastes, Job, and the Greek sapiential apocrypha. However, the biblical notion of the unique historical event as vehicle of revelation is absent and strange to this religious tradition. Consequently, scripture, or holy writings, must mean something quite different.

Muslims, on the other hand, have a very clearly defined scripture in the Qurʾan, which is believed to be the very Word of God or, as Smith puts it, the *ipsissima verba* (the very words) *of God himself,* written on tablets in eternity and delivered to humanity for all time by Muhammad, the last and greatest of the prophets. The Qurʾan is spoken in Arabic and cannot rightly be translated. The holy book, then, is not at all the same thing for Muslims as the Bible is for Christians. Rather, the Qurʾan corresponds (approximately) to what Christ is for Christians—the very revelation itself; it is for Muslims unambiguously the *norma normans non normata.* Whereas for Christians, the scripture bears witness to Christ, who is the Word, for Muslims, Muhammad brings the Qurʾan, which is itself identifiable with God's Word. For Muslims the *hadith*, which are essential but secondary traditions of the interpretation of the Qurʾan, are closer to what Christians generally mean by scripture.[26]

Closest to a Christian notion of scripture is, of course, the Jewish, since what Christians refer to as the Old Testament is more or less, in content, what Jews refer to as *Tanakh.* This term is an acronym for the three types or levels of sacred scripture: the Law, the Prophets, and the Writings. But we cannot simply equate the *Tanakh* with the Old Testament, since the books appear in a different order, and, of course, the Jews do not regard their scriptures as "old" in the sense of prior to something else. Neither does "testament" quite apply. Rather, the Jews think of their sacred scriptures as a whole as *Torah*, though that word can also be used to mean the first five books—the so-called Pentateuch, or the books of Moses. While the *T* of *Tanakh* signifies *Torah* as the first and most important part of the scripture, *Torah* as referring to the whole of the scriptures means essentially not "Law," as it is often translated, but more generally, "instruction" or "guidance." It is the whole message of God to humanity, instructing and guiding human beings concerning God's will for living.[27] For Jews, God's *davar* ("word") to the people comes mainly through the prophets, but decisive revelatory events in history are also basic, as they are also, derivatively, for Christians.

Smith tells us that it is normal for devotees of most religions to regard their scriptures with enormous reverence. Sometimes unheard-of memorization occurs; it is common, in fact, for Muslims to be able to recite the whole of the Qurʾan word for word, and for some Jewish rabbis to quote the Hebrew scriptures voluminously. Often the words of holy books are thought to have hidden meanings, the literal sense being nothing but an outer garment for profound truth hardly accessible to humanity. "It is altogether standard to feel," says Smith, "that this finite work held in the hand, or mind, enshrines much more than overtly appears. Buddhists, Jews, Muslims and others concur in locating ultimate truth and reality in every letter, every stroke of the pen."[28] It is true that Christians too have often regarded the Bible with similar awe and reverence.

It is important, then, to realize that, while many religions possess books that are held to be in some way sacred, when we speak of the many scriptures of many religions we are not talking simply about many instances of the same genre.

That as Christians we do not regard all the holy books of all the religions as scriptural for us does not imply that we despise them or dismiss their value or wisdom. They may indeed be very inspired and inspiring, more so than some parts of the Bible. We may well benefit greatly by reading and studying them, and God may indeed speak to us through them. Certainly God is not limited to our scriptures. If we take the biblical tradition seriously, we know that the God whom we worship is free and unconstrained, not tied down to Israel or the church. Reading these holy books of other religions (or, for that matter, the work of wise philosophers, novelists, or poets, whether Christian or not) may modify or even profoundly change our own theological understanding. It is worth noting that the ancient Greeks thought that poetry was inspired by God or the gods. Many kinds of literature, but perhaps most often the poetic, can lift us up out of the ordinary plane of living and afford inspiration for life. All the more, then, might the sacred books of other religions, which have guided millions of people for millennia, offer us wisdom and truth, and so evoke our regard and respect. Nevertheless none of these holy books can be scriptural for us as Christians, since they do not bear witness to the foundational events of our Christian faith. It is not that the Bible in all its parts is somehow superior to all the others. The point is that only the Bible is *constitutive* for us as a believing Christian community (in a manner similar to but not quite the same as the way in which the Qur'an is constitutive for Muslims as an Islamic community).[29] The testimonies of the Old and New Testaments have unique authority for us because they uniquely bear witness to Jesus Christ within the history of Israel. The Old Testament, for Christians, is the indispensable witness to God's special disclosure, covenant, and saving work with the people of Israel, out of which Jesus has come and without which we would lack all the categories necessary for understanding who Jesus is. Without it we could not speak of Messiah, Son of Man, Son of God, Emmanuel; nor of Spirit or law or covenant or salvation. Because they are foundational and constitutive for the church, they are essential to our specific identity as Christians. Kelsey's analysis of the content of the word "scripture" is illuminating here:

> Part of what it means to call a text or set of texts "scripture" is that its use in certain ways in the common life of the Christian community is

essential to establishing and preserving the community's identity. . . .
Part of what is said in calling a text or set of texts "scripture" is that it
is "authority" for the common life of the Christian community. "These
texts are authority for the church's common life" is analytic in "These
texts are the church's scripture."[30]

Kelsey's analysis is helpful, although he tends to downplay the question of truth
and of present inspiration. We need to acknowledge that the various religions,
drawing upon their different scriptures, also present different worldviews, different visions of reality. As we noted in chapter 6, they present differing notions of
time and history, of humanity and human need, of salvation and ways of life. To
respect them and their scriptures is to take their differences seriously. It is not
possible, then, to affirm all the truth claims of all the scriptures of the world.

Authority of Scripture: *Sola Scriptura*

That the Bible is constitutive of the Christian community, that is, that the
Old and New Testaments define what constitutes Christian faith, was the essential insight lying behind the Reformation principle of *sola scriptura* (by scripture
alone). Reformers such as Martin Luther, Menno Simons, and John Calvin in the
sixteenth century understood the unique constitutive position of scripture in the
church and tried to renew the church by attending to it closely. They sought to
discard accumulated doctrines and practices which they believed had no scriptural foundation and had become oppressive and destructive in the church. The
Bible was liberating in that it put Christians back in touch with the original well-
springs of their faith, in Israel and in Jesus. Thus they refused to recognize "traditions" based in the authority of popes and councils, or even of church fathers
or inspirational writers, as on a par with scripture. Listen to Luther's eloquent
and courageous words about this at Leipzig in 1521:

A simple layman armed with scripture is to be believed above a pope or
a council without it. As for the pope's decretal on indulgences, I say that
neither the church nor the pope can establish articles of faith. These
must come from Scripture. For the sake of Scripture we must reject
popes and councils.[31]

But Luther knew that Christian theology is not done by reference to scripture
only, and *sola scriptura* never meant that Christians should listen to the Bible and
nothing else. He himself honoured tradition—the creeds, the fathers, the doctors
of the church. He acknowledged the role of human reason and of faith experience
in Christian thought.[32] Tradition, reason, and experience certainly played influ-

ential roles in the establishment of Protestant "tradition." Yet these were means of interpreting scripture, and scripture *stands alone* (*sola scriptura*) for Protestants as incomparable source and authority for Christian faith and theology.

But what about this notion of authority where scripture is concerned? It has become a difficult word for many of us today. As we said in an earlier chapter, at the beginning of the twenty-first century in what is called our postmodern times, we have learned, quite rightly, to question all authorities. We do not automatically believe what our medical doctors tell us, nor our politicians, nor our church leaders. How can we expect intelligent, critically minded people to accept the authority of an ancient book? We have good reason to be suspicious of the "authority of the Bible." For much of our Christian history the authority of the Bible in the hands of authoritarian church leaders has been an instrument of coercive, hierarchical power. Still, after all the reservations have been entered, there is an appropriate kind of authority: the authority of a kind and wise parent, or of a truly learned and long-experienced person, or the truly inspired person. It was said of Jesus that he spoke "as one who had authority and not as the scribes" (Mt 7:29). Such authority is self-authenticating, not coerced or enforced upon others. It establishes itself by its own inherent life-giving power. The authority of Jesus was the authority of loving service, symbolized by his dramatic washing of the disciples' feet (Jn 13:3ff.), which de-divinized the authoritarian power of Caesar and Herod. The authority of the crucified Jesus for Christians, in the last analysis, depends on his resurrection, which brought love and power together in a gentle, noncoercive way. That is why the risen Christ could say to his disciples: "All authority in heaven and on earth is given to me" (Mt 28:18). It was the same liberating authority that was encountered by Moses in the burning bush, and was in turn exercised by Moses when he confronted the falsely divinized authoritarianism of the pharaoh. If "all authority" belongs to the God of exodus, present in the risen Christ, then clearly enough the Bible as such does not possess this authority. Its secondary authority derives from its witness to God's own authority in Christ. If the Bible has genuine and authentic authority, it is nothing but the empowering authority of a liberating God who addresses us by means of it, who, through the words and stories of scripture, frees our minds to think—frees us, paradoxically, even from the stultifying authority of the letter of a holy book.

Authority, I suggest, is more than an analytic concept implied logically in the concept scripture (as Kelsey would seem to suggest). Scripture only continues to be scripture and to carry authority because through it, we believe, God continues to address us in fresh and living ways. The words of the Bible have continued to speak to us, or should I say, God's living Word has continued to address us, through words of the Bible, down through our Christian history. To be more specific, it is precisely the life-giving character of the biblical message that gives it authority. It was just because the Bible spoke with liberating power that Luther found himself, in the sixteenth century, freed from the oppressive doctrines and practices of the medieval hierarchical church. Because Luther was released from fear and guilt by the scriptural message, the Bible became for him uniquely authoritative as source of the Word of God, the Word which, strictly speaking, is Christ himself. Again, God spoke a liberating, enlivening, and empowering Word, through the words of the Bible, to John Wesley at Aldersgate Street.[33] His heart was warmed and his personality transformed; he found new fire and energy for his work, and thus began in Britain the enormously fruitful evangelical awakening of the eighteenth century. The awakening brought with it new impetus for working people in the labour movement, inspiration for the anti-slavery and the antichild labour movements. Today, evangelicals, charismatics, liberationists, many feminists, many gay and lesbian folk, and countless ordinary church members continue to find liberation and empowerment in the words of the Bible. Thus it continues to carry unique authority in the church not only because it provides historical foundations and identity but because the Spirit of God continues to use it to call and to challenge, to console, and to give hope.

However, to say simply that the Bible *is* the Word of God is misleading, not only in the sense that it is secondary as witness to Christ. We may better say, though, that the words of the Bible *become* God's very Word again and again in the power of the Holy Spirit. Karl Barth tells us that the Word of God must be thought of as an event and miracle of God that does not come under our control. Therefore

> We cannot regard the presence of God's Word in the Bible as an attribute inhering once for all in this book as such and what we see before us as books and chapters and verses. Of the book as we have it, we can only say: We recollect that we have heard in this book the Word of God; we recollect, in and with the church, that the Word of God has been heard in all this book and in all parts of it; therefore we expect that we shall hear the Word of God in this book again. . . . Yet the presence of the Word of God itself, the real and present speaking and hearing of it, is not identical with the book as such. But in this presence something takes place in and with the book.[34]

That it is Jesus himself who *is* the Word, and not the Bible as such, is very important for our use of and interpretation of scripture. It is he who grasps us again and again as Lord, and it is he and his gospel that are truly and finally liberative for us as Christians. That is why Luther methodologically subordinated scripture to Christ and could even regard a canonical book, the Epistle of James, as an "epistle of straw," since, according to him, it did not "preach Christ." Christ is "Lord and King of scripture," and scripture is subordinate to and judged by Christ.[35] Thus Luther could say, "Christ . . . is the Lord of the sabbath, of the law, and of all things. . . . And the Scripture must be understood in favour of Christ and not against him. . . . Therefore, if our opponents attempt to use the Scripture against Christ we assert the authority of Christ against the Scripture."[36] Christ against the scripture! It is a liberating concept indeed, though no one knew better than Luther how utterly dependent he was on scripture for his knowledge of Christ.

In our own time, feminist theologians rightly have had much to say about the appropriate authority of experience, especially women's experience. But to emphasize women's specific experience and its significance for theology does not necessarily imply that Christian women should reject the authority of scripture. The feminist theologian Sandra Schneiders, for example, wants to claim for Christian women the scripture's normative status as witness to Jesus, who is himself liberative for women. She wishes to maintain for women the mooring of the contemporary community of faith in the foundational past, and she cherishes the scripture as basic for participation in the ecumenical community and for its rich resources for spirituality. But if the scripture is to be liberative for women, it cannot be regarded as a "semantic container of propositional revelation." When so regarded it is often oppressive and cannot be salvific for women. However, Schneiders writes, "if the text is understood as a text, that is, as human witness in human language to the human experience of divine event, then all the flexibility and power of the process of interpretation can be mobilized to liberate the text from its own limitations and women from the oppressiveness of the text."[37] It is not so much, then, that the Bible has authority for us, but that Christ has authority in and through the Bible. And the authority of Christ is precisely his power to liberate and give life. Authority need not be a matter of domination and power over us. Authority, after all, can also be authorizing and empowering.[38] Asian liberation theologian Aloysius Pieris also makes this point eloquently:

> Authority makes no external claims. Authority is competence to communicate freedom. Those who lack competence use power. "With whose authority?" asked the power-thirsty clerics from the Son of Man. . . . His authority was his freedom available to all who touched him. It is a self-authentication derived from a liberation-praxis.[39]

The authority of scripture, then, does not reside equally in every chapter and verse, or equally in every book. We have already seen that not all biblical texts are life-giving or liberating, and this implies that not all the words of scripture have authority for us. The authority or criteria question Is it biblical? cannot mean, Can it be proved by quoting chapter and verse? We do not establish the rightness of a course of action or the truth of a theological idea or doctrine simply by referring to some verses in the Bible. When we ask Is it biblical? we are asking whether a practice, a theology, a doctrine, an ethic, or whatever is defensible in terms of the biblical message as a whole, interpreted faithfully in the light of Christ. When faced with biblical proof-texting contrary to his own understanding, John Wesley liked to refer to "the whole tenor of scripture."[40] Sometimes people speak of "the thrust of scripture as a whole." These are, of course, rather vague concepts and can easily be used to avoid scriptural texts we dislike or to impose our theological system on scripture. We have to be careful not to be controlling in our handling of scripture, allowing it to say only what we want it to say. Nevertheless, when we actually work with scripture it becomes obvious that individual texts have to be interpreted in light of the whole; and the whole must be interpreted in light of individual texts, or, as Rudolf Bultmann once put it, we have to "understand the whole from the details, and the details from the whole."[41] The point about the authority of scripture is not that every verse of the Bible must be believed (as some biblicists argue) but that every part of the Bible must be read in light of the whole. Individual texts cannot by themselves establish policies, doctrines, or ethical precepts or authorization for action. Evidently, biblical texts have to be interpreted and indeed criticized. But according to what criteria should we criticize holy scripture?

Reading Scripture Critically

If the Bible is holy scripture, constitutive for us in the Christian community and an indispensable source of truth and liberation, and if we expect to hear a Word of God from it, on what basis can we question it? Should we not rather be questioned by scripture? How can we be confident, in criticizing scripture, that we are not proudly refusing to hear what we do not want to hear, simply imposing our prejudices on it? The following (fictitious, but partly remembered) discussion between theological students over lunch in the college cafeteria illustrates some of the ways in which Christians criticize scripture.

Conversation

JOHN: [A rather brash young chap in first-year theology] *OK my feminine friends, look what I found in 1 Timothy last night when I was doing my Baby Bible paper:* [Reading with authority and zest]

> Let a woman learn in silence with all submissiveness. I permit no woman to teach or to have authority over men; she is to keep silent. For Adam was formed first, then Eve; and Adam was not deceived, but the woman was deceived and became a transgressor. Yet woman will be saved through bearing children [hoots of laughter round the table as he points his finger at the women] if she continues in faith and love and holiness, with modesty. [1 Tim 2:11-15]

[With a flourish] *This is the Word of the Lord!*

THE MEN: *Thanks be to God!* [The men laugh out loud.]

DEBRA: [A particularly bright young woman, not amused] *Well, I guess that does it. I'll have to pack up my books and move out tomorrow. Maybe I'll go into law or something.*

JOHN: [Grinning ear to ear] *How about a little childbearing? That's what "the Word of the Lord" recommends.* [Debra swats John on the back of the head.]

JOHN: [Since Debra isn't smiling] *Hey, I was just joking!*

DEBRA: *Actually, I thought Paul said salvation was by "faith without works." What's this about salvation by childbearing? Sounds like work to me!*

JOAN: [A mature student in her final year] *Personally, I don't like 1 Timothy much. I prefer Galatians 3:28: You know:* "There is neither Jew nor Greek, there is neither slave nor free, there is neither male nor female. . . ." *Individual texts have to be interpreted by other texts, and in light of the whole biblical message, right? I say we have to critique 1 Timothy 2 in light of Galatians 3:28. And most especially, we have to interpret all biblical texts in light of our own experience of life!*

JOHN: *The systematics prof would say that's your "hermeneutical preference."*

JOAN: *Yes, and Elisabeth Fiorenza thinks we're entitled to our hermeneutical preferences. And we have to apply hermeneutical suspicion to the Bible itself as well as to interpretations of the Bible, because it was written by men!* [With pointing finger and protruding tongue]

DEBRA: *And Rosemary Ruether says we can find the divine only in what is liberative, and particularly, liberative for women (since we're more than half the human race!). The liberative prophetic tradition in the Bible has to be used as a norm by which to criticize the Bible itself. So we use the Bible to critique the Bible. She also says the prophetic themes of liberation and justice are central to the Bible, and on this basis,"many aspects of the Bible are to be set aside and rejected." If it doesn't liberate women, it's not divine! You should read* Sexism and God-Talk.[42]

JOHN: *Joan and Debbie have just finished that elective course on feminist theology. Now they think Elisabeth and Rosemary should be canonized. Chapter and verse please.*

BRIAN: [A doctoral student, age 30 or so, addressing Debra] *Yes, but liberating according to whom? I like Luther's hermeneutical principle better.*

DEBRA: *Of course you would, Luther was a man!*

BRIAN: *Luther said Christ is Lord and King of scripture. Texts that don't teach Christ are not apostolic. That's from his* Preface to the Epistles of St. James and St. Jude.

DEBRA: *Listen to him show off, just because he's a grad student.*

JOAN: *So what do you do with 1 Timothy 2, etc.? Get rid of it, right? I'm going to get my scissors right now!* [Ha Ha!]

JOHN: *Don't you just have to recognize that it was written for a particular time and place and kind of update it? Probably it made perfect sense in the early second century when women weren't very well educated. But it doesn't apply to us today.*

JOAN: *Oh no you don't! You're whitewashing the text, John! Just because it's in the Bible you have to make it right somehow. Look at all that stuff blaming women for all the evils of the world! Think how many so-called witches have been burned because of 1 Timothy 2 and Genesis 3! Why not face the fact that the church in the early second century was becoming more and more patriarchal, that the original liberation of women that Jesus initiated (and which Paul affirmed incidentally) was gradually being lost to the surrounding patriarchal culture? As far as I'm concerned, this text is not canon for me. And I have Barth's backing on that. I don't believe the Word of God ever spoke through that text! If I had a chance I'd campaign to have an ecumenical council decanonize it.*

BRIAN: *If you don't mind a little graduate wisdom here, let me point out that Luther did not whitewash texts. What he didn't like he threw out!* [Grinning, laughter, Yeah, Yeah! Hear, hear!] *Actually, I'm exaggerating. But he did say James was an epistle of straw and at least at one point recommended that it be removed from the canon. In other words, Luther had a canon within the canon. It's not the Bible as such, but the gospel of Jesus Christ that has authority for us. In fact I happen to have a volume right here in my bag.* [Smiles all around]

JOHN: *Brian has become a true Lutherophile.*

BRIAN: *All in favour of canonizing Luther say Aye. No, listen:* "What does not teach Christ is not apostolic, even though Peter or Paul teaches it. Again, what preaches Christ is apostolic, even though Judas, Annas, Pilate and Herod teach it." The Preface to the Epistles of St. James and St. Jude.[43]

JOAN: *Wow! But let's face it, for Luther the gospel of Christ was nothing but justification by faith. He didn't like James because he thought it taught justification by works and threatened his own spiritual security. For some of us the gospel has more to do with liberation here and now than justification and going to heaven.*

DEBRA: *Hey, hang on a second. I think old Martin and the feminists are closer than we realize. Sure, he's talking about this justification thing. But what does he mean by it? Liberation. Freedom. That's what Luther was after. Liberation from the oppressive burden of moral laws, and fear-mongering preaching, and oppressive structures of the church. That's what he found in the gospel. He didn't find it in James. He found it in Romans. And today we sure don't find it in Timothy. We find it in Galatians and Luke.*

BRIAN: *And maybe we should listen to each other's liberative texts and let them balance each other? I happen to think there's a connection between justification and liberation. If we don't connect them, our theology turns out to be nothing but legitimization for our own ideologies. I also think we should keep reading the texts that bug us. Someday they just might have something to say to us. That's why a christological hermeneutic is better than a vaguely liberative one.*

JOAN: *But a christological hermeneutic can be rather vague too. It depends on which Christ you're using. If you're using a feminist Christ, I mean the Jesus of the Gospels, who always affirms women and undermines stereotypes of women, then I agree to a christological hermeneutic. But that's not the Christ of most of Christianity, which has been quite comfortable with 1 Timothy 2.*

BRIAN: *True. But even without feminism we should have known that Christ broke down all the barriers that divide classes and races and the sexes from each other. Since he died for us all, he puts us all in the same boat.*

DEBRA: [Rolling her eyes] *I don't know what "died for us all" means. But you're right. It all comes down to christology in the end.*

JOAN: *I'm not so sure. To me it comes down to praxis in the end. What are the practical results of somebody's theology? I mean, Does it liberate me? Or anybody? Does it motivate me? People can be as christologically orthodox as you like, but if they turn out to be narrow-minded chauvinistic bigots, they can keep their christology!*

BRIAN: *But you evaluate the practical results in light of Christ, right? Things like love, equality, justice, peace, the reign of God. You learned those precepts from Christ, through the church, right? So if you're going to call yourself Christian you have to decide who Christ is and what he's all about, and what lifestyle follows. And that becomes your hermeneutical key to scripture as a whole. Mind you, though, your only source for deciding that is the scripture itself. It's a kind of circle.*

JOHN: *Now Brian's going round and round in circles, like some professors I know.*

JOAN: *I still say: "By their fruits you shall know them." That goes for theologies as well as people!*

As we have noted before, and as we see illustrated in this dialogue, scripture can be criticized through the higher, primary norm of Christ himself. The christological norm is prior to (while completely dependent on) the scriptural norm. Yet a practical or experiential criterion, or what we have called the praxis criterion, can be brought to bear as well. Is the text life-giving and liberating? How can it be interpreted in a life-giving and liberating way? The christological norm, I've suggested, properly governs the praxis criterion, which, in circular fashion, informs the interpretation of Christ himself.

In other words, God's scriptural story of Israel and of Christ meets with our myriad of human stories. We inevitably overlap here into the subject matter of the next chapter, that is, the contextuality of all theology, particularly of biblical interpretation. Douglas John Hall writes of theology as "the meeting of stories"—God's story and the human story. God's story, at least for Christians, is the "tradition of Jerusalem," the story of God's history with Israel and of the Jewish rabbi Jesus. The human story is its history of Promethean rebellion, an ever-changing drama, both magnificent and banal. "Theology lives *between* the stories—God's story of the world, and humanity's ever-changing account of itself and all things. *Theology is what happens when the two stories meet.*"[44] The concept of "hermeneutical circularity" is another way of understanding the dynamic of biblical/theological interpretation.

Hermeneutical Circularity

The foregoing dialogue, in fact any theological conversation or debate, can be illuminated by an analysis in terms of hermeneutical circle or spiral, a methodological concept used frequently in the liberationist theologies.[45] Hermeneutics, of course, has to do with interpretation, or methods or principles of interpretation. The circle is a descriptive concept having to do with the actual circular or dialectical interaction which characterizes all theological discourse (consciously or unconsciously).[46] "Spiral" simply means that the circle does not go just once around but continues again and again. Christ and scripture, the basic norms of Christian theology, constantly interact with present contexts, experiences, and circumstances. This circularity may be construed in various ways. I would describe it in this way:

First, the serious believer interprets all of her experience and the world around her through the lens of Christ and scripture. There is a sense in which disciplined faith-full theological interpretation begins there. That is because Christ and scripture (i.e., Christ as attested in scripture, and scripture interpreted through Christ) are revelatory of the divine, throwing light on creation, sin, salvation, and so on, but also on personal experiences of joy and suffering, and social, cultural, and economic circumstances. Yet at the same time these contexts, experiences, and circumstances throw light back on Christ and scripture. They pose questions to the ancient revelatory sources from here and now. They offer angles of vision or lenses through which scripture is read and through which Christ is understood and followed. They provide predispositions to emphasize certain aspects of Christ and to favour some biblical texts over others and certain interpretations rather than others. Thus a "circle" of mutual interaction occurs, moving back and forth from scripture to context, and from context to scripture. When we think of the circle as a spiral we emphasize that theology remains alive and dynamic, never settling down into mere static, fixed understanding. As long as we remain within faith, our biblical and theological understanding will continue to grow and shift. It is through this dynamic that scripture continues to speak to us a "living Word" through the inspiration of the Holy Spirit, in many new and different contexts and situations.

We may observe the functioning of hermeneutical circularity, with varying degrees of awareness, in the foregoing conversation among theological students. The young male student is cheerfully amused by the patriarchy and misogynism of a certain biblical text, while the young woman student is angered and depressed by it. He is comfortable with an updated contemporary interpretation, while she wants to reject it entirely. A young male graduate student gives more weight to Christ and scripture as normative than the mature female student, for whom her own experience of life and awareness of marginalization and praxis of emancipation are the bottom line. One should not generalize, of course, since in other conversations the roles of young men or mature women might be completely reversed. Preferably, the christological and praxis criteria need to be held together and understood in and through each other.

The hermeneutical circle or spiral may function for an individual's faith understanding in a very personal way, or in the life of a Christian faith community. We may note in the following stories a few real-life examples of hermeneutical circularity. A Christian man has a certain theology of pain and suffering, seeing it as a basically benign aspect of the good creation, something that warns us, disciplines us, and shapes our character for the better. Certain biblical texts have informed this understanding of suffering (e.g., Rom 8:18-28). But then his own wife suffers a dreadful, miserable illness, and this close-up, personal encounter with pain throws this theology into doubt. When she dies, the man in his loneliness loses his faith altogether for a time, feeling that his wife and he himself have been abandoned by God. Later he finds himself returning to scripture, rereading it in light of his experience and focusing now on other biblical texts, such as the book of Job and Jesus' cry of dereliction from the cross. He has moved around the hermeneutical circle and reached a deeper, more viable faith that is capable of facing the darkness of misery and despair, having brought scripture and his life experience together.[47]

A young Christian couple, possessing what may be called a serious "conservative" biblical faith, have entered into marriage on the supposition that the man is the head of the wife and that the wife should obey her husband, or at least acknowledge his final authority in all matters of importance. They have derived this from scripture (e.g., Eph 5:22). But the young woman begins to read feminist literature, encounters many feminist women, finds herself training for a learned profession, and begins to find the notion of the authority of her husband over her to be unacceptable. The young man also has begun to be uncomfortable, wondering what his headship actually amounts to in practice. Together, not without pain and struggle, they become aware of other scriptures that seem implicitly critical of Ephesians 5. They notice the freedom and equality that Jesus accords to women, the prominence of women among Jesus' followers, even as witnesses to the resurrection, and the essential oneness and equality of all people, bond and free, Jew and Greek, male and female, in Christ (Gal 3:28). They realize that the Ephesians text reflects an outmoded cultural view of the relation of women to men and that their faith in Christ need not bind them permanently to this view, but rather that, on the contrary, Christ liberates them from such a narrow understanding. Here, not only their own cultural experience of equality but the authority of Jesus over scripture liberates them for a more life-giving vision of their relationship. They too have traveled around the hermeneutical circle, having brought together the authority of scripture, under Christ, with the authority of their real-life experience.

A large Protestant denomination excludes "self-declared, practicing" homosexual men and women, not officially, but practically, from the practice of ordered ministry. They do so, at least in part, on the basis of scriptural texts that speak in condemning terms of sexual expression between members of the same sex (e.g., Rom 1:26-27; Lev 20:13; etc.). Yet, recognizing the involuntary "givenness" of their sexual orientation, many church members, including many gay or lesbian members themselves, begin to question whether it is fair and just to exclude homosexual persons from ordination. Extrascriptural sources of information are brought into play, including the stories of homosexual people, many of them church members, about their own life experience, and psychological and sociological studies throwing new light on the realities of sexual orientation. Through a process of consultation over a period of years, including scriptural study and prayer, the national ruling body of the denomination goes out on a limb and votes to make homosexual persons eligible for ordered ministry. Christ and scripture are not set aside. Rather, the Christ of scripture is seen as the friend of all marginalized and persecuted persons, not only the poor, lepers, women, and rejected tax collectors, but now of homosexual people too. Though no positive texts can be found that explicitly affirm gay or lesbian people, new, contemporary knowledge of sexual orientation is brought to bear on the interpretation of scripture, and many texts and stories are now interpreted in a way that encourages homosexuals to live courageously and authentically as the people they are.[48] Thus this ecclesial body has moved around the hermeneutical circle, rereading scripture in light of Christ, and in light of new information and experience.[49]

A prayer and study group, part of a Christian congregation in a southern African university, has become painfully aware of the historic connections between Christian missions and colonialism and the exploitation of black people by Christian white people. Though they love Jesus and feel deeply the reality of God in their lives, they begin to see the intimate connections also between Christianity and Western capitalism, which has so often utilized racism, legitimized by biblical texts, as an ideological means for the maximization of profit. A text like Deuteronomy 7:1-6, for example, depicts God not only forbidding intermarriage between God's people and foreign peoples but also commanding the utter destruction of defeated peoples. Genesis 11 (the story of the tower of Babel) is used to legitimize the "separate development" (and therefore, in practice, the unequal treatment) of people of different races.[50] Members of this group begin to recognize that a certain kind of very personal, individualistic theology of salvation and spirituality has often functioned to divert African people from vigorous defense of their human rights and from social and political struggles for justice. In light of historical studies and critical missiology they reflect on their own personal experiences of colonialism and begin to doubt whether they should continue to be Christians at all. However, with the help of black theologies, they begin to reread scripture in light of their new understanding, finding many liberative texts which affirm their anticolonialism and anticapitalism, especially the book of Exodus, and stories of Jesus as resisting oppression. They too travel around the hermeneutical circle and reach a deeper, more informed and relevant faith for their time and place.

The concept of a hermeneutical circle is not universally approved. It has been dismissed by the American theologian Hans Frei, for example, who argues for a view of theology as Christian "self-description," seeing the circle as a kind of subtle apologetic, attempting to correlate the radical givenness of the gospel to human self-understandings. Biblical hermeneutics, he thinks, has been assimilated to a general philosophical outlook on the human being as "language-bearer," thus subsuming biblical interpretation into a broader anthropological/philosophical agenda not governed by Christ or scripture.[51] A question-and-answer pattern or hermeneutical circle, he argues, accords to a certain existential preunderstanding "supposed special status as *the* indispensable conceptual or dialectical instrument for thinking Christianly."[52] This criticism has some pertinence, I think, to the so-called new hermeneutic of certain theologians under the influence of Heidegger and Bultmann, and serves as a worthwhile warning against the subordination of faith and theology to human self-understanding or preunderstanding. It is true that liberationist hermeneutics bears some resemblance to, and has learned from, the philosophical hermeneutics of Schleiermacher and Heidegger. Frei exhibits, however, virtually no awareness of liberationist or feminist theologies (whose authors' names are entirely absent from his indices) or of the personal/pastoral dimensions of biblical interpretation such as we have been suggesting here. Hermeneutical circularity, as a method used by such theologians as Jürgen Moltmann, Gustavo Gutiérrez, Juan Luis Segundo, James Cone, Letty Russell, Elizabeth Johnson, Kim Yong-Bok, and so on, cannot fairly be accused of subsuming Christ and scripture under alien philosophical or ideological agenda, not even a Marxist one.[53] The "ideological agenda" (if it may be so called) of the "option" for the poor, oppressed, and marginalized people is authorized precisely from Christ and scripture. It is because of Jesus Christ that the experiences of the oppressed should be placed into dynamic interaction with the texts. Indeed, I suggest, hermeneutical circularity is an essential feature of Christian theological self-description, which operates *a posteriori.* Theology *actually* occurs in this way, and it is naive to imagine that we ever approach biblical texts without questions and predispositions arising out of some particular context.

We noted in these stories the functioning together, in a dynamic interaction, of texts of scripture with actual life experience, as well as new knowledge, in particular contexts. This is what Clodovis Boff calls "socio-analytic mediation."[54] It means that theological reflection cannot be done in a way that is abstracted from real-life experience or from everything else that we know. This does not mean, however, that social analysis and life stories become theologically normative, on a par with Christ and scripture. Social analysis, for example, which is never value-free, has to be done from the perspective of faith. We will choose and discern among social analyses, causes, and strategies under the lordship of Christ.[55] We will seek to bring our predispositions and ideologies under the discipline of Christ, as attested in scripture. This implies that scripture is sufficiently rich and profound to speak to many new and different times and places. Even alongside the insight afforded by other written texts, it functions as the incomparable source of the gospel for the Christian community.

We shall have to explore further the notion of hermeneutical circle or spiral in our next chapter on contextuality.

CHAPTER 8

Is It Contextual?

"Now That Was a Breath of Fresh Air!" He Said

"Our new minister preached about creation today! He gave us a whole new slant on the creation stories in Genesis. I had no idea there was so much meaning in those old stories! He even made it relevant to the environmental crisis. Now that was a breath of fresh air!"

A theology that is life-giving and liberating will blow upon us like a breath of fresh air on a hot humid day. It sounds like a cliché, but we often hear it expressed of a theology, or theological viewpoint, as articulated in a sermon, book, or lecture. Sometimes we feel a certain staleness, having listened to a certain preacher for many years. Having assumed certain theological concepts for a long time, we may sense that our ideas and beliefs are no longer quite adequate, that they are somehow out of date or out of touch with our reality. We are no longer excited about our Christian faith. Then someone proposes a new way of thinking about God that seems so much more credible and relevant, and faith takes on new meaning. Perhaps something we have read, or a conversation we have had in a study group, has shown us a more adequate way to understand creation stories in the book of Genesis, and we find that it now fits better with our scientific understanding or our ecological concern. Perhaps we are shown a way of interpreting the Sermon on the Mount that challenges us in our social or political commitments. A new angle on salvation may enable us to relate more tolerantly and generously to other religions or to certain groups of people that we have found strange and alien. Perhaps we have been shown a deeper understanding of Jesus that seems more credible, and as a result a whole new, more exciting sense of the Christian mission opens up for us. Then the former theological concepts seem inadequate and uninteresting. Such experiences show us the need for contextuality in Christian thought.

We need, then, a life-giving and liberating contextuality, one that is centered and anchored in Christ and faithfully biblical.

Again, this is an *a posteriori* (after the fact) methodological precept. We know from within the experience of faith and theology that theological thought is never finished, that it must constantly adjust itself to changing circumstances and new knowledge. Again, as we said in relation to the interpretation of scripture, this is because theology lives from a living Word that reaches us by the breath of the Spirit. A hermeneutical circularity is at work, bringing scripture and context together in dynamic interaction, offering new meaning for new times, new places, and new circumstances. At the same time, we are anchored in the eternal God, who is constant and trustworthy, and in an ancient tradition that is more profound than the latest intellectual fashion. This is why the contextuality of theology needs to be governed from the rock-solid givenness of God's self-disclosure, from the Christic center, and from scripture, lest context take over, imposing its ideologies or alien agenda.

Within the concept of "contextuality" here I include both "contemporaneity" and the dimension of place and circumstance, as well as "experience" as operative factors in theology. Contextuality has to do with the whole social, economic, political, cultural, intellectual situation and circumstance of a particular time and place within which we hear scripture and think theologically.[1] It has to do with our experiences, as a community, of life in our particular time and place in history. At a personal level, it also has to do with the social location and experience of the individual—gender, race, sexual orientation, economic status, health and well-being, personality, and so on. A theology that is life-giving and liberating will have to address such particular personal or social experiences in order to be credible in its time and place. North American contextual theologian Douglas John Hall has written substantially about contextuality as an essential dimension of the theological task. We quote him here:

> To claim that Christian theology is by definition contextual is to insist that the *engagement* of the milieu in which theology is done is as such a dimension of the doing of theology. The attempt to comprehend one's culture—to grasp at some depth its aspirations, its priorities, its anxieties; to discern the dominant ideational motifs of its history; to distinguish its real from its rhetorical mores—all this belongs to the theological task as such.[2]

Hall's contextuality, then, like that of Paul Tillich, for example, attempts to relate faith to a whole culture or civilization in a particular age (that is, of course, one's own).[3] As we shall see, other contextual theologies relate faith to specific issues or the experiences and concerns of particular groups, often minority or marginalized groups.

The Authority of Context and Experience

I speak of "context" and "experience" together here. By experience we may mean the experience of the Holy Spirit, of receiving a revelatory Word—something we discussed in chapter 2.[4] Here I am interested in experience in the contemporary and contextual sense: the world and culture around us as they impinge on us in a particular time and place. We may ask: In what sense do context and contemporary experience carry authority in theology? What sort of weight do they, or should they, carry? Sometimes in theological discussion we hear people argue, "What you are saying is out of date. We can't possibly think that way any more. It goes against everything we know today about . . . world religions, or the evolution of life on this planet, or human sexuality, or the world economic system."

Contemporaneity and contextuality have to do with relevance and credibility. As David Kelsey puts it, "There are culturally conditioned limits to what either the theologian or [the] readers can find seriously imaginable. By 'seriously imaginable' I mean imaginable as a way of shaping my personal identity and the identity of any community that is personally important to me."[5] For example, for most of us today it is no longer seriously imaginable that God wills the institution of slavery or the subordination of women to men; or that God has preordained from all eternity that some of his human creatures should be damned to perdition; or that all non-Christians are condemned forever if they do not become Christians before they die; or that heretics should be burned at the stake; or that the Holy Spirit is the "author of scripture," and so on. All of these are beliefs or practices affirmed by most Christians for centuries, but today it is difficult to find anyone who will defend any of them. It was to a large extent the intellectual movement called the Enlightenment of the eighteenth century, and currents of thought that followed on later, that eventually made these concepts unthinkable. Yet aspects of the Enlightenment itself may be seen as long-overdue fruits of the gospel. Modern or postmodern Christians read and interpret the Bible in light of their own contemporary experience, and for better or worse we are post-Enlightenment people for whom it is unimaginable (barring enormous catastrophes) that we will ever go back to these things. Theology does change, and orthodoxy does shift from one age to another (though not necessarily always for the better). Probably within a century or two, even a decade or two, some of the ideas we now cherish will appear foolish. Perhaps many Christians will reject concepts that are contemporary and relevant for us, and return to older ones. Because of the limitations of the context and experience within which we live, we cannot even imagine what these might be.

As the stories we considered in the previous chapter indicate, there is a sense in which it is appropriate to speak theologically of the authority of context and experience. When we use the word "authority" in relation to Christ and scripture, we speak of the normativity of God's revelation. Context and experience, I suggest, are not normative in that sense, but nevertheless carry an undeniable authority in that their truth cannot be denied and must be reckoned with. This is not to set God and truth against each other, for wherever truth is, there is God. The Johannine Christ declares, "I am . . . the truth" (Jn 14:6). Most emphatically, Christ and truth cannot be separated. The most profound of the great novelists, Fyodor Dostoevsky, wrote poignantly about Christ and truth:

> I believe that there is nothing finer, deeper, more lovable, more reasonable, braver, and more perfect that Christ; and not only is there nothing, but there cannot be anything. More than that; if anyone told me that Christ is outside truth, and if it had been really established that truth is outside Christ, I should prefer to stay with Christ than the truth.[6]

The French Jewish/Christian mystic Simone Weil speaks paradoxically of this when she writes of the necessity for a rigorous love of truth: "Christ likes us to prefer truth to him because, before being Christ, he is truth. If one turns aside from him to go towards truth, one will not go far before falling into his arms."[7] We cannot be faithful to Christ by suppressing truth and reality, however that may be encountered. That is why a hermeneutical circle or spiral (as discussed in the last chapter) is necessary to relate the authority of Christ and scripture positively to the authority of present knowledge and experience. Or, to state the same point differently: the beautiful, powerful story of the Christ must be placed into dialogue with the stories of our own experiences of life.

When feminist Christians, for example, speak of the authority of women's experience, they mean, among other things, that awareness of their full equality with men is rock-bottom, non-negotiable truth. Neither biblical texts nor traditions could ever persuade them to think otherwise. Biblical texts that would seem to contradict this (and there are plenty of them) have to be rejected or critiqued.[8] Even if one criticizes scriptural texts by other scriptural texts (in accordance with *sola scriptura*), it is usually the praxis of "women's experience" that would set that critical move in motion.

People who have suffered greatly also know the authority of experience as incontrovertible. A Holocaust survivor, interviewed on television, was asked whether after her experience of the concentration camp she could still believe in God, answered simply: "Of course not. Not after what I've seen." In view of the unspeakable horrors that she had endured or seen—torture and random murder; painful medical experiments carried out on human beings; seemingly endless misery and despair; mental, physical, and spiritual brutalization, going on year after year with no divine intervention in sight—if she was ever to believe in God again it would have to be a very different sort of God than the one she had been brought up to believe in. The authority of her experience had simply refuted, undeniably, what she had been told in her childhood about the tender care and protection of the good and Almighty God.[9] She would have to reach a quite different notion of God's power.

Gay men or lesbian women will also typically speak of the authority of their sexual experience. They know that their persistent experience of sexual attraction to members of their own sex, probably from the time of childhood or early adolescence, is real and undeniable. Their own arduous, frustrating efforts to change have been futile. They know that, even if they remain celibate, they remain sexual beings with desires, dreams, and fantasies that they do not control. To cite biblical or traditional sources and to tell them that they should feel otherwise is irrelevant, and so they know that those sources either have to be rejected or understood differently if the truth is to be spoken and God's will discerned in this matter.[10] From the perspective of a half century ago, it is simply astounding that the theological ethics of so many mainstream Christians, and even of whole churches, have shifted to take account of these realities.

Liberation and political theologies often speak of "beginning with experience," and though that concept is controversial and rather ambiguous, they are making an important point about theological method.[11] Latin American and American black theologies frequently speak of "beginning with the experience of oppression," or "beginning with the experience of being black in America." The point is not to place context and experience totally in control of the theological enterprise, nor to compete with the normative status of Christ or scripture; it is to take these experiences seriously from the beginning, to place them into immediate dynamic contact with the sources of revelation.

In all of this we have to beware of mere faddism, of looking for something new for its own sake and opting for something superficial, perhaps an old heresy that was thought of long ago and rejected for good reasons. Some earlier modern ideas also now appear foolish to most of us today, for example, the great optimism of the Age of Reason that believed in the "perfectibility of man" and unlimited technological progress, or the fond hope of some social gospellers that by the end of the twentieth century—the "Christian century"!—the whole world would be Christianized and most social evils overcome through onward and upward moral progress. Much of this attitude remains with us in North America today, in what Hall calls "the officially optimistic society,"[12] in that many people, in a kind of numbness, simply refuse to confront the darkness all around them. As we saw in a previous chapter, some postmodern critics of modernity today seriously call into question many of the assumptions and attitudes of modernity that have become instruments of domination, both of people and of the environment. Others believe that both modernity and postmodernity have moved us toward moral and religious relativism, hedonism, nihilism, and a loss of reverence and respect for ancient wisdom.[13] The hermeneutical circle, then, will not always function in a liberalizing direction. Sometimes, in view of life's experiences, theology returns to older ideas that had been discarded but which again seem to be profound and true. A return to the Bible may correct what have become current or fashionable ideas. An example of this is the movement of neo-orthodoxy in the 1920s and '30s to insights that remain with us today, reemphasizing doctrines of sin and grace, incarnation and eschatology, reacting against an optimistic liberalism that came to appear superficial in tragic circumstances. A return to scripture, a rereading in light of events, may sometimes move us in what might be called a conservative, orthodox, or traditional direction. The actual contextuality of theology reminds us of the humanity and fallibility of theological thought—that theology, like all human knowledge and understanding, is partial and inadequate, always developing, always striving to correct itself and to relate to a changing social and cultural environment, always perspectively limited,[14] so that what is seriously imaginable keeps shifting. Whether our theology will be contextual is not a matter of choice. The question is whether we will do it unconsciously, unintentionally accommodating ourselves to dominant attitudes and ideologies that surround us, or whether we do it intentionally, governed by our primary norm, Jesus Christ, as attested in scripture. The Christic center is essential if our contextuality is to be prophetic rather than merely accommodating to the context around us.

I have said in previous chapters that an adequate Christian theology must be centered in and congruent with our best understanding of Jesus Christ, while recognizing that Christ is not a fixed norm that stands still. Christology itself must be contextual. I have also argued that Christian theology must be biblical, recognizing that this too is a complex concept, involving constant listening and new interpretation for the sake of hearing a fresh and living Word. It needs to be emphasized that the criterion of contextual adequacy does not function as authority or as normative in the same way as the previous two criteria questions (Is it founded in Jesus Christ? and Is it biblical?) because the contemporary context does not become normative for us. Most certainly, 2005 cannot become primarily determinative of our theological understanding. Karl Barth once said that it was necessary to choose between the Bible and 1933, and the mere mention of the year in which Hitler came to power and the context and religious ideology of Nazi Germany makes his meaning clear.[15]

Nevertheless, the livingness of God's Word in the power of the Holy Spirit and the dynamism of the discipline of theology demand that we are able to answer yes to the question, Is it contextual? By refusing to adopt 1933 as normative for his theology, Barth was acutely contextual for his time and place. We too must reject 2005 as normative. The dominant components of our context are not our norms: The American Empire and American way of life are not normative; corporate globalization and environmental destruction are not the up-to-date realities to which we want to conform. We do not wish to bless the trivialization and hedonism of much of the secularized world that surrounds us. To be contextual does not mean accommodating to or buttressing these realities. Yet we must listen to, and must address, our own day.

Having said this, we also emphasize that the contemporaneity and contextuality of theology are not merely something to be regretted, avoided, or minimized. "The recognition of necessity is the beginning of freedom," some wise person once said. So also, the acknowledgment that all of our perception and thought is angled and fragmentary is the beginning of the true knowledge of that Reality which transcends all of our limited perspectives. Moreover, specific times and places, though limited and limiting, also afford special opportunities and insights. We will never hear the gospel with the heart and mind of an enslaved gladiator of first-century Rome who responded to the apostles' preaching and became a Christian. His reality was so foreign to ours that we will never know precisely what the grace of Jesus Christ meant to him. We will never see the elevation of the eucharistic host with the eyes of a medieval Catholic peasant woman, never quite know what consolation, what joy, fear, or hope she derived from the Mass. We will not sing Charles Wesley's great hymn "Jesus Lover of My Soul" amidst a huge throng of hard-bitten, weeping, heart-warmed miners at a Methodist field meeting in eighteenth-century England. Their location and experiences of life in time, space, and circumstance give each of these people a very particular angle on the gospel of Christ, an angle that none of us will ever quite share. The context in which we have heard the message is undeniably an active, operative ingredient in our hearing of the Word and our understanding of it. We should not deplore this as a limitation, but delight in it as evidence of the many-faceted breadth and depth of the gospel, or, as Paul Ricoeur says, the "polysemic" character of biblical texts, that is, their "surplus of meaning" or their potential to convey multiple meanings.[16] This allows the text, by the activity of the Spirit, to speak powerfully and acutely to all sorts and conditions of men and women, whose differing circumstances give rise to different questions posed to the text.[17] Or, to turn the matter around, the text, as the instrument of the living Word, will question us in new and fresh ways depending on our particular context and experience.

Production of Meaning

It is axiomatic for any preacher that the tension between an ancient cultural milieu from which the biblical text emerged and the present situation in which we find ourselves requires a fertile rereading. Good preachers know this instinctively, even if they do not articulate it in terms of a hermeneutical principle. The Argentinian biblical scholar J. Severino Croatto has written very helpfully on this matter of contextual biblical interpretation. He insists that the Bible must be regarded not as a closed deposit of revelation that has already "said it all" but as a living text that speaks in fresh ways to the present.[18] Drawing upon basic concepts from Ricoeur, Croatto distinguishes between the intent of the ancient author and the meaning of the text for us today. If we cling exclusively to the intention of the author or redactor of the texts as their sole meaning, we risk "shutting up the message of the Bible in the past." The possibilities of the text do not stop with the thought of the author or redactor, nor does the present-day interpreter, theologian, or preacher merely repeat the text or explain what the author meant. Interpretation for here and now, says Croatto, must be more than repetition; it must also be "production of meaning."[19] The "distantiation," or distancing, between speaker and hearer occurs precisely in the act of writing, which, in the case of profound texts, provides a reservoir of meaning, that is, a polysemous richness of possible significations. The New Testament authors already did such a creative, christological rereading of Old Testament texts (the most important of these being, perhaps, the Christian rereading of Isaiah 53 to signify Jesus). Croatto states the matter nicely:

> One does not emerge from a text (exegesis . . .) with a pure meaning, gathered from within, as a diver might swim to the surface with a piece of coral in hand, or as one might take something from a bag or a trunk. One must first "get into" the text—a matter of *eisegesis*—with questions that are not always those of its author, from a different horizon of experience, which has significant repercussions on the *production* of meaning that constitutes a re-reading.[20]

Thus Croatto can go on to say that "all exegesis is also eisegesis," that is, "reading out" of the text involves "reading into" it. He does not mean that we should simply read into the text anything we like. We must attend "tirelessly" to "the world behind the text," that is, the world and intention of the author, and attempt to hear as accurately as possible what Jeremiah, Paul, or Luke was saying in his time and place. Yet we must also listen for a Word of God which the text may speak to the world "in front of the text," that is, the here-and-now. This implies, then, that we cannot read into the text without first reading out of it. Eisegesis must also be exegesis: "The two are inseparable in the act of the production of meaning that constitutes a reading."[21]

We may be immediately suspicious, or at least cautious, about the production of meaning, which could be a way of avoiding the challenge of the text, making it fit in with our preunderstanding, ideologies, or preferences. Surely the interpretation of scripture is essentially a listening, a receptivity. We do not want our preunderstanding to determine what the text may or may not say. In reading scripture we seek transcendence; we seek a Wisdom and Word which come to us from beyond ourselves, which offer grace and promise, instruction and demand that we cannot give ourselves. To speak of production of meaning may be valid if we keep in mind that our interpretation of scripture must continue to be a receptive listening, in the Spirit. However, to stay comfortably with the author's intention and message for his own time may not be the best way to listen; it may be a mere obscurantism, even a way of avoiding the import of the text for our own circumstances, a refusal to listen to what the Spirit is saying now. In another

book (as we noted in chapter 2) Croatto offered Latin American, contextual exe-
gesis/eisegesis of the exodus story. The liberationist use of these texts, whether
Latin American, South African, Korean, lesbian, gay, or feminist, moves far
beyond a re-presentation of the authors' intentions, yet may indeed be faithful,
challenging and promising, life-giving and liberating. Croatto's notion of the
relation of exegesis and eisegesis is akin to the whole concept of hermeneutical
circularity that we considered in the last chapter. We noted there already a number of examples of ways in which scripture has been read and re-read in light of
contextual experience and questions. To read out of the exodus texts a present
call of God to protest and rebel against colonial or capitalist systems is a kind of
eisegesis, but may be a faithful hearing of the text. To read the full equality of
women and men into Galatians 3:28 may go far beyond Paul's intention, yet this
eisegesis may be faithful exegesis. To read into the stories of Jesus' solidarity
with lepers or tax collectors a call to solidarity with gay and lesbian people might
well have been scandalous to the author of Luke, but may be, today, a true hearing of God's Word from the Lukan texts. There is no uncontroversial way of
doing such a rereading. There are no guarantees that one is getting it right; and,
of course, there is no one right interpretation. Contextual interpretation is risky,
but it is also unavoidable and inevitable if one is to hear a living Word. The best
way to discipline this controversial process is to be governed by the Christic center. We may ask of any given proposed interpretation of a biblical text: Is it congruent with our best understanding of Jesus Christ?

It is theology's fate and opportunity, then, to correlate, in some sense, the
authority of the Word of God (in scripture) and its essential content, Jesus Christ,
to the authority of truth that we encounter in many particular times, places, circumstances, and concerns. A breath of fresh air is always welcome. Theology at
its worst can become superficially stylish and "with it" or, on the other hand,
merely out of touch, stale, and deadly. We may note specifically the time dimension of contextuality.

Contemporaneity and Global Context

Contemporaneity, as an aspect of contextuality, has to do specifically with
timeliness. Jesus admonished his followers to "read the signs of the times" (Mt
16:3; Lk 12:56). When we do theology in a contemporary way, we seek to understand what is going on now and to hear the gospel message in terms of the now.
How does the turn of the first decade of the twenty-first century differ from the
1960s, the 1930s, the sixteenth century, the thirteenth, the fifth, the first century
C.E.? To read the written theologies from those times and to hear and feel the
great differences of idea and atmosphere make it dramatically evident how powerful a factor "the times" are to Christian thinking. If we read side by side, for
example, a text from Calvin and a text from Elizabeth Johnson on the same sub-

ject—say christology or the Trinity—we will notice a certain continuity but also an enormous difference, not only in style or form but in substance. It is not irrelevant that Johnson is a Catholic woman who lives in a postmodern world, a time of the emancipation of women and of ecological crisis, and that Calvin is a man who lived in a thoroughly patriarchal world, a leader of the vulnerable Reformed movement in the late Middle Ages, in a time of tumultuous religious and political turmoil. To understand the differences between them we have to ask about what was or is happening in the culture, in the economy, about political struggles, both in church and society.

A sign of the times in the early twenty-first century is that, to a considerable degree, many contextual factors have become more or less worldwide or global on our shrinking planet, so that, ironically, context has become global context. What are some of the realities of the early twenty-first-century global context that may, or should, have a bearing on our theology? A contemporary theology, alert to what is going on globally, will need to ask about the systems and structures of power in what is increasingly one world-system, and how these impact the lives of real people. The global picture is a dark one indeed.

One must first mention the AIDS crisis in Africa, colossal in its proportions and unimaginable in grief and pain. This colossal misery is evidently a very small matter to the minds of those who wield great power and influence. It is simply not a priority, even to compassionate and sensitive people, who hear rather little of it in the media. The increasing maldistribution of wealth and poverty in the world, of which the African misery is a part, and the felt powerlessness of certain cultural and religious populations are all part of a great nexus of fear and violence. One would have to note the ever more visible American Empire and its drive for control of oil in the world.[22] This is the priority of the most powerful, and this is what reaches us (under various disguises) on our television screens. This is closely accompanied by the struggle for survival and for peace in a world threatened by nuclear and other kinds of terrorism, and where some peoples are threatened with genocide. We may ask also about the relationship of the great world religions to one another, across the seas and continents and within our own local communities. We think especially of the growing tension and even hatred between many Muslims and many Christians and Jews, fed by the Israeli–Palestinian conflict and the events of September 11, 2001, and the subsequent Afghanistan and Iraq wars. Closely associated with these are the relation of capital and labour in a newly globalized world and the decline of the self-determination of nations and the power of democratic electorates in a world of *maquiladoras*—"free trade" zones. Beneath all of these is the most fundamental of all crises, that of the violent relationship of humankind to the environment and the real possibility of colossal breakdown and climate change.

Of particular interest to religious communities is the question of the place of religions and religious institutions in various contemporary societies, the widespread secularization and marginalization of faith communities in some (but not all) contexts. Within and across cultures there continue to be tensions over the relationship of the sexes and over problems of social violence. These are global human concerns. Of course, for anyone reading this book a few years hence, the way in which I have mentioned these particular concerns will already date me as a person writing very early in the twenty-first century. It also locates me within a particular ideological perspective and within a northern peripheral, increasingly dominated nation. Others will see the issues differently.

But the question of contemporaneity would not have been raised in quite the same way in past decades, and no doubt it will be raised differently in the future. It is clear enough, though, that a merely abstract understanding of creation and humanity, of woman and man, of Christ and church, of faith and salvation that does not intentionally relate to these concerns would be theologically inadequate. This does not mean that the content of faith and its proclamation are simply altered to suit the times. It means, rather, that various aspects of the message are emphasized over others, that certain interpretations become more relevant or credible than others, and that a fresh, new Word may be heard addressing us from the Bible.

A practical caveat is needed here. Preachers and theologians need not, should not, imagine that they are experts on the world situation. Most of us cannot become expertly knowledgeable about economic globalization or the state of contemporary art and literature. We cannot all be scholars of the world religions or the pros and cons of various plans for ecological survival. Most of us feel inept when it comes to political and social analysis. If we pose as experts on complex matters about which we know little, we may well damage our own credibility with our listeners and may even do harm by misleading people. Nevertheless, we should not make excuses for being ignorant of the world around us, and we need to take steps to keep informed—reading newspapers, but also finding alternative sources of information and insight, beyond the dominant media. The theologian and preacher needs to be a viewer of movies and a reader of novels. It is good if we can find time to be involved in political activity, perhaps as party members, participants in social-action organizations, and so on. All of this can be a daunting task, which, in terms of time and energy, would seem to negate any possibility of being competent interpreters of the Bible or doers of theology, let alone responsible, attentive pastors, church members, spouses, parents, friends. We have to accept our limitations and do the best we can. However, it must be said that preaching or theology that makes no stab at this will be hopelessly deficient.

That "the times" are a factor in theological thought is no longer by any means a new idea. As we have seen, the young Karl Barth already knew well, as early as 1914, the power of historical circumstances to alter one's theological stance. Similarly, Paul Tillich knew, fifty years ago, that the answers of the gospel message have to be addressed in a contemporary way to the questions and anxieties of a particular age. He suggested, in mid-twentieth century, in the wake of two world wars, Auschwitz, and Hiroshima (and influenced as he was by the existentialism of philosophy, literature, and the arts) that the predominant anxiety or existential concern of his time was emptiness, meaninglessness, and despair.[23] Certainly half a century later, emptiness, meaninglessness, and despair are still with us in abundance. Hall, building on Tillich's insight, speaks tellingly of "covert despair" as the pervasive ailment of our contemporary global context.[24] The breakdown of the optimism of modernity about human progress; the often repressed awareness of this among great numbers of people; the dim but often more or less unconscious realization that the human race cannot continue on for long in its present directions—these are deep underlying dimensions of experience to which theology and preaching must address themselves. Covert despair manifests itself often in denial or cynicism, apathy and passivity in the face of seemingly insoluble dilemmas. With the decline of modern hope, and lacking the energy for resistance, great numbers of people, deprived even of the depths of traditional religions, lapse into mindless consumerism—if they are in a position to do so—or into frenzied fear and violence. Noam Chomsky comments on large numbers of "depoliticized" Americans, but his description fits many Canadians and others around the world:

> they don't have faith in institutions, they don't trust anybody, they hate the government, they assume they're being manipulated and controlled. . . . Now that's not necessarily a movement to the *left*: that could be the basis for fascism too—it's a question of what people do with it. I mean, this kind of cynical, depoliticized population could easily be mobilized by Jimmy Swaggart [a televangelist] or it could be organized by environmentalists.[25]

At the same time, ironically, hope exists in our world, and not only among Christians. Vast numbers of people all over the globe have found meaning in new struggles for justice and liberty and for the wholeness and well-being of the earth. Great strides were made near the end of the twentieth century toward human emancipation—for example, in the new awareness of womankind and her potential almost all over the world through the feminist movements. This, surely, was one of the most profound revolutions of the twentieth century; from the perspective of a century ago, it would surely appear to be utopic, the realization of an impossible dream, though it has not by any means reached its completion. We have seen rebellions and revolutions, both triumphant victories and tragic defeats, arising out of the sheer refusal on the part of peoples, both in the (so-called) third world and in the old Communist world, and on the part of indigenous or minority peoples in the first world, to put up with long-standing tyrannies and inequities. The sudden end of apartheid in South Africa after a long struggle was unimaginable just a decade earlier. The increasing postcolonial awareness and energy among North American indigenous people are a sign of hope for the decades ahead.[26] New, widespread understanding of homosexual orientation and emancipation of gay and lesbian people from millennia of brutal persecution and inequality have been remarkable in recent years. In some first-world nations, especially in western and northern Europe and Canada, over a period of a few decades, social democratic achievements that occurred in the twentieth century—universal education, universal health care, universal pensions, maternity leave, care of the disabled, and so on—would have seemed to be pure utopia a few years before.[27] It will require a struggle, though, to defend these advances in the decades to come in view of the advance of free trade areas, globalization, and American/capitalist dominance in the world.

As democratic powers diminish, under the dominance of globalized capitalism, we see at local levels, in the lives of real people (even in Canada, which evidently has a much better social security system than the United States) increasing poverty, homelessness, and loss of access to medical care. Recent statistics show that in Canada 250,000 people experience homelessness during the course of a year; about 20 percent of the users of shelters are children! Again, about a quarter of homeless folk are aboriginal.[28] Increasing poverty in apparently prosperous urban and suburban areas is often hidden but shockingly real. Statistics published by the Halton Social Planning Council (concerning a suburban area near Toronto, including prosperous Oakville and Burlington) show that 11 percent of all children and youth live in poverty; 11 percent of women and 8 percent of men live in poverty. Since cutbacks in welfare payments and subsidized housing (from 1995) poverty means serious, measurable increases in malnutrition and the violent abuse of women.[29] These are but a few examples of a society that is becoming less humane and compassionate at the systemic level, with governments less capable of protecting and advancing the well-being of their citizens.

To name new and continuing struggles, however, should not blind us to what has been achieved or dampen our drive for utopic achievements in the future. As the modern faith in automatic progress breaks down, we may give thanks for such breakthroughs as the work of the Spirit of God among us, sometimes through the faithful service of Christian people and movements, sometimes through adherents of other religions or of no religion at all. South African theologian Russel Botman speaks of remaking Christian hope, "basing it anew in the new acts that God is doing in the world today." Such hope must be expressed as a category of grace, not of nature, so that "the hope Christians are called to confess in the twenty-first century differs radically from the hope manifested in the deterministic understandings of Marxism, modern capitalism, and the Enlightenment."[30]

But my purpose here is not to analyze substantially our turn-of-the-century times but to make a very simple and basic point about theological method. The best theologians have always tried to read the signs of the times and to relate their theologies (their understandings of faith) to what was going on around them. This was already true of the biblical authors and editors, for these too were theologians, whether prophets or seers, rabbis or scribes, evangelists or writers of epistles. It is obviously true of the great memorable theologians of church history—Augustine, Luther, Wesley, Barth—whose work was so notably contemporary that they brought forth articulations of the gospel that are still of interest to us today.

The work of the great theologians of the past shows us that fresh, contemporary theologies must at the same time maintain their memory of the originative events, experiences, and wisdom that have been handed down, must maintain stability and identity through time, and yet must also find ways of adapting and becoming relevant to changing circumstances. Theological thinking always involves some kind of interaction between that which is radically given (the original revelatory events and the authoritative testimony to those events) and new events and experiences through time.

Contemporaneity in the Bible and Tradition

Though explicit talk about contemporaneity and contextuality in theology is not very old, the reality itself is nothing new. We find warrant for it already in the Bible itself and observe it in the great thinkers of our theological tradition. Important biblical scholarship in the late twentieth century has made us more keenly aware of the functioning of context among biblical authors themselves. We note that Jesus spoke of "reading the signs of the times." We may note also that biblical authors show evidence of doing so and of shaping their message for the times they addressed. Old Testament scholar James Sanders, for example, has described what he calls a canonical process in ancient Israel, in which Torah functioned as rock-bottom authority and source of spiritual stability for the community, while the message was continually contextualized for new times and circumstances. The faith of Israel was not permitted to fossilize, and later prophecy and wisdom writings interacted dialectically with Torah, sometimes actually reshaping the literary content of Torah documents, and at the same time transforming elements of prophecy and wisdom materials to permit them to be contained within the dynamic of ongoing tradition.[31] Thus we hear the voice of God in the unofficial, unauthorized, and disruptive message of Amos or Jeremiah, or the consoling but fresh new message of an exilic Isaiah or Ezekiel. The prophets in fact address directly the political and social injustices and international affairs of the nation. The prophetic word, with all its freedom and novelty, is taken into the ongoing tradition, accompanying Torah and enriching it—even, we might say, modernizing and updating Torah.[32] Again, Gerald Sheppard has shown us that still later the Torah was restudied in sapiential (wisdom) categories, wisdom becoming a hermeneutical construct for interpreting Torah. Wisdom thought (present in the Hebrew wisdom books of the Bible, and the Greek apocryphal books of wisdom) functioned in the service of contemporaneity and contextualization. Sheppard's description of the mutual interaction of Torah and wisdom writings closely resembles what we have been referring to as the hermeneutical circularity of contemporary theology:

> Only by grounding wisdom in the interpretation of the superior canon-ical Torah traditions, could wisdom teachings (both canonical and non-canonical) retain an independent religious significance in any way comparable to that of the Torah in the post-exilic period. Conversely, these wisdom interpretations legitimate the Torah and its claim to per-vasive authority by demonstrating in practical terms how Torah narra-tive directly informs the concerns of wisdom.[33]

The wisdom and truth that God gives through creation and experience, the exer-cise of human observation and rational study, interact with the radical revelatory givenness of exodus and covenant in the Torah, the latter maintaining founda-tional canonical authority. New insight can be recognized by Israel only if it is found to be congruent with Torah. The way in which both prophecy and wisdom relate to Torah for ancient Israel resembles the way in which contemporary expe-rience and knowledge relate to the rock-bottom normativity of Jesus Christ in holy scripture for Christians, since, for Christians, new insight can be recognized only if it is found congruent with him.

The New Testament redaction critics have shown us a quite different but similar contemporizing process in the theologies of the early church. It is well known that theological development can be found from Paul's early to his later theology (from 1 Thessalonians to Romans) and from the theology of Mark to the theologies of Luke and John, as the first and second generations of Christian disciples adjusted to life of the Greco-Roman imperial world. Luke and John were contemporary theologians in their time seeking to hear a living, creative Word of hope in a time of disappointment about the return of the Lord, by lis-tening again and again to the Hebrew scriptures in light of the disciples' testi-mony to Jesus' life, death, and resurrection, and in light of their ongoing experience of life and the world. Both Luke and Matthew edit materials received from Mark for reasons of contemporaneity and add materials from other oral tra-ditions that they feel are of particular pertinence to their contexts. The letters of Paul and the Gospels adapt their messages not only in light of the delay of the expected *parousia,* but in view of the situation of the growing, increasingly Gen-tile Christian community. This was obviously a contemporizing and contextual-izing process, and in this sense these concepts have biblical warrant.

Contemporaneity has, of course, characterized Christian theology through the centuries. The postapostolic apologists continued the hellenizing process already visible in the New Testament. It was not enough for them merely to repeat again and again the content of John's Gospel. It would not have been enough for Augustine in fifth-century Christendom merely to repeat what was said by Athanasius in the fourth. Aquinas had to break new ground in the thirteenth century to address a new intellectual situation created by the renewed study of Aristotle. A few centuries later, Luther spoke and wrote with amazing contemporaneity to the pressing spiritual needs and ecclesiastical/political circumstances of sixteenth-century Germany. Again, John Wesley addressed the corruptions, cruelties, and spiritual deadness of urbanizing, industrializing eighteenth-century Britain, and those who followed him spoke and worked prophetically against slavery and child labour. Walter Rauschenbusch, in early-twentieth-century United States, developed a liberal social-gospel theology, building in part on Enlightenment thought, that spoke to conditions of poverty among the American urban working classes. Liberal theologians and biblical scholars swiftly, and courageously, adjusted Christian thought to newly learned scientific findings in biology, geology, and anthropology. Nellie McClung, a leader of an early form of twentieth-century feminism within the Canadian Methodist tradition, related the gospel to the newly awakening consciousness of women and to conditions of poverty and injustice.[34] In the next generation, Karl Barth and Reinhold Niebuhr, with their reaffirmations of aspects of classical theological tradition, together with outspoken comment about the affairs of their time, were acutely and powerfully contemporary and contextual, doing theology, as Barth said, with the Bible in one hand and the newspaper in the other. These earlier Christian leaders and thinkers of the past (and these are only a few among a vast number) would not have described their theologies as contemporary or contextual. They rarely thought in those categories. But today, partly because of our heightened historical consciousness, we can see plainly that all of them lived, thought, and wrote theology for their times.[35] Looking back on their work, we can observe the functioning of hermeneutical circularity, as incisive and fertile minds found new messages in the old scriptures that spoke to the needs of their changing worlds.

We believe and we think as people of our time. The permission to do so is in itself life-giving and liberating. It is both unfruitful and burdensome to strive to believe or to think as people of another time, and, I dare say, God calls us now to think theologically as authentic Christians at the outset of the twenty-first century. Having said all this, we must also recognize that contemporaneity has it limits and dangers. Contemporary theologies must be both valued and critiqued. We note that all of the great theological leaders mentioned above have much in common with each other, the later ones building on earlier ones. Matthew and Luke built on Mark. Augustine's theology is inconceivable without that of Athanasius. Rahner built on Aquinas, Barth on Luther and Calvin, Tillich on Hegel and Kierkegaard, and all of these on Augustine. This is because they all shared in something that transcends and unifies their separate and different epochs of history. This continuity exists not only among these great names, but also between ourselves and our own parents and grandparents, great-grandparents, and distant ancestors, who have passed on the Christian tradition for centuries. Obviously they, and we, had common foundations in Jesus Christ and scripture. Probably we are critical of all of them in one way or another, both theologians of the past and our own personal forebears, if we believe that some of their doctrines and practices were unfaithful and destructive of human well-being. The greatness of the leaders of our theological traditions has been not simply to reflect or flatter the spirit of their times. Rather they addressed their times with courage, sometimes against the stream. With hindsight we can see that, for some of them, their failure was precisely to reflect their contemporary cultures or contemporary philosophies too closely. For example, most theologians before the 1980s would be found today to be incorrigibly sexist. They reflected the sexism of their time, more or less unconsciously, and if they wrote in the same vein today they would be accused of heresy. And some of us would be critical of the reductive liberalisms that our predecessors adopted in the nineteenth and early (or late) twentieth centuries, which lost sight of the Christic center or lightly dismissed major elements of the biblical witness.

This implies that not all new contemporary developments can be seen as progress. Insofar as the historical theologians mentioned were great thinkers, their greatness was not merely to accommodate the dominant thought patterns and concepts of their time. Rather, their greatness was to address their times out of a center, standing on a firm foundation, which is Jesus Christ. Just as exodus and Torah remained the anchor for the updating of Hebrew faith in ancient times, so also contemporary theology cannot replace Jesus Christ as the center and foundation of Christian thought and life. Nor can "the times" become an additional norm or basis for Christian theology. The *Zeitgeist* is not the Word of God. *Vox populi* is not *vox Dei*. We may indeed believe that God is present and active in the worldly events of our time and that wisdom is to be derived from reflecting upon them. But these events do not for that reason become revelatory or normative on a level with the redemptive events of the life, death, and resurrection of Jesus Christ. It was to combat this idea that Karl Barth declared in the face of the contemporary pro-Nazi ideological theology of the German Christians in the early Hitler period that Christians would have to choose either "Scripture or 1933."[36] So also, there will be ways in which we have to choose between Jesus Christ and the dominant thought patterns of our time. Examples of bad contextual accommodationism are many: white apartheid theology in South Africa, American Reaganite theology (Falwell) or Armageddon theology (Lindsay) in the United States. Hall is making a similar point when he warns that the Christian message is "not just whatever anyone decides, one morning, that it should be!" No one has pleaded more eloquently than Hall for the contemporaneity and contextuality of theology, but it is he who deplores "a situation in which 'Christianity' is fair game for any who announce themselves as Christians," and he goes on to insist that the church has been "built upon the foundation of apostles and prophets, Christ Jesus himself being the chief cornerstone" (Eph 2:20).[37] There is no simple formula for avoiding the twin errors of obscurantism and faddism or for distinguishing between a prophetic contextuality and a merely accommodating contextuality. What Hall urges is that in our attempts to articulate an authentic Christian theology for today we must steadfastly "hold to Christ."[38]

The Contextuality of Place and Circumstance

What "holding to Christ" means will be quite different, however, not only from one individual to another but especially from one place or circumstance to another. We have come to realize in the last two or three decades that contextuality is more than contemporaneity; it also has to do with the dimension of place. It matters not only *when*, but also *where* a theology comes from. Contextuality also has to do with various particular circumstances or social locations that may coincide within one place or region and all the life experiences which that implies.

Again, what I am suggesting is not some *a priori* epistemological principle. The contextuality of place and circumstance is something we observe, *a posteriori,* about actual Christian thought. Probably it has been the liberation theologies of the third world and of first-world minorities, together with feminist theologies, that have demonstrated to us that the angle from which we see and interpret Jesus Christ depends considerably upon *where* we live and think and on the cultural, social, economic, and political location of our life. James Cone, in *God of the Oppressed*, taught us much about this when he spoke of doing theology out of the experience of being black in America. It is not only "American" in some broad generic sense, but "black American," and therefore a contextuality of both place and circumstance.

> For theology to be black it must reflect upon what it means to be black. Black Theology must uncover the structures and forms of the black experience, because the categories of interpretation must arise out of the thought forms of the black experience itself.[39]

The different kinds of explicitly contextual theology are now so numerous that we cannot begin to consider them all, but we may note here just a few of them, especially "black" and Korean theologies.

A prime example is the "womanist" theology of black women in the United States. The womanist theologians write out of their own specific contexts and experiences, insisting that black women's experience is not at all the same as that of white women and that white feminist theology cannot speak adequately to or for them.[40] Moreover, black men's theology too has tended to ignore the specific experience of black women. Black women have their own special stories. Experience, then, even black American experience, should not be generalized in a facile way. A womanist theologian such as Delores Williams, to name one among a number of significant womanist authors, offers distinctive and rich reflections on selected biblical texts. It is the biblical story of Hagar particularly (Gen 16; 21), generally much neglected, that speaks loudly to her of God in black women's experience of surrogacy and struggle for survival. In the Hagar texts, Williams finds theological meaning and truth about God and survival that no white man would ever have suspected. For Williams and other womanists, black women's literature and black women's "life-line politics," become lively, powerful sources for theological reflection.[41] Context and experience here, we observe, take on great authoritative weight as a hermeneutical perspective for the interpretation of scripture. More than that, black women's literature, especially fictional novels, alongside the Bible, becomes an important source of spiritual inspiration for black women's lives.[42]

Other black theologians think theologically out of scripture and Christian tradition very substantially, yet at the same time draw upon black experience, culture, and literature, as well as on their own black African religious heritage. For example, Karen Baker-Fletcher and Garth Kasimu Baker-Fletcher can speak of Jesus as the incarnation of God in high traditional terms as "the scandal of God with a body," and of Jesus as "fully human and fully God." At the same time, Jesus is "the greatest of the Ancestors."[43] Insights and perspectives are drawn from black literature, most notably Alice Walker's *The Color Purple,*[44] and from black American music, but also from African Traditional Religion, the original religion of the slaves. A generation of black male theologians too has arisen since Cone's generation; they have focused on, among other things, the stories of black slave experience and its theological significance for black people today. Dwight Hopkins, as one example of several in his generation, speaks not only of the contextual experience of black people as slaves but also of their spiritual or religious experience in the invisible institution of the slave church. Not only this history but also contemporary black fiction, music, and other aspects of black culture serve, together with scripture, as liberating sources for black theology today.[45] It is interesting that, according to Hopkins, in spite of the great weight he gives to black experience, history, and literature, "the slaves were radically centered on Jesus."[46] "Holding to Christ" is crucial, yet at the same time "context"—using the term broadly to include nonscriptural historical and contemporary texts—serves as a source for theology.

On the other side of the world we find Korean *minjung* theology, also a contextual theology of both place and circumstance, and preeminently a theology of stories.[47] It is Asian and therefore exhibits an openness to Asian religions, most especially Korean Shamanism; it is also a theology of the oppressed people. A prime example of a contemporary Korean *minjung* theogian is Kim Yong-Bock, who joins Christ and Bible with the needs and concerns of the Korean poor. It was the experience of the *minjung,* their stories of suffering, interwoven with biblical stories, that began to clarify for them the power of the gospel.[48] Kim speaks of the "social biography of the *minjung*," that is, their histories and personal stories, apart from which there can be no meaningful theology for them in their Korean context. While the Korean churches, founded mainly by North American missionaries, are often very conservative in a North American way, Kim appeals for a fresh and authentic Korean Christian theology:

> Our new Christian identity should seek new relationships with the Asian religio-cultural traditions, particularly those of the poor and oppressed people. The suffering and the *Han* (a Korean term for a deep sense of injustice amassed in the hearts of the people) of the Asian peoples as well as their lofty aspirations and penetrating imagination form the rich store of their religious and cultural stories.[49]

At the same time, Kim's Korean theology can be called Christ-centered in its own distinct way.[50] Korean Christians, with a not-so-distant history of brutal Japanese occupation, of the miseries of the Korean war and the splitting up of their nation, of internal oppressive and repressive governments and ongoing domination by the capitalist West, are lovers of the suffering, crucified Jesus. Thus Kim comments:

> It is our contention that the social biography of the people of God is essentially intertwined with the story of Jesus in the New Testament. Jesus the Suffering Servant, Jesus the Pascal Lamb and Jesus the Crucified are intrinsically intertwined with the stories of the *ochlos,* the poor, the sick and imprisoned. Therefore just as we cannot fully understand the story of the people of God, so we cannot fully understand the story of Jesus outside the context of the social biography of the people of God.[51]

A quite different kind of theology appears in the Korean feminist work of Chung Hyun Kyung. Chung's thought, resembling that of the womanists, insists upon the specificity of Korean women's *han*—their sense of oppression, humiliation, and deeply embedded resentment, as distinct from the *han* of Korean men. Seeking a theology of *han-pu-ri,* or "untanglement" or healing of *han,* she analyzes the sources of Korean women's oppression both in ancient Korean religions, especially Confucianism, and in Christianity. At the same time she draws positively on Shamanism and its ritual, truth-telling methods for the healing of *han,* describing her theology confidently as "survival liberation-centered syncretism."[52] She asserts that "liberation-centered Christianity and liberation-centered Shamanism are not totally separate realities. In some sense they are one reality that empowers the poor to fight for justice and freedom."[53] Drawing both on Shamanism and on her own personal stories and those of other Korean women, Chung speaks of what we are calling "contextual experience" as a powerful factor for her theological thinking. Speaking with Korean women about their lives and their faith, she found that

> Women talked about their concrete, historical life experience and not about abstract, metaphysical concepts. Women's truth was generated by their *epistemology from the broken body.* Women's bodies are the most sensitive receiver for historical reality. Their bodies record what has happened in their lives. Their bodies remember what it is like to be a *no-body* and what it is like to be a *some-body.*[54]

Of central importance, personally and theologically for Chung, was learning of her own surrogate mother and her mother's own painful story. It was a common thing: a woman's body had been used, instrumentally, to produce a baby, and was then discarded. It is impossible for Chung to do theology as though her mother's story did not exist. Most poignant and powerful, not only for Chung but for other Asian feminists, are perhaps the stories of the Korean "comfort women," forced into prostitution by the Japanese army during World War II.[55] Such stories make it very clear to Chung what constitutes good theology. The measure of good theology for her lies solely in the question: Is it life-giving and liberating? Specifically: What is life-giving and liberating for such women as these? For her, what we have called the "praxis criterion" is the absolute and unqualified bottom line. She is not concerned whether a theology is founded in Christ, in scripture, or in tradition: "The future of Asian women's theology must move away from Christo-centrism and toward life-centrism," she insists.[56] Chung articulates her methodological stance most clearly when she speaks explicitly of "text" and "context":

> Asian women theologians should realize that *we are the text,* and the Bible and tradition of the Christian church are the context of our theology. . . . The text of God's revelation was, is, and will be written in our bodies and our people's everyday struggle for survival and liberation. . . . The location of God's revelation is our life itself. Our life is our text, and the Bible and church tradition are the context which sometimes becomes the reference for our own ongoing search for God.[57]

This is an example, then, of an extreme methodologial contextualism which departs from the Christic center and from other normative sources—scripture and ecclesia. Chung's work is an example of what Croatto called "Present Reality as Primary Text."[58] It is impossible to read Chung without sympathy for the points she is making about present reality. She is very convincing about the crucial importance and power of contextual experience for any life-giving, liberating theology, and she is entirely correct about the inadequacy of so much of what she calls "orthodoxy" and the "missionary theology" that often, in many parts of the world, has functioned as a kind of cultural and religious imperialism. She is right, too, I believe, about the possibilities of syncretism, in the sense of bringing together or blending the most profound, life-giving elements of quite different religious traditions.[59] What we note, critically, is that she separates Jesus Christ from life and liberation—no doubt a reflection of the Christ that was introduced to her by inadequate theology and preaching. Yet, I have to say, such a separation is inadmissible for a Christian theology if it is to remain Christian. It is impossible to imagine a lasting, viable Christian faith that decenters the story of Jesus Christ.

One may note the positive feminist christology of Korean Canadian Grace Ji-Sun Kim, who resonates and empathizes entirely with Chung's experience and stories and borrows much from her syncretistic or multifaith approach. Yet she also affirms the power and importance of the Bible for Korean Christians and the possibilities of an inculturated, syncretized feminist wisdom christology for Korean North American women.[60] A sympathetic male Korean American commentator, Jeong Woo Kim, who also seeks a liberative Korean American theology in dialogue with American black theology, speaks of the actual liberating character of Christ and scripture for countless Korean people, especially as they entered the church during the long years of Japanese domination. The story of Korean people finding sustenance in Christ and scripture in a time of national suffering under brutal occupation is also worth hearing. He asks:

> Can "context" really become "text" for Christian faith? We may question whether these inclusive categories are really accountable to Korean Christians, for whom Christ and the Bible are liberating and life-giving. The Bible has normative significance not as an alien authority placed over our heads, but because we find life and freedom, grace and hope in and through its testimony.[61]

Of course we realize now, in the relative safety and security of our white Western world, that our theologies too are contextual. Gradually we are beginning to develop German, American, and Canadian, that is, first-world contextual theologies. Gradually white male Christians of the West and North have come to realize that our own particular theological angles, interpretations, and emphases are as contextual as anyone else's and that this must be more and more a conscious and intentional affair.[62]

Contextual theologies, as I suggested above, may be quite different but not disagree very much. They may be no more opposed than dollars, pounds, and yen. On the other hand, different contextual theologies *may* differ and disagree profoundly. Some American conservative evangelical theologies, very contextual in their own way, may be in sharp conflict with, for example, American black or womanist theologies, even to the point of mutual anathema.

Encounter on Ascension Day

Perhaps it would be helpful to illustrate theological contextuality of a very concrete sort by reconstructing (approximately) an actual conversation in which I was a participant when I worked as a pastoral chaplain and theology lecturer in the university in Lesotho (southern Africa) in the late 1970s and early '80s. Lesotho is a tiny, extremely poor, dependent third-world nation, at that time politically and economically very much under the thumb of apartheid South Africa. This dialogue will actually contain elements of a number of similar conversations, will involve fictional (but typical) characters, and for reasons of discretion I shall exclude myself from this reconstructed dialogue. The occasion of this particular conversation was a student strike at examination time, in which university students jeopardized their degrees and professional futures by refusing to write examinations, in protest against the arrest and imprisonment without trial of one of their lecturers. They knew that their government at that time was in large measure a puppet of the surrounding oppressive apartheid state. The lecturer had offended the powers that be, both of the local elite and of the neighbouring imperial authority, by openly criticizing in his classes both the national government and the domineering neighbour, and by being actively engaged in activities that were seen as threatening to their interests. This student protest and strike actually occurred on Ascension Day (a public holiday in that country), a day on which Christians gather in the midweek for a special service of worship. A substantial number of the Protestant congregation had gathered in the chapel for Ascension Day worship just across the road from the examination hall, where a large crowd of angry, clamorous students barred the entrance to examinations, demanding a fair trial or the release of their lecturer. The following dialogue reflects the strength and vitality of Christianity and knowledge of the Bible, as well as the lively state of political/theological debate in that country, and so takes a tone quite unfamiliar to us in the North and West. The very tone of the discussion reveals something of the contextual character of theological thought, particularly as it relates to christology. We note that since that time a great deal has changed in southern Africa, and so theological discourse has changed also. The conversation exhibits the contextuality of both time and place, as well as circumstance. We may note that the hermeneutical circularity is functioning in the discourse of each of the participants. In order to appreciate what is happening in the conversation, the reader will need to know something of the life circumstances of the interlocutors. Each has his or her own story, which shapes his or her responses to the Christian message.

Conversation

Thabo is a highly intelligent student in humanities and social sciences, twenty-two years of age, an active Christian and member of the Protestant congregation on that university campus. He was raised in a poor, Christian (Protestant) village family, and his mother was a deeply devout woman. Thabo grew up as part of a vibrant Christian congregation in a remote rural area of the country. His father was a migrant labourer in a South African mine, and he himself has spent time working in the mines. Since coming to the university, Thabo has imbibed something of southern African black liberation theology.[63]

Timothy is an American expatriate evangelical Christian, single in his early thirties, lecturer in mathematics. A member of a conservative American denomination, very patriotic and fearful of communism, he has come to Africa on a foreign aid contract to share his professional expertise, but also to share his enthusiastic Christian faith. He is involved with a Christian prayer and Bible study group on the campus.

Father John [the actual first name of a person well known in southern Africa, referred to but not present] is a greatly beloved white, Anglican missionary priest, actively engaged with the African National Congress (South Africa), who, because of his political activities, aid to refugees, and educational work through the church, had incurred the wrath of the South African security state. He had recently received a parcel bomb from South Africa and lost his right hand and nearly his life.

'Me (Mother, or Mrs.) Mohapi, a woman in her early sixties, is a well-educated and professional university administrator, the wife of a local African professor, mother of a large, grown-up family, devoted elder of the Protestant congregation. A member of the comfortable local African elite, she grew up under British colonialism and takes foreign domination for granted. Yet, as a compassionate and courageous member of the privileged class, 'Me Mohapi has been known to confront, personally, members of the government about their worst abuses.

Ntate (Father or Mr.) Moshe is a recently imprisoned lecturer in political science (referred to but not present). He is a local African academic of Marxist sympathies, who was raised in the Protestant church but has since left it. He has a reputation for expressing viewpoints critical of the national government and of neighbouring apartheid South Africa. ("Moshe" translates "Moses," a common name in that country.)

Lebohang is a young student bystander, raised in the local Roman Catholic Church, daughter of a middle-class elite family, but now, in her twenties, an intelligent and articulate leader among the Marxist students at the university.

Samuel is also a student bystander, raised in a Protestant family in a poor village, but now, having angrily rejected religion, he has espoused Marxism.

TIMOTHY: *Thabo my friend, what are you doing here with this noisy mob, don't you know it's Ascension Day? It's time for church.*

THABO: *Oh good morning, Ntate Tim. Dumela [Hello], 'Me Mohapi. O phela joang? [How are you?] Tim, do you truly expect me to leave the protest and go to church? Hela! They're going to be singing hymns about Jesus rising up in the sky on a cloud. Come on, man! I'm more interested in what's going on right here and now.*

TIMOTHY: *Worshiping with your congregation is much more important than getting mixed up with this political hullabaloo. Today we celebrate that Jesus was raised to the right hand of God in glory. He's the one who reigns over the world, and one day he will return to judge us all and set the world right. Thabo, you're respected by the other students. By leaving this crowd now and entering the church for Ascension Day worship, you'll be making a powerful witness for Jesus. All this political hubbub will not solve anything. If you're not careful you're just going to get yourself in trouble and end up in jail yourself, just like Ntate Moshe.*

THABO: [Heatedly] *Well, as far as I'm concerned Moshe is a hero. He had the courage to speak out and he's taking the consequences. This university badly needs teachers who will tell the truth. Just like Father John when he got the parcel bomb. Somebody has to speak the truth without fear of the consequences, and sometimes our non-Christian brothers are more courageous than we are. We can't just live in constant fear. Don't you remember? Jesus said, "Fear not." Otherwise our masters will have their way forever. The least we can do is back up Ntate Moshe by making a fuss about it. He's probably being beaten and tortured right now!*

TIMOTHY: *Let's face it, Thabo, your Father John was very indiscreet. His heart was in the right place, but he was very naive, one of the true innocents in this part of the world. Did he really think he could defy the government, and the power of South Africa as well, and get away with it? Remember, "Let every person be subject to the governing authorities. For there is no authority except from God." I tell you! Aiding and abetting communist guerrilla fighters from across the border! John should have stuck to saying Mass and preaching the gospel. And now that he's had to leave the country, what good can he do anybody? As for Moshe, he's just a demagogue of the worst kind!*

'ME MOHAPI: *Ach, Timothy, you're very harsh. But I'm afraid he's mostly right, Thabo. I feel bad about Ntate Moshe too. He's a good man. We'll be praying for him in church today. This afternoon the mothers' union members are going to visit his wife to pray with her. We've been through this kind of thing many times, mora oa ka* [my son]. *Eventually Ntate Moshe will be released, you'll see. They may hurt him, but he'll survive. God will be with him and strengthen him there in prison. But this strike won't do him any good, and you're in danger of missing your examinations, getting yourself expelled, sacrificing your whole future! You're going to get yourself in trouble here and in the end you'll lose anyway. Come on to church, we need you in the choir!*

THABO: [With folded arms and determined face] *I'm sorry, 'Me, this is where I belong today, and this is where I take my stand as a Christian. I do not wish to be rude, 'Me, but this is what the prophets would want and what Jesus would want. "Take away from me the noise of your songs and let justice roll down like waters." And, Ntate Tim, I am very disappointed with you in what you say about Father John. After all, Morena Jesu [the Lord Jesus] was rather indiscreet, wasn't he, with the scribes and Pharisees, and the Sadducees and Romans. Especially when he threw over the tables in the temple. Jesus was one of us black people. Like a black anyway. He was oppressed like us. What do you white men know about it? When Morena Jesu was raised from the dead, Molimo [God] showed us that he was his Son, and that the justice he stood for will one day be victorious over all injustice. He came to "set at liberty those that are oppressed" and "he will persist until he has brought justice to victory." Nothing can stop our struggle for freedom because God is with us.*

TIMOTHY: *Oh my goodness!* [Rolling up his eyes to heaven] *You've been listening to Desmond Tutu. You've been reading that liberation theology again.*

THABO: *Yes, and let me tell you, Ntate Tim, I think I find Jesus in Father John and Ntate Moshe, and right here in this protest, much more than I'll ever find him in those Ascension Day hymns and prayers. I think following Jesus and working for his kingdom means standing right here on this picket line. That's my Christian witness today.* [Thabo folds his arms.]

TIMOTHY: *It's all nonsense, Thabo. Jesus was no revolutionary. Jesus criticized the scribes and Pharisees for religious hypocrisy and legalism. They depended on their own righteousness and the law for their salvation rather than the grace of God. Maybe that's your problem too, since you think you have to be a hero in this hopeless protest. Such a good work will not save you, if that's what you think.*

THABO: [Laughing aloud in disbelief] *Come on, Ntate, I'm not interested in being saved. I never give it a thought. I just want to stand by my brother Moshe. He has stood up to the principalities and powers, just as Jesus did!*

TIMOTHY: *Jesus never took on the Roman Empire, Thabo. He said "My kingdom is not of this world." He was crucified for our sins as our Saviour so that we could be forgiven, so that we could be with him in heaven. You have to "seek first his kingdom, and all these things will be added unto you." Social justice and freedom will come to Africa when the people accept him as Lord and Saviour and walk in his ways. Africans must give up their drinking and immoral ways, and work hard everyday. That's the only way that social justice will ever come to this country, Thabo.*

LEBOHANG: *Oh really, Ntate, I can't stand here and listen to this rubbish any longer! It's because of people like you that I left Christianity behind, and I say Tsamaea hantle!* [Good-bye!] *What has Christianity ever done for the blacks of South Africa? Aren't they nearly all Christians? Don't they already work a whole lot harder than you ever did? Aren't their masters and white bosses nearly all Christians? What more religious Christian country could you ever find than sunny South Africa? But its ever-so-Christian regime is one of the most oppressive in the world! Colonialism, Christianity, and Capitalism, the three big Cs, they all go together, they've all worked hand in hand to defeat and exploit us as a people. And look at all those deluded students filing into that chapel over there to sing about Jesus in the clouds! It makes me sick. Marx said "religion is the sigh of the oppressed creature, the heart of a heartless world, the opium of the people." Instead of escaping into their prayers they should be here with us standing up for Ntate Moshe in prison. As for you, Thabo, you're wasting your time with these Christians. Why not come and join us tonight at our Marxist-Leninist study cell? Tonight we're reading* Marx's Economic and Philosophical Manuscripts.

SAMUEL: *That's right, Thabo. These* [f— expletive] *Christian bourgeois imperialists are trying to deceive you with their* [f— expletive] *religious ideology of the ruling class. They try to draw away our people by offering them the opium of the people. They want to enlist you on their side of the struggle for the dominance of bourgeois capitalism and the international capitalist elites, and to continue to exploit the toiling masses. This* [f— expletive] *foreign American lecturer here is an agent of the Western multinational corporation elites. Probably he is in the pay of the CIA. Of course some of these religious people are sincere, like Father John, but they are very unscientific. Only scientific socialism will liberate us, Thabo.*

'ME MOHAPI: [Waving her finger] *Oh you silly small boy, Samuel. All your Marxist talk doesn't fool me. And how dare you speak so rudely in my presence! You show no respect for your elders. You were brought up in church and you should know better. We Africans aren't going to be atheists and deny the presence of God. We know that our ancestors are in heaven with Molimo Ntate* [God the Father] *and Morena Jesu. And do you think we really want to trade our white capitalist masters for white communist ones who don't believe in Morena Jesu at all?* [Increasingly red in the face] *I know that you young people who call yourself Marxists have no morality. It's all an excuse for sexual laxity! Shame on you!* [Samuel hangs his head.]

THABO: *Hela! Here comes the Vice-Chancellor and a government representative.*

I'm on the negotiating team for the strikers. I have to go. Forgive me, 'Me Mohapi, I'll see you at prayers tonight. Tsamaeang hantle! [Good-bye!]

Conversation Analysis

The conversation reflects the high level of Christian piety and biblical knowledge that was common among Christians there, as well as the disillusionment felt with Christianity by many of the young, who at that time often turned to a faith in Marxism. There are a number of ways in which an analysis of the conversation illuminates the nature of Christian theological discourse and therefore theological method. First, it illustrates what we have been saying in previous sections of this chapter and the last about theological method and hermeneutical circularity.

1. The Christians in the discussion appeal to the Bible to back up or authorize their practical decisions and accompanying theological concepts; this is basic to Christian identity, and theological discussion cannot proceed at all without reference to the Bible, both Old and New Testaments. They naturally select their own favourite texts, exhibiting their hermeneutical preferences and interpreting them in ways that fit with their own existing theologies or ideologies.

2. The Christians also appeal to christological ideas: Who is Jesus? What is the nature of his work and salvation? What kind of obedience is he calling us to? This illustrates the centrality of Christ and christology for Christians, in that their christologies are basic and central to their concepts of the kingdom of God and are directly related to their sense of Christian discipleship and witness. They rightly challenge one another, on the basis of scripture, about the adequacy of their views of Jesus Christ.

3. Yet also, practical and ideological commitments to certain ways of thinking and acting have informed their theological concepts, including their christologies. They did not first arrive at a christology by some pure intellectual process (biblical exegesis, historical and doctrinal study, etc.) and then draw the appropriate practical conclusions. Each of them, with varying degrees of consciousness, is operating out of a social analysis of what is happening in that country and region. Practical and political ideas about what is going on and what strategies should be pursued have helped to shape their theologies. The questions that have troubled them, but also their own economic and political interests, are factors or ingredients in their thinking. They have heard the gospel differently (no doubt some more authentically than others) mainly because they have heard it from different social locations. In this sense their theologies are contextual.

4. Both their practical commitments regarding the nature of Christian witness and discipleship and the theological concepts used to back them up are related not only to their social locations but also to their varying personal stories. Timothy is a comfortable middle-class American, well paid as an expatriate lec-

turer, content with the way things are in his world, but, in the early '80s, frightened by the presence and power of communism around the globe and the visible presence of Marxism at this campus. This challenges both his political and religious security. He has come to Africa to help the poor people of the third world with his knowledge of mathematics and to share his understanding of the gospel. His conservative evangelical theology reflects this life experience and social location and at the same time informs his understanding of Christian discipleship and mission as well as his analysis of what is going on in the context. Thabo, on the other hand, is angry and discontent with the way things are going in his region of the world. He is politically oppressed, without a voice in the government of his country, unable to speak freely without danger of imprisonment and torture. His family is terribly poor and economically exploited (through migrant labour in the mines), and his country is dominated by foreign powers. He has a long life ahead of him and hopes for a radically different future. It is not surprising, then, that as a Christian he has hungrily devoured the black liberation theology that now informs his style of discipleship. 'Me Mohapi, a senior woman, has lived already for many years in a situation of oppression, yet she herself and her family, part of a small elite minority, are quite prosperous and comfortable. She has found ways, over the years, of coping with the humiliated condition of her people and of surviving spiritually and emotionally in an apparently hopeless situation. She can also be compassionate and courageous in defence of the people she cares about. Her middle-of-the-road theology informs her understanding of what she is called to do in the situation.

No doubt some are more right than others (more authentically biblical? more truly christological? more insightful in their contextual analysis?). We may feel that one or some of them are simply wrong. Nevertheless, each of them can learn something by listening to the faith experience and ideas of each of the others.

5. It is notable that people coming from almost identical contextual backgrounds may think and act very differently. The two young men, Thabo and Samuel, are both of Christian, African background and from poor village families, but they have reached very different stances with regard to Christian faith (though their politics are similar). It is obvious that very personal factors—of personality, of parents, of clergy they have known, of teachers, or of peers—also form part of the context or circumstances that individuals bring to questions of faith.

6. The non-Christian bystanders (Lebohang and Samuel) and participants in the dialogue teach us something very important about theological thought. Their challenge is indispensable (though one is much more intelligent and cogent than the other). Their critique sharpens our theological wits and makes us look more deeply into our own Christian faith and history. They keep us honest and help us to avoid glib pious talk. We have much to learn from them, for the Holy Spirit has been at work within them also. It is noteworthy that they too find their unity and identity in certain books and founding figures who have authority for them.

Instead of quoting from the Bible, they quote from the writings of Marx, whose words function to them as something comparable to a canon of scripture. They have replaced one faith with another that they find more credible and relevant to their situation. Lebohang operates out of a well-thought-out, well-informed Marxism; Samuel mouths slogans and operates with a kind of fundamentalist Marxism. We may note a certain similarity between Timothy and Samuel, and between Thabo and Lebohang.

The point of telling this story has been to illustrate the actual operation of contextuality, that is, factors of time and place, circumstance and social location, in the theological thinking and practical commitment of Christians. We would draw the wrong conclusions from this, however, if we decided that theology is just hopelessly mired in subjectivity, a merely arbitrary exercise of preference. From the beginning of this study I have said that theology must seek to be a rational discipline, that is, must discipline its thought in some conscious and reasonable way if it is to have credibility, integrity, and coherence. This is why context (like the times) cannot become simply an additional norm or foundation for Christian life and thought beside, or on a level with, Christ and scripture. One could hope that, with sustained dialogue, the Christian participants in this conversation may correct one another or at least modify one another's perceptions. A key function of *intra*-Christian theological dialogue is to purge out the ideological distortions that so often creep into theological thinking. Hopefully such dialogue can occur without diluting their views into a dull and tasteless mixture.

CHAPTER 9

Is It Ecclesial?

Our final methodological criterion for good theology is the ecclesia, the church or faith community. The ecclesial criterion means that we ask of any theological stance, way of discipleship, mission, form of worship, and so on: Is it *of the church?* Or, to enlarge upon that: Is it in critical continuity with the church's theological traditions and with the ecumenical Christian community throughout the world? Another classic way of putting the question is to ask: Is it catholic?

So stated, this is intentionally a very broad criterion in that, given the enormous breadth and variety of the Christian church throughout history and around the world, one could answer yes to a great variety of stances or practices. This criterion is not meant, then, to be a constricting straitjacket designed to confine Christians within narrow rules or strict theological boundaries. A theology that seeks to be Christ-centered and faithfully biblical is likely to be ecclesial as well, since an ecclesial theology is one that, in its listening to Christ and scripture, also takes the faith community seriously, including the historical community, sometimes called the "great cloud of witnesses" (Heb 12:1) of those who have gone before us and have passed on to us a rich tradition, both of active discipleship and theological thought.

In keeping with the basic christocentrism of our theological method, it is essential to point out that the ecclesia we speak of here is not simply the Church of God, but specifically the Church of Jesus Christ. We speak of the "churches of God in Christ Jesus" (1 Thess 2:14; cf. also Rom 16:16; Gal 1:22). The church is only the church if it is built on and defined by Jesus Christ, by his past, present, and future. Members gather in his name, are baptized in his name, receive his body and blood, and rejoice in his resurrection. "Where two or three are gathered in my name I am there among them" (Mt 18:20). To speak methodologically of an authority of the church is to speak of the authority of this community whose faith, worship, and mission are centered in him and founded in him. The confession of Jesus Christ, then, is constitutive of the church, and it is only as *Christ's* church that it can be a criterion for faith and theology.[1]

An ecclesial theology listens to the church's tradition and traditions, but also to that present, worldwide ecumenical community of Christians as it worships and struggles, thinks and confesses the faith in many places and circumstances around the world. Quite simply, a good theology will be one that has listened to the voices of the past and also to the diverse voices of the present. But this criterion too, like the others, must be understood dialectically with our praxis criterion: Is it life-giving and liberating? Certainly not every tradition is to be honoured or followed. A traditional or dominant practice or doctrine will be found wanting if it is destructive of life and liberty (these concepts being understood in and through Christ). This will entail listening especially to the voices of "the least of these," since Jesus identified himself especially with them (Mt 25:40, 45). The option for the poor and marginalized, then, comes into play as a critical hermeneutic when traditional and ecclesial criteria are considered. So also, the christological criterion must be at work here; that is, a traditional or dominant stance of the church cannot be allowed to stand if it is not congruent with our best understanding of Jesus Christ. Yet our typical circularity pertains here too: our best understanding of Jesus Christ depends on our listening to the church.

A full ecclesiology is not our task here; our interest is the way in which "church" functions in theological method. But we need to say what we mean by church. *Ek-klesia,* in the Greek New Testament is, literally, those who are "called out," that is, the gathering or assembly of believers. The ecclesia is the communion (*koinōnia*) of Christian people who share faith, hope, and love in union with Jesus Christ, through the *koinōnia* of the Holy Spirit. The church, then, is a community of the knowledge of God, of common worship and prayer, discipleship and mission. Christian people live out their discipleship not in isolation as individuals but in the community of "the body of Christ" (1 Cor 12; Rom 12) and therefore do theology also in community. This is why theology can never be a merely individualistic activity, since Christians, as members of Christ's body, are "members one of another" (Rom 12:5). Theology is done according to the gifts of the Spirit within the church, in the context of worship and prayer. To reiterate a point we have made at each earlier phase of our study, this is not an *a priori,* but an *a posteriori* (after the fact) judgment. Christian theology *actually* and essentially occurs within community. To compare the discipline of theology to other disciplines of knowledge and thought, we may refer to the ecclesia as "a community of verification."

The Ambiguity of "Tradition"

"Tradition" is an ambiguous and ambivalent term in the New Testament. In the last chapter we noticed that in the teaching of Jesus in the Gospels the term "tradition" is sometimes used pejoratively to speak of merely human traditions as opposed to God's truth, and this critical approach can be found still in the post-resurrection church (e.g., Col 2:8). But even in the earliest Christian literature we also find positive reference to tradition (2 Thess 12:15; 3:6; 1 Cor 11:2), where Paul speaks of the traditions of the gospel which he received and has handed on to the new churches. Thus we see that the question of the authority of tradition was already a controversial concept in the early church and has continued to be throughout Christian history.

"Tradition" is, literally, that which has been handed down, handed on, or handed over (Latin: *tradere*). Tradition, in methodological parlance, has come to be distinguished from scripture (though in one sense scripture is the first or earliest tradition). One can speak very broadly of Christian tradition, but there are many distinct Christian traditions throughout the world. The particular tradition within which a specific church family or communion lives may be seen as a kind of context that, like other aspects of context, functions as a source of predispositions for theology.

In discussions of theological method, "tradition" in the singular usually refers to the dominant theological doctrines and concepts that have reigned in the church through the centuries, through councils, creeds, and official confessions. It often refers more or less to commonly accepted orthodoxy (right teaching) that has shaped eccesial contexts—practically, liturgically, theologically—over the centuries. When we speak positively about tradition in this sense we honour the thought of the great theologians who have shaped our thought and practice decisively (though we would not all agree which ones should be placed on the list). It is impossible to avoid distinguishing between authentic understandings of the gospel and heresy—those that falsify or distort the message. In large measure theology is just this: distinguishing true from false, or better from worse, articulations of Christian faith. But we may also honour some of the heretics of history, who, though they were found to be in error (and we may or may not still think they were in error) made important contributions by putting forward solutions or formulations that helped the church to clarify its doctrine. One may well wish to honour some of the losers of the theological battles of the ancient church—Ebionites or docetists, Arius, Apollinaris, Nestorius, and others—who did their best to be faithful and through their efforts pushed others to sharpen their understanding of the person of Christ. Today we blush when we think of how the heretics of past generations were treated. In recent decades critical reflection on tradition has raised questions of whether "tradition" refers mainly to the views and practices of the "winners" of old theological controversies. Perhaps some of the time they won their battles for extraneous reasons, such as the support of an emperor, prevailing cultural attitudes, the dominance of males in the church's hierarchy, or rampant racial or religious prejudice. Theological traditions of anti-Judaism, for example, discoverable in many classic theologies and even in scripture,[2] have been found culpable in view of the atrocities of the twentieth century. Certain viewpoints expressed by great orthodox fathers, such as

Augustine, or great reformers and church founders, such as Calvin or Wesley, may now be thought to be erroneous, even heretical. Consider Augustine's rather dualistic (Platonic) attitude to body and soul, or Calvin's doctrine of double pre-destination, or Wesley's doctrine of Christian perfection. None of these is widely regarded today as orthodox teaching. If we consider the long historical support for the great evil of slavery, we see that for most of its history the church failed in orthopraxis (right practice) as well as orthodoxy. Or, if we consider the atti-tude of almost all historical theologians to womankind, we realize that heresy (distortion of the Christian gospel) has been almost universal on this topic until the late twentieth century. Feminist theologians especially have rightly criticized the long and hefty traditions of the theological abuse of women[3] and have searched not only the story of Jesus and the scriptures but also the church's minority traditions for a life-giving, "usable past,"[4] that is, Christian traditions that have supported the equality of women with men. Thus, we may speak of "minority traditions," which should now be regarded as orthodox. Streams of thought and activity that have not been regarded historically as orthodox are sometimes championed in contemporary theologies. I think, for example, not only of certain traditions of women's theology (often found in the medieval women mystics, for example, or the early-twentieth-century suffrage movement) but also traditions of social justice and care of the poor (e.g., St. Francis, the social gospel), or theology of the cross and of the suffering of God (in Luther). In recent years these have been rediscovered and brought forward as inspiring examples and precursors of where theology needs to go. Ideas that once seemed heretical have become orthodox.

Tradition as Context

Traditions do function as context, not only in the broad historical and ecu-menical sense but also in particular families or communions of the church and within certain times and places. That this chapter on this criterion is placed last in our study of method is no accident, given that this author is Protestant, and Canadian/North American at that. A Roman Catholic author, or perhaps even a European Protestant author, or certain Protestants in Korea or Africa may more likely have placed tradition and eccesial authority ahead of contemporary con-text, very close to scripture and to the Christic center. Further, that I have placed tradition within the wider concept of ecclesia together with contemporary ecu-menical voices would seem once again to subordinate and reduce the import of tradition as such for theological method. These choices no doubt reflect the author's own ecclesial context within a liberal North American denomination. Protestant tradition in general has not traditionally placed tradition very high as a norm for theology! Protestant tradition has a tradition of subordinating tradi-tion to scripture! The sixteenth-century Reformation, after all, was a massive criticism of accumulated traditions that existed in late medieval Catholicism and drew upon scripture as the source of liberation from oppressive traditions and established ecclesiastical authority. As a dyed-in-the-wool Protestant, this author stands unapologetically (though not uncritically) within this tradition.

Yet again, not only as a Protestant but also as a Canadian/North American, this author has a built-in contextual suspicion of tradition. Our ancestors (or at least some of them, both biological and spiritual) came to this continent to live in a new world free from oppressive and constricting traditions. The individualism of modernity, evident in Europe from Descartes on, becomes especially pronounced in North America. To live within this tradition of modernity (and even more so in some kinds of postmodernism) is to be automatically suspicious of official authority of any kind, especially the authority of old dogmas and creeds that seem to give prior authority to historic community over the present individual. As Hall puts it, with chagrin: "Before the tribunal of the self, the most sacred and time-honored teachings of religious communities are nothing but matters of taste and opinion."[5] Acknowledging such Protestant and North American predispositions, one must be self-critical and recognize that tradition cannot be ignored, that we are influenced by tradition more than most of us like to think, and that any Christian theological work supposes a tradition and takes up a position within the flow of tradition.[6] On the other hand, traditional*ism*, as a substitute for hearing for oneself God's own living Word, can be another form of spiritual laziness, even a kind of fideism, of believing and living comfortably "on the labours of others" who have gone before us.[7] In the light of the Christic center and what we have called the praxis criterion, we rejoice that many aspects of old traditions have already been widely discarded: slavery, the subordination of women, double predestination, and so on, and no doubt more will be discarded in the future. Possibly other aspects of older traditions will be recovered: perhaps a wider and deeper appreciation of the doctrine of the Trinity (which in recent years has been receiving new attention); perhaps a renewed appropriation of grace, or of eschatology. We need, then, to have a balanced attitude of respect for a rich heritage, while not absolutizing the understandings, practices, and formulations of the past.

Tradition (as I have been suggesting concerning my own methodological predispositions) functions in fact as an inevitable context for theology. Even if (like Descartes) we seek to shed all preunderstandings and start from scratch, as it were, we are who we are theologically in large measure because of the spiritual/religious context in which we grew up or were originally nurtured in faith. Even if we have rebelled against our personal formation, that against which we have reacted may still form us, perhaps unconsciously. But more commonly, we are shaped positively as Christians by our nurturing in some particular ecclesial tradition. What moves us and feeds us in worship, what inspires us to action and guides our decision making, both practically and intellectually, depends considerably on the forms of worship we are used to, the teachers and pastors who influenced us within a particular denomination, and the particular aspects of the broader Christian tradition that were emphasized in our original nurturing community. We may get a glimpse of this if we listen in on a conversation between two devout Christian women, both quite well informed and committed members of their respective churches. The one, Maria, is Roman Catholic; the other, Catherine, a member of a mainline Protestant denomination in the Reformed tradition. They are away on holiday together.

Conversation

MARIA: *Oh, it's Sunday tomorrow. I have to find out where the church is so I can go to Mass.*

CATHERINE: *Oh, a good idea! Maybe I'll go with you, or maybe there's a Protestant church around here somewhere. I must say, I admire your commitment to going to Mass. Is it expected? I mean, are you obligated to go even when you're away?*

MARIA: *Well, yes. But that's not why I go. I mean I'm not going to be punished or damned or anything if I don't make it. If I don't go to Mass I just miss it so much. I mean I just feel that it puts me in touch with God, you know? It sets me up for the week. When Jim and I were traveling abroad I didn't always manage to find a Catholic church, and when I'd missed it for two or three weeks I actually felt . . . sort of disoriented. I was actually hungry for it. I don't know. I can't quite explain it.*

CATHERINE: *No, I know what you mean. I feel that way too if I don't get to church for awhile. But we don't have communion every Sunday. I just like to be with the congregation. I enjoy the hymns and prayers and scriptures, and especially a good sermon.*

MARIA: *Yes, but for me it's really the Mass. It's nice if you know the people and have a good sermon and so on, but for me it's really the Mass that I need. If I went to church and there was no Mass I'd feel I hadn't been to church at all.*

CATHERINE: *Is that because for you the bread and wine are actually the body and blood of Christ? Like transubstantiation and all that?*

MARIA: *Well . . . yes. I realize it's symbolic and I can't give you a technical explanation of it like a priest could, but, yes, I feel I'm really receiving Christ himself. That's what I'm hungry for. It's not just a little bit of bread I'm eating. If I thought it was just a bit of bread I don't think I'd bother. And besides* [with an embarrassed smile] *I was brought up to think that's a horrible heresy!*

CATHERINE: *Well, yes, and I was always told that Catholics have some pretty crazy ideas!* [Both laughing] *But that's interesting. Communion is important to us too. We sing about meeting the Lord face to face, and we believe that Jesus is present with us in communion in a special way. Our minister says it's a special means of grace. But for me I guess it's the sermon. If I went to church and there was no sermon I'd feel I'd been cheated. The sermon is always based on the Bible, and I expect to . . . hear the Word of God, I guess. That's what sets me up for the week.*

We should not regret or deplore this influence of tradition. It is a richness that we have received. But it is valuable for us to recognize how it operates as a given in our consciousness and the role it plays in our theological thinking. Certain ideas, practices, or commitments are almost automatic for members of some traditions. Mennonites, for example, know they should be pacifists, and even if they have their personal doubts about total pacifism, they are almost automatically against any particular war. They would not object to a rousing pacifist sermon from their pastor, but a similar sermon from a mainline Protestant pastor might get him in trouble with his congregation. For most Protestants, it is not seriously imaginable that they could ever believe in the infallibility of the pope (even when that concept is properly qualified), while most Roman Catholics, even if they have their doubts about it (and even if they disagree with him), do not find the idea so absurd and will treat the pope's pronouncements with great respect. Moreover, among Roman Catholics one notices a greater respect for traditional dogma and for the creeds. A near universal willingness to perform the sign of the cross in the name of the Trinity speaks volumes about the place of tradition for most Catholic people. Mainline Protestants, if they are conservatives, reserve such respect for scripture and know that they should be reading the Bible daily. If they are liberals, they will tend to give very little weight at all to traditional dogmas or creeds but may have a very active conscience about being involved in charitable or social-justice action. And whether they recognize it or not, this too is a kind of tradition. Tradition as context is about the way our nurturing Christian communities predispose us to what we find credible or acceptable.

Tradition and Scripture

How should we construe the relation of tradition to holy scripture? How are they to be distinguished and used methodologically in such a way as to honour our primary norm, the life-giving Christ, and our christologically determined praxis criterion? We need an attitude to tradition that is life-giving rather that deadening or stultifying, one that liberates us to hear the living Word—Jesus Christ, in the power of the Spirit—from the scriptural witness. As we think of the

Holy Spirit speaking to us again and again in new ways from the scripture, we also need to recognize the continuing work of the Spirit in the ongoing life of the church through the authoritative teaching of church councils, of creeds, of practical leadership, and of teaching authorities. We should think of tradition not only as something from the past but as something that is constantly being shaped creatively in the present, to be handed on to the future. For example, in the early twenty-first century we can already speak of the tradition of social gospel theology, of the new tradition of Pentecostalism, of the tradition of neo-orthodoxy, of the young traditions of liberation and feminist theologies, and most recently of ecological theologies, which we have received from the century just behind us and which are very much alive today. In all of these cases, tradition and traditions were shaped in a positive relation to scripture. We have to think of tradition, then, not only as something from the very remote past but as something that is constantly growing and renewing itself.

Scripture itself, of course, is a tradition. It is the faithful witness of Israel and of the earliest church, *handing on* to succeeding generations its testimony to decisive revelatory, salvific events. Where the New Testament is concerned, it is accurate for Christians to refer to it as "the first tradition." We find church fathers as early as the second century citing as authoritative sources what we now treat as scriptural or canonical texts, and they did so because they regarded them as apostolic witness. This set it off as distinct from any later writings, in that the witness of the apostles placed them, and still places us, as close as possible to the originative revelatory events. To quote Robert Jenson once again, "If the apostles did not get it right, no one ever did."[8] A certain gray area exists, though, between the latest New Testament writings (perhaps the pastoral epistles) and writings of the so-called apostolic fathers—such figures as Clement of Rome (who wrote *1 Clement* about 96 C.E.) or Ignatius of Antioch (35-107), whose *Letter to Smyrna* may be earlier than some canonical texts.[9] As we saw in our chapter on the Bible, the definition of what should constitute canonical scripture has been controversial, and the exact ending point of the apostolic age is indefinite.

Nevertheless, a distinction has been drawn between scripture and tradition from very early times. The early father Irenaeus (c.130-c.200) in his *Adversus Haereses* (*Against Heresies*) distinguishes scripture from extrascriptural truths, or alleged revelations or traditions. We can see why he felt the distinction was necessary, since he was concerned to refute the ideas of the gnostics, who claimed special esoteric *gnōsis* or knowledge and cited the thoughts of their own leaders as authoritative. Irenaeus insisted that only the tradition derived from the apostles should carry weight in the church, and constantly he debates the gnostics using scriptural texts.[10] More than a century later, the great father of the Council of Nicaea, Athanasius (296-373), also argued for the sufficiency of scripture for the establishment of Christian truth and argued his trinitarian christology from scriptural texts.[11] We begin to see authority given to extrascriptural tradition in the theology of the Cappadocian theologian Basil of Caesarea (called

St. Basil the Great, 330-379). In his *On the Holy Spirit* Basil declared that some aspects of Christian truth are found not in scripture but equally in traditions of the church, including written and unwritten traditions, even secret oral traditions passed down by the apostles through their successors.[12] In the Latin West, Augustine (354-430) also speaks of the authority of extrascriptural oral tradition and ascribes much authority to the church as such, which moves the faithful to honour the authority of scripture. In turn, according to Augustine, the scripture refers the faithful back to the authority of the church and its oral apostolic traditions. Even here "apostolic" authority is foundational, since extrascriptural traditions are said to be apostolic in origin.[13] In later centuries Basil and Augustine were often cited in support of extrascriptural teachings and practices, and by the late Middle Ages, just prior to the Reformation, it was common for popes and bishops to regard their own authority as the authority of the church, more or less on a par with scripture. Now it was taught that the Holy Spirit abides with the church and continually gives her new inspiration. Debates raged among canon lawyers about the relative authority of popes and councils, while at the same time some theologians continued to press for the ultimate authority of scripture.[14] The parallel authority of tradition tended to hold sway, however, from about the time of Augustine. Early in the fifth century, Vincent of Lérins declared that the *regula fidei* (rule of faith) must hold sway for all interpretation of scripture or doctrine, so that one must look for "universality, antiquity, consent," and "that which has been believed everywhere, always and by everyone."[15]

It is not difficult to see how tradition understood in this way might function as guarantor of a deadening status quo. On the other hand, traditions might also proliferate, so that abuse of power might well occur, and many innovations in doctrine and practice might develop that are not congruent with Christ or scripture, nor contextual or life-giving in any constructive way. By the time of Luther in the early sixteenth century and even in the century before him, there were many who were concerned about the corruption both of doctrine and of practice and called for a return to the original apostolic sources. These included the defeated early protesters John Huss (1371-1415) and John Wyclif (1328-1384), both declared heretics because of their attacks on extrascriptural papal and ecclesiastical authority, and northern European humanists, like Erasmus (1466-1536) and Johannes Reuchlin (1454-1522), who remained Catholics through the Reformation period.[16] Martin Luther (1483-1546) was also declared a heretic and was placed under papal condemnation and slated for execution. He was, of course, the prime mover of the Reformation, and his assertion of scripture over tradition and church authority (a viewpoint shared by some others of his time) was basic to the whole movement.

As a scripture scholar and highly conscientious monk, Luther came to find many of the structures, teachings, and practices of the church deeply oppressive. He came to believe that the doctrine of the freedom of God's grace had been negated by the church's teachings about salvation as the reward of both faith and

good works, and that ecclesiastical rulers had abused their extrascriptural authority, distorting doctrines to buttress their own power and wealth. The story is well
known of the papal legate Tetzel coming to Luther's town of Wittenberg preaching the sale of indulgences for the forgiveness of sins, and for the release of
departed loved ones from purgatory—for a price! Against all of this, Luther
asserted his radical theology of justification by grace alone, through faith alone.
For him this was enormously liberating, and he had derived it from scripture,
especially from the letters of Paul. One could say that his doctrine of *sola scriptura*—the sole, sufficient, and incomparable authority of the Bible in the
church—derived from his own experience of liberation from oppressive teachings and practices of the church of his day. Scripture had authority because its
words had grasped his mind and heart and released him from despair, thus giving him life. Subsequent doctrines of sacraments and of the priesthood of all
believers flowed out of his scripturally based doctrine of justification. His
famous and courageous words in debate with the pope's representative, which we
already heard in our chapter on scripture, bear quoting once again: "A simple layman armed with scripture is to be believed above a pope or a council without
it. . . . neither the church nor the pope can establish articles of faith. These must
come from Scripture. For the sake of Scripture we must reject popes and councils."[17] Luther was not so naive, however, as to think that a Christian could simply read the Bible and come up easily with uncontroversial truth. He did think
that the Bible was essentially clear and could be read and understood by laypeo-
ple, since all believers are priests, and he insisted that no powerful individual
could dictate its correct interpretation. Nevertheless, he denied that individuals in
isolation could interpret the Bible correctly without the help of tradition or learning. Luther acknowledged the creeds and ecumenical councils of the ancient
church and frequently referred to church fathers, especially Augustine, to back
up his own interpretations of scripture. In debate with Cardinal Cajetan, Luther
acknowledged a certain traditional and ecclesial authority when he declared: "I
am not conscious of going against Scripture, the fathers, the decretals, or right
reason. . . . I may be in error, I submit to the judgment of the universities of Basel,
Freiburg, Louvain and, if need be, of Paris."[18] Yet, at Worms before the emperor,
Luther refused to recant his teachings unless persuaded by "the testimony of
Scripture and by clear reason."[19] Tradition and ecclesial authorities, then, were
not by any means dismissed by Luther, but they were not to be seen as independent authorities on a par with scripture. Their hermeneutical function is really the
elucidation of the meaning of scripture. *Sola scriptura* never meant that theology
was to be done by reading the Bible only and by itself, but it did mean that the
Bible was incomparable and *stood alone* as source of the gospel of Christ. We
have already seen, in our chapter on scripture, that Luther again subordinated the
words of scripture to Christ, who is "Lord and King of scripture."[20] We find in
Luther, then, a thoroughly Christ-centered theological method in which scripture,
interpreted under the authority of Christ, interacts with what we have called the

praxis criterion—Is it life-giving and liberating? He would never, of course, have asserted explicitly such a subjective criterion. For him, very clearly, it is Christ and scripture that inform us as to what is life-giving and liberating. While we may say that his substantive starting point and criterion for good theology is "Christ in scripture," we may nevertheless point out that his existential or experiential starting point was his sense of the liberation and life, joy and hope, which he derived from his study of the Bible.[21] At the same time, his interpretation of scripture—even if he was defiant against the ecclesial authority of his own time—was also ecclesial, in that it grappled with traditional sources and sought to be in dialogue with others in the Christian community.

We should note that the other major reformers closely resembled Luther on the doctrine of scripture and in their attitude to tradition. Calvin (as we noted in an earlier chapter) certainly held a very high doctrine of scripture as authored by the Holy Spirit. He often speaks of "traditions" or "human traditions" pejoratively referring to the "popish doctrine of the obligation of traditions."[22] Extrascriptural ecclesial traditions are not to be entirely and simply rejected, however. He frequently refers to the authority of church fathers, acknowledges the creeds and early councils without hesitation, and recognizes an authoritative ordained ministry in the leadership of the church. But all of this must be subordinated to and authorized by the authority of scripture as the Word of God.[23] It is noteworthy that Calvin was criticized by Servetus on the grounds that his doctrine of the Trinity was traditional and not scriptural, just as Luther was similarly criticized on the sacraments by Zwingli and Calvin, and that Luther, Calvin, and Zwingli were all criticized by the Anabaptists for supporting a traditional, unscriptural doctrine of infant baptism.[24] Thus, we see that the relation of tradition to scripture is not a simple matter. Despite the freedom and dynamism that often mark Protestant churches, an obvious weakness of the traditions of the Reformation has been their tendency to splinter into many groups, lacking a clear authoritative center of scriptural interpretation.

In response to the Reformation, the Roman Catholic Church at the Council of Trent (1546) took strong steps for the practical reformation of the church. It reacted strongly against *sola scriptura,* insisting, in line with Basil the Great, that the authority of tradition was not less than that of scripture, that both were from God and should be received with equal reverence. Beliefs and practices such as prayers for the dead, prayer to the saints, infant baptism, and the perpetual virginity of Mary could be taught on the church's authority without scriptural warrant.[25] This line of thought culminated in the nineteenth century with the promulgation of the doctrine of the immaculate conception of Mary (1854), and at the First Vatican Council (1870) the doctrine of the primacy and infallibility of the pope. In 1950 an encyclical of Pope Pius XII, *Humani Generis,* spoke of "two sources of revelation"—scripture and tradition—with the living magisterium or teaching authority of the church as a kind of third locus of theological truth, dependent on scripture and tradition. The great reforming council, Vatican II

(1962-1965), adopted an open, ecumenical stance toward other Christians and presented, in its document *Dei Verbum*, a view of a living and developing tradition and magisterium in dynamic relation to scripture. As Avery Dulles explains,

> Since the three are coinherent, no one of them can be used as a totally independent source to judge or validate the other two. Theologically, Scripture has no normative value except as read in light of tradition and under the vigilance of the magisterium. Tradition and magisterium, conversely, have no value except as referred to Scripture.[26]

Most Protestants would still have difficulty giving this much weight to either tradition or magisterium. But Protestants have not simply discarded traditional creeds and dogmas, or an authorized teaching office.

Creeds, Dogmas, and Teaching Office

Despite great ongoing differences between Catholics and Protestants on the relation of tradition to scripture, and major continuing disagreements about many doctrinal matters stemming in part from this difference, certain important similarities should be noted. An authentic Reformation concept of *sola scriptura* should recognize the active importance of tradition for the interpretation of scripture. We have seen this clearly in both Luther and Calvin. Protestant churches have usually acknowledged the ancient creeds and councils, and in fact have usually interpreted the scriptures through the lens of such traditions. The following preamble to the doctrinal statement of the United Church of Canada (1925) is fairly typical of the attitude of the classical mainstream Protestant churches on scripture and tradition:

> We build upon the foundation laid by the apostles and prophets, Jesus Christ Himself being the chief cornerstone. We affirm our belief in the Scriptures of the Old and New Testaments as the primary source and ultimate standard of Christian faith and life. We acknowledge the teaching of the great creeds of the ancient Church. We further maintain our allegiance to the evangelical doctrines of the Reformation.

It is interesting that, while Christ is chief cornerstone, scripture seems to have, here, the status of *norma normans*. In the second article, "Of Revelation," we find the same foundational authority ascribed to Jesus Christ, together with what seems now to be a very high doctrine of scriptural authority:

> In the fullness of time [God] has perfectly revealed Himself in Jesus Christ, the Word made flesh, who is the brightness of the Father's glory

and the express image of His person. We receive the Holy Scriptures of the Old and New Testaments, given by inspiration of God, as containing the only infallible rule of faith and life, a faithful record of God's gracious revelations, and the sure witness of Christ.[27]

In a Protestant document of the early twentieth century, the "infallible rule" that is "contained" in scripture appears to be a pointed rejection of the infallibility of the pope (promulgated at Vatican I in 1870). While scripture, as witness to God's revelation and Word and "the sure witness of Christ," is our most authoritative tangible source, we need to acknowledge that ancient creeds, later confessional statements, and even recent creeds used in liturgies actually carry considerable weight in the way we think theologically. It is not uncommon for theologians, theological students, or ministers to cite the Apostles' Creed or the Nicene Creed in the presentation of a theological argument. The reader will have noticed that in chapter 5 of this book I drew heavily upon both scripture and tradition, as well as contemporary context and experience, to articulate the identity and mission of Jesus Christ. Even when creeds are not mentioned, we tend to read scripture through the lens of traditional creeds, and to some degree this happens unconsciously. The creeds, especially if they are used often in worship, take on a certain authority. In my own denomination, a new creed, intentionally contemporary, dating from the 1960s and updated twice,[28] is well beloved and carries a kind of gentle implicit authority in theological conversation. To argue: "Even our new creed says . . ." is enough to clinch the argument in some Bible study meetings or theological seminars. The effect of this is that tradition and the wider faith community, whether ancient or recent, are brought to bear on the interpretation of scripture. This serves the unity of the community and its mission, in that individual opinions, sometimes rather wild and off-the-wall opinions, are to some degree constrained. This in itself is life-giving. When we stand and confess our faith together, we express our solidarity in one faith, not only in the local congregation but across wide boundaries of time and space. In the case of the ancient creeds, we express faith in ways that have stood the test of time, in words that have been uttered by our forebears for many centuries, and in ways that transcend particular nationalities and ideologies. This defends the church against fads and individualistic interpretations; helps to avoid old errors, long discarded for good reasons; and allows for a breadth and depth that would otherwise be missing.

A Lutheran theologian who speaks very positively of tradition and creed is Robert Jenson. For him, the creeds communicate *dogma,* the authoritative, permanent, and official teaching of the church. A creed is "a confessional formula that has acquired dogmatic standing."[29] Though "dogma" has become an extremely unpopular word, especially in relatively liberal denominations, it nevertheless functions among us, especially, as Jenson points out, at the point of baptism and confirmation, when people are asked: "Do you believe . . . ?" in relatively fixed liturgical forms. Questions at ordination too are asked in officially prescribed ways. It means that in fact not every belief is acceptable in the church and certain beliefs are not optional for members of the Christian community, especially its leadership. That is why the ancient councils often ended their pronouncements with words of condemnation for those who disagreed: "Let them be anathema!"

We are rightly uncomfortable today with harsh treatment of doctrinal dissenters; we are now much more aware of the fragility of our theological convictions and less inclined to cry "heresy!" We know that we all live in glass houses and that our own ideas could be judged heretical, if not today, then a decade or two from now. Yet we would deceive ourselves if we thought that dogma does not function within our communities. Even in very liberal congregations, there are limits to what one could say from a Christian pulpit about Jesus, about eternal life, or about the love of God. It would not be acceptable to the people, for example, to preach a Hindu doctrine of karma and reincarnation from most Christian pulpits, even if not a few members might privately hold such opinions. Dogma functions, in fact, in both conservative and liberal ways. In some circles and contexts, it is heretical to use inclusive gender language, either about humanity or about God. Yet in other contexts (often regional or national conferences or synods) it is heretical not to do so; it provokes scandal and indignation! Certain social and political stances are heretical (regarded as distortions or falsifications of the gospel message), for example, the theological defence of apartheid since the early 1980s or any denial of the full equality of women. Even if we dislike and avoid the word "dogma," the question of heresy is very much alive in our contemporary churches, which continue to be scenes of theological struggle.

Jenson perhaps goes too far, however, when he speaks of a dogma as an "irreversible rule of faith."[30] Surely this is to absolutize human formulations. We may indeed be very reluctant to consider overthrowing such basic ecclesial decisions as the creed of Nicaea. Even if we choose to use a different language or conceptuality (e.g., if we no longer find its language of "substance" or "being" very useful), we may still wish to affirm its intent concerning the unity of Jesus Christ with God.[31] But we do not continue to affirm this simply because Nicaea said so. The doctrine of the incarnation of God in the flesh of Christ, as we have seen, is itself a radical biblical teaching, asserting the absolute importance of earthly, fleshly existence and God's solidarity and unity with the poor and victims.[32] Ancient creeds and other traditional confessional statements are not beyond criticism. It is common, for example, for Christians of liberationist perspective to criticize the creeds for passing so quickly from Jesus' birth of the virgin to his death under Pontius Pilate. What of his liberating, life-giving ministry of teaching, preaching, healing, and solidarity with the poor? What of the political significance of his struggle with the powers of the day and his political death? These elements of the life and death of Jesus of Nazareth were sorely neglected in the traditional creeds and have been downplayed in the preaching and the teaching of the churches for centuries.[33] It is also possible for established creedal traditions, if weighted too heavily, to become a factor of staleness. Creeds should not become a substitute for scripture or for fresh hearing of scripture. Creeds and confessions, if people are unduly committed to them, may even quench the working of the Spirit and God's speaking, here and now, in and through the Scripture,[34] and so foster a faith that is anything but life-giving. What we need is a *critical* continuity with the church's creedal traditions.

And what of the church's ongoing teaching authority? The Roman Catholic Church, as we have seen, forthrightly locates its teaching authority in the magisterium of pope and bishops, exercised through encyclicals and Vatican instructions, enforced by bishops in their dioceses and episcopally ordained priests. The term "magisterium" carries a connotation of domination, mastery, and rule that is unpalatable to Protestants, who tend to imagine that they have no magisterium. Yet Protestants do in fact have authoritative bodies, whether houses of bishops, general assemblies or councils, general synods, and so on, which exercise authority in relation to both theological and practical questions. Even when these bodies are democratic in structure, they do function as a kind of magisterium or teaching authority. Protestants would find it unthinkable that any such teaching authority could be in any sense infallible, since, after all, the whole Reformation was premised on the reality that by the sixteenth century the magisterium of Rome had gone seriously wrong both in practice and in doctrine and needed to be corrected by a return to scripture. Nevertheless, without some recognized teaching authority, there is no one to defend the church against false teaching or individualistic opinion. As Jenson points out, "the church must have a voice with which to speak for herself to her own members. To affirm this, we need not commit ourselves about a mandated or appropriate *location* of teaching authority." One need not affirm Rome as the divinely ordained locus of true teaching. It has been obvious to Protestants since the time of the Reformation that Rome provided no guarantee of truth. Yet Jenson goes on, "it is again the teaching authority by which Scripture and dogmatic texts can assert themselves."[35]

We need to add, though, that the teaching authority also performs a necessary function when it promotes new understandings necessary for a new time. At critical moments, fresh, contextual, and prophetic teaching may come forth even from a minority synod, such as the 1934 Barmen Declaration against Nazi religious ideology in Germany, or an international confessional body such as the World Alliance of Reformed Churches against the heresy of apartheid in 1982. The ruling body of a confessional communion may not only defend ancient orthodoxy but also authoritatively set forth new teaching that is believed to be implied by our commitment to Christ. I think, for example, of the official encouragement of inclusive language and the ordination of women and of gay and lesbian people (the latter two innovative decisions taken by the United Church of

Canada in 1936 and 1988 respectively). Here Jesus' own option for the marginalized comes into play. To cite another example: to officially promulgate, in creedal form, "to live with respect in creation" in a time of ecological crisis is another example of fresh teaching by a church's teaching authority that is life-giving and liberating.[36]

An aspect of the functioning of the church's teaching authority is the institution of ordained ministry. In the earliest church the apostles fulfilled a unique authoritative function of leadership and teaching, but it was especially when the apostles died that the church needed to govern itself and defend its authentic teaching in various institutional ways, including the canon of scripture, the creeds, and structures of recognized leadership. Thus arose the notion of an authoritative apostolic succession. It became abundantly clear, however, during the time of the Reformation, that such a succession to the apostles, through laying on of hands by bishops in a perpetual succession from the apostles, did not guarantee authentic or faithful teaching or Christian practice. The church's apostolicity was not ensured by a juridical process of ordination, but depended on the fresh working of the Spirit in and through faithful people. Calvin argued that "the pretence of succession is vain, if posterity do not retain the truth of Christ." True apostolicity, then, "is not founded upon the judgments of men or the priesthood, but upon the doctrine of the Apostles and Prophets (Eph ii. 20)."[37] Centuries later, Jürgen Moltmann, in the same Reformed tradition, has suggested that the apostolicity of the church should be conceived of not only in terms of continuity with apostolic doctrine but also in terms of the apostolic mission. "Apostle" (from the Greek *apostellō*) means one who is "sent" on a mission:

> The historical church must be called "apostolic" in a double sense: its gospel and its doctrine are founded on the testimony of the first apostles, the eyewitnesses of the risen Christ, and it exists in the carrying out of the apostolic proclamation, the missionary charge. The expression "apostolic" therefore denotes both the church's foundation and its commission.[38]

This Reformed understanding of apostolicity replaced episcopal authority with scriptural authority, both for teaching and practice. Not only the ordained ministers but the whole church participates in this apostolicity, and therefore Bible reading and study have always been encouraged for the laity. Nevertheless, scripture requires interpretation. Not only the Roman Catholic and Orthodox, but also the Lutheran, Baptist, Mennonite, Reformed, Anglican, Methodist, and Pentecostal traditions (among others) honour various traditions of ordered ministry, recognized beyond the local congregation, with individuals who function authoritatively as bishops or as pastors. While no specific pattern for such ordering is divinely mandated, this kind of office of ecclesial supervision is warranted in scripture, which speaks of the *episkopos* and *presbyteros* (1 Tim 3:1-2; 5:19; Tit 1:7; 1 Pet 5:1), supervisors and elders who, through their office, exercise a kind of magisterial authority for the church. This too is an important and indispensable aspect of ecclesiality, which functions as a gift of the Spirit to the church. As we have seen, gifts of the Spirit include "the utterance of wisdom . . . and the utterance of knowledge according to the same Spirit" (1 Cor 12:8). In Romans 12 Paul mentions, among other functions, prophecy, ministering (serving), teaching, exhortation, leading, all tasks associated (though not exclusively) with what have come to be called "clergy." Ephesians mentions "gifts" that some are apostles, some prophets, some evangelists, some pastors and teachers, and their function is clear: "to equip the saints for the work of ministry" (Eph 4:11-12). Since all Christians are called to ministry and mission, and all are equally priests in the "priesthood of all believers" (1 Pet 2:5; Rev 1:6; 5:10), the task of what we have come to call ordered or ordained ministers is to "equip the saints" for their all-important ministries in the world.

To acknowledge the importance of ordained office is not to suggest that the being (*esse*) of the church depends on this office. The Protestant churches generally have found no christological or biblical grounds for believing that such office is *constitutive* of the church, since it is only Christ's presence and the confession of Christ by the people that constitute a community of people as a church of Jesus Christ.[39] Nevertheless it is surely for the *bene esse* (well-being) of the church that such an office exists and that part of its task is to serve the integrity of the church's faith and theology.

We would emphasize again, however, that the teaching authority of ordered ministers, who are authorized to preach and teach and administer sacraments in the congregation and to offer pastoral care, is not *solely* to defend established traditions, but also to speak and lead in new and prophetic ways under the inspiration of the living Christ, through the Spirit.

Unity, Catholicity, and Ecumenicity

I suggested at the beginning of this chapter that a good theology is ecclesial in the sense that is "of the church"—in critical continuity with the church's traditions and with the ecumenical Christian community throughout the world; that is, it should be "catholic theology." The premise here is that the church is essentially one, as in Paul's vision of the church: "in one body we have many members" (Rom 12:4); "in one Spirit we are all baptized into one body" (1 Cor 12:13). According to John's Gospel, Jesus prayed "that they may all be one. As you, Father, are in me and I am in you, may they also be in us, that the world may believe" (Jn 17:21). The texts teach us that the unity and peace of Christ's followers are a hope derived from the unity of the triune God. The Letter to the Ephesians, which so emphasizes the breaking down of all the barriers of human alienation and the hope for one new humanity through Christ, also appeals to Christians to lead a life

> with all humility and gentleness, with patience, bearing with one another in love, making every effort to maintain the unity of the Spirit in the bond of peace. There is one body and one Spirit, just as you were called to the one hope of your calling, one Lord, one faith, one baptism, one God and Father of all, who is above all and through all and in all. (Eph 4:2-6)

It is for good reason, then, that Christians have always aspired to be one and at peace as (in the words of the Nicene Creed) "one, holy, catholic and apostolic." In all of these marks of the church, whereby it seeks to measure its own authenticity, the church has never "arrived," is always seeking and hoping to be true church. Its unity is in Christ, for there is only one Body of Christ, yet in actuality this unity is never fully realized; it is something the church strives for, hopes for, and prays for. The church's holiness or sanctification also derives from the holiness of Christ (1 Cor 1:30); it can never claim to be holy in itself, yet it strives to realize a measure of Christ's holiness in its own life.[40] The church's apostolicity, as we have discussed above, is its faithfulness to the apostolic message and mission, and this too can never be taken for granted or guaranteed, but must be striven for and struggled for. But what is the church's catholicity? And why must a good theology be "catholic theology"?

Not a New Testament term for the church, the Greek *katholikos* means general, comprehensive, or universal. The church father Justin Martyr used the term in this sense to speak of a "catholic resurrection" and "catholic prayer," referring to the hope for universal resurrection and prayers for all people. It was also used early in the second century by Ignatius of Antioch to distinguish a true from a false, heretical, or apostate church.[41] The catholicity of the church, then, has to do with its continuity and identity through all its differences. Karl Barth suggests that a church is catholic as "true church activating and confirming its identical being in all its forms."[42] If a church is not catholic, it is perhaps heretical, apostate (unfaithful) or simply parochial, cut off from the larger body of the Christian people. But "catholic" need not be seen as primarily a disciplinary or restrictive concept. Positively, a church is catholic when it is open to the universality of God's reign, when it is as inclusive as possible, straining after the universal inclusivity of God's love for the whole world in Jesus Christ. In this sense it is, like the church's unity and holiness, an eschatological dimension, having to do with the universal, unlimited breadth of Christ's mission.[43] It is unfortunate that Protestants of various kinds have often allowed the term "catholic" to be surrendered to the Roman Catholic Church and have allowed the term to be contrasted with the generic "Protestant." "Protestant" has its own positive meaning, from

Latin *protestatio* and *protestari,* referring to those who solemnly declare, bear witness, or protest,[44] and has come to be used to refer to almost all non–Roman Catholics in Western Christianity. However, Christians of all the major families or communions of churches seek to be "catholic," genuinely members of the one body of Christ, and therefore part of the one, holy, universal, and apostolic church.

Not only the church as such, but a Christian theology will also strive to be catholic when it seeks to express faith at one with the whole church of Jesus Christ through time and throughout the world. The term "ecumenical" has in recent years taken on a similar meaning. The church is extended throughout the "whole inhabited earth" (*oikoumenē*) and therefore an "ecumenical" theology will seek to be open to expressions of faith from all over the world. Everyone is limited in this respect, of course, since no finite mind can attend to *all* the voices. While such listening implies the search for a kind of orthodoxy or right teaching, as well as a kind of orthopraxis or right practice, I suggest that it does not imply, necessarily, a conformity to *dominant* teachings and practices. Orthodoxy and dominance should not be equated, given that orthodoxy or right teaching is never final, but always shifting and dynamic, responding to the living Word of a living God. A truly catholic and ecumenical church, I suggest, listens for what the Spirit has taught all the churches, is open to all traditions and to the churches of all times and places. Perhaps we need especially to be open to those most unlike us, those whose perspectives most sharply challenge our own. Reformed listening to Orthodox, Orthodox listening to Anabaptist, Catholic listening to Pentecostal, and so on, may serve the catholicity of the church profoundly. However, quite apart from denominational or traditional divides, those aligned with dominant traditions or contexts need to be open especially to minority or marginalized voices. Protestants especially, whether Lutheran, Mennonite, or Reformed, should know this, in that their traditions began as small, beleaguered minorities, accused of heresy and threatened with death and damnation. Those who are genuinely catholic may sometimes have to stand alone, as Luther did, declaring, "Here I stand. I cannot do otherwise. God help me." This does not mean that every minority movement is genuinely catholic or that no serious heresies or apostasies exist. It does mean that the majority can be wrong, that catholicity cannot be measured by mere numbers, but must be measured by faithfulness to Christ.

Here, too, our praxis criterion—Is it life-giving and liberating?—must come into play, since Christ is the one who liberates and gives life. Listening to the voices of "the least of these," with whom Christ is identified, will be essential to an ecclesial and catholic theology. Thus, a North American, white, male theologian, if he wishes to be catholic, must especially listen to women, to people of colour, to theologies that arise out of situations of poverty and marginalization, and to people who live and articulate faith out of very different cultural contexts.

POSTSCRIPT

At the outset I proposed to offer a theological method that was Christ-centered and praxis-oriented, a liberationist method that was also rationally defensible. I offered criteria questions by which a Christian might check out a theology as to its adequacy, its faithfulness, its relevance. Dialogues attempted to illustrate the interaction of differing theological stances and their accompanying methods. All this has been in aid of reaching and laying hold of God's truth for our time and place, to distinguish rationally between good and bad theologies.

But the great danger of all methodological discussion in theology is that one will lay out the blueprint for a "system"—a kind of intellectual mastery of the divine: Follow this method and you will find God! If I have done this I will have brought down upon my head the ridicule of one of my theological heroes, Søren Kierkegaard. How he laughed at the system builders of his day who tried to organize Christian truth into a rational and highly abstract set of concepts:

> It is as if Christianity also had been promulgated as a little system, if not quite as good as the Hegelian, it is as if Christ—aye, I speak without offense—it is as if Christ were a professor, and as if the Apostles had formed a little scientific society.[1]

Kierkegaard's ironic scorn is poured out especially upon the philosopher G. E. Lessing:

> Were he living in these times, now that the System is almost finished, or at least under construction, and will be finished by next Sunday: believe me, Lessing would have stretched out both hands to lay hold of it. . . . But then, the System also has more to offer than God had in both hands; this very moment it has more, to say nothing of next Sunday, when it is quite certain to be finished.[2]

But to defend myself against Kierkegaard's pointing finger, I quote my own words from the introduction: "I claim no absolute correctness for this construal of theological criteria" (p. 17). Again, I said in chapter 1: "We emphatically do not seek here to build a system of closed and completed concepts. While theologies usually try to be 'systematic' in the sense that they seek internal coherence, method in theology should not be seen as a quest for security and completeness, because it offers no guarantee of truth, no simple formula for 'getting it right.'" *Pace,* Kierkegaard! The theological task will never be finished, and certainly not by next Sunday. Jesus Christ, as bottom-line criterion and primary norm, does not constitute a principle for some eternally fixed set of theological truths. If he is the living Word and Wisdom of God he will constantly break through all our systems, and even our methods, however carefully thought out!

I have contended that methodological discussion is indispensable for theology if we are to be intentional, self-aware, and self-critical in our Christian life, thought, and witness. However, the limits of methodological discourse and the impossibility of a universally acceptable system of theology may be dramatized by a conversation with my imaginary Sheila and Dennis, whom you met in chapter 1. They were kind enough to read my manuscript draft and give me feedback. I wanted to know whether I had helped them understand each other, or whether reading the book had budged them at all from the opposing stances they took at that national board meeting. So we met one Saturday morning for breakfast at a favourite restaurant. After the initial pleasantries, the conversation went something like this.

Conversation

AUTHOR: *Well, it was kind of you both to read my manuscript. I know you're both busy people with plenty of other things to read.*

SHEILA: *Oh I enjoyed it, Harold. Thanks for asking. I must say, I learned a lot. I think I do understand Dennis better than I did before. I mean, I see where he's coming from, not that I agree with him. But I'm still digesting it. I'm still not sure whether I'm convinced.*

AUTHOR: *I can't ask for much more than that!*

DENNIS: *Yes, an interesting effort, Harold. It's quite a balancing act you've done.*

AUTHOR: [With a smile] *I prefer "dialectic" to "balance," if you'll forgive the jargon. The problem with balancing between more conservative and more liberal or radical views is that you tend to dilute or compromise the concerns of both sides and end up watering down both. A dialectic tries to hold together apparent opposites or poles in tension. Rather like Chalcedon, you know? You try not to let the one side of the duality compromise the other.*

SHEILA: *The two sides being . . . ?*

AUTHOR: *You know, on the one hand the normative or authoritative sources—Christ, scripture, tradition—and on the other, present context, questions, stories, contemporary knowledge, and problems that may or may not be directly dealt with in the classic sources. The hermeneutical circle. Some people put the weight on the one side and some put it on the other. Or, to put it differently, the dual bottom line: the christological criterion and the praxis criterion. You know: Is it congruent with our best understanding of Jesus Christ? Is it life-giving and liberating? They have to be kept together and understood through each other. But I'm being didactic as usual. Occupational hazard. I'm here to listen to you.*

DENNIS: *Yes, I put the weight on the side of the authoritative sources, no apologies. I'm not so sure you've succeeded, Harold. In fact—why be polite?—I'm sure you haven't. You do defend some classical orthodox stances, like the incarnation and the Trinity. I have my doubts about the social Trinity, by the way. And I like the way you sock it to the pluralists (though you're really a little fuzzy on that one too). But in the last analysis, let's face it, you're really some kind of liberal. Your ideological prejudices have definitely got the upper hand over the scriptures!*

AUTHOR: *Oh, you think so?*

DENNIS: *Definitely, on the practical things that matter, the outcome of it all! You support gay and lesbian ordination, for example. Next thing you'll be supporting gay marriage as well! To do that you have to do some weird contortions with the scriptures. I mean, come on! "Production of meaning?!" "Exegesis is eisegesis?!" You can make the Bible say anything you like! This is a perfect example of deciding beforehand what you think—on purely extraneous extrabiblical grounds—and then reading it into the text. Having compassion on social outcasts is one thing. Giving your blessing to a sin like homosexual relations is quite another! There's no way you'll find anything like that in the Bible!*

SHEILA: *I'm not convinced he needs to find it in the Bible. Anyway, he didn't say that Leviticus or Romans actually approved of homosexuality. He said you have to go beyond authorial intent. You also have to let different scriptures balance and correct each other. Like on another issue: How are you going to read 1 Timothy 2, about women being silent in the church? If you go by that text, you'll have to exclude women from ordination as well!*

DENNIS: *Completely different case! There's no sin in being a woman!*

SHEILA: *Well, thanks a lot!* [Laughter all around] *But let's face it, on your grounds, seventy-five years ago, you would have had to oppose the ordination of women!*

AUTHOR: [Since Dennis has his arms folded in front of him and a determined look on his face] *It's plain I'm not going to get you to agree on gay and lesbian ordination. But what about the basic thrust of the book? The dual bottom line? Does it work for you?*

SHEILA: *As in: Is it founded in Jesus Christ? and Is it life-giving and liberating?*

AUTHOR: *You got the message, Sheila!*

SHEILA: *Obviously, the second question is the important one for me. I put the weight on the side of present questions, stories, contemporary knowledge—life and liberation if you like. I'm still thinking about the first one. I still have to think more about christology. I can't say I'm convinced that Jesus is truly God, but I guess I understand the whole idea a little better than I did before. I still have to think through the implications of not believing in it. I appreciate a lot of what you're saying over against the pluralists, but I'm not sure Paul Knitter may not be right! Let's say I'm still thinking about the Christic center, but definitely, the bottom line for me is human and environmental well-being.*

DENNIS: *So you don't really need to be a Christian at all, Sheila. You can work at your various social-justice causes quite nicely with or without Jesus Christ!*

SHEILA: [Hesitating] *Well . . . , it's true that I have friends outside the church who care about the same social-justice and environmental issues that I do. But I also believe in God, Dennis, and I love Jesus and the church, and the Bible, and I cherish the Christian heritage—at least some aspects of it. My faith motivates my social causes.* [With a rueful smile] *So you won't get rid of me that easily. I have as much right to be part of the church as you have!*

AUTHOR: *Absolutely! We need both of you in the church!*

DENNIS: *Now you sound like one of those liberal bishops who celebrates the variety of theologies and doesn't want anybody to leave because we can't afford to lose them! But no, Sheila, seriously, we need you and the kind of challenge you bring to the church.* [She smiles and bows] *But I'd just like to convert you to a solid Christian faith.* [Nervous laughter] *To get back to your so-called dual bottom line, Harold. It seems to me that to make a norm out of "life-giving and liberating" is just a great big Trojan horse! You can justify anything that way. Syncretism, revolutions, universal salvation, you name it. Make Christ say things he never said. It's wide open to ideology! You can drive a truck through it!*

AUTHOR: *You're mixing your metaphors, Dennis.*

DENNIS: *But honestly, Harold, you want to have your cake and eat it too! I think you've basically got a liberal theology with a polite nod to orthodoxy and tradition.*

AUTHOR: *You're right on there. Absolutely. I want to have my cake and eat it too!*

SHEILA: *What about that chapter on christology, Dennis? You call that a nod to tradition? It was Nicaea and Chalcedon through and through. Bodily resurrection? Christ dying for our sins? Sounds pretty conservative to me! With a nod to the liberationists! But I must say, I was surprised to find out how orthodox some of these feminists and liberationists are!*

The conversation went on for some time. No doubt it will continue to go on at many times and in many places and circumstances.

NOTES

Introduction

1. See Gregory Baum, *Religion and Alienation: A Theological Reading of Sociology* (New York: Paulist, 1975) chapter 9; also, idem, *Essays in Critical Theology* (Kansas City: Sheed & Ward, 1992).

2. From an American black spiritual, quoted by Dwight N. Hopkins, *Shoes That Fit Our Feet: Sources for a Constructive Black Theology* (Maryknoll, N.Y.: Orbis Books, 1997) 28.

3. Ibid., 29.

4. Jeffrey Stout, *Ethics after Babel: The Languages of Morals and Their Discontents* (Boston: Beacon, 1988) 163.

5. See Moltmann's comments about this in *God in Creation: An Ecological Doctrine of Creation,* trans. M. Kohl (London: SCM, 1985) xiv-xv; also his methodological volume *Experiences in Theology: Ways and Forms of Christian Theology,* trans. M. Kohl (Minneapolis: Fortress, 2000) xiv-xvi.

6. Peter Abelard, *A Dialogue of a Philosopher with a Jew and a Christian,* trans. P. J. Payer (Toronto: Pontifical Institute of Medieval Studies, 1979).

7. Mark Klein Taylor, *Remembering Esperanza: A Cultural-Political Theology of North American Praxis* (Maryknoll, N.Y.: Orbis Books, 1990) 4.

1. Criteria of Theological Adequacy

1. Karl Marx, *Theses on Feuerbach,* in Karl Marx, Friedrich Engels, *Selected Works,* vol. 1 (Moscow: Progress Publishers, 1977) thesis XI, 15.

2. Elisabeth Schüssler Fiorenza, *Rhetoric and Ethic: The Politics of Biblical Studies* (Minneapolis: Fortress, 1999) 17.

3. For a discussion of the Frankfurt school theorists Theodor W. Adorno, Max Horkheimer, Jürgen Habermas, and the Latin American radical educationist Paulo Freire, see M. Stackhouse, *Apologia: Contextualization, Globalization and Mission in Theological Education* (Grand Rapids: Eerdmans, 1988) 84-105.

4. Marx, *Theses on Feuerbach,* thesis II, 13.

5. See Harold Wells and Patricia Wells, *Jesus Means Life* (Toronto: CANEC, 1982).

6. This view is expressed by Colin Gunton, *The Christian Faith: An Introduction to Christian Doctrine* (Oxford: Blackwell, 2002) x. A very different sort of theologian, Gus-

tavo Gutierrez, expresses the same view in *The God of Life,* trans. M. J. O'Connell (Mary-knoll, N.Y.: Orbis Books, 1991) xi-xviii.

7. James Cone made this point very clearly many years ago in his *God of the Oppressed* (New York: Seabury, 1975). He spoke not generally of the poor or marginal-ized but specifically, from his black American context, of "black experience": "The con-vergence of Jesus Christ and the black experience is the meaning of the Incarnation. Because God became man in Jesus Christ, he disclosed the divine will to be with human-ity in our wretchedness. And because we blacks accept his presence in Jesus as the true definition of our humanity, blackness and divinity are dialectically bound together as one reality" (p. 35).

8. Gregory Baum, *Religion and Alienation: A Theological Reading of Sociology* (New York: Paulist, 1975), 196.

9. Robert W. Jenson protests "the besetting sin of Protestant . . . theology that escapes control by any determinate object and makes the gospel be whatever is 'justifying' or 'healing' or 'liberating' or whatever such value the theologian finds her- or himself affirm-ing" (*Systematic Theology,* vol. 1, *The Triune God* [New York: Oxford University Press, 1997] 12).

10. George Grant, "A Platitude," in *Technology and Empire* (Toronto: House of Anansi, 1969) 138.

11. See Donald A. D. Thorsen, *The Wesleyan Quadrilateral: Scripture, Tradition, Reason and Experience as a Model of Evangelical Theology* (Grand Rapids: Zondervan, 1970). See comments of Albert C. Outler on the "Wesleyan quadrilateral": "More than once I have regretted having coined it for contemporary use, since it has been so widely misconstrued" ("The Wesleyan Quadrilateral—in John Wesley," *Wesleyan Theological Journal* 20, no. 1 (Spring 1985): 16.

12. Anselm of Canterbury, *Proslogion,* preface, 1, in *Anselm: Basic Writings,* ed. S. N. Deane (LaSalle, Ill.: Open Court, 1968). See a major discussion of Anselm's under-standing of faith and reason by Karl Barth, *Anselm: Fides Quaerens Intellectum: Anselm's Proof of the Existence of God in the Context of His Theological Scheme,* trans. I. W. Robertson (London: SCM, 1960).

13. This is discussed by David Tracy in *The Analogical Imagination* (New York: Crossroad, 1981).

14. See Gregory Baum, "David Tracy: Pluralism and Liberation Theology," in *Essays in Critical Theology* (Kansas City: Sheed and Ward, 1994) 38-39.

15. See David Tracy, *The Blessed Rage for Order: The New Pluralism in Theology* (Minneapolis: Winston Seabury Press, 1975) chapter 1.

16. For a thorough discussion of experience in theological method, see Jeong Woo Kim, "The Theological Function of Experience: Method in Black American and Korean Theologies" (Th.D. diss., Knox College, Toronto School of Theology, 2002).

17. Eberhard Busch, *Karl Barth: His Life from Letters and Autobiographical Texts,* trans. J. Bowden (Philadelphia: Fortress, 1976) 81-92.

18. Debate has raged among Barthian scholars concerning the question of his radi-calism. See Friedrich-Wilhelm Marquardt, who argues that Barth's theology is funda-mentally determined by his socialism ("Socialism in the Theology of Karl Barth," in *Karl Barth and Radical Politics,* ed. George Hunsinger [Philadelphia: Westminster, 1976]). On the other hand, Helmut Gollwitzer argues that Barth never seriously connected his poli-

tics thoroughly to his theology, exhibiting a "bourgeois slant" (see "The Kingdom of God and Socialism in the Theology of Karl Barth," in ibid., 106, 111). See also George Hunsinger, "Karl Barth and Liberation Theology," in *Disruptive Grace: Studies in the Theology of Karl Barth* (Grand Rapids: Eerdmans, 2000); also Harold Wells, "Theology of the Cross and the Theologies of Liberation," in *Toronto Journal of Theology* 17, no. 1 (Spring 2001), 147-66.

19. David H. Kelsey, *The Uses of Scripture in Recent Theology* (Philadelphia: Fortress, 1975) 137.

20. See J. Wentzel Van Huysteen, *The Shaping of Rationality: Toward Interdisciplinarity in Theology and Science* (Grand Rapids: Eerdmans, 1999).

21. Paul Ricoeur, *Freud and Philosophy: Essay on Interpretation,* trans. D. Savage (New Haven: Yale University Press, 1970) 32-36.

22. I refer to Martin Heidegger, Wilhelm Dilthey. See Karl Mannheim, *Ideology and Utopia: An Introduction to the Sociology of Knowledge* (New York: Harcourt, Brace & Co., 1936).

23. Karl Marx and Friedrich Engels, *The German Ideology,* ed. R. Pascal (New York: International Publishers, 1947) 39.

24. Ibid., 34.

25. See the discussion of Heidegger's hermeneutics by Anthony C. Thistelton, "The New Hermeneutic"; also Thomas W. Gillespie, "Biblical Authority and Interpretation: The Current Debate on Hermeneutics," both in *A Guide to Contemporary Hermeneutics: Major Trends in Biblical Interpretation,* ed. Donald K. McKim (Grand Rapids: Eerdmans, 1986) 93-94, 196-97.

26. Thomas S. Kuhn, *The Structure of Scientific Revolutions* (Chicago: University of Chicago Press, 1962).

27. José Míguez Bonino, *Doing Theology in a Revolutionary Situation* (Philadelphia: Fortress, 1975) 91.

28. Elisabeth Schüssler Fiorenza, *Bread Not Stone: The Challenge of Feminist Biblical Interpretation* (Boston: Beacon, 1984) xi.

29. George A. Lindbeck, *The Nature of Doctrine: Religion and Theology in a Postliberal Age* (Philadelphia: Westminster, 1984).

30. Paul Tillich described the "anxiety of meaninglessness, emptiness and despair" as the distinctive anxiety of modern times (*The Courage to Be* [New Haven: Yale University Press, 1952]). See a recent discussion of widespread "covert despair" as "pervasive" in the global society of the early twenty-first century by Douglas John Hall, "Despair as Pervasive Ailment," in *Hope for the World: Mission in a Global Context,* ed. Walter Brueggemann (Louisville: Westminster John Knox Press, 2001) 83-93.

2. Revelation and Faith

1. Mordecai Richler, *Son of a Smaller Hero* (Toronto: McClelland & Stewart, 1989) 11.

2. Daniel Migliore, *Faith Seeking Understanding: An Introduction to Christian Theology* (Grand Rapids: Eerdmans, 1991) 19.

3. See Karl Barth's discussion of the objectivity and subjectivity of revelation, *Church Dogmatics,* vol. 1, pt. 2, ed. G. W. Bromiley and T. F.Torrance (Edinburgh: T & T Clark, 1956).

4. J. Severino Croatto, *Exodus: A Hermeneutics of Freedom*, trans. S. Attanasio (Maryknoll, N.Y.: Orbis Books, 1981) chapter 2.

5. Mircea Eliade, *Cosmos and History: The Myth of Eternal Return* (New York: Harper, 1959) 67-69.

6. Croatto, *Exodus,* 15-16.

7. The experience of the ineffable and the holy is not exclusive, by any means, to Jewish or Christian religious experience. Certainly comparable stories of revelatory experience can be found elsewhere in the history of religion. See Rudolf Otto on the theophany of the burning bush (*The Idea of the Holy,* trans. J. W. Harvey [New York: Oxford University Press, 1958] 75).

8. Croatto, *Exodus,* 12.

9. Eliade, *Cosmos and History,* 104, 161.

10. See Paul Ricoeur, "The Dialectic of Event and Meaning," in *Interpretation Theory: Discourse and the Surplus of Meaning* (Fort Worth: Texas Christian University Press, 1976) 8-12.

11. Paul Ricoeur, "The Hermeneutical Function of Distanciation," in *Hermeneutics and the Human Sciences,* ed. and trans. J. B. Thompson (London: Cambridge University Press, 1981) 131-44.

12. J. Severino Croatto, *Biblical Hermeneutics: Toward a Theory of Reading as the Production of Meaning,* trans. R. R. Barr (Maryknoll, N.Y.: Orbis Books, 1987) especially chapter 2.

13. Ibid., 22-23.

14. Ibid., 23.

15. Jürgen Moltmann, *Theology of Hope: On the Ground and the Implications of a Christian Eschatology,* trans. J. W. Leitch (London: SCM, 1965) chapter 3.

16. Paul Tillich, cited by Douglas John Hall, *Thinking the Faith: Christian Theology in a North American Context* (Minneapolis: Augsburg, 1989) 414.

17. Karl Barth, *Church Dogmatics,* vol. 2, pt. 1, trans. and ed. G. W. Bromiley and T. F. Torrance (Edinburgh: T & T Clark, 1957) 4-5.

18. Edward Schillebeeckx, *Jesus: An Experiment in Christology,* trans. H. Hoskins (New York: Crossroad, 1979), part II, chapter 2.

19. José Comblin, *The Holy Spirit and Liberation,* trans. P. Burns (Maryknoll, N.Y.: Orbis Books, 1979) 1-7.

20. Paul Tillich, *The Dynamics of Faith* (New York: Harper and Row, 1957) 101.

21. Hall, *Thinking the Faith,* 173-74.

22. Reinhold Niebuhr, *The Nature and Destiny of Man* (New York: Scribner, 1964) 2:75; quoted by Hall, *Thinking the Faith,* 177.

23. Moltmann, *Theology of Hope,* 18-19.

24. Jon Sobrino, *Jesus the Liberator: A Historical-Theological View,* trans. Paul Burns and Francis McDonagh (Maryknoll, N.Y.: Orbis Books, 1993) 92-93.

25. Richard A. Horsley, "Rhetoric and Empire—and I Corinthians," in *Paul and Politics: Essays in Honour of Krister Stendahl,* ed. Richard A. Horsley (Harrisburg: Trinity Press International, 2000) 90-103.

26. "Faith is precisely the contradiction between the infinite passion of the individ-

ual's inwardness and the objective uncertainty. . . . If I wish to preserve myself in faith I must constantly be intent upon holding fast the objective uncertainty, so as to remain out upon the deep, over seventy thousand fathoms of water, still preserving my faith" (Søren Kierkegaard, *Concluding Unscientific Postscript*, trans. David Swenson [Princeton: Princeton University Press, 1941] 182).

27. Wolfhart Pannenberg, *Metaphysics and the Idea of God,* trans. P. Clayton (Grand Rapids: Eerdmans, 1990).

28. Wolfhart Pannenberg, *Basic Questions in Theology: Collected Essays,* vol. 2, trans. G. H. Kehm (Philadelphia: Fortress, 1971) 32.

29. Ibid., 7.

30. See discussion of "success" and the church by Douglas John Hall, *The Future of the Church* (Toronto: United Church Publishing House, 1989) 34-37. See also a good discussion of the power dynamics of the spread of Christianity in western Europe in the early medieval period, in David Bosch, *Transforming Mission: Paradigm Shifts in the Theology of Mission* (Maryknoll, N.Y.: Orbis Books, 1991) 214-30.

31. See St.Thomas Aquinas's "five ways" in *Summa Theologiae,* vol. 2, trans. Blackfriars (London: Burns Oates and Washbourne, 1963) 13-18.

32. Martin Luther, *Heidelberg Disputation,* in *Luther's Works,* vol. 31, ed. H. J. Grim (Philadelphia: Muhlenberg Press, 1957) 41.

33. Ibid., 51.

34. Ibid., 52-53.

35. Ibid., 53.

36. Ibid., 55.

37. Ibid., 55-56.

38. Luther, Sermon of Feb. l, 1517, in *Luther's Works,* 51:24.

39. See Abraham Heschel, *The Prophets* (New York: Harper & Row, 1962) vol. 2, chapters 1-3; also Jürgen Moltmann, *The Trinity and the Kingdom:The Doctrine of God,* trans. M. Kohl (London: SCM, 1981) chapter 2.

40. In a lecture at McMaster University in the 1960s.

41. H. Stendhal, quoted by Jürgen Moltmann, *The Crucified God: The Cross of Christ as the Foundation and Criticism of Christian Theology*, trans. R. A. Wilson and J. Bowden (London: SCM, 1974) 225.

42. Albert Camus, *L'homme révolté* (Paris: Gallimard, 1951), quoted by Moltmann, *The Crucified God,* 221-22.

43. Ibid., quoted, 226.

44. Moltmann, *Crucified God,* 221.

45. Dietrich Bonhoeffer, *Letters and Papers from Prison,* ed. Eberhard Bethge (London: SCM, 1953) 360.

46. C. S. Lewis, *Mere Christianity* (London: G. Bles, 1952) 42.

47. John Updike, *Self-Consciousness: Memoirs* (New York: Alfred A. Knopf, 1989) 229.

48. Jon Sobrino, *Christology at the Crossroads: A Latin American Approach,* trans. J. Drury (Maryknoll, N.Y.: Orbis Books, 1978) 220-21.

49. Moltmann, *The Crucified God,* 201.

50. Ibid., 227.

3. Faith as Rational

1. Douglas John Hall, *Thinking the Faith: Christian Theology in a North American Context* (Minneapolis: Augsburg, 1989) 402.

2. See Alvin Plantinga and Nicholas Wolterstorff, eds., *Faith and Rationality* (Notre Dame, Ind.: University of Notre Dame Press, 1983); Alasdair MacIntyre, *Whose Justice? Whose Rationality?* (Notre Dame, Ind.: University of Notre Dame Press, 1988).

3. The point is made by J. Wentzel Van Huysteen, *The Shaping of Rationality: Toward Interdisciplinarity in Theology and Science* (Grand Rapids: Eerdmans, 1999) 141.

4. Ibid., 150.

5. Ibid., 2, 131.

6. Hall, *Thinking the Faith,* 389.

7. *Karl Barth's Table Talk,* ed. John Godsey (Richmond: John Knox Press, 1963) 31.

8. Margaret Rose, "Defining the Post-Modern," in *The Post-Modern Reader,* ed. Charles Jencks (New York: St. Martin's Press, 1992); Charles Jencks, *What is Post-Modernism?* (New York: St. Martin's Press, 1989); J. Richard Middleton and Brian Walsh, *The Truth Is Stranger Than It Used to Be* (Downers Grove, Ill.: InterVarsity, 1995).

9. Stanley J. Grenz, *A Primer in Postmodernism* (Grand Rapids: Eerdmans, 1996) 20-21.

10. Ibid., 37-38.

11. Craig Van Gelder, "Mission in the Emerging Postmodern Condition," in *The Church between Gospel and Culture: The Emerging Mission in North America,* ed. George R. Hunsberger and Craig Van Gelder (Grand Rapids: Eerdmans, 1996) 113-38.

12. Francis Bacon, *Novum Organum,* part 2, trans. and ed. J. Spedding (London: Longmans, 1887-1901) 4:147. See the ecofeminist discussion by Rosemary Radford Ruether, *Gaia and God: An Ecofeminist Theology of Earth Healing* (San Francisco: HarperSanFrancisco, 1992); see also Harold Wells, "The Flesh of God: Christological Implications for an Ecological Vision of the World, *Toronto Journal of Theology* 15, no. 1 (Spring 1999): 50-68.

13. Douglas John Hall, *Professing the Faith: Christian Theology in a North American Context* (Minneapolis: Fortress, 1993) 145.

14. See Karl Lowith, *From Hegel to Nietzsche: The Revolution in Nineteenth Century Thought,* trans. D. E. Green (New York: Doubleday, 1941).

15. Friedrich Nietzsche, *The Will to Power,* ed. W. Kaufmann, trans. W. Kaufmann and R. J. Hollingdale (New York: Random House, 1967).

16. See the discussion of Marx, Nietzsche, and Freud by Paul Ricoeur, in *Freud and Philosophy: Essay on Interpretation,* trans. D. Savage (New Haven: Yale University Press, 1970) 240-42.

17. Friedrich Nietzsche, *Thus Spake Zarathustra: A Book for All and None,* trans. A. Tille (London: T. F. Unwin, 1908) 6.

18. Ibid., 86, 87.

19. Friedrich Nietzsche, *The Genealogy of Morals: An Attack* (1887) in *The Birth of Tragedy and the Genealogy of Morals,* trans. Francis Golffing (New York: Doubleday, 1956) 297.

20. Friedrich Nietzsche, *Beyond Good and Evil: Prelude to a Philosophy of the Future,* ed. R.-P. Horstmann et al. (Cambridge: Cambridge University Press, 2002) 44, 45.

21. George Grant, "Nietzsche and the Ancients," in *The George Grant Reader,* ed. William Christian and Sheila Grant (Toronto: University of Toronto Press, 1998) 293. This high estimate of Nietzsche's philosophical achievement is shared by Alasdair MacIntyre, *After Virtue: A Study in Moral Theory* (Notre Dame, Ind.: University of Notre Dame Press, 1984) 113: "In five swift, witty and cogent paragraphs he disposes of what I have called the Enlightenment project to discover rational foundations for an objective morality."

22. Grant, "Nietzsche and the Ancients," 294.

23. Grenz, *Primer in Postmodernism,* 124.

24. See Michel Foucault, *The Archaeology of Knowledge,* trans. A. M. S. Smith (New York: Pantheon, 1972); also *The Order of Things: An Archaeology of the Human Sciences* (New York: Random House/Pantheon, 1971).

25. Foucault, quoted by Grenz, *Primer in Postmodernism,* 135.

26. Jacques Derrida, in *Margins of Philosophy*, trans. Alan Bass (Chicago: University of Chicago Press, 1982), quoted by Grenz, *Primer in Postmodernism,* 149.

27. See Grenz, *Primer in Postmodernism,* 45-49.

28. Jean-Francois Lyotard, *The Postmodern Condition: A Report on Knowledge,* trans. G. Bennington et al. (Minneapolis: University of Minnesota Press, 1984) 46.

29. Ibid., 41-47.

30. Ibid., 45-47.

31. Gregory Baum, "Postmodern Discourse and Social Responsibility," in *Essays in Critical Theology* (Kansas City: Sheed & Ward, 1994) 89.

32. Gregory Baum, "Critical Theology: Replies to Ray Morrow," in *Essays in Critical Theology,* 14.

33. Perhaps some of the best postmodern thought is found in feminist authors, such as Elisabeth Schüssler Fiorenza, who may be described as "critical modern." A radical hermeneutic of suspicion is combined with a forthright liberationist commitment to certain universal values. She is so described by Loraine MacKenzie Shepherd, *Feminist Theologies in a Postmodern Church: Diversity, Community and Scripture* (New York: Peter Lang, 2002) chapter 2.

34. Mark C. Taylor, *Erring: A Postmodern A/theology* (Chicago: University of Chicago Press, 1984); idem, *Hiding* (Chicago: University of Chicago Press, 1997); Mark Kline Taylor, *Remembering Esperanza: A Cultural-Political Theology for North American Praxis* (Maryknoll, N.Y.: Orbis Books, 1990).

35. See Mary McClintock Fulkerson, *Changing the Subject: Women's Discourses and Feminist Theology* (Minneapolis: Fortress, 1994). Her work is discussed by Loraine MacKenzie Shepherd (*Feminist Theologies in a Postmodern Church,* chapter 3), who offers a definition of "poststructuralist": "Often used interchangeably with postmodern, but usually in reference to literary theory and deconstruction. This philosophy states that language constructs, rather than describes, reality. Language cannot refer to anything outside of itself. It is based upon contrasting differences, describing what something is and, by extension, is not" (p. 237).

36. MacIntyre, *Whose Justice?*

37. Thomas Oden, *After Modernity . . . What? Agenda for Theology* (Grand Rapids: Zondervan, 1990).

38. Ronald Thiemann, *Constructing a Public Theology: The Church in a Pluralistic*

Culture (Louisville: John Knox Press, 1991); Stanley Hauerwas, "The Church's One Foundation is Jesus Christ her Lord Or, In a World Without Foundations all we have is the Church," in *Theology Without Foundations: Religious Practice and the Future of Theological Truth,* ed. Stanley Hauerwas, Nancey Murphy, and Mark Nation (Nashville: Abingdon, 1994); John Milbank, *Theology and Social Theory: Beyond Secular Reason* (Oxford: Basil Blackwell, 1990).

39. Stanley J. Grenz and John R. Franke, *Beyond Foundationalism: Shaping Theology in a Postmodern Context* (Louisville: Westminster John Knox Press, 2001) 23.

40. Alvin Plantinga, "Reason and Belief in God," in *Faith and Rationality,* ed. Plantinga and Wolterstorff, 48.

41. See Grenz and Franke, *Beyond Foundationalism,* 23.

42. Anselm of Canterbury, *Proslogium,* in *Anselm: Basic Writings,* trans. S. N. Deane (LaSalle, Ill.: Open Court, 1968) 3. Before him Augustine had also said, "If you cannot understand, believe in order that you may understand" (*Sermo* cxviii, cited by M. C. D'Arcy, S.J., "The Philosophy of St. Augustine," in M. C. D'Arcy et al., *Saint Augustine* [Cleveland: World Publishing, 1961] 159).

43. Anselm's original title for *Proslogium.* Anselm speaks of "One who contemplates God and seeks to understand what he believes" (*Proslogium,* Preface, 1). See Karl Barth's treatment of Anselm's ontological argument: *Anselm: Fides Quaerens Intellectum: Anselm's Proof of the Existence of God in the Context of His Theological Scheme,* trans. I. W. Robertson (London: SCM, 1960).

44. Anselm, *Proslogium,* 3.8.

45. Ibid., 3.9.

46. Nicholas Wolterstorff, "Can Belief in God Be Rational?" in *Faith and Rationality,* ed. Plantinga and Wolterstorff, 141.

47. Thomas Aquinas, *Summa Contra Gentiles,* ed. English Dominican Fathers (London: Burnes, Oates and Washbourne, 1924) chap. 6, 11-13.

48. Ibid., 11.

49. David Tracy, *Blessed Rage for Order: The New Pluralism in Theology* (New York: Winston Seabury Press, 1975) 7.

50. David Tracy, *The Analogical Imagination: Christian Theology and the Culture of Pluralism* (New York: Crossroad, 1981) 57.

51. Ibid.

52. John Updike, "Pigeon Feathers," in *Pigeon Feathers and Other Stories* (New York: Alfred A. Knopf, 1962) 116-50.

53. T. F. Torrance, "The Influence of Reformed Theology on the Development of Scientific Method," in *Theology in Reconstruction* (London: SCM, 1965).

54. René Descartes, *Meditations and Other Metaphysical Writings,* ed. and trans. Desmond M. Clarke (New York: Penguin, 1998), Meditation 2.

55. See the incisive criticism of Cartesian "self"-oriented knowledge and dualism by John Macmurray, *The Self as Agent* (Amherst, N.Y.: Humanity Books, 1999) and *Persons in Relation* (Amherst, N.Y.: Humanity Books, 1999).

56. John Locke, *An Essay Concerning Human Understanding* (Oxford: Clarendon Press, 1894) 121-23.

57. See reference to Blaise Pascal in MacIntyre, *After Virtue,* 54.

58. William C. Placher, *The Domestication of Transcendence: How Modern Thinking about God Went Wrong* (Louisville: Westminster John Knox Press, 1996) 1-17.

59. Søren Kierkegaard, quoted from his *Journals* (1841) in *Provocations: Spiritual Writings of Kierkegaard,* trans. and ed. Charles E. Moore (Farmington, Pa.: Plough Publishing House, 1999) 273. It is interesting that even Kierkegaard is willing to admit the possibility that demonstrations or proofs, while ambiguous, may be "able to lead someone—not to faith, far from it, but to the point where faith might come into existence. At best they are able to help someone become aware and come into the tension where faith breaks forth: Will you believe or will you be offended?" (cited in *Provocations,* 269).

60. See Ricoeur, *Freud and Philosophy,* 236-38, 240-42.

61. C. F. von Weizsacker, *The World View of Physics* (London: Routledge & Kegan Paul, 1952) 132. See discussion by T. F. Torrance in *God and Rationality* (London: Oxford University Press, 1971) 205.

62. Michael Polanyi, *Personal Knowledge* (London: Routledge & Kegan Paul, 1958) 151.

63. Thomas Kuhn, *The Structure of Scientific Revolutions* (Chicago: University of Chicago Press,1970).

64. Van Huysteen, *Shaping of Rationality,* 34.

65. Kuhn, *Structure of Scientific Revolutions,* 92.

66. Van Huysteen, *Shaping of Rationality,* 38-39.

67. Ibid., 185.

68. Ibid., 163.

69. Ibid.

70. William Placher, *Unapologetic Theology* (Louisville: Westminster John Knox Press, 1989) 34.

71. Quintus Septimius Florens Tertullianus (Tertullian) in *De Carne Christi,* 4-5, in *The Early Christian Fathers,* ed. and trans. Henry Bettenson (London: Oxford University Press, 1963) 173.

72. Quoted by Plantinga, "Reason and Belief in God," 87.

73. Luther, *Lectures on Galatians* (3:6) in *Luther's Works,* vol. 26, ed. J. Pelikan (St. Louis: Concordia, 1963) 228.

74. Ibid.

75. Luther, at the Diet of Worms, quoted by Roland H. Bainton, *Here I Stand: A Life of Martin Luther* (Nashville: Abingdon, 1950). See *Luther's Works,* 32:112.

76. Brand Blanshard, *Reason and Belief* (London: George Allen & Unwin, 1974) 165, 182.

77. See Hans Frei, "Eberhard Busch's Biography of Karl Barth," in *Karl Barth in Review,* ed. H.-M. Rumscheidt (Pittsburgh: Pickwick Press, 1981) 103.

78. Note Frei's use of Erich Auerbach on "realistic narrative" in *The Identity of Jesus Christ* (repr., Eugene, Ore.: Wipf & Stock, 1997) 7.

79. Ibid., 40-45.

80. Hans Frei, *The Eclipse of Biblical Narrative* (New Haven: Yale University Press, 1974) 1-16.

81. Placher, *Unapologetic Theology,* 163. A similar appreciative criticism comes from Trevor Hart, who asks how Frei's rather "formalist" approach to scriptural texts relates to the real world in which we live. How do these biblical stories relate to the truth of the reality of the situation in the world? "This question will not go away while we continue to take seriously the question of truth in our attempts to think theologically" (*Faith*

Thinking: The Dynamics of Christian Theology [Downers Grove, Ill.: InterVarsity Press, 1996] 33).

82. Frei, *The Identity of Jesus Christ,* 183.

83. George A. Lindbeck, *The Nature of Doctrine: Religion and Theology in a Postliberal Age* (Philadelphia: Westminster Press, 1984) 18.

84. Ibid., 33.

85. Ibid., 18.

86. George A. Lindbeck, "The Gospel's Uniqueness: Election and Untranslatability," in *The Church in a Postliberal Age,* ed. James J. Buckley (Grand Rapids: Eerdmans, 2002).

87. Van Huysteen, *Shaping of Rationality,* 76.

88. Lindbeck, *The Nature of Doctrine,* 130-31.

89. Ibid., 16.

90. Ibid.

91. Douglas John Hall, "On the Contextuality of Christian Theology," *Toronto Journal of Theology* 1, no. 1 (Spring 1985): 3-26.

92. Lindbeck, *Nature of Doctrine,* 16.

93. Ibid., 105.

94. Ibid., 134-35.

95. Mark Kline Taylor, *Remembering Esperanza,* 33-34.

96. See the critical comments on Lindbeck by Amy Plantinga Pauw, "The World is Near You: A Feminist Conversation with Lindbeck," *Modern Theology* 50, no. 1 (April 1993): 45-56.

97. See Van Huysteen's arguments with Thiemann, Milbank, and others (*The Shaping of Rationality,* 72-77, 81-85). See Kathryn Tanner, who argues that the postliberal makes the "mistake" of projecting onto the object studied "what its own procedures of investigation requires—a coherent whole." Thus, "[t]he method of study itself thereby validates the conclusions of the theologian while disqualifying the people and practices it studies from posing a challenge to those conclusions" (*Theories of Culture: A New Agenda for Theology* [Minneapolis: Fortress, 1997] 76).

98. See the critical comments on Lindbeck by Alister E. McGrath, *A Passion for Truth: The Intellectual Coherence of Evangelicalism* (Downers Grove, Ill.: InterVarsity Press, 1996) 135; also idem, "An Evangelical Evaluation of Postliberalism," in *The Nature of Confession: Evangelicals and Postliberals Together,* ed. T. R. Phillips and D. L. Okholm (Downers Grove, Ill.: InterVarsity Press, 1996) 40.

99. See the criticism of Lindbeck by Hart, *Faith Thinking,* 85-89. See also George Hunsinger, "Truth as Self-Evolving: Barth and Lindbeck on the Cognitive and Performative Aspects of Truth in Theological Discourse," *Journal of the American Academy of Religion* 61, no. 1 (1993): 12-29.

100. Kathryn Tanner may be described as a postliberal theologian in that she often seems unconcerned about referentiality. However, see her *God and Creation in Christian Theology: Tyranny or Empowerment* (Oxford: Blackwell, 1988) 12.

101. I am indebted here to Hall, *Thinking the Faith,* chapter 6.

102. See the meticulous methodological work of Clodovis Boff for whom "reason" is an important concept: *Theology and Praxis: Epistemological Foundations,* trans. R. R. Barr (Maryknoll, N.Y.: Orbis Books, 1987) 109-10, 191-92.

103. George Grant, "Pursuit of an Illusion: A Commentary on Bertrand Russell," in *The George Grant Reader,* ed. Christian and Grant, 334.

104. See the reference to Pascal by Bertrand Russell, *A History of Western Philosophy* (New York: Simon & Schuster, 1959) 691; see also MacIntyre, *After Virtue,* 76.

105. On the Frankfurt school, see Ronald J. Schindler, *The Frankfurt School Critique of Capitalist Culture* (Aldershot: Hants, 1998).

106. Charles Taylor, *The Malaise of Modernity* (Concord, ON: House of Anansi, 1991) especially chapter 2; see also Nicholas H. Smith, *Charles Taylor: Meaning, Morals, and Modernity* (Cambridge: Polity Press, 2002).

107. See Hall, *Thinking the Faith,* 390-91.

108. George Grant, *Time as History,* ed. William Christian (Toronto: University of Toronto Press, 1995) 65.

109. Van Huysteen, *Shaping of Rationality,* 218-19. On the "fiduciary" character of all knowledge, see Lesslie Newbigin, *Truth to Tell* (Grand Rapids: Eerdmans, 1991); also Polanyi, *Personal Knowledge.*

110. T. F. Torrance, "Theology in the Scientific World," in *God and Rationality*, 93.

111. See Harold Wells, "Social Analysis and Theological Method: Third World Challenge to Canadian Theology," in *A Long and Faithful March*, ed. H. Wells and R. Hutchinson (Toronto: United Church Publishing House, 1989) 210-12.

112. I use the word "object" cautiously, in view of Grant's warning that the language of subjects and objects is one of the ways through which the beauty of the world has been obscured for us. "Object," he points out, means literally something that we have thrown over against ourselves: *jacio* (I throw), *ob* (over against). In German, *Gegenstand* (object) is that which stands against. Thus Grant sees the language of "object" as tending toward reason as project, and rationality as dominant, technological science. Grant believes that "if we confine our attention to anything as if it were merely an object, it cannot be loved as beautiful . . . the professors concerned want to share the prestige of objectivity with their colleagues from the mastering sciences. . . . Only as anything stands before us in some relation other than the objective can we learn of its beauty and from its beauty" (*Technology and Justice* [Toronto: House of Anansi Press, 1986], 36, 40-41).

Yet we need not surrender the important language of objectivity to technological reason, for we do need language to express the relationship of the knower to that which is known. In the case of Jesus Christ as God's Word made flesh, what we must cherish is the fact that God has graciously and mercifully become "object" for us, yes, even "over against" us, as one of us, in our flesh.

113. See Walter Brueggemann, *The Creative Word: Canon as Model for Biblical Education* (Philadelphia: Fortress, 1982) chapter 4.

114. T. F. Torrance, "The Word of God and the Response of Man," in *God and Rationality*, 142.

4. Is It Founded in Jesus Christ?

1. The Barmen Confession, in *The Church Confronts the Nazis: Barmen Then and Now*, ed. H. G. Locke (Lewiston, N.Y.: Edwin Mellen Press, 1984) 22-23.

2. Jon Sobrino speaks of Jesus Christ in this way. Jesus is *norma normans non nor-*

mata in his whole person and practice (*Jesus the Liberator: A Historical-Theological View,* trans. P. Burns and F. McDonagh [Maryknoll, N.Y.: Orbis Books, 1993] 53). Traditionally, scripture, or the Spirit speaking through scripture, has more often been regarded as *norma normans non normata.* See Stanley J. Grenz and John R. Franke, *Beyond Foundationalism: Shaping Theology in a Postmodern Context* (Louisville: Westminster John Knox Press, 2001) 63-68. See also chapter 7 below.

3. "Whole Christ" here does not refer to the Catholic doctrine of Christ as *caput et membra* (head and members). Elizabeth Johnson suggests this line of thought when she argues that Christ cannot be "reduced" to the historical individual Jesus of Nazareth. Christ, she says, "is a corporate personality, a relational reality, redeemed humanity" (*She Who Is: The Mystery of God in Feminist Theological Discourse* [New York: Crossroad, 1992] 72). Here she seems to evoke a high ecclesiology of the church *as Christ,* or church as *incarnatus prolongatus* (prolongation of the incarnation), though her concern as a feminist theologian is to avoid identifying "the Christ" with the male historical Jesus. Miroslav Volf rejects this notion of the *totus Christus,* since it is incompatible with *solus Christus.* He insists that "the church is not the subject of salvific activity with Christ; rather Christ is the *only* subject of such salvific activity" (*After Our Likeness: The Church as the Image of the Trinity* [Grand Rapids: Eerdmans, 1998] 164). That is, only Christ is the Saviour. The church is sinful, standing in need of salvation, and cannot save the world. While the church is "in Christ" and "in the Spirit," the church *is not* Christ. The "whole Christ" as I use the term here, however, refers to Jesus of Nazareth in his historical existence, now risen and exalted as the Christ, present with us in and with the Holy Spirit.

4. A good recent discussion of this can be found in the work of two contrasting "historical-Jesus" scholars: Marcus Borg and N. T. Wright, *The Meaning of Jesus: Two Visions* (San Francisco: HarperSanFrancisco, 1999). Note also Borg's distinction between the "Pre-Easter Jesus" and "Jesus as Spirit Person" in *Meeting Jesus Again for the First Time: The Historical Jesus and the Heart of Contemporary Faith* (San Francisco: HarperSanFrancisco, 1994) 20-31, 31-39.

5. A recent massive but controversial effort of this kind is that of John Dominic Crossan, *The Historical Jesus: The Life of a Mediterranean Jewish Peasant* (San Francisco: HarperSanFrancisco, 1991). A rich account of Jesus in the context of the Roman Empire is Richard A. Horsley, *Jesus and Empire: The Kingdom of God and the New World Disorder* (Minneapolis: Fortress, 2003).

6. See the arguments of Luke Timothy Johnson, *The Real Jesus: The Misguided Quest for the Historical Jesus and the Truth of the Traditional Gospel* (San Francisco: HarperSanFrancisco, 1996).

7. A good example of disagreements between two scholars on many questions regarding the historical Jesus is Borg and Wright, *Meaning of Jesus.* Note also, for example, the disagreement between Borg and E. P. Sanders on the question of Jesus' eschatology: Marcus J. Borg, *Jesus in Contemporary Scholarship* (Harrisburg, Pa.: Trinity Press International, 1994) chapter 3; idem, *Meeting Jesus Again for the First Time,* 29; and E. P. Sanders, *The Historical Figure of Jesus* (London: Allen Lane, Penguin, 1993) 261-64.

8. Geoffrey Wainwright insists on the intimate association of worship and theology in *Doxology: The Praise of God in Worship, Doctrine, and Life* (New York: Oxford University Press, 1980).

9. Paul Newman, *A Spirit Christology: Recovering the Biblical Paradigm of Christian Faith* (Lanham, Md.: University Press of America, 1987) 15, 204.

10. David R. Newman, *Worship as Praise and Empowerment* (New York: Pilgrim Press, 1988) vii.

11. Jon Sobrino, *Christ the Liberator: A View from the Victims*, trans. P. Burns (Maryknoll, N.Y.: Orbis Books, 2001) 323-24.

12. "A New Creed" of The United Church of Canada, 1968; revised 1980, 1994.

13. Clodovis Boff, *Theology and Praxis: Epistemological Foundations*, trans. R. R. Barr (Maryknoll, N.Y.: Orbis Books, 1987) 192-93.

14. The point is made by Jürgen Moltmann in *Experiences in Theology: Ways and Forms of Christian Theology*, trans. M. Kohl (Minneapolis: Fortress, 2000) 294-95.

15. Gustavo Gutiérrez, *A Theology of Liberation: History, Salvation, and Politics*, trans. and ed. C. Inda and J. Eagleson, 2nd ed. (Maryknoll, N.Y.: Orbis Books, 1988) xxxiv.

16. For an account of ecological theology among evangelicals, see Robert Booth Fowler, *The Greening of Protestant Thought* (Chapel Hill: University of North Carolina Press, 1995), 17, 39-44.

17. A prime example here is Matthew Fox, *Creation Spirituality* (San Francisco: HarperSanFrancisco, 1991); also, more recently, idem, *Sins of the Spirit, Blessings of the Flesh* (New York: Harmony Press, 1999).

18. Jürgen Moltmann, *God in Creation: An Ecological Doctrine of Creation*, trans. M. Kohl (London: SCM, 1985); idem, *The Way of Jesus Christ: Christology in Messianic Dimensions*, trans. M. Kohl (London: SCM, 1990); Leonardo Boff, *Cry of the Earth, Cry of the Poor*, trans. P. Berryman (Maryknoll, N.Y.: Orbis Books, 1997); Douglas John Hall, *Imaging God: Dominion as Stewardship* (Grand Rapids: Eerdmans, 1986); idem, *The Steward: A Biblical Symbol Come of Age* (Grand Rapids: Eerdmans, 1990).

19. Rosemary Radford Ruether, *New Woman and New Earth: Sexist Ideologies and Human Liberation* (San Francisco: Harper & Row, 1975).

20. Elizabeth A. Johnson, *Women, Earth, and Creator Spirit* (Philadelphia: Fortress, 1985).

21. Thomas Berry, "Twelve Principles for Understanding the Universe and the Role of the Human in the Universe," in *Thomas Berry and the New Cosmology*, ed. A. Lonergan and C. Richards (Mystic, Conn.: Twenty-Third Publications, 1987) 107.

22. Thomas Berry, with Thomas Clarke, *Befriending the Earth: A Theology of Reconciliation between Humans and the Earth* (Mystic, Conn.: Twenty-Third Publications, 1991) 54, 76.

23. Thomas Berry, *Piracy in America: Profiteering in the Public Domain* (Atlanta: Clarity Press, 1999).

24. Sallie McFague, *Life Abundant: Rethinking Theology and Economy for a Planet in Peril* (Minneapolis: Fortress, 2001) 30.

25. Sallie McFague, *Super, Natural Christians: How We Should Love Nature* (Minneapolis: Fortress, 1997) 1-15.

26. Ibid., 15-16.

27. Sallie McFague, *The Body of God: An Ecological Theology* (Minneapolis: Fortress, 1993) xi.

28. Ibid., 162.

29. Ibid.

30. Ibid., 28, 137; idem, *Life Abundant,* 169.

31. This accusation was leveled notably by Lynn White, who charged that Christian-

ity is the "most anthropocentric religion in the world" ("The Historical Roots of Our Ecological Crisis," *Science,* March 10, 1967, 1203-07). See also Gordon Kaufman, "Problem for Theology: The Concept of Nature," *Harvard Theological Review* 65 (1972): 337-66; also Fox, *Creation Spirituality.* Rosemary Radford Ruether, while not rejecting these arguments altogether, notes that modern scientific and technological developments leading to environmental disaster also have roots in Greek philosophy and science (*Gaia and God: An Ecofeminist Theology of Earth Healing* [San Francisco: HarperSanFrancisco, 1992] 22-31). See also Ronald A. Simpkins, *Creator and Creation: Nature in the Worldview of Ancient Israel* (Peabody, Mass.: Hendrickson, 1994); Stephen Bede Scharper, *Redeeming the Time: A Political Theology of the Environment* (New York: Continuum, 1997); Paul Santmire, *The Travail of Nature: The Ambiguous Ecological Promise of Christian Theology* (Philadelphia: Fortress, 1985).

32. Martin Luther, *That These words of Christ "This is my Body," Etc. still stand firm against the fanatics* (1527) in *Luther's Works,* vol. 37, ed. R. H. Fischer (Philadelphia: Muhlenberg, 1961) 59. We must note, of course, that Luther distinguished radically between this general presence of God in all creation and God's identity with the humanity of Jesus.

33. I developed this argument at greater length in an article that I am paraphrasing here: Harold Wells, "The Flesh of God: Christological Implications for an Ecological Vision of the World," *Toronto Journal of Theology* 15, no. 1 (Spring 1999): 51-68.

34. See this argued by Jürgen Moltmann, *The Way of Jesus Christ: Christology in Messianic Dimensions,* trans. M. Kohl (London: SCM, 1990) 246-63.

35. See this argued by Douglas John Hall, *Imaging God: Dominion as Stewardship* (Grand Rapids: Eerdmans, 1986) 185-86.

36. For a recent study of neo-orthodox theology, see Douglas John Hall, *Remembered Voices: Reclaiming the Legacy of "Neo-Orthodoxy"* (Louisville: Westminster John Knox Press, 1998).

37. Karl Barth, *Church Dogmatics,* vol. 2, pt. 2, ed. G. W. Bromiley and T. F. Torrance (Edinburgh: T & T Clark, 1957) 4-5.

38. Gutiérrez, *Theology of Liberation,* xiii.

39. Gustavo Gutiérrez, "Liberation Praxis and Christian Faith," in *The Power of the Poor in History* (Maryknoll, N.Y.: Orbis Books, 1983) 61.

40. Gustavo Gutiérrez, *The Truth Shall Make You Free* (Maryknoll, N.Y.: Orbis Books, 1990) 88.

41. E.g., Chung Hyung Kyung, *Struggle to Be the Sun Again: Introducing Asian Women's Theology* (Maryknoll, N.Y.: Orbis Books, 1994) 9.

42. Elizabeth Johnson is a trinitarian feminist theologian who espouses what might be called a high christology of Jesus as divine and human. Nevertheless, she does not seek to be Christ-centered, but begins instead with the Spirit and makes the "lens of women's flourishing" her fundamental norm (see *She Who Is,* chapters 1 and 2).

43. See, e.g., Jacquelyn Grant, *White Women's Christ and Black Women's Jesus: Feminist Christology and Womanist Response,* American Academy of Religion Series 64 (Atlanta: Scholar's Press, 1989) 212-13; Maria Clara Bingemer, "Trinity from the Perspective of a Woman," in *Faith Born in the Struggle for Life: A Re-Reading of Protestant Faith in Latin America Today,* ed. Dow Kirkpatrick, trans. L. McCoy (Grand Rapids: Eerdmans, 1988); Pamela Dickey Young, *Feminist Theology/Christian Theology: In Search of Method* (Minneapolis: Fortress, 1990) 78-80.

44. Letty M. Russell, "Exploring the Context of our Faith," in *Changing Contexts of our Faith,* ed. Letty M. Russell (Philadelphia: Fortress, 1985); see also idem, *Household of Freedom: Authority in Feminist Theology* (Philadelphia: Westminster, 1987) 30.

45. *Household of Freedom,* 23, 53.

46. Letty M. Russell, *Church in the Round: Feminist Interpretation of the Church* (Louisville: Westminster John Knox, 1993) 41, 42.

47. Ibid., 38.

48. Douglas John Hall, *Thinking the Faith: Christian Theology in a North American Context* (Minneapolis: Fortress, 1989).

49. See Douglas John Hall, *God and Human Suffering: An Exercise in the Theology of the Cross* (Minneapolis: Augsburg, 1986).

50. Douglas John Hall, "Despair as the Pervasive Element," in *Hope for the World: Mission in a Global Context* (Louisville: Westminster John Knox Press, 2001) 83-93.

51. Hall, *Thinking the Faith,* 409.

52. Douglas John Hall, *Professing the Faith: Christian Theology in a North American Context* (Minneapolis: Fortress, 1993) 363-64.

53. John B. Cobb Jr., "Toward a Christocentric Catholic Theology," in *Toward a Universal Theology of Religion*, ed. Leonard Swidler (Maryknoll, N.Y.: Orbis Books, 1988) 88.

54. Ibid., 99.

55. John B. Cobb Jr., "Beyond Pluralism," in *Christian Uniqueness Reconsidered: The Myth of a Pluralistic Theology of Religions* (Maryknoll, N.Y.: Orbis Books, 1990) 90-91.

5. *Apologia* for the Christic Center

1. I shall not follow the long-standing historical practice of expounding the work of Christ as prophet, priest, and king. This *munus triplex* (threefold office) was especially developed by Calvin (see *Institutes of the Christian Religion,* vol.1, trans. H. Beveridge [London: James Clarke, 1962] bk. 2, xv, 1-6, 425-32). While this schema is valid, it seems not particularly useful for our methodological purpose. However, Christ's resurrection as Messiah establishes Christ as king; his dying for us is his priestly office; his teaching and revelation of the triune God are a part of the prophetic office.

2. Rudolf Bultmann, "The New Testament and Mythology," in *Kerygma and Myth: A Theological Debate,* ed. H.-W. Bartsch, trans. R. H. Fuller (London: SPCK, 1953), 1-44. See the response of Karl Barth, "Rudolf Bultmann: An Attempt to Understand Him," in *Kerygma and Myth,* vol. 2, ed. H.-W. Bartsch, trans. R. H. Fuller (London: SPCK, 1962), 83-132.

3. Jürgen Moltmann discusses this in *Theology of Hope: On the Ground and Implications of a Christian Eschatology,* trans. J. W. Leitch (London: SCM, 1965) 172-82.

4. Mircea Eliade, *Patterns in Comparative Religion,* trans. R. Sheed (Cleveland: World Publishing, 1958) 98-99.

5. Mircea Eliade, *Cosmos and History: The Myth of the Eternal Return* (New York: Harper, 1959) 143.

6. Hans Frei cites Erich Auerbach, *Mimesis* (Princeton: Princeton University Press, 1968) in *The Identity of Jesus Christ: The Hermeneutical Bases of Dogmatic Theology,*

2nd ed. (Eugene, Ore.: Wipf & Stock, 1997) 7. See also Hans Frei, *The Eclipse of Biblical Narrative: A Study in Eighteenth and Nineteenth Century Hermeneutics* (New Haven: Yale University Press, 1974).

7. Frei, *Identity of Jesus Christ,* 174.

8. Ibid., 59-60.

9. Ibid., 59.

10. This is approximately the view of John Hick, *The Metaphor of God Incarnate: Christology in a Pluralistic Age* (Louisville: Westminster John Knox Press, 1993) 25.

11. Major debates have raged about the nature of the appearances of the risen Jesus to Paul and to the other disciples and about the question of the empty tomb. See, e.g., Gerald O'Collins, *Jesus Risen* (New York: Paulist, 1987); James D. G. Dunn, *Jesus and the Spirit* (London: SCM, 1975); Raymond E. Brown, *The Virginal Conception and Bodily Resurrection of Jesus* (New York: Paulist, 1973); Helmut Koester, *Introduction to the New Testament,* vol. 2: *History and Literature of Early Christianity* (Philadelphia: Fortress, 1982); Pheme Perkins, *Resurrection: New Testament Witness and Contemporary Reflection* (New York: Doubleday, 1984); G. Luedemann, *The Risen Jesus,* trans. J. Bowden (Minneapolis: Fortress, 1994); John Dominic Crossan, *Jesus: A Revolutionary Biography* (San Francisco: HarperSanFrancisco, 1994); N. T. Wright, *Christian Origins and the Question of God:* vol. 2, *Jesus and the Victory of God* (Minneapolis: Fortress, 1996); idem, *The Resurrection of the Son of God* (Minneapolis: Fortress, 2003); Marcus Borg and N. T. Wright, *The Meaning of Jesus: Two Visions* (San Francisco: HarperSanFrancisco, 1999).

12. Elizabeth A. Johnson, *She Who Is: The Mystery of God in Feminist Theological Discourse* (New York: Crossroad, 1992) 163.

13. Elizabeth A. Johnson, "Redeeming the Name of Christ," in *Freeing Theology: The Essentials of Theology in Feminist Perspective,* ed. Catherine Mowry LaCugna (San Francisco: HarperSanFrancisco, 1993) 132.

14. Johnson, *She Who Is,* 159, 164; see also Jürgen Moltmann, *The Way of Jesus Christ: Christology in Messianic Dimensions,* trans. M. Kohl (London: SCM, 1990) 252-56.

15. An opposing view can be found stated by Wolfhart Pannenberg, who comes close to arguing that the resurrection can be demonstrated as at least a highly probable historical event; see *Jesus God and Man,* trans. L. L. Wilkins and D. A. Priebe (Philadelphia: Westminster, 1974).

16. See a dramatized, fictional debate about this between Barth, Bultmann, Pannenberg, and Moltmann, by Daniel Migliore, *Faith Seeking Understanding: An Introduction to Christian Theology* (Grand Rapids: Eerdmans, 1991) appendix B.

17. Celsus, quoted by Origen in *Against Celsus* 2.60.62 in *Ante-Nicene Fathers,* vol. 4 (Edinburgh: T & T Clark, 1990) 455, 456.

18. This is the emphasis of Jon Sobrino, *Christology at the Crossroads: A Latin American View,* trans. J. Drury (Maryknoll, N.Y.: Orbis Books, 1976) 253-56.

19. E. P. Sanders, *Jesus and Judaism* (Philadelphia: Fortress, 1985) 240.

20. Wright, *Jesus and the Victory of God,* 110.

21. Marcus Borg, "Jesus as Prophet of the Kingdom of God," in *Meaning of Jesus,* ed. Borg and Wright, 74-75.

22. Note Albert Schweitzer, *The Mystery of the Kingdom of God* (1901; London: A. & C. Black, 1925); idem, *The Quest of the Historical Jesus: A Critical Study of its Progress from Reimarus to Wrede* (1906; London: A. & C. Black, 1954); Ernst Käsemann,

Essays on New Testament Themes (1960; London: SCM, 1964); Joachim Jeremias, *New Testament Theology: The Proclamation of Jesus* (New York: SCM, 1971); James M. Robinson, *A New Quest of the Historical Jesus* (London: SCM 1959); John Dominic Crossan, *The Historical Jesus: The Life of a Mediterranean Jewish Peasant* (San Francisco: HarperSanFrancisco, 1991); Wright, *Jesus and the Victory of God;* Marcus Borg, *Meeting Jesus Again for the First Time* (San Francisco: HarperSanFrancisco, 1994).

23. Richard A. Horsley, *Jesus and Empire: The Kingdom of God and the New World Disorder* (Minneapolis: Fortress, 2003) 108.

24. See Borg and Wright, *Meaning of Jesus,* part 7.

25. Sobrino, *Christology at the Crossroads,* chapter 3.

26. Crossan, *Jesus: A Revolutionary Biography,* 113.

27. Jon Sobrino, "Central Position of the Reign of God in Liberation Theology," in *Systematic Theology: Perspectives from Liberation Theology,* ed. Jon Sobrino and Ignacio Ellacuria, readings from *Mysterium Liberationis* (Maryknoll, N.Y.: Orbis Books, 1996) 38-74.

28. Ibid., 64.

29. See Gustavo Gutiérrez, "Option for the Poor," in *Systematic Theology,* ed. Sobrino and Ellacuria, 22-37.

30. Ibid., 42.

31. Moltmann, *Theology of Hope,* 161.

32. Jürgen Moltmann, *Experiences of God,* trans. M. Kohl (Philadelphia: Fortress, 1980) 11-12.

33. See Jon Sobrino's discussion of the recognition of faith in Jesus as Messiah before and after the resurrection: *Christ the Liberator: A View from the Victims,* trans. P. Burns (Maryknoll, N.Y.: Orbis Books, 2001) 98-110.

34. See Rosemary Radford Ruether, *Faith and Fratricide: The Theological Roots of Anti-Semitism* (New York: Seabury, 1974).

35. Perhaps most notable in this respect has been Jürgen Moltmann, whose theology of hope emphasizes that which is yet to come in the salvation of the world. See his discussion of "The Resurrection and the Future of Jesus Christ," in *Theology of Hope,* chapter 3. See also his discussion of Jewish-Christian Dialogue in *The Way of Jesus Christ,* 28-37.

36. Moltmann, *Way of Jesus Christ,* 32.

37. Gregory Baum, in his introduction to Ruether, *Faith and Fratricide,* 17-18.

38. See Leonard J. Greenspoon, "The Origin of the Idea of Resurrection," in *Traditions in Transformation: Turning Points in Biblical Faith* (Winona Lake, Ind.: Eisenbrauns, 1981).

39. I borrow the concept of "vulnerable God" especially from William C. Placher, *Narratives of a Vulnerable God: Christ, Theology, and Scripture* (Louisville: Westminster John Knox Press, 1994).

40. John Hick argues that the doctrine of the divinity and humanity of Jesus is a metaphor (*Metaphor of God Incarnate,* chapters 4-7).

41. Jürgen Moltmann makes this point in *The Crucified God: The Cross as the Foundation and Criticism of Christian Theology,* trans. R. A. Wilson and J. Bowden (London: SCM, 1974) 222-23.

42. Gregory of Nyssa, *Address on Religious Instruction,* 24, trans. C. Richardson, in *Christology of the Late Fathers,* E. R. Hardy (Philadelphia: Westminster, 1954) 301.

43. See Moltmann's discussion of the Jewish kabbalistic teaching about God's *Shekinah*—the indwelling of God's glory with the people in times of suffering and humiliation, which is God's own humiliation with them. Moltmann discusses Jewish authors on this question: Abraham Heschel, Gershom Sholem, and Franz Rosenzweig (*The Trinity and the Kingdom: The Doctrine of God* [San Francisco: Harper & Row, 1981] 25-30).

44. See Sobrino, *Christology at the Crossroads,* 219.

45. T. F. Torrance points out that, in view of Einsteinian physics, "space" can no longer be regarded as a container or receptacle. To be "in space," then, is not to be locked into a limited place or area. Space, rather, is open-ended, and it is possible to conceive of God "entering" space and time without becoming trapped by our finite circumstances. See *Space, Time, and Incarnation* (London/New York: Oxford University Press, 1969).

46. See Karl Barth, *The Humanity of God* (Atlanta: John Knox Press, 1960) 46-52.

47. See *The Church Teaches: Documents of the Church in English,* ed. and trans. J. F. Clarkson (Rockford, Ill.: Tan Books, 1973); for commentary, see also J. N. D. Kelly, *Early Christian Creeds* (London: Longmans, Green, 1950).

48. Something comparable to this approach to the doctrine of the incarnation can be found in Donald Baillie, *God Was in Christ: An Essay on Incarnation and Atonement* (London: Faber & Faber, 1955).

49. Catherine Mowry LaCugna, *God for Us: The Trinity and Christian Life* (San Francisco: HarperSanFrancisco, 1991) 257, 259. She refers to John Macmurray, *Persons in Relation* (New York: Harper & Brothers, 1961).

50. Johnson, *She Who Is,* 165.

51. *Perichōrēsis* may be translated literally as "circling around," indicating a mutual relation or interaction. It was translated into Latin as *circumincessio,* or *circuminsessio,* insitting, or circular indwelling. See *The Oxford Dictionary of the Christian Church,* ed. F. L. Cross (London/New York: Oxford University Press, 1957); and *The Oxford English Dictionary,* vol. 2.

52. Gregory of Nazianzus, Letter 101, trans. C. G. Brown and E. A. Swallow, in *Nicene and Post-Nicene Fathers,* 2nd series, vol. 7 (New York: Christian Literature Co., 1893) 439-43.

53. See *Church Teaches,* ed. and trans. J. F. Clarkson; also J. N. D. Kelly, *Early Christian Doctrines* (London: A. & C. Black, 1977).

54. Gregory of Nazianzus, Letter 101, in *Nicene and Post-Nicene Fathers,* 2nd series, vol. 7, 440.

55. Johnson, *She Who Is,* 153.

56. Mary Daly, *The Church and the Second Sex* (New York: Harper & Row, 1975) 38.

57. Johnson, *She Who Is,* 152.

58. See Rosemary Radford Ruether, "Can a Male Savior Save Women?" in *Sexism and God-Talk* (Boston: Beacon, 1983) 137.

59. See Jacquelyn Grant, *White Women's Christ and Black Women's Jesus: Feminist Christology and Womanist Response,* American Academy of Religion Academy Series 64 (Atlanta: Scholar's Press, 1989) 212-14. See also Karen Baker-Fletcher and Garth Kasimu Baker-Fletcher, *My Sister, My Brother: Womanist and Xodus God-Talk* (Maryknoll, N.Y.: Orbis Books, 1997). The Baker-Fletchers argue that Spirit- or creation-centered theology is not antithetical to Christ-centeredness and a theology of Jesus as "fully God" (pp. 85-87).

60. See Karl Barth, *Church Dogmatics,* vol. 1, pt. 2, trans. and ed. G. W. Bromiley and T. F. Torrance (Edinburgh: T & T Clark, 1956) 153-58.

61. Paul Tillich, *The Courage to Be* (New Haven: Yale University Press, 1952).

62. For a positive account of sacrifice, see Abraham Heschel, *The Prophets,* 2 vols. (New York: Harper & Row, 1962) 1:195-98.

63. Propitiation (appeasement) and expiation (cleansing) are often distinguished, but some scholars argue that they are essentially the same. See Timothy Gorringe, *God's Just Vengeance* (Cambridge: Cambridge University Press, 1996) 38.

64. See Wright, *Jesus and the Victory of God* (Minneapolis: Fortress, 1996) 582.

65. See J. H. Charlesworth, ed., *The Old Testament Pseudepigrapha,* vol. 2 (New York: Doubleday, 1985).

66. W. H. Auden, *For the Time Being: A Christmas Oratorio* (London: Faber & Faber, 1953) 116.

67. Other prophetic contexts denounce sacrifices, e.g.: Mic 6:7-8; Amos 5:21-24; Is 43:22-24; Jer 9:10; Ps 40:6, 50:8; etc.

68. For example, C. F. Whitley argues that the canonical prophets rejected the sacrificial cult entirely (*The Prophetic Achievement* [London: A. R. Mowbray, 1963] 63-92). Abraham Heschel strongly argues that the prophets intended not to abolish sacrifices but to ethicize them, calling for sincerity in their performance (*Prophets,* vol. 2, chapter 11).

69. Crossan, *Jesus: A Revolutionary Biography,* 66-70.

70. Anselm of Canterbury, *Why God Became Man,* in *A Scholastic Miscellany: Anselm to Ockham,* ed. and trans. Eugene R. Fairweather (Philadelphia: Westminster, 1956) book 1, chapter 14, 122.

71. Ibid., 112.

72. Peter Abailard, *Exposition of the Epistle to the Romans,* III, in *Scholastic Miscellany,* ed. and trans. Fairweather, 276.

73. Johnson, *She Who Is,* 158.

74. See Dorothee Soelle, *Thinking about God: An Introduction to Theology* (Philadelphia: Trinity Press International, 1990) 120; see also Mary Grey, *Redeeming the Dream: Feminism, Redemption and the Christian Tradition* (London: SPCK, 1989) 11-14; and Rita Nakashima Brock, "And a Little Child Will Lead Us: Christology and Child Abuse," in *Christianity, Patriarchy, and Abuse,* ed. Joanne Carlson Brown and Carole R. Bohn (New York: Pilgrim Press, 1989).

75. William Placher, *Jesus the Savior: The Meaning of Jesus Christ for Christian Faith* (Louisville: Westminster John Knox Press, 2001) 139.

76. Sobrino, *Christology at the Crossroads,* 209.

77. Horsley, *Jesus and Empire*, 126.

78. Ibid., 127.

79. For a thorough exploration of the conditions surrounding the death of Jesus, see John Dominic Crossan, *Who Killed Jesus? Exploring the Roots of Anti-Semitism in the Gospel Story of the Death of Jesus* (San Francisco: HarperSanFrancisco, 1995).

80. See Borg and Wright, *Meaning of Jesus,* 77-107.

81. See Wright, *Jesus and the Victory of God,* 540-611.

82. See Barth, *Church Dogmatics,* vol. 4, pt. 1, trans. and ed. G. W. Bromiley and T. F. Torrance (Edinburgh: T & T Clark, 1956) 281, 306.

83. Jürgen Moltmann speaks of "death in God" in *Crucified God,* 207.

84. Sobrino, *Christology at the Crossroads,* 202.

85. Jon Sobrino, *Jesus the Liberator: A Historical-Theological Reading of Jesus of Nazareth* (Maryknoll, N.Y.: Orbis Books, 1993), 228-29.

86. See Harold Wells, "Theology for Reconciliation," in *The Reconciliation of Peoples: Challenge to the Churches,* ed. Gregory Baum and Harold Wells (Maryknoll, N.Y.: Orbis Books, 1997).

87. Barth, *Church Dogmatics,* vol. 4, pt. 1, 211-83.

88. Placher, *Jesus the Savior,* 141.

89. Harold Wells, "Not Moral Heroes: The Grace of God and the Church's Public Voice," in *Doing Ethics in a Pluralistic Society: Essays in Honour of Roger C. Hutchinson,* ed. Phyllis D. Airhart, Marilyn J. Legge, and Gary L. Redcliffe (Waterloo, ON: Wilfrid Laurier University Press, 2001) 93.

90. It is widely held (though certainly not universally) that the virgin conception of Jesus by the Holy Spirit is not necessarily a biological fact, but a theological statement, expressing the first Christians' conviction that he was Son of God in his very identity, from his very beginning. Only Matthew and Luke report this; there is nothing of it in Paul or John or elsewhere in the New Testament. His divinity or status as Son does not depend, then, on this concept. The fact that other ancient figures were considered to have been miraculously conceived (e.g., Alexander the Great, the Buddha) suggests a legendary or mythical element here.

91. Johnson, *She Who Is,* 80-81.

92. See Elizabeth A. Johnson, "Jesus the Wisdom of God: A Biblical Basis for Non-Androcentric Christology," *Ephemerides Theologicae Lovanienses* 61 (1985): 261–94.

93. Daly, *The Church and the Second Sex,* 38; see also idem, *Beyond God the Father: Towards a Philosophy of Women's Liberation* (Boston: Beacon, 1973) 37.

94. Elizabeth A. Johnson, "The Incomprehensibility of God and the Image of God Male and Female," *Theological Studies* 45 (1984): 441-65.

95. See the arguments for Father, Son, and Holy Spirit as God's name: Robert Jenson, *The Triune Identity* (Philadelphia: Fortress, 1982); Elizabeth Achtemeier, "Exchanging God for 'No Gods,'" in *Speaking the Christian God,* ed. Alvin Kimel (Grand Rapids: Eerdmans, 1992); Deborah Belonick, "Revelation and Metaphors: The Significance of the Trinitarian Names Father, Son, and Holy Spirit," *Union Seminary Quarterly Review* 40 (1985): 31-42.

96. Catherine Mowry LaCugna, "God in Communion with Us," in *Freeing Theology: The Essentials of Theology in Feminist Perspective,* ed. Catherine Mowry LaCugna (San Francisco: HarperSanFrancisco, 1993) 107.

97. Ellen Charry, "Is Christianity Good for Us?" in *Reclaiming Faith: Essays on Orthodoxy in the Episcopal Church and the Baltimore Declaration,* ed. Ephraim Radner and George R. Sumner (Grand Rapids: Eerdmans, 1993) 225-46.

98. See Johnson, "Jesus, the Wisdom of God," 261-94.

99. Douglas John Hall makes this point in *Professing the Faith: Christian Theology in a North American Context* (Minneapolis: Fortress, 1993) 61.

100. On the relation of Christ and Spirit, see Jürgen Moltmann, *The Spirit of Life: A Universal Affirmation,* trans. M. Kohl (Minneapolis: Fortress, 1992) 306-9.

101. Council of Constantinople. See *Church Teaches,* ed. Clarkson; also Kelly, *Early Christian Creeds.* For the work of Basil of Caesarea, see St. Basil the Great, *On the Holy Spirit,* trans. D. Anderson (Crestwood, N.Y: St. Vladimir's Seminary Press, 1980).

102. Karl Barth makes this point several times in *Church Dogmatics,* vol. 1, pt. 1, trans. G. T. Thomson (Edinburgh: T & T Clark, 1936) 474, 513, 533.

103. LaCugna, *God for Us,* 212.

104. See a useful discussion of this by Placher, *Narratives of a Vulnerable God,* 57.

105. Karl Rahner, *The Trinity* (New York: Herder & Herder, 1970) 21-24, 82-103.

106. See Placher, *Narratives of a Vulnerable God,* 72.

107. Augustine developed his doctrine of the Trinity in his famous *De Trinitate* (*On the Trinity*); see Migliore, *Faith Seeking Understanding,* 69.

108. John of Damascus, *De Fide Orthodoxa,* cited and discussed by Moltmann, *Trinity and the Kingdom,* 174-75.

109. Johnson, *She Who Is,* 192.

110. Immanuel Kant, *The Conflict of the Faculties,* quoted in Placher, *Narratives of a Vulnerable God,* 57.

111. Jürgen Moltmann makes this point in *The Trinity and the Kingdom,* 8.

112. See Leonardo Boff, *Trinity and Society,* trans. P. Burns (Maryknoll, N.Y.: Orbis Books, 1986); John D. Zizioulas, *Being as Communion: Studies in Personhood and the Church* (Crestwood, N.Y.: St. Vladimir's Seminary Press, 1997).

113. Moltmann, *Crucified God,* 227.

114. Ibid., 244.

115. Quoted by Moltmann, *Trinity and the Kingdom,* 195.

116. Ibid.

117. Ibid., 198; see also L. Boff, *Trinity and Society,* 11.

118. See Moltmann, *Crucified God,* 332.

119. L. Boff, *Trinity and Society,* 16.

120. Johnson, *She Who Is,* 216. Note similar comments by another feminist theologian: Anne E. Carr, *Transforming Grace: Christian Tradition and Women's Experience* (San Francisco: Harper, 1990).

121. Both Barth and Rahner avoid using the word "persons" for the trinitarian three, wishing to avoid an individualistic, modern notion of "person," lest the three be thought of as three gods. They prefer to speak of "modes," while not wishing to be modalists in the Sabellian sense. See Barth, *Church Dogmatics,* vol. 1, 1, 348ff.; Rahner, *Trinity,* 103-15; see also Moltmann's criticism in *The Trinity and the Kingdom,* 139-44.

122. See criticisms of Moltmann on this point by George Hunsinger in his review of *The Trinity and the Kingdom,* in *The Thomist* 47 (January 1983): 129-39; also Walter Kasper, *The God of Jesus Christ,* trans. Matthew O'Connell (New York: Crossroad, 1984) 379.

123. Moltmann, *Trinity and the Kingdom,* 146-47.

124. Zizioulas, *Being as Communion,* 16, 88, 101.

125. Leonardo Boff, *Cry of the Earth, Cry of the Poor,* trans. P. Berryman (Maryknoll, N.Y.: Orbis Books, 1997) 156.

126. Ibid., 157.

6. The Challenge of the Pluralist Theologies

1. Korean feminist Chung Hyun Kyung argues for a "survival-liberationist-centered syncretism" in *Struggle to Be the Sun Again* (Maryknoll, N.Y.: Orbis Books, 1994) 9. See further discussion in chapter 8 below.

2. These categories were layed out by Alan Race, *Christians and Religious Pluralism* (London: SCM, 1983, 2nd ed. 1994). A later statement of these categories is offered by Diana L. Eck, *Encountering God: A Spiritual Journey from Bozeman to Banaras* (Boston: Beacon, 1993).

3. Paul F. Knitter has proposed recently to speak rather of various models: the Replacement, Fulfillment, Mutuality, and Acceptance models (see his *Introducing the Theologies of Religions* [Maryknoll, N.Y.: Orbis Books, 2002]).

4. For example, Gavin D'Costa argues that the so-called pluralists are actually "liberal modern" exclusivists (see his *The Meeting of Religions and the Trinity* [Maryknoll, N.Y.: Orbis Books, 2000] 20-24).

5. For example, Lesslie Newbigin, who would generally be regarded as an exclusivist, would object to being so labeled. He would admit to being exclusive with regard to the unique, unsurpassable Christ as Saviour of the world; however, he thinks that in other respects he is inclusivist and pluralist (see *The Gospel in a Pluralist Society* [Grand Rapids: Eerdmans, 1989] chapter 13).

6. This whole matter is discussed helpfully by Harold Coward in *Pluralism in the World Religions: A Short Introduction* (Oxford: Oneworld, 2000).

7. Some examples of theologians and publications that may be regarded as exclusivist are the following: Karl Barth, in his discussion of "Religion as Unbelief" in *Church Dogmatics,* vol. 1, pt. 2, trans. and ed. G. W. Bromiley and T. F. Torrance (Edinburgh: T & T Clark, 1958); Hendrik Kraemer, *Religion and the Christian Faith* (London: Lutterworth, 1956); Carl Braaten, *No Other Gospel! Christianity among the World's Religions* (Minneapolis: Fortress, 1992); Newbigin, *Gospel in a Pluralist Society;* John Stott, *Calling Christian Leaders: Biblical Models of Church, Gospel, and Ministry* (Leicester: Inter-Varsity, 2002); idem, *Making Christ Known: Historical Mission Documents from the Lausanne Movement, 1974-1989* (Grand Rapids: Eerdmans, 1997).

8. Diana L. Eck, for example, vigorously opposes any understanding of pluralism as relativism, pointing out that pluralists cannot avoid at times speaking in an inclusivist way, in that Christian pluralists still wish to hold on to specifically Christian commitments (*Encountering God,* 180, 195).

9. Some significant authors and publications (beyond the authors we are discussing here at length) that might be described as pluralist are the following: Eck, *Encountering God;* Raimon Panikkar, *The Cosmotheandric Experience: Emerging Religious Consciousness* (Maryknoll, N.Y.: Orbis Books, 1993); Aloysius Pieris, *Love Meets Wisdom: A Christian Experience of Buddhism* (Maryknoll, N.Y.: Orbis Books, 1988); Stanley Samartha, *One Christ—Many Religions: Toward a Revised Christology* (Maryknoll, N.Y.: Orbis Books, 1991); Leonard Swidler, ed., *Toward a Universal Theology of Religion* (Maryknoll, N.Y.: Orbis Books, 1987); Marcus J. Borg, *The Heart of Christianity: Rediscovering a Life of Faith* (San Francisco: HarperSanFrancisco, 2003).

10. Some authors and publications that might be described as inclusivist are the following: Karl Rahner, "Christianity and the non-Christian Religions," in *Theological Investigations,* vol. 5, trans. H.-K. Kruger (Baltimore: Helicon, 1966) 115-34; John Cobb, *Christ in a Pluralistic Age* (Philadelphia: Westminster, 1975); Gavin D'Costa, *Theology and Religious Pluralism: The Challenge of Other Religions* (Oxford: Basil Blackwell, 1985); idem, *Meeting of Religions and the Trinity;* idem, ed., *Christian Uniqueness Reconsidered: The Myth of a Pluralistic Theology of Religions* (Maryknoll, N.Y.: Orbis Books, 1990); J. A. DiNoia, *The Diversity of Religions: A Christian Perspective* (Wash-

ington: Catholic University of America Press, 1992); Jacques Dupuis, *Toward a Christian Theology of Religious Pluralism* (Maryknoll, N.Y.: Orbis Books, 1997); S. Mark Heim, *Salvations: In Search of Authentic Religious Pluralism* (Maryknoll, N.Y.: Orbis Books, 1995).

11. The documents of Vatican II can be found on the Internet: www.vatican.va (Archives/Documents of Vatican II). See especially *Lumen Gentium* and *Nostra Aetate.* For analysis of Vatican II and subsequent official Vatican documents, see Dupuis, *Toward a Christian Theology of Religious Pluralism.*

12. See comment of Gregory Baum, "The Church's Mission in Asia: A Catholic Perspective," *Laval theologique et philosophique* 58, no. 11 (February 2002)**:** 89-101.

13. "Dominus Jesus: On the Unicity and Salvific Universality of Jesus Christ and the Church," *Origins,* vol. 30, no. 14 (Sept. 14, 2000): 209-19. For critical response, see Stephen J. Pope and Charles Hefling, eds., *Sic et Non: Encountering Dominus Jesus* (Maryknoll, N.Y.: Orbis Books, 2002).

14. See Douglas John Hall, *Why Christian? For Those on the Edge of Faith* (Minneapolis: Fortress, 1998) 146-52.

15. S. Mark Heim also chooses these three and discusses them more thoroughly than I do in *Salvations: Truth and Difference in Religion.*

16. John Hick, *God and the Universe of Faiths* (New York: St. Martin's Press, 1973).

17. John Hick, *God Has Many Names* (London: Macmillan, 1980).

18. Hick argued this persuasively in "The Non-Absoluteness of Christianity," in *The Myth of Christian Uniqueness: Toward a Pluralistic Theology of Religions,* ed. John Hick and Paul F. Knitter (Maryknoll, N.Y.: Orbis Books, 1987) 23-24.

19. See John Hick, *An Interpretation of Religion* (New Haven: Yale University Press, 1989).

20. *The Myth of God Incarnate,* ed. John Hick (Philadelphia: Westminster, 1977).

21. John Hick, *The Metaphor of God Incarnate: Christology in a Pluralitic Age* (Louisville: Westminster John Knox Press, 1993) 23.

22. Ibid., chapter 5.

23. Ibid., 12; see also 105.

24. Ibid., 105.

25. Ibid., 98.

26. Ibid., 162.

27. Hick, *Interpretation of Religion,* 325.

28. D'Costa, *Meeting of Religions and the Trinity,* 26.

29. This argument is stated at length by Heim, *Salvations: Truth and Difference in Religion,* 23-35. He argues the point even more radically in his later book *The Depth of the Riches: A Trinitarian Theology of Religious Ends* (Grand Rapids: Eerdmans, 2001).

30. Hick, *Interpretation of Religion,* 369-70.

31. Heim, *Salvations,* 42.

32. Wilfred Cantwell Smith, *Towards a World Theology: Faith and the Comparative History of Religion* (Philadelphia: Westminster, 1981) 4.

33. Ibid., 18.

34. Ibid., 171.

35. Ibid., 168-69.

36. Wilfred Cantwell Smith, *The Meaning and End of Religion* (New York: Macmillan, 1964).

37. Wilfred Cantwell Smith, *The Faith of Other Men* (New York: New American Library, 1963).

38. Wilfred Cantwell Smith, *Faith and Belief* (Princeton: Princeton University Press) 12.

39. David Zub, "Rediscovering a Critical Theology of Religion: Religious Pluralism and Theology of the Cross" (Th.D. diss., Emmanuel College, Toronto School of Theology, 2001) 176-77.

40. Smith, *Towards a World Theology,* 113.

41. Zub, "Rediscovering a Critical Theology of Religion," 177.

42. Wilfred Cantwell Smith, "Theology and the World's Religious History," in *Toward a Universal Theology of Religion,* ed. Swidler, 55.

43. Kana Mitra, "Theologizing through History?" in *Toward a Universal Theology of Religion,* ed. Swidler, 81.

44. See Smith's major discussion of scriptures in many religions in *What Is Scripture? A Comparative Approach* (Minneapolis: Fortress, 1993). Smith is well aware of how differently scriptures function in various historic traditions.

45. Smith, *Towards a World Theology,* 44.

46. Ibid., 114; see also "Theology and the World's Religious History," 70-71.

47. Mitra, in "Theologizing through History?" 81.

48. Smith, *Towards a World Theology*, 177.

49. Smith, *Faith of Other Men,* 133.

50. Smith, *Towards a World Theology,* 176.

51. Heim, *Salvations,* 54.

52. Ibid., 56.

53. For more discussion of syncretism, the reader may consult Josue A. Sathler and Amos Nascimento, "Black Masks on White Faces: Liberation Theology and the Quest for Syncretism in the Brazilian Context," in *Liberation Theologies, Postmodernity, and the Americas,* ed. David Batstone, Eduardo Mendieta, Lois Ann Lorentzen, and Dwight N. Hopkins (New York: Routledge, 1997); Diego Irarrazaval, *Inculturation: New Dawn of the Church in Latin America* (Maryknoll, N.Y.: Orbis Books, 2000). See also Carl F. Starkloff, *A Theology of the In-Between: The Value of Syncretic Process* (Milwaukee: Marquette University Press, 2002).

54. Gavin D'Costa discusses the pluralist thought of the Hindu thinker Sarvapelli Radhakrishnan (1888-1975), whom he identifies as "Neo-Hindu" (*The Meeting of Religions and the Trinity,* chapter 2). See also Coward's discussion of pluralism in Hinduism in *Pluralism in the World Religions,* chapter 5.

55. Paul F. Knitter, *No Other Name? A Critical Survey of Christian Attitudes toward the World Religions* (Maryknoll, N.Y.: Orbis Books, 1985).

56. Paul F. Knitter, *One Earth, Many Religions: Multifaith Dialogue and Global Responsibility* (Maryknoll, N.Y.: Orbis Books, 1995).

57. Paul F. Knitter, *Jesus and the Other Names: Christian Mission and Global Responsibility* (Maryknoll, N.Y.: Orbis Books, 1996).

58. *The Uniqueness of Jesus: A Dialogue with Paul F. Knitter,* ed. Leonard Swidler and Paul Mojzes (Maryknoll, N.Y.: Orbis Books, 1997); Knitter, *Introducing Theologies of Religions* (Maryknoll, N.Y.: Orbis Books, 2002).

59. Knitter, *Jesus and the Other Names,* 25.

60. Knitter, *One Earth, Many Religions,* 19.

61. Ibid., 15.

62. Paul F. Knitter, "Toward a Liberation Theology of Religions," in *The Myth of Christian Uniqueness: Toward a Pluralistic Theology of Religions,* ed. John Hick and Paul F. Knitter (Maryknoll, N.Y.: Orbis Books, 1987) 193.

63. Ibid., 199.

64. Knitter, *One Earth, Many Religions,* 127.

65. See D'Costa's criticism of Knitter on this point (*The Meeting of Religions and the Trinity,* 30-40).

66. The point is made by Heim, *Salvations,* 95.

67. Knitter, *Jesus and the Other Names,* 61.

68. Ibid., 67.

69. Ibid., 76.

70. Ibid., 75.

71. Ibid., 61.

72. Paul F. Knitter, "Five Theses on the Uniqueness of Jesus," in *Uniqueness of Jesus,* ed. Swidler and Mojzes, 7.

73. Knitter, *Jesus and the Other Names,* 74.

74. Ibid., 73.

75. Knitter, "Five Theses on the Uniqueness of Jesus," 14-15.

76. Knitter, *Jesus and the Other Names,* 93.

77. Knitter, "Five Theses on the Uniqueness of Jesus," 11.

78. Knitter, *Jesus and the Other Names,* 133.

79. See D'Costa, *Meeting of Religions and the Trinity,* 35-36.

80. See Jon Sobrino, *Christ the Liberator: A View from the Victims,* trans. Paul Burns (Maryknoll, N.Y.: Orbis Books, 2001) chapter 10. See also Jürgen Moltmann, *The Way of Jesus Christ: Christology in Messianic Dimensions* (London: SCM, 1990) chapters 1 and 3.

81. Jon Sobrino, *Jesus the Liberator: A Historical-Theological View,* trans. P. Burns and F. McDonagh (Maryknoll, N.Y.: Orbis Books, 1993) 244.

82. I enlarge on this idea in "Not Moral Heroes: The Grace of God and the Church's Public Voice" in *Doing Ethics in a Pluralistic Society: Essays in Honour of Roger Hutchinson,* ed. Phyllis Airhart, Marilyn Legge, and Gary Redcliffe (Waterloo, ON: Wilfrid Laurier University Press, 2002).

83. Knitter, *Jesus and the Other Names,* 87.

84. Knitter, "Five Theses on the Uniqueness of Jesus," 15.

85. Knitter, *Jesus and the Other Names,* 169.

86. D'Costa, *Meeting of Religions and the Trinity,* 37, 39.

87. Wilfred Cantwell Smith, "Sharing the Qurʾan and the Bible and the Word of God," in *On Sharing Religious Experience,* ed. Gerald D. Gort et al. (Grand Rapids: Eerdmans, 1992) 57.

88. Knitter, *Introducing Theologies of Religions,* 217.

89. Diana Eck, as a pluralist, argues this in *Encountering God,* 180.

7. Is It Biblical?

1. Jon Sobrino, *Jesus the Liberator: A Historical-Theological View*, trans. P. Burns and F. McDonagh (Maryknoll, N.Y.: Orbis Books, 1993) 53, 63.

2. Stanley J. Grenz and John R. Franke, *Beyond Foundationalism: Shaping Theology in a Postmodern Context* (Louisville: Westminster John Knox Press, 2001). Grenz and Franke argue that the "biblical message" is the basic norm for theology, or, more precisely, "the Spirit speaking through scripture" (pp. 57-64). Lutheran theologian Robert Jenson also speaks of the canon of scripture as *norma normans non normata* (*Systematic Theology,* vol. 1, *The Triune God* [New York: Oxford University Press, 1997] 26). Roman Catholic Roger Haight, S.J., states that, almost universally in the history of the church, scripture has been regarded as the *norma normans non normata* (*The Dynamics of Theology* [New York: Paulist, 1990] 89-94). This would seem to be something of an exaggeration with regard to the Roman Catholic tradition. At any rate, he goes on to argue at length that the normativity of scripture must be understood differently today. Liberationist Clodovis Boff also speaks of scripture as *norma normans,* while noting that it is not *non normata* (*Theology and Praxis: Epistemological Foundations,* trans. R. R. Barr [Maryknoll, N.Y.: Orbis Books, 1987] 136).

3. Daniel Migliore, *Faith Seeking Understanding: An Introduction to Christian Theology* (Grand Rapids: Eerdmans, 1991) 42.

4. T. F. Torrance, *Theological Science* (London: Oxford University Press, 1969).

5. Karl Barth, *Anselm: Fides Quaerens Intellectum*, trans. I. W. Robertson (London: SCM, 1960) 28.

6. John Calvin, *Institutes of the Christian Religion*, bk. 1, vii, 4 (vol. 1), trans. H. Beveridge (London: James Clarke, 1962) 71.

7. John Calvin, *Commentary on Romans,* cited by Karl Barth, *Church Dogmatics,* vol. 1, pt. 2, ed. and trans. G. W. Bromiley and T. F. Torrance (Edinburgh: T & T Clark, 1956) 520.

8. Luther, though capable of being critical of canonical books, could also refer to God as the "author" of scripture. See discussion of these other authors, together with Wesley, by R. Larry Shelton, "John Wesley's Approach to Scripture in Historical Perspective," *Wesleyan Theological Journal* 16, no. 1 (Spring 1981): 23-25.

9. John Wesley, *The Character of a Methodist,* in *The Works of the Rev. John Wesley,* vol. 8 (London: Wesleyan Conference Office, 1872) 340.

10. Wesley, *Works,* 8:198; see also 11:373.

11. Barth, *Church Dogmatics,* vol. 1, pt. 2, 531.

12. William Placher, *Narratives of a Vulnerable God: Christ, Theology, and Scripture* (Louisville: Westminster John Knox Press, 1994) 91.

13. William Shakespeare, *The Merchant of Venice,* Act I, Scene 3.

14. G. E. Lessing, quoted by E. Schillebeeckx, *Jesus: An Experiment in Christology* (New York: Seabury, 1979) 585.

15. Calvin, *Institutes,* I, bk. 1, vii, 4 (vol. 1) 72.

16. See Barth on proclamation as a form of the Word of God in *Church Dogmatics,* vol. 1, pt. 1, trans. G. Thomson (Edinburgh: T & T Clark, 1936) 98-111.

17. Jenson, *Systematic Theology,* vol. 1, *The Triune God,* 30.

18. Ibid., 27.

19. See Brevard S. Childs, *The New Testament as Canon: An Introduction* (London: SCM, 1984) 25.

20. Calvin, *Institutes* I, vii, 1 (vol. 1) 68.

21. On the openness of the canon, see Karl Barth, *Church Dogmatics,* vol. 1, pt. 2, ed. T. F. Torrance and G. W. Bromiley (Edinburgh: T & T Clark, 1956) 476-81. See also the discussion of the canon by Brevard Childs, *Introduction to the Old Testament as Scripture* (Philadelphia: Fortress, 1980). On the acknowledgment of Scripture, see Calvin, *Institutes,* I, vii, 2 (vol. 1) 69.

22. Barth, *Church Dogmatics,* vol. 1, pt. 2, 473-81; this quotation, 479-80.

23. Jenson, *Systematic Theology,* vol. 1, *The Triune God,* 28.

24. Wilfred Cantwell Smith, *What Is Scripture? A Comparative Approach* (Minneapolis: Fortress, 1993) 147, 185.

25. Ibid., 133.

26. Ibid., 46.

27. Ibid., 101.

28. Ibid., 233.

29. "Constitutive" is the term used by David Kelsey regarding the nature of scripture (*The Uses of Scripture in Recent Theology* [Philadelphia: Fortress, 1975]).

30. Ibid., 89.

31. Martin Luther, translated and paraphrased by Roland Bainton, *Here I Stand* (Nashville: Abingdon, 1950) 117. See *Luther's Works*, vol. 31, ed. H. J. Grim (Philadelphia: Muhlenberg Press, 1957) 313.

32. Harold Wells, "The Making of the United Church Mind" (Part II), *Touchstone* 8, no. 1 (January 1990): 17-29.

33. *Journal of John Wesley,* May 24, 1738. See Albert C. Outler, ed., *John Wesley* (New York: Oxford University Press, 1964) 66.

34. Barth, *Church Dogmatics,* vol. 1, pt. 2, 530.

35. Martin Luther, *Preface to the Epistles of St. James and St. Jude,* in *Luther's Works,* 35:395-98.

36. *Luther's Works,* 34:112.

37. Sandra M. Schneiders, "The Bible and Feminism," in *Freeing Theology: The Essentials of Theology in Feminist Perspective,* ed. Catherine Mowry LaCugna (San Francisco: HarperSanFrancisco, 1993) 51.

38. Letty M. Russell, *Household of Freedom: Authority in Feminist Theology* (Philadelphia: Fortress, 1987).

39. Aloysius Pieris, *An Asian Theology of Liberation* (Maryknoll, N.Y.: Orbis Books, 1988) 86.

40. Commenting on Romans 12:6, John Wesley, *Explanatory Notes upon the New Testament* (London: Epworth, 1950) 569.

41. Rudolf Bultmann, *History and Eschatology* (Edinburgh: Edinburgh University Press, 1957) 111.

42. See Rosemary Radford Ruether, "Feminist Theology: Methodology, Sources, and Norms," in *Sexism and God-Talk: Toward a Feminist Theology* (Boston: Beacon, 1983) 22-27.

43. *Luther's Works,* 35:395-98.

44. Douglas John Hall, *Thinking the Faith: Christian Theology in a North American Context* (Minneapolis: Augsburg, 1989) 89-91.

45. See, e.g., Juan Luis Segundo, *The Liberation of Theology*, trans. J. Drury (Dublin: Gill & Macmillan, 1976) 8; Gustavo Gutiérrez, *A Theology of Liberation*, trans. C. Inda and J. Eagleson (Maryknoll, N.Y.: Orbis Books, 1988); Russell, *Household of Freedom*, 53; Russell also speaks of the "spiral" in *Church in the Round: Feminist Interpretation of the Church* (Louisville: Westminster John Knox Press, 1993) 34.

46. The concept of "hermeneutical circle" finds philosophical background in Martin Heidegger, who spoke of the "historicality" of all understanding, of the inevitable presuppositions and preunderstanding in all works of interpretation, and he distinguished between the original sense of a text and its meaning for contemporary readers. On Heidegger, see Donald K. McKim, *A Guide to Contemporary Hermeneutics: Major Trends in Biblical Interpretation* (Grand Rapids: Eerdmans, 1986) 93, 196. A century earlier, Friederich Schleiermacher had already spoken of the preknowledge and horizons that precede any act of interpretation (ibid., 163).

47. The example is inspired by the movie *Shadowlands,* the story of C. S. Lewis and his wife. See Lewis's book *A Grief Observed* (London: Faber & Faber, 1963).

48. For an interpretation of the stories of Saul, David, and Jonathan from a "queer" perspective, see Theodore W. Jennings, "YHWH as Erastes"; also "Yahwist Desires: Imagining Divinity Queerly," in *Queer Commentary and the Hebrew Bible*, ed. Ken Stone (Cleveland: Pilgrim, 2001) 36-74.

49. The example I have in mind is the United Church of Canada in the decision of its General Council in 1988. See the church's study document "Toward a Christian Understanding of Sexual Orientation, Lifestyles, and Ministry," Report of the Division of Ministry Personnel and Education and the Division of Mission in Canada, February 19, 1988; see *Record of Proceedings of the Thirty-Second General Council* (Victoria, August 1988) (Toronto: United Church of Canada, 1988).

50. For a discussion of the use of biblical texts for the defense of apartheid in South Africa, see John W. DeGruchy and Charles Villa-Vicencio, *Apartheid Is a Heresy* (Grand Rapids: Eerdmans, 1983) chapters 8 and 9.

51. See Hans Frei, *The Identity of Jesus Christ: The Hermeneutical Bases of Dogmatic Theology* (Eugene, Ore.: Wipf & Stock, 1997) 59-60.

52. Hans Frei, *Types of Christian Theology,* ed. George Hunsinger and William C. Placher (New Haven: Yale University Press, 1992) 154.

53. I argued this point regarding the hermeneutical circle of Juan Luis Segundo. See Harold Wells, "Segundo's Hermeneutical Circle," in *Journal of Theology for Southern Africa* 34 (1981): 25-32; also "Ideology and Contextuality in Liberation Theology," in *Liberation Theology and Sociopolitical Transformation,* ed. J.-G. Antezana (Burnaby, BC: Simon Fraser University Press, 1992) 53-68.

54. C. Boff, *Theology and Praxis,* chapter 2.

55. This dynamic is discussed more thoroughly in my article "Social Analysis and Theological Method: Third World Challenge to Canadian Theology," in *A Long and Faithful March: 'Towards the Christian Revolution' 1930s/1980s,* ed. Harold Wells and Roger Hutchinson (Toronto: United Church Publishing House, 1989).

8. Is It Contextual?

1. For a thorough exploration of the concept of contextuality in theology, see Stephen B. Bevans, S.V.D., *Models of Contextual Theology* (Maryknoll, N.Y.: Orbis Books, 1994). Bevans speaks of various models of contextual theology: translation, anthropological, praxis, synthetic, transcendental. The contextuality I speak of in this book is primarily what he calls the "Praxis Model," chapter 6.

2. Douglas John Hall, *Thinking the Faith: Christian Theology in a North American Context* (Minneapolis: Augsburg, 1989) 75.

3. See Hall's characterization of North American context in *Thinking the Faith,* chapter 3. He speaks of these "components of our context": the end of the Constantinian era, religious pluralism, the theological impact of Auschwitz, Marxism and the revolution of the oppressed, the rebellion of nature, the nuclear crisis, apocalyptic consciousness, and the rise of religious simplism.

4. For a substantial discussion of this distinction, see Jeong Woo Kim, "The Theological Function of Experience: Method in Black American and Korean Theologies" (Th.D. diss., Knox College, Toronto School of Theology, 2002) 220-28.

5. David H. Kelsey, *The Uses of Scripture in Recent Theology* (Philadelphia: Fortress, 1975) 171-72.

6. F. Dostoevsky, in a letter to Madame von Wisine, quoted by George Grant, *Technology and Justice* (Toronto: House of Anansi, 1986) 69.

7. Simone Weil, *Waiting for God,* trans. E. Craufurd (New York: Harper & Row, 1973) 69.

8. Rosemary Radford Ruether, "Method and Sources in Feminist Theology," in *Sexism and God-Talk* (Boston: Beacon, 1983).

9. See a discussion of "Questioning the Father Almighty," by Douglas John Hall, *Professing the Faith: Christian Theology in a North American Context* (Minneapolis: Fortress, 1993) chapter 2.

10. See Richard Cleaver, *Know My Name: A Gay Liberation Theology* (Louisville: Westminster John Knox Press, 1995) especially chapter 2.

11. For a discussion of starting point in theology, see Harold Wells, "Ideology and Contextuality in Liberation Theology," in *Liberation Theology and Sociopolitical Transformation,* ed. J.-G. Antezana (Burnaby, BC: Simon Fraser University Press, 1992) 53-68.

12. Douglas John Hall, *Lighten Our Darkness: Toward an Indigenous Theology of the Cross* (Philadelphia: Westminster, 1976) chapter 1.

13. As we saw in chapter 3 of this book, there are different kinds of postmodernists, including Foucault, Derrida, etc., who, following Nietzsche, reject both the optimism and rationalism of the Enlightenment, moving toward a kind of nihilistic relativism. But some conservative Christians also want to be postmodern in their own way; see, e.g., Thomas Oden, *After Modernity . . . What? Agenda for Theology* (Grand Rapids: Zondervan, 1990) 46; George Grant, *Technology and Empire: Perspectives on North America* (Toronto: House of Anansi, 1969); and chapter 3 of this book.

14. For a rich discussion of the perspectival character of all human thought, see Paul Ricoeur, *Fallible Man,* trans. C. Kelbley (Chicago: Henry Regnery, 1967) 29-37.

15. Karl Barth, "The Situation—1933-1934," in *The German Church Conflict* (London: Lutterworth, 1965) 37.

16. Paul Ricoeur, "The Task of Hermeneutics," in *Hermeneutics and the Human Sciences* (London: Cambridge University Press, 1981) 43-62; see also idem, "Philosophical Hermeneutic and Theological Hermeneutics," *Studies in Religion* 5, no. 1 (1975-76): 14-33.

17. J. Severino Croatto, *Exodus: A Hermeneutics of Freedom*, trans. S. Attanasio, (Maryknoll, N.Y.: Orbis Books, 1981) 3.

18. J. Severino Croatto, *Biblical Hermeneutics: Toward a Theory of Reading as the Production of Meaning*, trans. R. R. Barr (Maryknoll, N.Y.: Orbis Books, 1987) ix.

19. Ibid., 9-10.

20. Ibid., 66.

21. Ibid., 67.

22. See the analysis of the American author Noam Chomsky, in his book *9/11* (New York: Seven Stories Press, 2001). For further substantial analysis of the functioning of American power in the world, see *Understanding Power: The Indispensable Chomsky*, ed. Peter R. Mitchell and John Schoeffel (New York: New Press, 2002).

23. Paul Tillich, *The Courage to Be* (New Haven: Yale University Press, 1952) 46.

24. Douglas John Hall, "Despair as Pervasive Ailment," in *Hope for the World: Mission in a Global Context*, ed. Walter Brueggemann (Louisville: Westminster John Knox Press, 2001) 83-93.

25. Chomsky, *Understanding Power*, 68.

26. For a theological expression of this awareness, see Laura E. Donaldson, "The Breasts of Columbus: A Political Anatomy of Postcolonialism and Feminist Religious Discourse," in *Postcolonialism, Feminism, and Religious Discourse*, ed. Laura E. Donaldson and Kwok Pui-lan (New York: Routledge, 2002) 41-61.

27. For a substantial discussion of this, see Harold Wells, *A Future for Socialism? Political Theology and the "Triumph of Capitalism"* (Valley Forge: Trinity Press International, 1996) chapter 7.

28. See Jamie Swift, Jacqueline M. Davies, Robert G. Clarke, and Michael Czerny, *Getting Started on Social Analysis in Canada*, 4th ed. (Toronto: Between the Lines, 2003) chapter 3.

29. *Report Card 2000: Child Poverty in Halton* (Burlington: Halton Social Planning Council, 2000). Statistics derived from Statistics Canada.

30. Russel Botman, "Hope as the Coming Reign of God," in *Hope for the World*, ed. Brueggemann, 74.

31. See James Sanders, *Torah and Canon* (Philadelphia: Fortress, 1972); idem, "Adaptable for Life: The Nature and Function of Canon," in *Magnalia Dei: The Mighty Acts of God*, ed. F. M. Cross, W. Lemke, and P. Miller, Jr. (Garden City: Doubleday, 1976) 531-60; see also Brevard S. Childs, *Introduction to the Old Testament as Scripture* (Philadelphia: Fortress, 1979).

32. See Joseph Blenkinsopp, *Prophecy and Canon* (Notre Dame: University of Notre Dame Press, 1977).

33. Gerald Sheppard, *Wisdom as Hermeneutical Construct* (Berlin: Walter de Gruyter, 1980) 13. See also Walter Brueggemann, *The Creative Word* (Philadelphia: Fortress, 1982) 112. Note also Elizabeth Johnson's treatment of Hebrew and apocryphal Greek wisdom literature as contextualization: "Jesus the Wisdom of God: A Biblical Basis for Non-Androcentric Christology," *Ephemerides Theologicae Lovanienses* 61 (1985): 261-94.

34. See Nellie McClung, *In Times Like These* (1915; repr., Toronto: University of Toronto Press, 1972).

35. Douglas John Hall, "On Contextuality in Christian Theology," *Toronto Journal of Theology* 1, no. 1 (Spring 1985): 6.

36. Barth, "The Situation—1933-1934," 37.

37. Douglas John Hall, *The Future of the Church* (Toronto: United Church Publishing House, 1989) 99-100.

38. Ibid., 87-89.

39. James H. Cone, *God of the Oppressed* (New York: Seabury, 1975) 18.

40. Note that Jacquelyn Grant, a pioneer of womanist theology, argues that white feminist theology is concerned with fulfillment, while black womanist theology is concerned with survival. She even accuses white feminism of being racist in its neglect of black women's experience. See Jacquelyn Grant, *White Women's Christ and Black Women's Jesus* (Atlanta: Scholars Press, 1989) 195, 199-201. Latin American women's theology, or *mujerista* theology, has appeared also, questioning the sexist character of much liberation theology. See Ivone Gebara, *Out of the Depths: Women's Experience of Evil and Suffering* (Minneapolis: Fortress, 2002).

41. Delores S. Williams, *Sisters in the Wilderness: The Challenge of Womanist God-Talk* (Maryknoll, N.Y.: Orbis Books, 1993); see also idem, "Women's Oppression and Life-line Politics in Women's Religious Narratives," *Journal of Feminist Studies in Religion* 1, no. 2 (Fall 1985); idem, "Black Women's Literature and the Task of Feminist Theology," in *Immaculate and Powerful: The Female in Sacred Image and Social Reality,* ed. Clarissa W. Atkinson et al. (Boston: Beacon, 1985).

42. For example, the use of Toni Morrison's *Beloved* (New York: Alfred A. Knopf, 1987) by Karen Baker-Fletcher and Garth Kasimu Baker-Fletcher in *My Sister, My Brother: Womanist and Xodus God-Talk* (Maryknoll, N.Y.: Orbis Books, 1997); also the use of the screenplay and film of Julie Dash—see Julie Dash, *Daughters of the Dust: The Making of an African American Women's Film* (New York: New Press, 1992), in *My Sister, My Brother,* 89-91.

43. Baker-Fletcher and Baker-Fletcher, *My Sister, My Brother,* 86, 89, 94.

44. Alice Walker, *The Color Purple* (New York: Harcourt, Brace, Jovanovich, 1982).

45. Dwight N. Hopkins, introduction to *Cut Loose Your Stammering Tongue: Black Theology in the Slave Narratives,* ed. Dwight N. Hopkins and George L. Cummings (Maryknoll, N.Y.: Orbis Books, 1991); see also Dwight N. Hopkins, *Shoes That Fit Our Feet: Sources for a Constructive Black Theology* (Maryknoll, N.Y.: Orbis Books, 1993).

46. Hopkins, *Shoes That Fit Our Feet,* 29.

47. Commission on Theological Concerns, Christian Conference of Asia, ed. *Minjung Theology: People as the Subjects of History* (Maryknoll, N.Y.: Orbis Books, 1981).

48. Kim Yong-Bock, *Messiah and Minjung: Christ's Solidarity with the People for New Life* (Hong Kong: Christian Conference of Asia, 1992) 4.

49. Ibid., 61.

50. See an account of Kim Yong-Bock's contextual method by Jeong Woo Kim, "The Theological Function of Experience," 113-34.

51. Kim Yong-Bock, *Messiah and Minjung,* 33. See also an earlier essay by Kim, "Messiah and Minjung," and the programmatic contextual essay of Suh Nam-Dong, "Towards a Theology of *Han*;" in *Minjung Theology: People as the Subjects of History.*

52. Chung Hyun Kyung, "Following Naked Dancing and Long Dreaming," in *Inher-*

iting Our Mothers' Gardens: Feminist Theology in Third World Perspective, ed. Letty M. Russell et al. (Philadelphia: Westminster, 1988) 62-63.

53. Chung Hyun Kyung, "Opium or the Seed for Revolution? Women-Centered Religiosity in Korea," in *The Power of Naming: A Concilium Reader in Feminist Liberation Theology,* ed. Elisabeth Schüssler Fiorenza (Maryknoll, N.Y.: Orbis Books, 1996) 277-78.

54. Chung Hyun Kyung, *Struggle to Be the Sun Again: Introducing Asian Women's Theology* (Maryknoll, N.Y.: Orbis Books, 1994) 104.

55. See her discussion of this in "Your Comfort vs. My Death," in *Women Resisting Violence: Spirituality for Life,* ed. Mary John Mananzan, Mercy Amba Oduyoye, Elsa Tamez, J. Shannon Clarkson, Mary C. Grey, and Letty M. Russell (Maryknoll, N.Y.: Orbis Books, 1996) 129-40.

56. Chung, *Struggle to Be the Sun Again,* 66.

57. Ibid., 111.

58. Croatto, *Biblical Hermeneutics*, 5-6.

59. A large literature exists about the question of syncretism, which cannot be considered at length here. The term, which has long been used in a pejorative way to refer to inappropriate mixing of religions, is now frequently used more positively. While Chung's is a survival-centered syncretism, others speak of a "Christ-centered syncretism." See M. M. Thomas, "The Absoluteness of Jesus Christ and Christ-Centered Syncretism," *Ecumenical Review* 37 (1985): 387-97. Leonardo Boff, who also seeks a Christ-centered syncretism, speaks of the inevitability of syncretism: "Pure Christianity does not exist" (*Church, Charism, and Power: Liberation Theology and the Institutional Church* [New York: Crossroad, 1985] 92). See also Harold Wells, "Korean Syncretism and Theologies of Interreligious Dialogue: The Contribution of Kyoung Jae Kim," *Asia Journal of Theology* 12, no. 1 (April 1998): 56-76. For a full methodological and missiological consideration of syncretism, see Carl F. Starkloff, *A Theology of the In-Between: The Value of Syncretic Process* (Milwaukee: Marquette University Press, 2002).

60. Grace Ji-Sun Kim, *The Grace of Sophia: A Korean North American Women's Christology* (Cleveland: Pilgrim Press, 2002), 19-41, also chapter 7.

61. Jeong Woo Kim, "The Theological Function of Experience," 178.

62. We have noted the explicit and intentional North American contextual theology of Douglas John Hall. We may note his specifically Canadian contextual theology in *The Canada Crisis* (Toronto: Anglican Book Centre, 1980). For a discussion of other Canadian contextual theologies, see Harold Wells, "Contextual Theology and Peoplehood: Toward African/Canadian Theological Dialogue," *Africa Theological Journal* 21, no. 2 (1992): 146-63.

63. The person characterized here under a fictional (but common) name may recognize himself, though his story here is partly fictional as well. He did eventually spend time in prison, but is now a highly placed official, and a very constructive one, in the government of his country, after a post-apartheid democratic breakthrough.

9. Is It Ecclesial?

1. The point is well made by Miroslav Volf, *After Our Likeness: The Church as the Image of the Trinity* (Grand Rapids: Eerdmans, 1998) 146, 248.

2. See Rosemary Radford Ruether, *Faith and Fratricide: The Theological Roots of Anti-Semitism* (New York: Seabury, 1974), and the introduction by Gregory Baum, 1-22.

3. A good compendium of sources on both negative and positive theological traditions concerning women can be found in Leonard Swidler, *Biblical Affirmations of Woman* (Philadelphia: Westminster, 1979).

4. Letty Russell, *Household of Freedom: Authority in Feminist Theology* (Philadelphia: Westminster, 1987).

5. Douglas John Hall, *Thinking the Faith: Christian Theology in a North American Context* (Minneapolis: Augsburg, 1989) 268.

6. Note the importance accorded to tradition by the Roman Catholic liberationist Clodovis Boff, *Theology and Praxis: Epistemological Foundations,* trans. R. A. Barr (Maryknoll, N.Y.: Orbis Books, 1987) 139.

7. Hall, *Thinking the Faith,* 445.

8. Robert W. Jenson, *Systematic Theology,* vol. 1, *The Triune God* (New York: Oxford University Press, 1997) 27.

9. *1 Clement* is known to have been read in the church at Corinth along with the scriptures, around 170 C.E. (*Oxford Dictionary of the Christian Church,* ed. F. L. Cross [New York: Oxford University Press, 1997] 360).

10. Irenaeus, *Against the Heresies,* in *Ante-Nicene Fathers,* vol. 1, trans. A. Roberts (Edinburgh: T & T Clark, 1993) bk. 1; bk. 5: xx, 547-48.

11. Athanasius, *Contra Gentes* (Leiden: E. J. Brill, 1984).

12. St. Basil the Great, *On the Holy Spirit* (Crestwood, N.Y.: St. Vladimir's Seminary Press, 1980) 98-99.

13. See reference to Augustine by Heiko Oberman, *The Harvest of Medieval Theology* (Grand Rapids: Baker, 2000) 369-73; also Stanley J. Grenz and John R. Franke, *Beyond Foundationalism: Shaping Theology in a Postmodern Context* (Louisville: Westminster John Knox Press, 2001) 95-98.

14. Grenz and Franke, *Beyond Foundationalism,* 95-98.

15. Vincent of Lérins, *The Commonitory of Vincent of Lérins, for the Antiquity and Universality of the Catholic Faith against the Profane Novelties of All Heresies,* cited by Volf, *After Our Likeness,* 265-66.

16. See Alister McGrath, *The Intellectual Origins of the European Reformation* (Oxford: Basil Blackwell, 1987).

17. Martin Luther translated and paraphrased by Roland Bainton, *Here I Stand* (Nashville: Abingdon, 1950) 117; found in *Luther's Works,* ed. H. J. Grim (Philadelphia: Muhlenberg Press, 1957) 31:313.

18. Quoted by Bainton, *Here I Stand,* 95.

19. *Luther's Works,* 32:112.

20. Luther, *Preface to the Epistles of St. James and St. Jude,* in *Luther's Works,* 35:395.

21. For a discussion of Luther's theology of the cross in relation to liberation theologies, see Harold Wells, "Theology of the Cross and the Theologies of Liberation," *Toronto Journal of Theology* 17, no. 1 (Spring 2001): 147-66.

22. See Jean Calvin's attack on "the cruelty of the pope and his adherents . . . in tyrannically oppressing and destroying souls" (see *Institutes of the Christian Religion,* bk. 4, x, 1-26 [vol. 2] trans. H. Beveridge [London: James Clarke, 1962]).

23. Calvin, *Institutes,* bk. 4, x, 27-32.

24. See Grenz and Franke, *Beyond Foundationalism,* 99.

25. See Avery Dulles, *The Craft of Theology: From Symbol to System* (New York: Crossroad, 1995) 87-89.

26. Ibid., 98.

27. The United Church of Canada, *The Manual* (Toronto: United Church Publishing House, 1991) 11-12.

28. The "New Creed" of The United Church of Canada was established in 1968, reworded for inclusive language in 1982, and updated to include "respect for creation" in 1994. "We are not alone, we live in God's world. We believe in God: who has created and is creating, who has come in Jesus, the Word made flesh, to reconcile and make new, who works in us and others by the Spirit. We trust in God. We are called to be the Church: to celebrate God's presence, to live with respect in Creation, to love and serve others, to seek justice and resist evil, to proclaim Jesus, crucified and risen, our judge and our hope. In life, in death, in life beyond death, God is with us. We are not alone. Thanks be to God."

29. Jenson, *Systematic Theology,* vol. 1, *The Triune God,* 36.

30. Jenson can also speak of "irreversibly established rites" (ibid., 34).

31. Grenz and Franke, *Beyond Foundationalism,* 124.

32. Jon Sobrino, *Christ the Liberator: A View from the Victims,* trans. P. Burns (Maryknoll, N.Y.: Orbis Books, 2001) 260-63, 270-74.

33. For a rich discussion of the creeds by a liberation theologian, see Leonardo Boff, *Jesus Christ Liberator: A Critical Christology for our Time,* trans. P. Hughes (Maryknoll, N.Y.: Orbis Books, 1978) chapter 10.

34. Grenz and Franke, *Beyond Foundationalism,* 124-29.

35. Jenson, *Systematic Theology,* vol. 1, *The Triune God,* 40.

36. I refer to the aforementioned creed of the United Church of Canada, amended with the addition of these words in 1994.

37. Calvin, *Institutes,* bk. 4, ii, 2-4, (vol. 2), 306, 309.

38. Jürgen Moltmann, *The Church in the Power of the Spirit: A Contribution to Messianic Ecclesiology,* trans. M. Kohl (London: SCM, 1977) 358. See discussion of the church's apostolicity also by Karl Barth, *Church Dogmatics,* vol. 4, pt. 1, trans. and ed. G. W. Bromiley and T. F. Torrance (Edinburgh: T & T Clark, 1956) 715-25.

39. See Volf, *After Our Likeness,* 248.

40. For helpful treatments of the church's oneness and holiness, see Moltmann, *Church in the Power of the Spirit,* 337-47, 352-57.

41. Justin, *Dialogue with Trypho* 81.4; Ignatius of Antioch, *Letter to Smyrna* 8; cited by Moltmann, *Church in the Power of the Spirit,* 347, 349.

42. Karl Barth, *Church Dogmatics,* vol. 4, pt. 1, 702.

43. Moltmann, *Church in the Power of the Spirit,* 349.

44. The term "Protestant" originates from the Diet of Speyer in 1529, when Lutherans opposed the annulment of an earlier decree allowing princes to manage religious affairs in their own territory. The term has the positive sense of solemnly declaring, vowing, or bearing witness, as well as protesting against something. See *Oxford Dictionary of the Christian Church,* ed. F. L. Cross (Oxford: Oxford University Press, 1997) 360.

Postscript

1. Søren Kierkegaard, *Concluding Unscientific Postscript: A Mimic-Pathetic-Dialectic Composition, An Existential Contribution by Johannes Climacus.* Responsible for Publication: S. Kierkegaard [Copenhagen, 1846], trans. David F. Swenson, introduction by Walter Lowrie (Princeton: Princeton University Press, 1941) 193.

2. Ibid., 97.

INDEX

accountability
  and rationality, 82
action and thought
  dialectical relation of, 14, 24-25
Anselm of Canterbury
  on faith, 19-20
  on God as feudal lord, 160-61
  ontological argument for God of, 93
anti-Semitism, Christian, 146-48, 163
Apostles' Creed, 282
apostolic succession, 285-86
Aquinas. *See* Thomas Aquinas
Arius/Arianism, 150, 175
Athanasius, 151
  on scripture and tradition, 277
Augustine
  on scripture and tradition, 278
authority
  of context, 242-46
  of experience, 230, 242-46
  and postmodernism, 84
  of scripture, 218-19, 227-31
  of tradition, 277-78

Baker-Fletcher, Garth, 258
Baker-Fletcher, Karen, 258
Barmen Declaration (1934), 118, 131, 284
Barth, Karl
  on authority of scripture, 217, 229
  Christ-centered theology of, 131-32, 213
  contextuality of, 245, 256
  development of theology of, 25, 295n. 18
  on knowledge of God, 53
  on reason, 83
basileia. See reign of God
Basil of Caesarea
  on scripture and tradition, 278

Baum, Gregory
  on Christian anti-Semitism, 147
  on postmodernist philosophers, 90
Berry, Thomas
  as ecological theologian, 126-27
Bible
  authority of, as dangerous idea, 218-19
  interpretation of, 217-18, 231-34
  and theological adequacy, 213-39
  See also authority; scripture
Bingemer, Maria Clara
  and Christ-centered theology, 133
Boff, Clodovis
  on liberation theology, 124-25
  on theology and experience, 239
Boff, Leonardo
  and Christ-centered theology, 132
  liberationist/ecological theology of, 126
  and Social Trinitiy, 177-80
Bonhoeffer, Dietrich
  idea of "cheap grace" of, 158
  as inspiring teacher, 221
  on theodicy, 76
Borg, Marcus
  on Jesus' understanding of his death, 163
Buddhism
  scriptures of, 224
Bultmann, Rudolf
  on resurrection, 139
  on scripture, 231

Calvin
  on apostolic succession, 285
  on scripture, 216, 221, 224, 227
Camus, Albert
  on theology of cross, 75-76
canon of scripture. *See* scripture: canon of

Frei, Hans (*cont.*)
  on faith statements, 103-4, 302n. 81
  on resurrection narratives, 139-41
Freud, Sigmund
  idea of religion of, 87
  on rational perceptions of reality, 29
Fulkerson, Mary McClintock
  as poststructuralist, 91

gender
  and doctrine of Trinity, 171-72
  and incarnation, 154-55
  See also feminist theologians
global context, 248-53
gnostics, 153
God
  arguments for existence of, 92-97
  communicating with humans, 42-47
  as Father, 170-72
  human alienation from, 156-59
  as Jesus' *Abba,* 152-53, 160, 168-71
  Jesus as, 148-49
  knowledge of: mode of, 113-14; and
    revelation, 53-54
  and question of theodicy, 74-79
  self-revelation of, 38, 45-47
  Spirit of, 66-67
  and theology, 23-27
  as Trinity, 168-80
  See also Jesus Christ; Holy Spirit;
    Trinity
gospel
  contrasted with human wisdom, 69-
    70
Grant, George
  on Nietzsche, 88
  as postmodern thinker, 91
  on rationality, 108-9
  on word "object," 304n. 112
Grant, Jacquelyn
  and Christ-centered theology, 133
Gregory of Nazianzus
  on humanity of Jesus, 154
  and *perichōrēsis,* 153
Grenz, Stanley
  on pluralism of postmodernity, 85
Gutiérrez, Gustavo
  Christ-centered theology of, 132

and hermeneutics, 238
on prayer and worship, 125

Hall, Douglas John
  on cognitive priority of revelation, 80
  and contextuality, 91, 126, 134, 241
  on cynicism, 60
  on tradition, 274
Hart, Trevor
  on Hans Frei, 104, 302n. 81
Hauerwas, Stanley
  as American postliberal, 92, 107
Hegel, G. W. F.
  absolute idealism of, 87
Heidegger, Martin
  and hermeneutical suspicion, 29
  and postmodern philosophy, 86
Heim, S. Mark
  on John Hick, 189-90
hermeneutical circularity
  and contextuality, 241
  philosophical background of, 321n.
    46
  and scripture, 235-39
hermeneutical suspicion
  and liberation theology, 29
  Martin Heidegger and, 29
  and modern philosophy, 28-29
Heyward, Carter
  theological foundation of, 133
Hick, John
  as pluralist theologian, 184-90
Hinduism
  sacred writings of, 224-25
history
  periods of, 84
Holy Spirit
  faith as gift of, 66-67
  as God's presence, 119
  Jesus and, 168-74
  as *Ruah,* 150-51, 172
  See also God; Jesus Christ; Trinity
homoi-ousios (of *like* substance), 150
homo-ousios (of one substance), 151
hope
  faith as, 58-61
Hopkins, Dwight
  on slaves and Jesus, 3

and rationality, 112
relativizing of, 30

unicity of church, 286-88
United Church of Canada
doctrinal statement of, 281-82
"New Creed" of, 327n. 28
Updike, John
on silent God, 77

Van Huysteen, J. Wentzel, 105
on rationality, 82, 108
on scientific knowledge, 98
Vatican I, 280
Vatican II
and interreligious dialogue, 183
on scripture and tradition, 280-81
Vincent of Lérins
on scripture and tradition, 278
Volf, Miroslav
on *totus Christus,* 305n. 3

Weil, Simone
on Christ and truth, 243
Weizsacker, C. F. von
on scientific knowledge, 97

Wesley, John
on scripture, 216, 229
Williams, Delores
on story of Hagar, 257-58
Wisdom, divine (*Sophia*)
and Jesus, 153
and Trinity, 171-72
wisdom, human
contrasted with foolishness of gospel,
69-70
Wittgenstein, Ludwig
and postmodern philosophy, 86
Wolsterstorff, Nicholas
as critic of modern thought, 92
worship, Christian
Christ-centeredness of, 122-25
Wright, N. T.
on Jesus' understanding of his death,
163
on resurrection, 142
Wyclif, John, 278

Young, Pamela Dickey
and Christ-centered theology, 133

Zizioulas, John
and Social Trinity, 177